PLAY THERAPY
An Introduction

KARLA D. CARMICHAEL, PhD
University of Alabama

PEARSON

Merrill
Prentice Hall

Upper Saddle River, New Jersey
Columbus, Ohio

Library of Congress Cataloging-in-Publication Data
Carmichael, Karla D. (Karla Delle)
    Play therapy: an introduction / Karla D. Carmichael.
        p. cm.
    Includes bibliographical references and index.
    ISBN 0-13-097418-8
    1. Play therapy. I. Title.
    RJ505.P6C365 2006
    618.92'891653—dc22   2005001714

Vice President and Executive Publisher: Jeffery W. Johnston
Publisher: Kevin M. Davis
Editorial Assistant: Sarah Kenoyer
Production Editor: Mary Harlan
Production Coordination: Thistle Hill Publishing Services, LLC
Design Coordinator: Diane Lorenzo
Cover Designer: Ali Mohrman
Cover image: SuperStock
Production Manager: Laura Messerly
Director of Marketing: Ann Castel Davis
Marketing Manager: Autumn Purdy
Marketing Coordinator: Brian Mounts

This book was set in Sabon by Carlisle Communications, Ltd. It was printed and bound by R. R. Donnelley & Sons Company. The cover was printed by R. R. Donnelley & Sons Company.

Photo Credits: Karla D. Carmichael, pp. 1, 6, 10, 13, 19, 26, 29, 34, 38, 41, 51, 61, 65, 69, 102, 134, 144, 148, 158, 162, 173, 177, 182, 185, 190, 195, 201, 206, 210, 214, 217, 218, 220, 223, 225, 229, 233, 236, 241, 246, 250, 254, 264, 267, 268, 271, 275, 280, 282; Judy Irvine, pp. 3, 109, 126, 132, 138, 186; Valoree Sainker, pp. 48, 56, 93, 97, 259; Rick Kottman, pp. 71, 80, 87; Patricia Murphree, pp. 89, 120, 149, 153; Rebecca How, p. 104; Bernard Guerney, pp. 114, 118; Joy Burnham, pp. 164, 169.

Pearson Prentice Hall™ is a trademark of Pearson Education, Inc.
Pearson® is a registered trademark of Pearson plc
Prentice Hall® is a registered trademark of Pearson Education, Inc.
Merrill® is a registered trademark of Pearson Education, Inc.

Pearson Education Ltd.
Pearson Education Singapore Pte. Ltd.
Pearson Education Canada, Ltd.
Pearson Education–Japan

Pearson Education Australia Pty. Limited
Pearson Education North Asia Ltd.
Pearson Educación de Mexico, S.A. de C.V.
Pearson Education Malaysia Pte. Ltd.

10 9 8 7 6 5 4 3 2 1
ISBN: 0-13-097418-8

To my parents, G. Carlton and Lula D. Carmichael, who have supported and encouraged me in all the endeavors of my life.

ABOUT THE AUTHOR

Karla D. Carmichael, PhD, is an associate professor at the University of Alabama. She received her degree in counselor education from The University of North Texas in 1982, where she specialized in family and child therapy. She is the co-founder and founding president of the Alabama Association for Play Therapy (AAPT). She served as the executive director of AAPT from 1993 to 2005. Carmichael has served as secretary-treasurer for the National Association for Play Therapy board of directors. Prior to moving to Alabama, Carmichael taught counselor education at Sul Ross State University in Alpine, Texas. She was an elementary school counselor in both Midlothian and Killeen, Texas. She currently teaches introduction to play therapy, advanced play therapy, psychological assessment, and program development and management. She is the clinical director of the Counselor Education Clinical Laboratory. She has published and presented nationally in the field of play therapy.

PREFACE

This text provides a firm theoretical, ethical, and clinical basis for play therapy. In order to become a registered play therapist, a mental health related professional must receive specific preparation in play therapy history, theory, techniques/methods, and applications to special populations and ethical practices. This text presents this basic knowledge clearly and objectively.

Play Therapy: An Introduction grew out of my own experience of teaching an introductory course in play therapy for the last 20 years. Each text I used had many good points but also lacked much of the information my students required. Many colleagues in the field of play therapy expressed the need for a general text that would provide an unbiased overview of the profession.

The information in the text is organized in the way I present the material to my class. Chapter 1 traces the historical background of play therapy. The second chapter provides a nondirective starting point for any laboratory or practica that may be a part of the course. I debated the exact location of this chapter. My idea for placing it so early in the book was to prepare students who already have a mental health background about what to expect during their practicum experience. Choosing to focus Chapter 2 on a child-centered philosophy was based on the training models with which I am most familiar in counselor education. As students incorporate new learning from the different theories, their own integrated theories of play therapy will emerge. Chapter 2 is intended as merely a starting point, not a destination.

The theoretical chapters that follow are arranged as nearly as possible to parallel the parent theory's appearance historically. For example, Adlerian play therapy emerged as a separate theory after child-centered play therapy, but it appears earlier in the text because Adlerian individual psychology preceded Rogers's client-centered theory.

The clinical chapters on assessment, diagnosis, research, and legal/ethical issues appear at the end of the text. Assessment is divided into two areas: informal and formal. I also teach assessment at my university, so the topic is a personal priority for me. The informal assessments are some of the most enjoyable experiences in my introductory class. I have summarized the ones that my colleagues and I use.

Chapter 14 on diagnosis draws heavily from Rita Wicks-Nelson and Allen Israel. A single chapter cannot even begin to explore diagnosis, but it does provide novice clinicians with an introduction, and I hope to make them hungry for more knowledge. Based on the research and the suggested interventions, I describe which play therapy theories might be more effective. All types of play therapy have been used with almost all of the DSM categories of childhood disorders, however, with some success.

No text would be complete without some portion devoted to research and ethics. The research reported in Chapter 15 is very limited because it has only recently become a major emphasis in the field. Play therapy is making the transition from a discourse of practice to a discourse of quantitative and qualitative research outcome-based inquiry. The two meta-analysis studies cited represent the current indications of the viability of play therapy as an intervention.

I served on the committee that drafted the first standards of practice for the Association of Play Therapy. The intention behind those early meetings and the initial draft was to move play therapy from an interesting medium to a specialty in the mental health–related professions. The inclusion of the standards of practice in the appendix furthers that recognition.

The final chapter was developed because of the growing need to apply play therapy theories across cultural boundaries. This chapter proved to be the most challenging, because so little relevant information was available at the time of its writing.

As I complete the writing of this textbook, I find so many more things that need to be included. But as I was taught to say when I went to defend my dissertation, "Alas, these topics are another study."

ACKNOWLEDGMENTS

I wish to thank the following people who agreed to serve as models to help illustrate this book:

- Jane Mastromonico, play therapist, Huntsville Child and Family Center, Huntsville, Alabama and her friends, Christian Niemi, Cameron Niemi, and Alexander Stephens.
- Theresa M. Clark, play therapist, The Amelia Center, Birmingham, Alabama, and friends, Sarah Johnson, Michael Johnson, Emily Street, and Amber Porter.
- Billy Kirkpatrick, graduate student, University of Alabama, Tuscaloosa, Alabama.
- Joy Burnham, therapist and assistant professor, University of Alabama, Tuscaloosa, Alabama, and daughters Kelly and Abbey.
- Graduate Play Therapy Class, The University of Alabama, Gadsden, Alabama, Brenda Douglas, Angela Forbus, Sally Garrett, Sonja George, Jose Jimenez, Cheryl Matthews, Kelley Mizic, Deirdre Nelson, Ray Pickard, and Casey Williams.
- Terry Kottman, play therapist and theorist, The Encouragement Zone, Cedar Falls, Iowa, and son Jacob.
- Garry Landreth, play therapist and theorist, Center for Play Therapy, Denton, Texas, and friend Emily How.

- Mark Leggett, therapist, Assistant Professor, The University of Alabama, Tuscaloosa, Alabama.
- Janice White, Owens House, Columbiana, Alabama, and daughters Raven and Ashlyn.
- Winnie Lowe-Davis, play therapist, Owens House, Columbiana, Alabama.
- Louise Guerney, play therapist and theorist, National Institute of Relationship Enhancement, Bethesda, Maryland, and her grandchildren.
- Sharita Gilliam, The University of Alabama, Tuscaloosa, Alabama, and her children, Christopher, Mikhael, and Jordan.
- Eidele Sainker, play therapist, Summit Psychotherapy PC, Huntsville, Alabama, and grandson Rudy.
- Mee Ying Lam, and son, Leon Nguyen, Cleburne, Texas.
- G. C. Carmichael, my father, Cleburne, Texas.
- Donna and Richard Flight, graduate students, The University of Alabama, Tuscaloosa, Alabama, and their children Maegan, Sarah, and Jacob.
- Jamie Satcher, professor, The University of Alabama, Tuscaloosa, Alabama.
- Lafacial Wilson, doctoral student, The University of Alabama, Tuscaloosa, Alabama.
- Mary C. Templeton, doctoral student, The University of Alabama, Tuscaloosa, Alabama, and friend Hanna McCook.
- Poppy Moon, play therapist in private practice and doctoral student, The University of Alabama, Tuscaloosa, Alabama.
- Angela Jenkins, graduate student, The University of Alabama, Tuscaloosa, Alabama.
- Kim Skelton, graduate student, The University of Alabama, Tuscaloosa, Alabama.

Drawings used in this book were completed by Kelly and Abbey Burnham.

I would also like to thank the reviewers of this edition for their insights and comments: Virginia B. Allen, Idaho State University; Christopher Brown, Southwest Texas State University; John D. Cerio, Alfred University; Teresa M. Christensen, University of New Orleans; M. Harry Daniels, University of Florida; Michael Duffy, Texas A&M University; Marijane Fall, University of Southern Maine; Betty Katsekas, University of Southern Maine; Faith H. McClure, California State University, San Bernadino; Dale Pehrsson, Oregon State University; Phyllis Post, University of North Carolina, Charlotte; Deanne C. Ray, Texas A&M University, Commerce; Joseph C. Rotter, University of South Carolina; Cathy Woodyard, Texas Woman's University.

DISCOVER THE COMPANION WEBSITE ACCOMPANYING THIS BOOK

THE PRENTICE HALL COMPANION WEBSITE: A VIRTUAL LEARNING ENVIRONMENT

Technology is a constantly growing and changing aspect of our field that is creating a need for content and resources. To address this emerging need, Prentice Hall has developed an online learning environment for students and professors alike—Companion Websites—to support our textbooks.

In creating a Companion Website, our goal is to build on and enhance what the textbook already offers. For this reason, the content for each user-friendly website is organized by topic and provides the professor and student with a variety of meaningful resources. Common features of a Companion Website include:

For the Professor—

Every Companion Website integrates **Syllabus Manager™**, an online syllabus creation and management utility.

- **Syllabus Manager™** provides you, the instructor, with an easy, step-by-step process to create and revise syllabi, with direct links into Companion Website and other online content without having to learn HTML.
- Students may logon to your syllabus during any study session. All they need to know is the web address for the Companion Website and the password you've assigned to your syllabus.
- After you have created a syllabus using **Syllabus Manager™**, students may enter the syllabus for their course section from any point in the Companion Website.
- Clicking on a date, the student is shown the list of activities for the assignment. The activities for each assignment are linked directly to actual content, saving time for students.
- Adding assignments consists of clicking on the desired due date, then filling in the details of the assignment—name of the assignment, instructions, and whether it is a one-time or repeating assignment.

- In addition, links to other activities can be created easily. If the activity is online, a URL can be entered in the space provided, and it will be linked automatically in the final syllabus.
- Your completed syllabus is hosted on our servers, allowing convenient updates from any computer on the Internet. Changes you make to your syllabus are immediately available to your students at their next logon.

For the Student—

- **Counseling Topics**—17 core counseling topics represent the diversity and scope of today's counseling field.
- **Annotated Bibliography**—includes seminal foundational works and key current works.
- **Web Destinations**—lists significant and up-to-date practitioner and client sites.
- **Professional Development**—provides helpful information regarding professional organizations and codes of ethics.
- **Electronic Bluebook**—send homework or essays directly to your instructor's email with this paperless form.
- **Message Board**—serves as a virtual bulletin board to post—or respond to— questions or comments to/from a national audience.
- **Chat**—real-time chat with anyone who is using the text anywhere in the country—ideal for discussion and study groups, class projects, etc.

To take advantage of these and other resources, please visit the *Play Therapy: An Introduction* Companion Website at

www.prenhall.com/carmichael

RESEARCH NAVIGATOR: RESEARCH MADE SIMPLE!

www.ResearchNavigator.com

Merrill Education is pleased to introduce Research Navigator—a one-stop research solution for students that simplifies and streamlines the entire research process. At www.researchnavigator.com, students will find extensive resources to enhance their understanding of the research process so they can effectively complete research assignments. In addition, Research Navigator has three exclusive databases of credible and reliable source content to help students focus their research efforts and begin the research process.

How Will Research Navigator Enhance Your Course?

- Extensive content helps students understand the research process, including writing, Internet research, and citing sources.
- Step-by-step tutorial guides students through the entire research process from selecting a topic to revising a rough draft.
- Research Writing in the Disciplines section details the differences in research across disciplines.
- Three exclusive databases—EBSCO's ContentSelect Academic Journal Database, *The New York Times* Search by Subject Archive, and "Best of the Web" Link Library—allow students to easily find journal articles and sources.

What's the Cost?

A subscription to Research Navigator is $7.50 but is **free** when ordered in conjunction with this textbook. To obtain free passcodes for your students, simply contact your local Merrill/Prentice Hall sales representative, and your representative will send you the Evaluating Online Resource Guide, which contains the code to access Research Navigator as well as tips on how to use Research Navigator and how to evaluate research. To preview the value of this website to your students, please go to www.educatorlearningcenter.com and use the Login Name "Research" and the password "Demo."

Brief Contents

CHAPTER 1   Introduction   1

CHAPTER 2   Beginning the Play Therapy Session   19

CHAPTER 3   Psychoanalytic Play Therapy   51

CHAPTER 4   Adlerian Play Therapy   71

CHAPTER 5   Jungian Analytical Play Therapy   89

CHAPTER 6   Child-Centered Play Therapy   104

CHAPTER 7   Gestalt Play Therapy   120

CHAPTER 8   Relationship Play Therapy   134

CHAPTER 9   Cognitive-Behavioral Play Therapy   149

CHAPTER 10   Child Developmental Play Therapies   164

CHAPTER 11   Ecosystems Play Therapy   186

CHAPTER 12   Family and Filial Play Therapy   201

CHAPTER 13   Assessing Children in Play Therapy   218

CHAPTER 14   Diagnosis and Treatment   236

CHAPTER 15   The Law, Ethics, and Research   254

CHAPTER 16   Cultural Sensitivity and Play Therapy   268

Contents

CHAPTER 1 Introduction   1

What Is Play Therapy? 2

Historical Development 3

    Roots in Special Education 3

    Mental Health and the Child Guidance Movement 4

    Prevention of Cruelty to Children 4

    Psychoanalytic Beginnings 5

    Release Therapy 9

    Relationship Therapy 10

    Nondirective Therapy 11

    Limits as Therapy 12

    Erik Erikson 12

    Play Therapy in Schools 13

Toward a Professional Identity 13

The Purpose of a Theory 17

Summary 18

CHAPTER 2 Beginning the Play Therapy Session   19

Toy Selection 19

Setting Up the Playroom 25

Organizing the Toy Display 29

Professional Intake, Disclosure, and Documentation 30

    Intake 30

    Informed Consent 30

    Custody Issues 32

    Consent to Treat 33

    Confidentiality 33

Case Notes and Treatment Planning   36
Other Points to Ponder   39
Conducting the Session   39
Responding to the Child in Play Therapy   42
Setting Limits   44
When Limits Are Violated   47
Manipulation   47
Power Struggles   48
The Good-Bye Session   49
The Good-Bye Personal Note   50
Summary   50

CHAPTER 3   Psychoanalytic Play Therapy   51

Introduction   52
Freud and Little Hans   52
Klein and the Berlin School   55
Anna Freud and the Vienna School   57
Lowenfeld   60
Toy Selection   63
Role of Therapist   64
Structuring the Session   66
Limits   67
Parent Involvement   67
Termination   68
Assessment and Techniques   69
Summary   70

CHAPTER 4   Adlerian Play Therapy   71

Introduction   72
Toy Selection   74
Role of the Therapist   74
Structuring the Session   77
Limits   80
Parent Involvement   81
Termination   83
Assessment and Techniques   84
Summary   88

CHAPTER 5   Jungian Analytical Play Therapy   89

Introduction   90
Toy Selection   92

Role of the Therapist   94
Structuring the Session   98
Limits   100
Parent Involvement   100
Termination   101
Assessment and Techniques   101
Summary   103

CHAPTER 6   **Child-Centered Play Therapy**   104

Introduction   105
Toy Selection   109
Role of the Therapist   110
Structuring the Session   113
     Stages of CCPT   113
Limits   115
Parent Involvement   116
Termination   117
Assessment and Techniques   119
Summary   119

CHAPTER 7   **Gestalt Play Therapy**   120

Introduction   120
Toy Selection   124
Role of the Therapist   125
Structuring the Session   127
Limits   129
Parent Involvement   129
Termination   130
Assessment and Techniques   131
Summary   133

CHAPTER 8   **Relationship Play Therapy**   134

Introduction   134
Toy Selection   135
Role of the Therapist   136
Structuring the Session   137
Limits   141
Parent Involvement   144
Termination   147

Assessment and Techniques   148
Summary   148

CHAPTER 9   Cognitive-Behavioral Play Therapy   149

Introduction   150
Toy Selection   151
Role of the Therapist   152
Structuring the Session   154
Limits   155
Parent Involvement   156
Termination   156
Assessment and Techniques   157
   Parent-Report Measures   157
   Intelligence and Personality Measures   157
   Play Assessments   159
   Behavioral Techniques   159
   Cognitive Techniques   161
Summary   163

CHAPTER 10   Child Developmental Play Therapies   164

Introduction   165
Developmental Play Therapy   167
   Toy Selection   167
   Role of the Therapist   167
   Structuring the Session   168
   Limits   170
   Parent Involvement   171
   Termination   171
   Assessment and Techniques   172
Theraplay   172
   Toy Selection   173
   Role of the Therapist   173
   Structuring the Session   174
   Limits   179
   Parent Involvement   180
   Termination   182
   Assessment and Techniques   183
Summary   185

CHAPTER 11   Ecosystems Play Therapy   186

Introduction   186
Toy Selection   187

Role of the Therapist   189
Structuring the Session   190
Limits   192
Parent Involvement   193
Termination   194
Assessment and Techniques   195
Summary   200

CHAPTER 12   Family and Filial Play Therapy   201

Introduction   202
Play Therapy Paradigm for Family Therapy   202
Conjoint Play Therapy   204
Family Play Therapy   204
Dynamic Family Play Therapy   205
Strategic Family Play Therapy   208
Filial Therapy   211
Linking Parents to Play Therapy   215
Summary   217

CHAPTER 13   Assessing Children in Play Therapy   218

Introduction   219
Drawing Assessments   219
Interview Assessments   227
      The Puppet Interview   228
      The Dollhouse Interview   229
Storytelling Assessments   230
      Projective Questions   234
Structured Interviews   234
Summary   235

CHAPTER 14   Diagnosis and Treatment   236

Introduction   236
Anxiety Disorders   237
      Social Phobia   237
      Separation Anxiety   238
      Generalized Anxiety Disorder   239
      Panic Disorder   239
      Post-traumatic Stress Disorder   239
      Obsessive-Compulsive Disorder   240
      Treatment   241

Mood Disorders   242
    Bipolar Disorder   242
    Separation and Loss   244
    Suicide   244
    Treatment   244
Conduct Disorder   245
    Oppositional Defiant Disorder   246
    Treatment   247
Attention-Deficit/Hyperactivity Disorder (ADHD)   247
    Treatment   248
Language and Learning Disorders (LLD)   248
    Treatment   249
Mental Retardation   249
    Treatment   251
Pervasive Developmental Disorders   251
    Autism   251
    Rett's Disorder   251
    Childhood Disintegrative Disorder   251
    Asperger's Disorder   252
    Treatment   252
Summary   253

CHAPTER 15   **The Law, Ethics, and Research**   254

Introduction   255
Legal and Ethical Guidelines   255
History of Children's Rights   256
Landmark Court Cases in Children's Rights   257
Ethical Issues in Play Therapy   259
Research   265
Summary   266

CHAPTER 16   **Cultural Sensitivity and Play Therapy**   268

Introduction   268
Toy Selection   272
Role of the Therapist   272
Structuring the Session   274
Limit Setting   278
Parent Involvement   278
Termination   280
Assessment   281
Summary   282

APPENDIX A   *Association for Play Therapy Standards of Practice*   283

APPENDIX B   *How to Become a Registered Play Therapist*   293

APPENDIX C   *How to Become a Registered Play Therapist Supervisor*   296

REFERENCES   299

NAME INDEX   317

SUBJECT INDEX   322

Note: Every effort has been made to provide accurate and current Internet information in this book. However, the Internet and information posted on it are constantly changing, so it is inevitable that some of the Internet addresses listed in this textbook will change.

CHAPTER 1

INTRODUCTION

The play therapist begins observations of the child as soon as the child arrives for the session.

In this chapter we define play therapy, review the history of mental health services for children, and outline the history of psychotherapy with children. Play has been an integral part of psychotherapy with children, but not until recent decades did play therapy become a distinct specialization among mental health workers. With this growth in the field and the many adaptations of personality theory, the play therapist is encouraged to develop a personal theory for working with children.

WHAT IS PLAY THERAPY?

Play therapy has grown out of a need to provide intervention to children with problem behaviors. Traditional therapies have required clients to be verbal participants in their own therapy. Because of the language development of children, however, traditional therapies, which require verbalizations of emotions and events, have had limited application. The child's lack of ability in using verbal symbols or words has greatly limited the development of traditional therapies with children. Children are believed to conceptualize the world in which they live at a much higher level than their verbal development. Thus the use of tangible manipulatives appeared to be the optimal method to help children communicate with the therapist those feelings, events, and ideations that are beyond their language development.

Play therapy has grown beyond the simple use of toys for communication in a playroom to include most of the expressive forms of therapy: art, music, dance, drama, movement, poetry, and storytelling. Although the mainstay of therapy is still the playroom with its selection of symbolic toys, the play therapist has greatly expanded the medium for nonverbal and verbal expression.

Play therapy has gone beyond the one-on-one relationship between a therapist and a child. First, the client may be an infant or an elderly person. Second, the therapist may become a consultant/teacher to parents, teaching/training parents to provide the actual therapy as in filial therapy. Third, the number of children or clients seen at one time may be greater than the one-on-one relationship, as in group play therapy.

Play therapists use music, art, poetry, literature, drama, and storytelling in addition to the selection of toys, but they are not considered music therapists, art therapists, drama therapists, or dance therapists. These therapeutic specialties require specific training and certification or licensure. Although the play therapist may borrow some of the techniques, the play therapist is always a play therapist.

The term *play therapy* often leads professionals unfamiliar with child therapy to misunderstand what play therapy is. The emphasis is not on the word *play,* but rather on the term *therapy.* Play therapy is an intervention, based on theoretical premises and accepted as a recognized therapy. The process may appear simple on the surface, but the depth of the therapy is challenging and requires a great deal of training to do it successfully. Play therapy is very different from the play interview used by many interviewers in the realm of child sexual abuse. The play interview is intended to help the child disclose evidence leading to the conviction of an offender. Play therapy is designed to provide the child with skills and experiences that will assist him or her in overcoming behavior difficulties and/or adjustment problems or reducing trauma.

Play therapy is the use of toys to take the place of words in telling the child's story and in expressing the child's emotions. It assists the child in making the abstract concrete through the medium of tangible items. The Association for Play Therapy's definition is "the systematic use of a theoretical model to establish an interpersonal process wherein trained play therapists use the therapeutic powers of play to help clients prevent or resolve psychosocial difficulties and achieve optimal growth and development."

Play therapy uses toys to establish an interpersonal process, to help children prevent or resolve difficulties, and to achieve maximum growth and development.

HISTORICAL DEVELOPMENT

Treatment of children is a relatively new concept in the mental health field. The child mental health movement appears to be a phenomenon of the 20th century (Kanner, 1948). The first attempt to understand child behavior was not in the area of mental health, but rather in the field of mental retardation.

Roots in Special Education

In 1799 Jean Itard attempted to educate the Wild Boy of Aveyron, who was thought to be raised by wolves. Itard thought that by teaching the Wild Boy to read, write, and function in society, he could establish that nurture is greater than nature in the educational process. Although Itard was only moderately successful in teaching the Wild Boy to function in society, he was successful in establishing a methodology for teaching the mentally retarded. Edwin Seguin in the 19th century continued and expanded work with the mentally retarded by research into causes, nature, and treatment (Achenbach, 1974). Residential schools were built for the mentally retarded in the United States. The first school for the mentally retarded was built in Massachusetts in 1848, followed by a second in New York in 1851. These institutions differed in that they were educational facilities rather than asylums. The initial goal was to train the retarded to function in society and then to return them to their homes. Although the goal of the so-called state school was to develop functioning individuals, by the end of the 19th century, the school had become a custodial treatment facility (Morris & Kratochwill, 1983).

Mental Health and the Child Guidance Movement

In 1901, the juvenile psychopathic institute was established in Chicago under the leadership of William Healy. The institute concentrated on studying juvenile offenders. Social workers, psychologists, and psychiatrists worked together in an interdisciplinary setting on particular cases, examining the multiple factors contributing to each child's behavior disorders.

In 1906, Lightner Witmer established the first child guidance clinic at the University of Pennsylvania preceding the publication of Beers's book, which provided the impetus of concern for mental health care.

Early in the 20th century, several concerns in mental health came to the forefront: the mental hygiene movement, child guidance clinics, and dynamic psychiatry. Clifford Beers (1908) published *A Mind That Found Itself*. His book related his experiences when he was hospitalized for depression and suicidal tendencies. Beers described the maltreatment of patients in state hospitals. The book was widely read, raising the level of awareness of the deplorable state of mental health treatment.

Especially significant was the interest of many prominent professionals and their advocacy of the need for change. The National Committee for Mental Hygiene was formed to provide information to the public concerning state hospital conditions, to improve mental health treatment methods, and to sponsor research on the prevention and treatment of mental illness. As an outgrowth of this mental health movement, mental hygiene programs began in schools and child guidance clinics were developed (Morris & Kratochwill, 1983).

As the chronology later in the chapter gives testament, many researchers and early mental health and social workers were seeking solutions to similar problems in isolation. Under the guidance and encouragement of the National Committee for Mental Hygiene, about 500 child guidance clinics were established by 1930, which allowed possible solutions to be shared and examined (Morris & Kratochwill, 1983).

Prevention of Cruelty to Children

Another movement during this period of time that impacted the cause of children's welfare was a move against child abuse. Historically, child abuse was considered a "family matter," and laws were not enacted to protect children until the late 1880s. First of all, children were considered the property of their parents, and second, severe physical punishment was considered necessary. The biblical phrase "spare the rod and spoil the child" was the justification for the treatment of children during this period. The first program to help abused children was organized in New York City (Kempe & Kempe, 1984) in 1871.

Mary Ellen Wilson, a foster child, suffered horrible atrocities at the hands of her foster mother. In New York's Hell's Kitchen of the 1860s and 1870s, no help was available for a little girl lost in this nightmare of existence. Etta Angell Wheeler, a social worker, heard of the little girl's plight and convinced Henry Bergh, founder of the American Society for Prevention of Cruelty to Animals, to remove the child on a warrant that was intended to remove a dog. Wilson became the first child to be removed from her home for child abuse. Her story is poignantly told in *Out of the Darkness: The Story of Mary Ellen Wilson* (Shelman & Lazoritz, 1998, 2000).

Through this landmark court case in 1874, the Society for the Prevention of Cruelty to Children was born. The case resulted in legislation passed in 1875 requiring police and courts to assist in protecting children from cruelty. By 1880 over 30 chapters of the Society for the Prevention of Cruelty to Children had been established in the United States and 15 in other countries (Gordon, 1985).

By 1909 the White House Conference on Children stated that a vital part of child protection was to work with parents to prevent abuse and neglect from reoccurring (O'Brien, 1980). Finally, by 1968, all 50 states had enacted laws that require reporting of child abuse. In 1974 the Child Abuse Prevention and Treatment Act was signed into law, creating the National Center on Child Abuse and Neglect (O'Brien, 1980).

Psychoanalytic Beginnings

Dynamic psychiatry was introduced by Sigmund Freud in Europe and by Adolph Meyer in the United States. The advocates of dynamic psychiatry believed that current behavior originates in the person's past. This viewpoint placed new emphasis on childhood experiences. In therapy, the patient explores past experiences. Therapists interpreted a cause-and-effect relationship between the current behavior patterns and their childhood experiences of their patients. Even though this therapy emphasized childhood experiences so heavily, children were not seen at first. Because of the focus on childhood and its effects on adult behavior, sufficient interest developed among professionals that created a new interest in observing children (Morris & Kratochwill, 1983).

Hug-Hellmuth, Melanie Klein, Anna Freud, and Margaret Lowenfeld all took up the challenge to work with children in the early 20th century. Their work was based on the concept that if neurotic behavior patterns are formed in early childhood, early intervention is indicated as a course of action to prevent adult difficulties. However, these founding mothers did not agree on how children are affected or the role of play in the child's treatment.

Hermine Hug-Hellmuth.   Hermine Hug-Hellmuth is considered the very first play therapist and the first practicing child psychoanalyst. She appears in many texts under forms of her name: Hug, Hug-Hellmuth, Hug von Hellmuth, and Hug von Hugenstein. Much of this confusion may be because Hug-Hellmuth chose to be somewhat of a mystery. History has no picture of her, and until the latter part of the 1900s, no biography. MacLean and Rappen (1991) wrote that she was one of the first women to earn a doctorate in physics from the University of Vienna. Prior to a degree in physics, she was a teacher with both secondary and elementary teaching qualifications that emphasized the sciences. Hug-Hellmuth has been credited as the first therapist to make observations in child development from the psychoanalytic point of view. She was the third woman to be accepted into the prestigious Vienna Psychoanalytic Society and the first non-Jewish member. (MacLean & Rappen, 1991).

Hug-Hellmuth was murdered in 1924 at age 53 by her nephew. Her will requested that nothing should ever be written about her or her work. Thus she was mentioned mostly in passing in a few texts on the history of child psychoanalysis. However, she did publish six papers (MacLean & Rappen, 1991).

Hermine Hug-Hellmuth was one of the first to report findings that children exhibited gender differences in play preferences.

At the close of World War I, the work of Hug-Hellmuth emerged in the child therapy field and provoked a change in the analysis of children. Until this time, children had been chiefly psychoanalyzed using adult techniques. Hug-Helmuth viewed the analysis of children and adults as "the restoration of the psyche to health and equilibrium which have been endangered through influences known and unknown" (Hug-Hellmuth, 1921, in MacLean & Rappen, 1991, p. 287). She stated that the purpose of analysis is more than to free the child of suffering, but also to provide the child with moral and aesthetic values. Hug-Helmuth said the aim of child analysis is character analysis, which she equated with education (MacLean & Rappen, 1991).

Hug-Hellmuth listed three considerations that make children different from their adult counterparts in therapy. First, the child does not come willingly to therapy, but rather because his or her parents have given up hope of other interventions. Second, the child is not suffering from past experiences, but present ones in the child's environment. Finally, children do not wish to give up the power of their naughtiness (MacLean & Rappen, 1991).

Hug-Hellmuth demanded that play be used in the analysis of children 7 years of age or younger (Lebo, 1955). She stated,

> When dealing with children of seven or eight years of age, the analyst can often pave the way by sharing in the play activities, and thus he can recognize several symptoms, peculiar habits and character traits; and in the case of these very young patients, very often play will enact an important part throughout the whole treatment. (MacLean & Rappen, 1991, p. 294)

Hug-Hellmuth did not formulate a distinct method of play therapy, but it is known she used play as a basis for much of her analysis. In 1924 she gave a 12-part lecture series, translated as "New Ways to the Understanding of Youth," at a conference in Leipzig and Vienna. The lectures, aimed at parents, teachers, educators, school physicians, kindergarten teachers, and social workers, were her final publications (MacLean & Rappen, 1991).

The ninth lecture, "Children's Play" (MacLean & Rappen, 1991), states the principles of observation that Hug-Hellmuth most likely used in her observations in child psychoanalysis. Hug-Hellmuth said that in free play the child discloses with spontaneity and originality. She believed that only in play is the child uninhibited because other activities are forced by models and discipline. And through play, the child can approach serious matters with less anxiety.

According to Hug-Hellmuth, the reason children play is to fulfill their wish to be adults; therefore, adults always serve as the model for the play. The motives of this play could be learning gender roles or even revenge toward adult domination. The role of the play depends on what childhood experiences are of concern to the child. (MacLean & Rappen, 1991).

Play allows the child to free all the different drives. Because Hug-Hellmuth's theory was drive oriented, the analyst could not understand play in a teleological (goal-directed) or operational sense. To limit play to goals and operations would negate the importance and satisfaction of the drives and impulses displayed in the play. Free play is much like fantasies and dreams with suppression, displacement, condensation, symbolization, identification, and rationalization exhibited (MacLean & Rappen, 1991). Play begins with a real situation, but the child manipulates the reality in play to change the passive role to an active one. Through this paradigm shift, the child discharges the affect that has not been directed in a meaningful manner.

The child's play, according to Hug-Hellmuth (MacLean & Rappen, 1991), provides the observer with insight into the child's imaginings, wishes, and challenges that discipline attempts to suppress. She said of specific types of play: "Fighting and catching games represent the early developing possessive drive; all kinds of competition, being physical or mental, are nurtured by the narcissistic drive for honor" (p. 194).

She explained further that the child needs to be ensured success in play situations because of feelings of inferiority or the need to be superior. The child suffers from either the over- or underestimation of ego values. She also believed that in all fighting and competitive games sadism, masochism, and malice are expressed in behavior not allowed in other forms of play.

Children who play theater or drama games are most likely to suffer from exhibitionism, according to Hug-Hellmuth (MacLean & Rappen, 1991). She believed costumes, processions, funerals, gymnastics, and sports reflect a need for "lustful watching and self-exposure" (p. 195).

The physical and psychological nature decides the child's behavior in play, by influencing the choices, preferences, and games that the child engages. The overly neat and the anal retentive child may spend most of the time arranging the toys. This arranging and ordering behavior displays itself in adult life with scheduling and organization. The little collector saves things up and is the original anal-erotic. The child who starts lots of games but never finishes one or cleans up after a game may have difficulties in concentration. Her observation would later be one of the identifying characteristics of attention-deficit/hyperactive disorder.

Hug-Hellmuth noted that gender preferences are observed in play. She felt that the preferences are because of identification with specific social gender roles. She expressed the observation that if left uninhibited and not socially educated, children do not make gender preferences in play. The more social contact the child has, the more the social gender roles are observed in the play.

Hug-Hellmuth (MacLean & Rappen, 1991) said that only children tend to have conflicts between wanting to overcome their loneliness and losing their position of attention. When there is loss of attention, the only child may feel lonely even among peers. And if the child does find someone with whom to play, the only child may overwhelm the playmate "with the energies of his unsatisfied instinctual life" (p. 198). This insatiable need for expression leads the child to a lack of what Hug-Hellmuth calls "the soul's resting point," which she said was important to avoid being ill or miserable. The only child would only find resolution if the seriousness and playfulness are balanced and this balance is identified in the child's play.

Although Hug-Hellmuth expressed strong opinions, she did not formulate a therapeutic structure; nor did she apply her ideas to children under 6 years of age (Landreth, 1987). She saw play as a way to traverse the communication gap between the therapist and the child. In addition, Hug-Hellmuth accentuated educational features in working with children. Educational emphasis continued but did not have guidelines and applications until the work of Melanie Klein (Lebo, 1955).

Conflict Among Early Play Therapists.   Klein said of Hug-Hellmuth; "H. Hug-Hellmuth, who had the honorable distinction of having been the first to undertake the systematic analysis of children, approached her task with the certain preconceptions in her mind, which she also retained to the last" (Klein, 1975a, p. 140). Many of Klein's writings (Klein, 1975a, 1975b, 1975c; Klein, Mannuzza, Chapman, & Fyer, 1992) are predicated with statements reflecting her view on the work of Hug-Hellmuth (MacLean & Rappen, 1991) and Anna Freud (Freud, 1909/1955, 1928, 1959, 1964, 1965, 1967; Freud & Baines, 1946; Freud & Clark, 1928; Freud & Low, 1931, 1935). Margaret Lowenfeld was also a recipient of Klein's contempt for other perceptions of the psychological and developmental treatment of children (Levy, 1938; Urwin & Hood-Williams, 1988).

Klein's differences in opinion with her contemporaries resulted in two distinct schools of child analysis based on her work and the work of Anna Freud. The crux of the distinction rested in the perceived development of the superego and ego of the child. The followers of Klein would come to be known as the Berlin school; the followers of Anna Freud would come to be called the Vienna school.

Margaret Lowenfeld (Levy, 1938) was a contemporary of Anna Freud and Melanie Klein. She developed a form of child psychotherapy that differed in emphasis from psychoanalytic therapy at the time. She stressed that play not only can help a child master or gain control over emotional conflicts or confusion but also provides access to the cognitive processes of children's thinking (Urwin & Hood-Williams, 1988).

The controversy among these three women did a great deal to diversify the treatment of children and to stimulate further work with young children. Their theories are treated in more detail later in this text.

Release Therapy

Structured play scenarios were devised in the 1930s. Two therapies that gained importance were release therapy (Solomon, 1938) and active play therapy (Lebo, 1955). In release therapy (Levy, 1938) interventions are selected on the basis of what traumatic incident the child has experienced. The therapist's role is to encourage the child to reenact the scene. Establishment of a relationship with the therapist is not necessary for successful therapy (Levy, 1938). Through this reenactment, release therapy (Solomon, 1938) was used in the following manner:

> The therapeutic device was simply to restore the situation in which the patient was attacked, releasing what was occasioned by it, repeating it to the point where the fears could be discharged and aggression—in other words, to enable the child to complete an act which had been blocked presumably by fear. (p. 141)

Active play therapy (Solomon, 1955) was introduced as a contemporary therapy. The active play therapy technique provides a method of symbolic substitutions that allows the child to enjoy the activity while releasing the child's rage. When the child uses a toy to release frustrations symbolically, the child externalizes his or her impulses onto another object. Through the act of externalizing the child's impulses, the need for acting out behavior in real-life situations is released. With the release of the frustration, the child is afforded the opportunity to solve problems in a more realistic manner and within the safety of the playroom (Solomon, 1948). A child progresses through seven observable periods in active play therapy:

1. Contact with the child's thinking.
2. Abreaction of the anxiety and aggressive impulses.
3. Working through dependent wishes.
4. Affording alternatives to the feeling of impending tragedy.
5. Release of tender impulses in an atmosphere of acceptance.
6. Alleviation of the sense of guilt.
7. Crystallization of the ego's structure in terms of reality. (Solomon, 1948, p. 407)

Solomon used play therapy to redirect the acting-out behavior into a more positive social-oriented behavior while helping children "to separate out anxiety over past traumas and future consequences from the reality of their present life situations" (Hambridge, 1955, p. 6).

Structured play therapy (Moustakas, 1959; Moustakas & Schalock, 1955) was patterned much like Levy's work. According to Hambridge (1955), a "therapist acts to focus attention, to stimulate further activity, to give approval, to gain information, to interpret or to set limits" (p. 106). He warned that the technique should be used with selectivity and is sometimes inappropriate for use. Hambridge (1955) suggested the following as appropriate scenarios: a baby at the mother's breast (sibling rivalry), balloon bursting (release aggression), peer attack, punishment, separation, genital differences (dolls modified with clay genitalia), controlling parent, seeing his parents during sexual intercourse, birth of the baby (using a hollow doll with pelvic opening), specific threats, acting out a dream, and other individualized play. His structured situations were introduced after the relationship was established with the child. Hambridge (1955) waited until he felt the child was strong enough to handle the directness of the procedure. After the play scenario was provided and played out, the child was allowed to debrief using a free playtime (Hambridge, 1955).

Relationship Therapy

Rank (1936), Allen (1939, 1942), and Taft (1933) became known as the relationship therapists. Rank (1936) did not formulate a theory to work with children; rather, his theory was adapted to the therapist-child relationship. Because Rank did not work with children, his theory espoused a belief that the quality of the relationship between the therapist and the adult client is therapeutic. This belief that the relationship is the therapy was later applied to work with children.

Therapists may use structured play therapy in preparing a child for court appearances.

This concept of the client-therapist relationship was taken further by Allen (1942), who was one of the first to emphasize being fully human with the child. The psychoanalytic view of being distant, unseen, and objective was cast aside in favor of a strong relationship between the client and therapist.

Following this contention was the belief that the relationship of the therapist to the client has curative powers. As a result, the emphasis was heavily on the interactions of the child and therapist in the realities of the present moment. These therapists still retained a strong tie to the psychoanalytic theory of attachment and individuation. According to the theory of attachment, children have a difficult time separating from the mother, which results in either a clinging child or a child unable to relate to others. Individuation is the realization that the child is independent of the mother and capable of independent action, movement, or thought. If the child does not individuate appropriately, he or she might become either too dependent or too detached. Moustakas (Rogers, 1942) was included in this group by Schaefer and O'Connor (1983) because Moustakas emphasized the necessity of the therapist helping the child individuate in the secure relationship with the play therapist.

Nondirective Therapy

Rogers (Dorfman, 1951) expanded and extended the work of the relationship therapist into what he termed *nondirective therapy*, which became client-centered therapy (Dorfman, 1951). In Rogers's classic text, *Client-Centered Therapy* (1951), Elaine Dorfman (Axline & Carmichael, 1947) contributed to the chapter entitled "Play Therapy." Dorfman basically reviewed the work done by Axline (Bixler, 1949).

Axline (1947) was a student and a colleague of Carl Rogers. Using what she had learned from Rogers, Axline (1947) developed what would become known as child-centered play therapy. Her eight basic principles of nondirective play therapy have become what Schaefer and O'Connor (1983) have termed "the credo of the approach" (p. 7). Those principles are paraphrased here:

1. A therapist must develop a warm, friendly relationship with the child, in which good rapport is established as soon as possible.
2. A therapist accepts the child exactly as he or she is.
3. A therapist establishes a feeling of permissiveness in the relationship so the child feels free to express his or her feelings completely.
4. A therapist is alert to recognize the feelings the child is expressing and reflects those feelings back to him or her in such a manner that the child gains insight into the behavior.
5. A therapist maintains a deep respect for the child's ability to solve some problems if given an opportunity to do so. It is the child's responsibility to make choices and to institute changes.
6. A therapist does not attempt to direct the child's actions or conversation in any manner. The child leads the way; the therapist follows.
7. A therapist does not attempt to hurry therapy along; therapy is a gradual process and recognized as such by the therapist.

8. A therapist establishes only those limitations that are necessary to anchor the therapy to the world of reality and to make the child aware of his or her responsibility in the relationship. (pp. 73–74)

Limits as Therapy

Bixler (1959) wrote an article entitled "Limits Are Therapy," introducing the belief that by setting limits properly, the child develops a sense of security and trust in adults. Through consistent limit setting, the child is provided with a safe environment to express the self without fear of self or of retaliation. In addition, the therapist maintains a positive attitude toward the child because the therapist does not have to tolerate aggressive, hostile, or destructive behavior.

Ginott (Ginott, 1961, 1994) was a proponent of this method. He was one of the first to use play therapy with a group of children (Ginott, 1965, 1969a; Ginott, Ginott, & Goddard, 2003). Ginott's work led him to formulate some basic ideas about effective communication with children and teenagers. A major emphasis in his books is how to set appropriate and effective limitations on the child's behavior. He presented principles of effective communication in his books *Between Parent and Child* (1965, 1969a), *Between Teachers and Children* (1972, 1993), and *Between Parents and Teenager* (1969b).

Erik Erikson

Erikson (1950) invited 10- to 12-year-old boys and girls in California to construct an "imaginary moving picture" on a tabletop. The toys to choose from included such materials as a doll family, a policeman, a Native American, a monk, an aviator, wild animals, domestic animals, doll furniture, cars, trucks, and a large assortment of wooden blocks. Erikson was surprised that with only a moment of reflection, the children constructed their "moving pictures." Having observed nearly 450 cases, Erikson indicated that the play constructions were personality revelations. Erikson found that boys' constructions and girls' constructions differed along the lines of topography and design.

Male constructions were characterized by outward and upward projections, which Erikson interpreted as a learned desire to achieve high standing and to be aggressive, mobile, and independent, the prevalent stereotype of the male role of the time. To Erikson, these projections had a phallic quality that paralleled the male genitals (Monte, 1987).

Female constructions showed girls as preoccupied with house interiors and enclosed, static space, which reflected the dominate culture's stereotyped role of the female in taking care of the home, bearing children, and rearing children in peaceful confines. Again, Erikson saw these constructions as indicative of the female genitals (Monte, 1987).

Thus Erikson believed the child's play construction was evidence of a predisposing effect of the individual's sense of his or her body. To a limited degree, Erikson was saying anatomy is destiny. Erikson's original study has undergone criticism in the political changes that have emerged since it was first accomplished. Replications of the study have not supported Erikson's findings. His greater contribution to the field

Play therapists may use toys to produce what Erikson termed "moving pictures" on tabletops to help gain insight into the thoughts and feelings of children.

of play therapy has been his theory of the eight stages of psychosocial development theory (Erikson, 1950).

Play Therapy in Schools

In the 1960s guidance and counseling programs became established in elementary schools. Professional journals, such as the *Elementary School Guidance and Counseling Journal,* were established by the American Personal Guidance Association, later called the American Association for Counseling and Development, eventually called the American Counseling Association. Prior to this time the writing in the area of play therapy had focused on private practice with emotionally disturbed children. With the increased demand for counselors in the elementary schools, writings by counselor educators began to appear in the literature. Alexander (1969), Landreth, Jacquot, and Allen (1968), Muro and Dinkmeyer (1977), Myrick and Holdin (1971), Nelson (1970), and Waterland (1970) championed the use of play therapy to meet the developmental needs of school children. These authors believed play therapy is not just for the maladjusted but for the child needing preventative interventions.

TOWARD A PROFESSIONAL IDENTITY

Play therapy has continued to gain acceptance and prominence in working with children. In 1980 the Center for Play Therapy was established in Denton, Texas, under the direction of Garry Landreth. The center houses the most complete library of play therapy publications.

The Association for Play Therapy (APT) was envisioned by Charles Schaefer and Kevin O'Connor in 1982 as a forum for professionals using play interventions as the primary mode of therapy for children. On the organizational board of directors were Charles Schaefer, Kevin O'Connor, Garry Landreth, Louise Guerney, Ann Jernberg, Eleanor Irwin, and Eileen Nickerson. The organization had 25 charter members. In June 1982 the Association for Play Therapy Newsletter was first published. The initial APT conferences were local or regional. The first executive director was Kevin O'Connor, who provided guidance for the organization through his academic office at the California School of Psychology in Fresno. The first National/International APT conference began in New Jersey in 1984 and continued to meet annually in the New York area until 1987. In 1987 the Fifth National APT Conference was held in Denton, Texas.

Following the 1987 conference, the site of the annual national conference has been in different states and regions each year. The Association for Play Therapy was formalized in early 1986 and continues to provide national and international conferences. The initial appointed board members were Garry Landreth, Louise Guerney, and John Allan. Charles Schaefer was the chairman of the board and Kevin O'Connor, the executive director. The founding board members were selected because they comprised the leaders in the field of play therapy at the time. Each of the original board members has made a significant contribution to the field of play therapy and an even greater contribution to the growing professional identity of the profession through their service on the APT board.

In 1990 a developing national certification and training criteria became the work of the APT. With the hope of establishing the criteria for training that would lead to the recognition of play therapy as a specialty in the field of psychotherapy, the association has gone about the work of providing registration, supervision, and recognition for the play therapist's work with children. The number of play therapists trained every year is growing, as is the greater demand for training facilities. The projected number of play therapists presently listed as members of the APT is well over 2,000.

In 2000 a total of 33 states had state branches affiliated with the APT. Two international branches, in British Columbia and South Africa, are affiliates. APT recently developed a dual membership program in which a person is required to be both a state and a national member. The organization continued to advocate play therapy's growth as a specialty and profession with the adoption of its Professional Practice Guidelines in 2000.

In 2003 the APT set up as a separate entity the Play Therapy Foundation, dedicated to the furthering of research and promotion of play therapy. The foundation continues to grow and sponsor activities to enhance the promotion and dissemination of play therapy research.

Highlights in the historical development of child therapy are summarized in the child psychotherapy and play therapy timeline. The increasing importance of studying children and their mental health can be seen with the rapid growth of interest in children in the twentieth century. As we are entering the 21st century, this interest in children's mental health and social concerns continues to grow and expand.

Child Psychotherapy and Play Therapy Timeline

1762   Jean-Jacques Rousseau publishes *Emile* and makes observation that play is important in understanding children.

1799   Jean Itard writes about the study of the Wild Boy of Aveyron, one of the first case studies of child development, education, and nature versus nurture studies.

1848   First school built for the mentally retarded in Massachusetts.

1851   School built for the mentally retarded in New York.

1871   First program to help abused children in New York.

1880   Thirty-three societies for Prevention of Cruelty to Children had been established.

1901   Juvenile psychopathic institute established in Chicago.

1903   Sigmund Freud publishes his theory of psychosexual stages.

Froebel writes in his *The Education of Man* that play has both conscious and unconscious purposes.

1906   Lightner Wittmer establishes the first child guidance clinic at the University of Pennsylvania.

1907   Freud's *Sexual Enlightenment of Children* published, which first mentions Little Hans.

1908   In his *On the Sexual Theories of Children*, Freud states that the study of Little Hans presents "irrefutable proof of the correctness of a view towards which the psycho-analysis of adults had long been leading me."

1909   Freud publishes the entire case study of Little Hans in his paper, *Analysis of a Phobia in a Five-Year-Old Boy*.

1910   White House Conference on Children states that a vital part of child protection is to work with parents to prevent abuse and neglect.

1913   Hug-Hellmuth begins interpreting children's play in analysis.

1919   Melanie Klein begins using play techniques in her analysis of children under 6.

1921   Hug-Hellmuth urges the use of play materials in the analysis of young children.

1922   Anna Freud introduces her techniques of child analysis.

1924   Hug-Hellmuth gives a series of lectures entitled "New Ways to the Understanding of Youth," in which she advised that play allows a child to approach serious matters with less anxiety.

1928   Margaret Lowenfeld founds the Children's Clinic for the Treatment and Study of Nervous and Difficult Children, which recognizes the importance of children's play.

1933   David Levy introduces experimental play method.

1934   Fredrick Allen applies relationship therapy to work with children using noninterpretative methods. In the "Psychiatric Physical Examination," the child pretended to be a physician and examined himself or herself and then provided a diagnosis (Allen, 1934).

1935   Lowenfeld publishes *Play in Childhood*.

1936   Bender and Woltman introduce group play therapy through the use of puppets.

1937   Bender and Woltman introduce Gestalt play therapy using plastic material in working with emotionally disturbed children.

1938   Solomon develops his active play therapy.

Levy begins publishing articles about a technique called release therapy.

1939   Lowenfeld first describes the world technique, which will become "sand play."

1940   Baruch writes about using play therapy as part of the educative process.

(continues)

1941	Bender and Woltman describe the first use of music in play therapy.
	Baruch is the first to suggest that teachers be trained to provide play therapy.
1942	Masani introduces behavioral play therapy.
1947	Virginia Axline writes about nondirective play therapy based on Carl Rogers's theory.
1948	Solomon hypothesizes that a child progresses through seven phenomena in active play therapy.
1949	Bixler writes that limits are therapy.
1950	Bach provides dramatic play therapy with adult groups.
1952	Lauretta Bender publishes *Child Psychatric Techniques*.
1955	Hambridge introduces structured play therapy.
	Moustakas develops relationship play therapy.
	Rabinovich introduces the use of play therapy for child victims of abused children.
1957	Levitt publishes figures that do not support the contention that psychotherapy with children is more effective than nonintervention.
1958	Dorfman contributes a chapter in Rogers's *Client-Centered Therapy* entitled "Play Therapy."
1961	Ginott says "the play of a child is talk with toys as words" and provides guidelines for group play therapy.
1964	Bernard Guerney publishes an article entitled "Filial Therapy: Description and Rationale."
	Alexander introduces the first school-centered play therapy program.
1966	Marcus introduces costume play therapy, which asks the child to develop a story or scene using the costume.
1968	Gardner introduces the mutual storytelling method.
1974	Yura and Glassi describe the Adlerian application of play therapy.
1976	Louise Guerney publishes *Training Manual for Parents: Instruction in Filial Therapy*.
	Schaefer begins to define what becomes known as prescriptive play therapy with the publication of *The Therapeutic Use of Child's Play*.
1978	John Allan describes the application of Jungian theory in looking at serial drawings.
	Oaklander introduces a description and application of Gestalt play therapy.
1979	Jernberg introduces *Theraplay: A New Treatment Using Structured Play for Problem Children and Their Families*.
1980	The Center for Play Therapy is established in Denton, Texas.
1982	Association for Play Therapy (APT) is conceptualized by Kevin O'Connor and Charles Schaefer.
1986	The Association for Play Therapy is formalized.
1991	Landreth publishes *The Art of the Relationship*, which describes the application of child-centered theory to play therapy.
	O'Connor describes the theory of ecosystems play therapy.
1992	Brody describes developmental play therapy as a dialogue of touch.
1999	APT writes its first Standards of Practice.
	Bratton and Dee summarize the indications of play therapy from the research to date.
2000	APT publishes Practice Standards.
2001	APT expands services to include limited play therapy training and continuing education through electronic courses.

The Purpose of a Theory

This text was written to help the novice play therapist develop the theoretical and professional foundations needed for the provision of play therapy. Most important in formulating a solid foundation for therapy is the understanding and development of a personal theory. The purpose of a theory has always been to provide an underpinning for the interventions a therapist uses with the client. Think of the theory as a sort of coat rack that supports and holds up the philosophical coats of personality development, role of the therapist, model of pathology, treatment goals, interventions, and major assumptions. Without this structure, the coats would be tossed about the floor haphazardly and difficult to find when needed.

Although it is possible to wear someone else's coat or philosophical construct for the time being, we return to the familiar and comfortable time and again. When you develop your personal theory of therapy, those most comfortable ideologies are the constructs that underpin your unique theory. Early on in the study of theories, a therapist may try on many different coats, but one style of therapy will always fit better and be more comfortable. Even those therapists who feel they must be in fashion, so to speak, will perhaps flit toward each new style of therapy only to return in a pinch to the most comfortable. During this time of study, you must learn what is most comfortable and fits best. A theory becomes a second skin that dominates and guides the therapist within the world of therapy, and, for many, within the world at large.

Without a theory, you do not have a direction. Many therapists may claim they do not have a theory. If this is true, then their activities and interventions with the clients are unpredictable, unplanned, and unstable. Many others claim to be eclectic because they believe a theory makes them lose flexibility in working with clients. The term *eclectic* is used too often as synonymous with "I have no clue what I am doing, so I will say I do everything." True eclectics will discover that their interventions and beliefs about normal and abnormal behavior fall within a cluster of theories (e.g., psychodynamic, cognitive-behavioral, behavioral, humanistic, systems, communications, etc.). A theory is not rigid attendance to only one set of thoughts. It is a growing and expanding body of constructs that are assimilated and accommodated into your perception of the world of therapy.

Piaget discusses how children take information they gain from the world and place it into an organization of categories that are already known to them, expanding the definition of the category and thus assimilating the concept or construct. When children come upon a new concept or construct, they examine the concept and construct and either discard it or build a new category for this new experience. The latter is accommodation. Constructs and concepts of therapy are also accommodated and assimilated by the therapist. As new learning and new experiences take place, your personal theory of therapy is honed and sharpened into a structured guidebook.

The theories presented here will help you look at the different ways to be with children in a therapeutic relationship. Some of the theories are very structured and direct the child in a specific direction. At the other end of the continuum, the therapist is merely in the presence of the child and allows the "child to find his or her own way" in therapy. The role of the therapist is equally contrasted from activity specific to allowing the child to choose the activity. A major point of departure in the theoretical orientation is whether the therapist serves as a playmate or as an observer in the role of the therapist. Many points of departure exist among the theories. As you read them, decide for yourself what fits you best. In statistics, the term *goodness of fit* is used to describe statistical concepts. I challenge you to explore the goodness of fit in the theories presented here and those you will encounter in future learning experiences.

SUMMARY

In a century of play therapy development, the concept has moved from an extension of adult therapy to a specialized field. The field has grown from a few persons practicing in isolation to a recognized profession with standards for registration and standards of practice. Research has grown from individual case study reports based on observation to complex research designs involving many children. The field has expanded to include parent training in support of the therapy process and extended into training parents to be play therapists for their own children. Play therapy continues to grow and develop as a profession and specialization for work with children.

With this growth of the profession, many theoretical orientations have emerged for the delivery of play therapy to its child clients. With this proliferation of many theories, you as the the play therapist are advised to become aware of the most common theories and to develop your own personal theory of play therapy.

CHAPTER 2

Beginning the Play Therapy Session

A comfortable waiting area helps to relieve the stress that parents and children experience while waiting for the therapy session.

This chapter first discusses the selection, organization, and logistics of setting up your first playroom. Second, the issues of initial interview, informed consent, and other accountability issues are presented. Finally, an example of how a child-centered first session might begin is provided.

Toy Selection

The selection of toys is presented first because many therapists work without a physical playroom. The number and size of the toys you select depends on the age of the children you see and the availability of a playroom. Many therapists who move about from location to location find that a large canvas bag or plastic box is sufficient for what they need. The quality of therapy does not depend on the quality or quantity of the toys.

The more generic the individual toys, the more they are open to the child's interpretation. Therefore, in selecting toys, try to acquire toys that are not associated with specific well-known characters. This need for generic figures is presented as a guideline and is not set in stone, however. With some children, characters with distinct roles that label them as evil or as heroes are often preferred. Therefore, in selecting toys, choose items that clearly have evil qualities and those that clearly have hero qualities, as well as those that can be both good and evil.

Toys for the playroom are not usually mechanical or computer generated. The mechanical games interfere with the process of therapy when the child becomes more focused on making the toy work properly and less focused on the expression of fantasy play. The child can become so frustrated with the toy that valuable therapy time is lost. Similarly, computerized toys allow the child to become absorbed in the toy and not communicate with the therapist in a meaningful way. Unless the child communicates either through play or words, the therapy session is just another play session without therapeutic value.

Cleanliness has become an issue because of the fear of contagious diseases. Select toys that can be washed in disinfectant, if necessary. Stuffed animals are often seen in playrooms. Although they offer a soft and cuddly surface, unless these can be laundered or dry-cleaned regularly, it is best to avoid them. An exception is sometimes made when the child is allowed to bring his or her own stuffed animal or given a personal stuffed animal. When a stuffed animal is necessary for the progression of therapy, you might either have a freshly dry-cleaned one or a new one available for this child. Baby bottles and pacifiers were often used in playrooms in the past. Unless you have a way to always offer a sterilized version, it is best to avoid these. Some play therapists do keep a good supply of sterilized bottles in sterile plastic bags, if they feel this is an important addition to the playroom or necessary for a particular child's play.

Noisy toys can present special problems in schools or office suites shared with others. The sound of bouncing balls or the falling of blocks can be readily handled by purchasing sponge versions. Drums, hammer and nails, musical instruments, and so on, are best avoided if you are providing therapy in an area where noise interferes with being a good neighbor.

Guns pose a special problem. People feel strongly on both sides of the argument of whether guns ought to be presented in the play materials. The argument is that children will be less likely to resort to guns to settle differences if they are not allowed to play with guns. The other proponents claim that children will make guns out of their fingers and hand if toy guns are not provided. Whether or not you offers guns in the play materials is a personal choice. Be aware that some parents strongly object to their child playing with guns. You may want to remove the gun with some children and have it available to others, depending on the therapeutic value of the gun to the child.

Many therapists have phobias about snakes, spiders, or bugs. Although the plastic variety of scary animals is usually included in most play therapy materials, you are not required to have them. If you have a snake phobia, do not include the snake in the selection. The relationship between you and the child is paramount.

Finally, in the same vein, do not have any toy or art supply that would inhibit your acceptance of the child. If the floor is carpeted, paint may not be an option. The same is true of little bits of modeling material that can be ground into the floor. Sand can be problematic because it will wear out a carpet or tiles prematurely. Many therapists have substituted other materials for sand, modeling material, and so on. If you are fearful of the damage to the surroundings, eliminate the possibility of damage so you can focus solely on the child, not on the environment. Another alternative is to move the child and the activity to another place. One therapist allows children to play with paint, finger paints, and a water hose at the back of her office building. The need for the child's expression is met, and the damage element is removed.

Many therapeutic games are commercially available. Although the role of these games is unquestioned in assessment and in skill development, their therapeutic value may be dubious. Many therapists untrained in play therapy rely heavily on these games because they are easy and quick answers to very complicated problems. Some play therapists have many of these games available for use in their offices but may not have them available as a matter of course in the playroom. Avoid board games that have definite winners and losers. The literature does present the use of card games, chess, checkers, and even a typewriter as therapeutic, but the question becomes "Would something else have gotten the same result or a better result?" Again, whether you use a board game with specific rules depends on your philosophy and your ability to relate to the child.

Landreth (1982, 1991, 2002) offers guidelines to assist the therapist in judging whether a toy is therapeutic or not. He suggests that toys:

1. Help the child to express a variety of feelings.
2. Help the child to express personal creativity.
3. Are interesting to the child.
4. Promote expression and exploration in play.
5. Can be used to communicate nonverbally.
6. Can be employed without given rules or traditions.
7. Allow the child work with ambiguous issues.
8. Can take a lot of rough treatment without breaking.

Norton and Norton (1997) offer the following guidelines for selecting toys for the playroom:

1. Toys must be sanitary.
2. Toys must be relationship oriented.
3. Toys must represent the reality in the child's life.
4. Toys should provide for projective play.
5. Toys should enable children to go into fantasy play.
6. Toys should encourage decision making.
7. Toys should enable children to create.

Different authors (Barnes, 1996; Landreth, 1991; Norton & Norton, 1997) have provided lists of essential playroom toys. Barnes (1996) suggests the following toys.

Barnes's Suggested Toy List

boxes	crayons	drawing paper	construction paper
nontoxic glue	fabric	string	pipe cleaners
empty berry boxes	thread	old clothes	sunglasses
safety scissors	puppets	bird's nest	rocks
glass gemstones	wild animals	domestic animals	human figures
primitive animals	tools	fences	marbles
farm equipment	buildings	fantasy figures	spiritual beings
country people	people	sand box	conflict figures

Norton and Norton (1997) provide not only a list of toys, but also what each toy may symbolize in play. Their toys are selected based on this schema of symbolic meaning. For our purposes here, the symbolism is too burdensome to explore. This aspect is discussed later in the symbolism of play. Their list of toys follows.

Norton and Norton's Suggested Toy List

airplanes	planes	art supplies	baby bottles
binoculars	balls	blankets	blocks
books	boxes	broken toys	camera
costumes	dolls	doctor's kit	dinosaurs
doll family	games	finger paints	flashlight
grooming tools	guns	kitchen utensils	knives
magic wand	keys	model cars	play money
monster figure	paints	musical instruments	pillow
playing cards	puppets	puzzles	soldiers
large box or tent	sword	tape recorder	targets
stuffed animals	phones	construction toys	tools

Norton and Norton's list is extensive, but each item has a special reason for inclusion in the playroom using their modality of play therapy.

Norton and Norton (1997) also provide an abbreviated list of portable toys.

Norton and Norton's Suggested Portable Toy Kit List

airplane	animals (domestic)	balls	animals (wild)
cars	clay	doctor's kit	dolls
doll house	family figures	guns	knives
money	musical instruments	paints	puppets
stuffed bear	telephone		

Landreth (1991, 2002) provides what he considers the minimum that will fit into a tote bag. His list of toys for a portable playroom follows.

Landreth's "Tote Bag" Toy List

crayons	doll	clay
rubber knife	toy soldiers	small car
handcuffs	two play dishes	two toy cups
black Halloween mask	sponge ball	spoons
small airplane	pipe cleaners	bendable figure
wooden craft sticks	dart gun	cotton rope
nursing bottle	bendable doll family	telephone
aggressive puppet	transparent tape	doll house furniture
small cardboard box	blunt scissors	costume jewelry
newsprint		

The items considered to be available in the playroom or the expanded list include additional toys.

Landreth's Expanded Toy List for Therapeutic Playrooms

doll bed	doll clothes	pacifier
chalkboard	chalk	colored chalk
toy refrigerator	toy stove	dishes
pitcher	dishpan	plastic food
empty fruit cans	eraser	egg cartons
empty vegetable cans	sponge	towel

(continued)

Landreth's Expanded Toy List for Therapeutic Playrooms—continued

purse and jewelry	broom	dust pan
silverware (toy)	soap	brush
comb	crayons	pencils
transparent tape	paper	paste
toy watch	building blocks	paints
easel	newsprint	paintbrushes
pipe cleaners	tongue depressors	ATV vehicle
tractor	boat	(can actually be ridden)
trucks	cars	bus
pounding bench	xylophone	cymbals
drum	fireman's hat	assorted hats
pine log	hammer and nails	sandbox
large spoon	funnel	sieve
pail	rubber snake	alligator
bop bag	suction darts	target board
toy machine gun	two telephones	medical kit
play money	cash register	hand puppets
tinker toys	tissues	

Comparisons of the lists show some basic items that are considered in all playrooms and some that are specific to the author of the list. One special group of toys that are not mentioned by any of these authors are those that are topically, culturally, or environmentally specific. Those people working in spiritual settings may wish to include objects like rosaries, Bibles, crosses, menorahs, Star of David, prayer rugs, and so on, that are reflective of the child's religious background.

Another consideration would be culturally specific items. In Mexican American communities, you could include a chocolate whip, a stone seed grinder, a tortilla press, and a grill in the kitchen choices. In Native American communities, you would definitely want to have miniatures of animals native to the area. Feathers, stones, pieces of leather, types of pottery, and other materials that are common in their daily life would be helpful. If you use feathers, purchase them from a craft supply because it is against the law in many states to pick up bird feathers from wild birds.

With Native Americans, a description of what should be included varies greatly because there are many nations of Native Americans and they do not always share a common heritage or find the same objects meaningful (Carmichael, 1991). Snakes in some Native American cultures symbolize death. After contact with death symbols, some tribes prescribe a cleansing ritual that can be financially costly to the parents of the child. A therapist who is not from the Native American culture or who is from a different tribe would be prudent to check the meaning of the various animals and artifacts used within the playroom.

In the Pacific Islands, you would also want to include objects specific to their culture. Dolphins, sharks, outrigger boats, surfboards, shells, exotic flowers, and other common elements of their environment need to be included in the playroom. This culture also has taboos that may be unintentionally crossed by the therapist who was not reared in the culture. Therefore check with someone familiar with the culture to make sure no taboo objects are in the playroom that traditionalists believe harm the child (Carmichael, 1991).

In working with children from many cultures, learn what items are important to different cultures. When asked, many people of the community can provide guidelines on what type of toys are unique to their culture and help locate miniatures of important symbols from their background. A good place to shop for culture-specific toys is in a market dealing exclusively with this culture. Most large cities have specialized markets where toys and culturally specific items can be found. Museum, zoo, and aquarium gift shops also provide some unique options (Carmichael, 1991).

Some general guidelines also apply. Remove toys that are broken or have missing pieces, unless there is some particular therapeutic value to the damaged toy. An example is a doll with a broken leg. A therapist reattached the doll's leg and put a cast on it, which made the doll usable again. Sometimes the damaged toy can be therapeutic, but generally it is best to remove toys that have broken or missing pieces. Children may spend valuable time in therapy trying to find a missing part or fixing a broken toy. Although this too can be therapeutic, it may also be inhibiting the child's expression and providing frustration that is not therapeutic.

If you see children with disabilities in your practice, figures that are in wheelchairs, wear glasses or hearing aids, or use crutches or other devices that signal a disability may be helpful. Several doll makers have these toys available. Large toy stores or an Internet search will help locate the dolls you need. One company even offers these special dolls in different ethnic characteristics. Another alternative is to take a soft doll to someone who can make the device for the doll. Although it may be expensive, you can make a realistic cast.

Band-aids, stretch bandages, and arm slings can be made that will fit most of the larger dolls for hospital play. Ambulances, operating rooms, hospital rooms, and other rescue miniatures are available for work with children facing surgery, hospital stays, or chronic illnesses. These miniatures may be helpful in working with children who have gone through a traumatic experience that required medical assistance.

SETTING UP THE PLAYROOM

Most therapists do not have the luxury of designing their playrooms from the building plans. However, you may have the chance to choose appropriate rooms or even have a room remodeled for play therapy. Most of you will have to adapt to the space available in a section of a private office. Whether you are designing from the ground up or adapting a temporary space, there are guidelines you will want to follow. The space that Landreth (1991, 2002) suggests is a room about 12 by 15 feet. Playrooms need to be large enough to accommodate the child's activities but small enough that the child is always within easy visual range.

Many play therapists may not have the opportunity to design and use a therapeutic playroom and may have to adapt a corner of an office space for toys and play materials.

The first consideration is to make sure the space is free from interruptions and private. Barnes (1996) describes the playroom as a "safe place." The space needs to be more than emotionally safe. The electrical outlets must have child safety devices. The furniture should be sturdy enough to take a child climbing without tipping over. Shelves need to be attached to the wall or of sufficient strength not to endanger the child. Check the room for sharp corners, protruding nails, and other hazards for cuts and scrapes. The heating and air conditioning need to be adequate. If you use open windows and window fans, these need to have screens on the windows and protective screening too small for fingers to get to the blades of the fan. Space heaters are not recommended at all. Open windows must have protection so the child cannot fall. When possible, avoid a room with windows to the outside and windows in doors. If necessary, ask your local fire marshal to come and inspect your playroom for dangers.

The playroom should be away from the main flow of traffic in the building. Children make noise even in the best of circumstances. Locate the playroom in an area where it disturbs the fewest people. The noise from the playroom needs to be far enough away from the reception area so the waiting parent cannot hear the child. Not being able to hear outside the door is preferable for purposes of confidentiality. It is not therapeutic for parents, visitors, or other clients to hear what is happening in the playroom.

The floor is best made of vinyl tile or even bare cement. These floors stand up to the hard abuse of a playroom. Carpet may keep the noise down, but it also limits the possible kinds of activities. When selecting flooring, take into account ease of cleaning, durability, and replacement cost. Several new flooring materials offer a natural wood look with low maintenance and durability. A vinyl sheet may be placed on the floor in the painting area to protect the floor from staining. A discarded vinyl window shade works well as an area drop cloth.

The preferred wall covering is washable and stain resistant. Vinyl wall coverings are adequate if a wall covering is used. The smoother the surface, the easier the surface is to clean. Painted surfaces should be enamel. Although many therapists are tempted to paint murals on the walls of windowless playrooms, this is not a good idea. Avoid bright colors, gem colors, and somber colors. Color affects mood in ways that are not fully understood. In addition, bright colors affect hyperactive children negatively. Therefore, the best color is a shade of white to cream. The playroom is not a place to make an interior decorator statement.

The room should have adequate low shelving to display the toys and materials. Where possible, these need to be of substantial quality to hold the weight of the child either sitting or standing on the shelves. Because the child will sometimes climb up on them, make sure the shelves are secured. The room will need an adult chair and appropriate seating for the child. A child-size table/work area is desirable with chairs. The shelves and furniture should be made of sturdy wood with a long-lasting finish. The type of finish used for a roller rink floor, commercial floor, or laminated floor is suitable for the tabletops and shelves. Fabric-covered chairs are not recommended for the playroom because they are difficult to keep clean. Sturdy plastic or hard wood chairs are best.

The lighting needs to be adequate. Recessed lighting with protective guards is preferred. Children may not intentionally throw a ball that hits a light but their aim is often less than ideal. Protect children from the possibility of breaking a light fixture and broken glass.

Access to water may be desirable. Again, if you wish to include water play, a child-height sink needs to be available or you may place a pitcher of water in the playroom. If you do have water, you will need paper towels and paper cups. An argument can be made for having an adjoining lavatory with water closet and sink. The lavatory allows the child to go to the toilet without leaving the playroom. Of course, this adjoining facility should have a door affording the child privacy for toileting.

Most training facilities have a one-way mirror and sound system leading to an adjoining observation room. Although this setup allows better supervision, it is not necessary. Many parents want to observe their child, if such a facility is available. You must determine what is most therapeutic for the child when deciding if observers are allowed or not. The one-way mirror does allow for videotaping of the sessions for supervision or for case review. An observation room is recommended if possible because the benefits outweigh the handicaps.

The chalkboard has mostly been abandoned in favor of the whiteboard and markers because the latter does not use chalk. Many children and therapists are allergic to chalk dust or any dust. The erasable markers need to be nontoxic and in a variety of colors. An appropriate eraser needs to be available. If the whiteboard does not come with a tray along the bottom of the board, talk to your lumberyard about the best material to use to make one or have one made. The proper height for the board, according to Landreth (1991, 2002), is about 21 inches from the floor to the bottom of the board.

In public schools and agencies with limited budgets and many child referrals, few play therapists have a playroom. Several arrangements have been developed for the portable playroom, however.

You can use a canvas bag. Several companies sell these preassembled. However, you may find that assembling your own kit is as effective and less expensive. The bag needs to have a few well-chosen toys: possibly a sponge ball, two small cars, a rescue vehicle, a doll family, finger puppets, dishes for two, baby doll, clay, crayons, pencil, paper, wild animals, domestic animals, small gun, and toy soldiers. A monster or other animal that may represent some sort of danger is appropriate. The kit need not be extensive to provide therapy. When limited by budget or space, purchase the basics and then add later, if more toys are necessary and you have the room.

Another portable play therapy room can be developed from an audiovisual aid cart or library cart with rollers. A personal favorite is a two-shelf abandoned audiovisual cart with doors and a lock, but open shelving works equally well. The toys can be permanently displayed on the shelves of the cart. Then the cart may be pushed from place to place in the building, where room is available. This method works well if you are in the same building consistently. To screen the toys from view when not in use, consider these methods:

1. Make a skirt with an elastic top that goes around the cart and firmly grips the top of the cart.
2. Attach a curtain by gluing hook and loop fasteners around the top of the cart.
3. Upholster the cart with a fabric box with a zipper on one side.

The toys do not have to be screened from view. However, many therapists working in schools or agencies with children are often doing other types of interventions other than play therapy, and screening the toys may prevent distractions for the child.

One counselor in the public schools who moved from school to school used a cardboard box covered with adhesive-backed paper that could be carried from site to site. The box was stored in the trunk of the car until it was needed each day. Most of the so-called playrooms were unheated stages, book rooms, the dead end of a hallway, or other storage facilities. In addition to the toy box, a fan was necessary for warm weather and an electric heater for winter. These facilities usually did not have electricity, so a heavy-duty extension cord of 20 or more feet was part of the kit.

Electric heaters and fans were common in classrooms in the 1970s; however, these appliances do pose a danger to children. If your agency or school allows them, be sure to take special precautions. If possible, avoid places that do not have adequate heating, cooling, and fresh air. If you must use them, be especially careful and do not stay in the room with an electric heater in the winter for long periods of time. Be sure your room is adequately ventilated. You must consider the safety of the child

Play therapists may find it necessary to develop portable play therapy kits to take to locations outside the office or playroom.

first in selecting any makeshift playroom. The second feature is confidentiality. The area needs to be private.

ORGANIZING THE TOY DISPLAY

The playroom builds an atmosphere of security because everything is always the same. The toys are always in the same general place. The furniture arrangement remains consistent. The toy selections and their arrangement vary little from session to session. The predictability of the playroom creates a stable environment for the child, which may be the only constant in his or her life.

The toys are usually assigned to specific shelves or spaces according to their overall category. Aggressive toys may all be on one shelf. Vehicles may all be on another shelf. Place all people figures, including dolls and doll clothes, on yet another shelf. Dressup clothes, jewelry, men's ties, hats, wigs, and other costume selections may be in a box, trunk, shelf, or small closet. The kitchen or home items should all be grouped together.

Avoid putting all the so-called boy toys on one set of shelves and all the so-called girl toys on another. Arrange the toys in categories, but do not organize the categories to imply right or wrong use. The categories or centers are simply to help you put the toys back into the same general area each time at the close of the play session. Having items in categories helps the child know where to seek a specific toy.

Most therapists arrange the rooms much like centers in kindergartens are arranged. A home center is developed in one corner of the playroom with the doll bed, the kitchen set, and table and chairs. Another space is designated for creative arts and has all of the art supplies located there. Some playrooms have music centers with musical instruments. Another space may be designated for water play. A large sturdy plastic child's wading pool full of sand may be the sand play center. Shelved toys are typically placed against one wall. The middle of the playroom is usually left open with room for the child to move about and play at will.

The organization is not therapy and does not have to have mystical significance. The fact that the organization and predictability does not change is therapeutic. With a systematic way of presenting the toys, it becomes easier to locate them or to replace toys in predictable places for them to be found. The subtle message to the child is one of predictability and security in the therapeutic session.

PROFESSIONAL INTAKE, DISCLOSURE, AND DOCUMENTATION

Intake

Intake is the term given to the initial data gathered in public and private agencies before the client is actually seen in the therapeutic session. Intake procedures vary from therapist to therapist and agency to agency. Some of these procedures are extensive; others are relatively short. The purpose of the intake is to help the therapist see the context of the concern that has caused the adults to seek treatment for the child.

Basic to most intake responsibilities are the informed consent agreement, client contact information, and the reason for referral. Beyond these three items, state laws, insurance requirements, and personal preferences emerge to dictate what other data is collected. A universal standard for these procedures does not exist. However, if you take private or government insurance payments for your services, you must meet the Health Insurance Portability and Accountability Act (HIPAA) of 1996 (PL 104-191), which has set minimal requirements in such areas as information security and disclosure. Generally, the standards require that clients have the right to access their records, restricts information disclosed to a third party to a minimum, and establishes safeguards concerning disclosure to public health, research, and law enforcement. Records must be secure. Per HIPAA, improper uses or disclosures under the rule may gander civil or criminal sanctions. What follows are some general guidelines offered in conjunction with HIPAA requirements for consideration.

Informed Consent

Informed consent is a disclosure of practice designed to assure that the client is submitting to treatment with a full understanding of the techniques, theory, and financial arrangements for treatment. Most informed consent forms also contain a disclosure statement stating that not all clients respond to treatment or that they may require additional services beyond therapy, specifically consultation with a medical doctor or psychiatrist. The time, meeting place, cost, and the scheduling process information is summarized. The therapist's expectations about missed sessions is explained. You may have in the informed consent a statement that a client is charged for any session not cancelled 24 hours in advance. You may also include a statement about what the client can expect if you cannot meet at the scheduled session. Public agencies may not have statements like these but rather how many sessions a client may miss before being dropped from the schedule. Public agencies may also have statements saying the agency reserves the right to reassign a client to another therapist in the event of time or other conflicts.

The therapist's qualifications are usually summarized, especially in private practice. Any special qualifications and training are described. Any theoretical bias that might impinge on the effectiveness of therapy or might be found disrespectful to the client is discussed. These potentially offensive biases might include such topics as a bias against divorce counseling, a feminist philosophy, or a Bible-based theory. Certificates and licenses need to be displayed in a highly visible area for verification of the therapists' credentials. Many therapists describe their theoretical orientation and what they expect of the client during the session. Relationship limitations are usually discussed along with the expectations of the client. The client is assured that no unusual or experimental techniques will be used in the course of treatment without the expressed permission of the legally responsible parties. Basically, you assure the client that any part of the therapeutic relationship will not be used for your social or financial gain beyond the established fee. You establish that a therapeutic relationship precludes any other social, business, physical, experimental, or emotional relationship forever. If you practice in a small town, this issue may have to be adapted.

If you work for an agency, these documents are likely to be already in place. However, review them periodically to make sure they meet changing state and federal laws.

An outline of the type of information required by HIPA is summarized in the following figure.

Notice of Privacy Practices Effective April 14, 2003

A   Introduction to my clients

B   Privacy and the laws about privacy

C   What I mean by your "medical information"

D   How I use your medical information

E   Procedures if you wish to access or amend your information

F   How your protected health information will be used and disclosed

G   Uses and disclosures requiring your authorization

H   Uses and disclosures *not* requiring your consent or authorization

I   Confidentiality regarding minors

J   An account of disclosures I have made

K   If you have problems or questions

Custody Issues

Custody issues must be addressed to protect the child and the therapist. You need to ascertain clarification of custody and establish the identify of the custodial parent or legal guardian. Only this legally designated party can grant permission for treatment. The exception occurs when court-ordered for treatment or evaluation. In the former, you need to request a copy of the divorce decree or custody hearing that establishes who has custody. In the case of joint custody, both parties need to be treated equally no matter who is actually paying for treatment. When possible, both parents need to be included and kept informed during the treatment process. Your client is the child and you must provide services in the child's best interest.

In the latter case of court-ordered therapy, you will be required to submit a written report to the court about the progress of treatment and make a recommendation "in the best interest of the child." When the court allows the parents to be part of the treatment, keep them informed and included. However, if parental rights are temporarily suspended, you are responsible to the judge. If you are unsure, call the judge's office and request a copy of the orders and clarification of its limitations.

A number of years ago, a therapist received a court order to evaluate both parents for the purpose of establishing custody. The judge designated the therapist an "officer of the court." This designation is one of the most powerful in most states. An officer of the court may function without parental permission and may remove the child at any time. This power is in existence until the court order is rescinded. In this particular case, the court order was in effect until the children reached majority. Age of majority varies from state to state, but basically, it is the age at which the legal system determines the child is an adult. The outcome of this story was not a happy one. A year after custody was given to the mother, the therapist had the children removed by Child Protective Services because of inadequate supervision and medical care. The child custody was given to the father and stepmother. However, at this writing, the court order is still in effect for the youngest child, who the therapist hears from regularly.

An attorney *ad litum* is an attorney appointed to represent the child. The attorney does not necessarily have the same authority as a guardian. The attorney's position is to advise the child legally and to make sure the child's rights are not violated. The attorney *ad litum* adds another layer of protection to the child's rights, in addition to guardianship. Be sure to include all legally responsible adults in information about the child's treatment and to secure the appropriate releases and permission for treatment. Get everything in writing and file the documents in the child's record.

Because the laws involving child custody vary greatly from state to state, what is presented in this section is very limited. Those of you in private practice need to consult with an attorney specializing in family law in the state where you practice. How you function may be affected by how the state handles custody issues. Agencies usually have policies in place that define these issues that have been written in consultation with a family attorney. Laws change, and these policies and documents used need to be reviewed periodically to reflect changes that may have occurred.

Consent to Treat

Consent to treat means you need a document that summarizes and describes the proposed treatment procedures. It may not be enough just to have the parents read this document. In the event of parents whose dominant language is not English, the document must be in their native language or presented through a translator. The translator's relationship to the parents needs to be documented along with contact information and acknowledgment of their understanding of the document. In working with parents from various cultural backgrounds, an open discussion of any cultural/religious limitation concerning treatment is advised.

A school counselor sent a consent form home with a first-grade child, asking for permission to provide play therapy. The parent could not read the form and called the counselor at school to have the form explained. The counselor answered the questions and clarified the form. When the permission form was returned, the mother had someone write above her signature, "My child may not be put to sleep." Within this family's culture, hypnosis was considered a channel for demon possession. Although the counselor felt she had clearly explained play therapy, she respected the parent's right to place a limitation on the process. The mother was assured in a follow-up phone call that the therapist would not use relaxation techniques, hypnosis, meditation, visualization, or subliminal materials in the course of treatment. Objections to these particular techniques may be expressed by specific religious sects also.

The form should confirm that you have described the methods, philosophy, and limitations of the therapy. In addition, the form needs to state that the parents were allowed to ask questions and have them answered to their satisfaction. Any limitation to therapy needs to be recorded. The information must be provided to both parents and their signatures secured. In the case of a divorce, make every effort to obtain both parents' permission for the treatment of a minor child. A certified letter sent to the nonparticipant parent with a copy of the permission can be helpful. In the event that both signatures are not available, be sure the parent/guardian signing has custody/guardianship of the child. Again, ask for confirmation in writing.

The child needs to have the therapy described fully in language appropriate to his or her understanding and developmental level. A recommended book for this purpose is *The Child's First Book of Play Therapy* (Nemiroff & Annunziata, 1990; Nemiroff, Annunziata, & Scott, 1990), available from the American Psychological Association (APA). Therapist-developed coloring books, pamphlets, and sticker books can be used to address children's concerns. The child may also sign a statement of consent to treatment. Having the child do so gives the child a subtle message of empowerment and personal responsibility. The message to the child is that he or she will be treated as an important client with a personal relationship with the therapist and has a significant responsibility in therapy. To be treated with this degree of respect is often a unique role for the child coming to therapy.

Confidentiality

A general statement to the effect that all content of sessions is held in confidence, as provided by the statues of the state, is usually required. **Confidentiality** may be

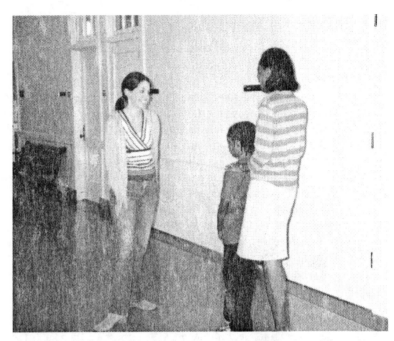

The therapist may find that reminding the parent and child of the confidentiality agreement before entering the playroom may be helpful to establishing rapport with the child and parent.

breached when the client is dangerous to self or others. Minor children do not actually have confidentiality from their parents. If parents request information about the child, the information must be given. This disclosure is basically limited to what is written about the child.

Some therapists choose to provide information about their procedures in dealing with court orders, subpoenas, and court testimony. Generally, the therapist contacts the client and asks for a signed release of information. However, if court ordered to appear or forward records, the therapist can comply without the client's permission. Inclusion of a client permission statement is a matter of preference. If court ordered to appear or send records, you must comply or suffer legal ramifications.

Another area of concern about confidentiality is in the process of third-party payments. The confidentiality of the client and his or her family may be breached when insurance companies are billed. Many of these companies require reports that require a diagnosis and progress report before paying the therapist or reimbursing the insured. Because of this confidentiality issue, many therapists avoid the issue by not taking third-party payments. Other therapists assure clients that they will report only what is required to procure the services for the client. Whichever way a therapist or agency decides to deal with the issue, the client's family needs to be informed, so they may make a judgment about how much of their privacy they wish to surrender to a third party.

A statement of confidentiality provides the parent and child with a clarification about who will have access to the information in the records maintained by the therapist. The therapist assures the legally responsible guardian that records will not be released without a signed release. However, if the legally responsible guardian wishes to have specific information released to a doctor, school, or other agency, the therapist needs to have a release of information available for the client.

The exceptions to this confidentiality need to be discussed with the parents and child. The exceptions are in the case of suspected child abuse, the therapist has a duty to report; in the case of potential harm to self or others, the therapist has a duty to warn; and in the case of court orders, the therapist may have to produce records or testify. In the latter case, several professional codes of ethics require the therapist to ask the court for privilege, which means the therapist asks the judge if he or she may be excused from testifying or producing information because it may threaten the therapeutic relationship. Only the judge may grant privilege, so the therapist may have to appear in court to request it.

The most important statement to the parent is that what the child says and does in therapy will be kept in confidence between the child and the therapist. However, if there are ways the therapist feels the parent may help the child, these suggestions will be provided to the parent. What I actually say to the parents or legal guardians might be something like this:

> Your child and my sessions are confidential. I will not tell you what the child does or says in the session. I would like to ask you not to question the child about what has happened in the session, as a way of you supporting the child's treatment. If I have suggestions about how you might help your child during treatment, I will share these with you. I will keep you informed of the progress in the ten minutes either before the session or following the session. I will not discuss the child's treatment or parenting suggestions without the child present. I will not release information to a third party without your written permission, except in the case of suspected abuse, harm to self or others, or court ordered. If court ordered, I will do my best to protect the child and your family within the legal perimeters of the best interest of the child.

I feel strongly that the child is the client; therefore, the child is accorded the same respect that an adult would be in the therapeutic environment. I do not allow parents to discuss the child or the treatment without the child present. I do excuse the child if the parents are going to discuss their marriage or financial difficulties. I find this policy avoids a lot of trust issues between the child and me. If something needs to be shared with the parents, I discuss what I am going to say and explain what I feel makes this important to discuss with the child prior to discussing it with the parents. Therapists feel differently about this aspect of confidentiality and about the role of the therapist in relationship with the parents.

Once again, confidentiality laws may vary by state. Check with an attorney familiar with family law and parents' rights concerning confidentiality. Most agencies have guidelines and policies in place that will direct you. Review these confidentiality practices and policies periodically to assure that the intent of the law is being fulfilled.

Case Notes and Treatment Planning

Case notes are required to document what happens in the therapeutic relationship. The documentation allows you to maintain evidence of competent treatment of the client, to provide other professionals with knowledge of the direction of the therapy, and to provide evidence in a court of law. Each and every note in the documentation needs to be written with the kind of preciseness you would expect to use if the records were subpoenaed for a court case. Although most records will never go to court, a court case with children is possible (Swenson, 1993). What to say and what not to say in documentation is often a confusing and frustrating skill to develop. The importance of appropriate documentation has received a great deal of attention with third-party payment demands and with the insistence on accountability. Well-written documentation can impart accountability, corroborate appropriate service delivery, and support clinical decisions (Cameron & Turtle-Song, 2002).

POMR stands for *problem-oriented medical records* and describes the type of records kept by many health care professionals, including those in mental health care. The POMR in mental health facilities or agencies usually contain the clinical assessment, problem list, treatment plan, and progress notes. The clinical assessment includes all formal and informal evaluations (i.e., intake interview, problem statement, developmental history, social history, family history, tests results, diagnosis, and recommendations) (Cameron & Turtle-Song, 2002).

The problem list is developed from those concerns identified from the developmental and family history. These problems may come from interviews, appraisals, and assessments from day care workers, schoolteachers and counselors, and pediatricians, as well as others who may have contact with the child. The problems are then indicated as either active, which means they are current problems, or inactive, which means they have been resolved (Cameron & Turtle-Song, 2002).

The treatment plan consists of the goals and objectives written in behavioral terms. Two types of goals are recorded. Long-term goals are intended to indicate the expected outcomes of therapy. The long-term goal is broken down into small behavioral goals that can be achieved in one or a few sessions. These behavioral goals leading to the desired outcome or long-term goal are called short-term goals (Cameron & Turtle-Song, 2002).

An accepted format for case notes or progress notes is illustrated by the acronym **SOAP**, which stands for *subjective, objective, assessment,* and *plan.* The SOAP note format set the precedent for the alternative case note models of data, assessment, and plan (DAP), individual educational plans (IEP), functional outcomes reporting (FOR), and narrative notes (Kettenbach, 1995). Another adaptation that appears in the literature is **STIPS**, which stands for *signs and symptoms, topics discussed in therapy, interventions used, progress of client,* and *special issues* (Prieto & Scheel, 2002). Any one of these recording methods is acceptable. SOAP is more fully discussed here because it preceded the other formats historically.

The *subjective* part of the note includes the child's feelings, appearance, concerns, play themes, materials used, observations with significant others, thought processes, and creative and graphic representations. The subjective part of the record reflects what has been told or shown to the therapist. This section should keep direct quotes to a minimum, using only key words or brief phrases. The verbs *reports, states, says, describes, provides, represents, indicates,* and *complains of* can help make case notes flow better and still communicate the meaning fully. You do not have to refer to yourself as "the therapist" (Cameron & Turtle-Song, 2002). This section is roughly parallel to the signs and symptoms of STIPS (Prieto & Scheel, 2002).

The *objective* part of the note consists of two types of data: the counselor's observations and outside written materials. The child's graphic materials might be considered as written materials and included in this area. To be objective, the information must be stated as facts without interpretation. The objective material of the case note must be what any reasonable person could observe through the five senses of taste, touch, smell, hearing, or sight. You do not use labels but may describe behaviorally the observation (Cameron & Turtle-Song, 2002). The topics discussed are summarized in this section also (Prieto & Scheel, 2002).

Assessment is a summary of your clinical thinking or hypotheses about the child's problem. This section allows for clinical impressions. Some play therapists may prefer to keep shadow or personal notes that record clinical impressions. Shadow or personal notes can be problematic because a second set of records may leave the client's documentation without a logical progression of evaluation, planning, and treatment. This absence of data may leave therapists with no evidence of their competency in the event of a lawsuit (Swenson, 1993). One set of records is recommended that details the logic and progression of the treatment and progress (Cameron & Turtle-Song, 2002).

The *plan* section describes the therapeutic interventions used. The plan usually has two parts that describe the action taken and a prediction of the outcome of the action. The next appointment information, treatment progress, referrals, and treatment direction for the next session are some of the types of information recorded in this section. The SOAP section A corresponds to the intervention and progress sections in the STIPS format (Prieto & Scheel, 2002).

Prieto and Scheel (2002) provide the additional section on *special issues*. This section is intended to record suicidal ideation, homicidal threats, concerns about referrals, medications, abuse issues, reports to special agencies, reports made to protective agencies or other judges of professional competency, and legal and ethical considerations. The special issues section is intended to "raise a red flag" that the therapist needs to monitor critical issues in this case (Prieto & Scheel, 2002).

The APT Standards of Practice are very clear about what should and should not be included in the child's clinical records. The Section A.D of the Association for Play Therapy (2000) Standards of Practice (Appendix A) states,

> Play therapists practicing independently shall document sessions with clients so that the most recent progress notes reflect the following:
>
> 1. Current developmental level of functioning, i.e., cognitive, play, affective
> 2. Long- and short-term goals of treatment
> 3. Verbal content of sessions relevant to behavior and goals
> 4. Observed play themes and materials used
> 5. Graphic images relevant to client behavior and goals, i.e., sketches of sand trays, drawings, photographs, videotapes, etc.

The play therapist will want to review and record case notes immediately after the session concludes before important events in the session fade from memory.

6. Changes in thought process, affect, play themes, and behavior
7. Interventions with significant others, i.e., adjunct therapy, referrals, etc.
8. Suicidal or homicidal intent or ideation
9. Observations of child with significant others
10. Level of family functioning and environment
11. Conditions of termination

SOAP and STIPS notes can offer a guideline in both maintaining records that are helpful to the treatment of clients and showing evidence of the level of competency of treatment the child received. Although the SOAP notes appear to be complete, the addition of the special issues suggested by Prieto and Scheel (2002) appear to improve greatly the overall case record.

If you are in doubt and uncertain of the laws in your state about case records and the type of items to be included, contact an attorney who can provide the required guidance about the limits of disclosure of records. Most public agencies have developed their documents under the direction of legal counsel.

James (1997) suggests that all records be kept a minimum of 3 years past the child becoming legally an adult. The records need to be in long-term storage and in a secure location. James suggests two locks; one inaccessible to cleaning crews and a locked file. Adult records need to be saved at least 10 years. Check with the laws in your state to ascertain if a longer period of time is required. The HIPAA standards may affect this practice, so be alert to changes at the national level in record keeping. If in doubt, consult with an attorney.

Other Points to Ponder

After-hour availability is another necessity. Whether you are practicing alone or within an agency, the family and child need a way to contact you in an emergency. An answering service, beeper, or cell phone number are all viable ways to be available for emergencies. Many cell phone companies are offering email messages directly to the cell phone, so a client might email a short message to the therapist explaining the emergency. Be aware that resentful and potentially dangerous clients have harassed and even harmed therapists who have given their private phone numbers and/or addresses. Make your method of emergency contact somewhat indirect. In the event that you will be out of town or unavailable, provide an alternative contact. You might leave a recorded message on the office phone like this:

> You have reached the office of . . . Our office hours are from . . . to . . . If you have an emergency, you may contact me at the following number . . . In the event that you have immediate needs, please go to your hospital emergency room for treatment. If you wish to make an appointment, please leave your name and number and I will contact you during office hours. If you are calling to cancel an appointment, please stay on the line and leave your name and number after the signal.

If you are out of town, the message might sound like this:

> You have reached the office of _____ . I will be out of town until _____. If you have an emergency, please contact my colleague, _____ , at _____ or go immediately to your hospital emergency room. If you wish to make an appointment, please leave your name and phone number. I will not be making any appointments until after _____ (date).

These two examples are presented as suggestions. You might want to include more information or provide other scenarios.

CONDUCTING THE SESSION

The most frightening experience for the inexperienced counselor is the appearance of the first child client. Even a seasoned clinician who has not done previous work with a child may experience sweaty palms and a pervasive feeling of inadequacy.

The question that seems most prevalent is What do I say to the child? The answer may differ from theory to theory, but basically the initial responses are about equal. Differences are discussed in other chapters. But for now, let us begin with the more simplistic of the theories to master, that of nondirective play therapy.

Usually the child will not have arrived alone or have been self-referred. Whether you are working in a clinic or a public agency, usually some limited form of intake has established why the child is being seen by a counselor for play therapy. You should have a clear-cut statement of why the child is seeking therapy and the description of a specific problem. Having in mind what the referral source is concerned about will help you observe the child's play. It is best not to make the child wait to enter the playroom. Any interviews that may have been needed for information are better completed prior to the first visit of the child or by another competent person during the child's session in another office. The parent is not usually invited to observe the session but rather encouraged to return to pick the child up at a later time.

As the child enters your facility, greet him or her warmly. If the child is very small, squat to the child's eye level so the child can see your face. Introduce yourself and comment favorably on something the child is wearing or on an interest the parent has shared in the interview.

An initial session might begin as follows: The parent has brought Bryan, a 6-year-old, into the waiting room of a small development center. Bryan has been reported as showing aggressive behavior in the first-grade class of his elementary school. Bryan's father left the home about 6 weeks before Bryan began first grade. No aggressive behavior was reported in his kindergarten class. (Enter Bryan and Mother. You come from another room into reception area.)

"Hello, Bryan," you say as you move toward the child. You squat down to his eye level. "You certainly have on a cute dinosaur shirt today."

"I like dinosaurs," Bryan responds, ducking his head.

"We have some dinosaurs in our playroom. Your mom said you are going to spend some time in the playroom with me today." Use this as a transition to move Bryan away from the mother and toward the playroom. Concluding this statement, take the child's hand and lead him toward the playroom. "Your mom will be back to pick you up at 3 o'clock."

Establish that the playroom is an interesting place for children. In addition, explain that you two will be together until his mother returns. Knowing what time the parent will be back helps the child feel more secure about the situation. Announcing when the parent will return covertly cues the parent about your expectation for picking up the child without distracting the child.

Move the child toward the playroom without further comment. If the child is hesitant, allow the parent to follow part of the way down the hall and then step between the child and the parent as they get to the playroom. Before opening the playroom door, introduce yourself and announce the rules. These rules are provided before the playroom door is opened, so the child will not be distracted by the toys and will hear the rules. Many elementary school teachers turned play therapists like to have the child repeat the rules. This assures the child's understanding, but it may be overemphasis on the limitations rather than the therapeutic value of the session.

The scenario might continue as follows:
(The mother has departed as you and Bryan proceed toward the playroom. The mother has reassured Bryan she will be back at 3 o'clock.)

(At the playroom door.) "Bryan, this is the playroom. I am Miss Blake."

You may allow the child to call you by your first name, if that is the policy of the clinic, school, or agency. However, some cultures are offended by allowing a child to address an adult by a personal name rather than a title. What the child calls you is a matter of personal taste, culture, or policy in most places. In the South, the first name of an adult is often preceded by "Miss," "Mister," or "Doctor." Having given the child a name to call you, you proceed to explain the three rules in the playroom:

1. You may not leave until time is up.
2. You may not break any of the toys on purpose.
3. You may not harm yourself or me.

The therapist gives the general rules outside the door, while the child's attention can still be focused on what the therapist is saying to the child.

Bryan giggles, which is typical, at the last rule because for most children hitting an adult seems like a very strange idea. Bryan nods that he does understand what you have said.

You open the door and set the tone for the session by what you say to the child. A suggestion of what to say is "In here you may do many of the things you would like to do."

It is very important that you do not say Bryan can do *anything* he wants to do because this will later allow Bryan to say to you, "But you said I could do *anything* I wanted to do."

In the special language of the playroom, you attempt to be exact in communicating with the child. Saying exactly what you mean allows you to be consistent with the child's expectations. The child will always know this adult is special because the concrete language used conveys an unambiguous meaning.

Upon entering the playroom, take a chair nearest the door, which will afford a complete view of the room and the child's activities. Do not move from this location except when it is necessary to convey interest in what the child is doing. Many play therapists express a desire to sit on the floor, but this may imply an overly casual relationship. You want to maintain a position that allows the child to feel you can empower the child, and you are a helpful adult but not a playmate.

Generally, you do not play with the child. If asked to play, you respond, "That is something you can do. I am here to watch."

When the child truly may need someone to play with, (e.g., as in checkers), allow the child to decide where to move the checkers and then let the child move the game pieces. You might suggest that perhaps the child could pretend to play with one of the dolls or the punch toy as a partner.

Avoid playing with the child to circumvent being manipulated into situations that may not be therapeutic, for example, pitching a ball. If you concede to playing ball with the child, you then have to decide whether to let the child win or not. In addition, what will winning mean to the child about your competence and what will losing do to the self-concept of the child? The rules are not absolute, but you must make decisions based on what is therapeutic for this child.

A simple act in play therapy can have long-reaching repercussions. Manipulation is often the strongest goal of the child's behavior. An example is a 10-year-old African American young man who spent three 50-minute sessions having the play therapist catch a ball and keep score. Catching a ball and keeping score does not give the play therapist material to reflect, but it is an effective way to keep the play therapist from finding out anything about the child's problems.

Your responses to the child should be aimed at reflecting the underlying feeling of the child's play. Axline (Axline & Carmichael, 1947) says that play is the language of the child. So you must consider the play as a form of language. The nondirective models for responses provided by Myrick (Myrick & Holdin, 1971) and Carkhuff (2003) apply to the types of responses you would make to the child's play.

RESPONDING TO THE CHILD IN PLAY THERAPY

Myrick and Holdin (1971) discuss that the lowest level of responses are those of advising or evaluating, analyzing or interpreting, and reassuring or supporting. Myrick and Holdin (1971) list the most facilitative responses as those that question, clarify or summarize, and reflect or understand a feeling.

In play therapy, the advising or evaluating response would reflect that the child was either good or bad. Included in this category would also be those responses that would tell the child how a game is played or label a particular item.

Here is an example of the advising response: Bryan holds a snake up to you and asks, "What is this?" An advising or teaching response would be to say, "It's a snake," but a clarifying response would be "It may be whatever you want it to be."

The latter response is more facilitative because it is consistent with letting the child lead the way and with what you have already said about the playroom being a place where the child may do many of the things he or she wishes. The response does not say to the child that we deal only with adult reality here, nor does it prevent the child from making the object something very different from what the child knows it already to be.

Evaluating responses are those that are the easiest to do accidentally. When a child shows you an art project, the typical adult response is to say, "That's good." The child then attempts to work for adult approval and see how many "that's good" comments can be obtained. A clarifying response might be that the child has used a lot of yellow or an I message: "I like this part most over here," indicating with the hand the portion of the painting the counselor finds most appealing or interesting. These are comments on the product and not related to the child's personality.

Analyzing and interpreting represents an attempt to give meaning to behaviors that may not exist. An example could be that of assuming a meaning of an action. For instance, the child buries the father figure in the doll family. You respond in an analyzing manner when you say, "You are really angry with your dad." The figure may not be the dad. It is simply a doll until the child indicates it is the dad or gives it another name. A reflection of feeling or understanding of a feeling response could be, "You looked angry when you buried the doll." The child can now agree or correct you. The doll will remain "the doll" until the child gives it a name. Otherwise, any other assumption on the part of the adult could be considered analyzing and interpreting.

Well-meaning and nurturing play therapists have the most difficulty not making reassuring or supportive comments. The danger lies in reassurances that comfort may be grounded in false hope. Things in the child's life may not get better and the child's behavior may not be "OK."

In this category falls the ever-present I-know-exactly-how-you-feel statement. If supportive and reassuring statements had worked in the past, the child would not be seeing a play therapist presently. In addition to being a poor response, statements rob the child of experiencing competence. For example, when a child is having a problem opening a box or jar, you could respond, "That's hard to open. It's OK. I'll open it for you." The child has been robbed of the experience of self-competency. You will improve the response by waiting until the child asks for assistance and then only loosen the top so the child can complete the job. You can respond, "You can do this for yourself now."

Summarizing may sound much more complicated than it really is. A summary statement can be a simple statement like, "Looks like you played with a lot of different toys today." In a few words you summarize what the child has done in the playroom. You can use the summary statement to assure the child that you understand what has been communicated. The summary statement represents a recapitulation of the child's activities.

Silence can become overpowering in the playroom, especially for children who are unsure of what is expected of them in this unfamiliar situation. The object of the session is not to structure the child, but it should not be an anxiety-provoking situation either. Several comments are appropriate early in the session if the child seems to be hesitant to speak. These should not be much closer together than about 10 minutes, or you might use one of the following statements with the child who is hesitant to talk or to play with the toys:

"Sometimes it's a little hard to get started."

"If you want to talk, that is one of the things you may do."

"New places are sometimes a little scary at first."

"This is a little different than what you thought."

"In here you may talk, or you may be silent."

"You do not seem really sure of what to expect in here."

If the child does not respond after the second or third probe, you can assume the child does not wish to talk. You may find it helpful to reassure the child that he or she can choose to talk or not to talk inside the playroom.

Sarcasm is not appropriate in the playroom. Children have a very fragile self-concept in this situation. The purpose of the playroom experience is to develop a better self-concept, not to have the child question self-value. Children appreciate humor. You may find it therapeutic to laugh at a rather simple joke. However, children like to tease people they are fond of and like to have the attention of an adult's teasing, if it affirms the child's positive image of self.

Encouragement is often used in the playroom, but be careful not to allow your encouragement to take a judgmental or evaluating tone. Encouragement may follow situations where the child has expressed an emotion that is positive or after the performance of a task/stunt the child has not been able to do previously. Encouragement statements may sound like these:

"Your eyes light up when you are happy."

"You could not do that last week."

"I can see you are getting better at that."

"You seem to be using more colors in your paint."

"You seem happier now."

Play therapy, like all other forms of therapy, relies on the same skills used with adults. The only difference is that with children, the language is expressed in a physical form rather than through words. The child's play is language. The special skills of reflection, understanding, questioning, and summarizing are as applicable here as in any other form of therapy. Your language must be clear, concise, and age appropriate to the child's level of understanding. Another skill beyond that of responses is that of confrontations in the form of setting limits.

Setting Limits

Limits provide the child with a sense of security in the playroom. Rules in any situation define the parameters of the possible exploration of one's feelings, environment, and relationships. Bixler (1949) entitled his classic article "Limits Are Therapy," which reflects the importance of the limits to the therapeutic process.

Bixler (1949) states that limits are necessary for the protection of the child both physically and emotionally. These may include both verbal and nonverbal interactions in the playroom. Bixler suggests that the client be limited to activities that will not cause the agency or clinic to become chaotic. He advocates the protection of person and property. In addition, he indicates that the idea of rules being different in relationships outside the playroom seems to be conveyed more accurately when limits are set in the playroom. Children seem to generalize better to outside situations if there are uniformly reinforced rules in the playroom.

Children do not seem to have an ability to learn long lists of rules. Therefore, Bixler (1949) illustrated rules in short and manageable phrases. Wording must be very concise because young children do interpret rules very literally.

Bixler (1949) and Landreth (1982, 1991, 2002) suggest that only three basic rules be presented to the child initially:

1. You may not leave until time is up.
2. You may not break anything on purpose.
3. You may not hit the therapist.

Bixler (1949) states his rules to be "—Children are not supposed to (1) destroy any property or facilities in the room other than play equipment; (2) attack the therapist in any physical sense; (3) stay beyond the time limit of the interview; (4) remove toys from the play room; (5) throw toys or other materials out of the window" (p. 136).

Here are some rules that are enforced uniformly as they are needed:

1. Children may not take home a toy from the playroom, but they may take home an art project.
2. Children may not paint toys. Specific areas are designated for painting in this day and age of caring.
3. Children may not prolong their stay at the end of a session.
4. Neither the child nor therapist may smoke.
5. Starting small fires is unacceptable; no matches or lighters are allowed in the playroom.
6. Children are not allowed to read books or to do homework.
7. No purposeful destruction of property, whether furniture, toys, or property of the therapist. (The only exception being the tearing of paper drawings the child has made himself/herself.)
8. Throwing objects other than a sponge toy is not acceptable.
9. No squirting water on the therapist.
10. No tying the therapist up or handcuffing.
11. No hugging for long periods of time or fondling even for short periods of time by the child or therapist.
12. No completely undressing.
13. No eating or drinking either things brought into the therapy room or those already in the playroom, with the exception of the nursing bottle.
14. No urinating or defecating on the floor.

These rules are in accordance with many of those behaviors found by Ginott and Lebo (1963) to be generally not acceptable. Special circumstances require additional rules. Because of the carpeting and personal tolerance, some therapists do not provide the child with toys that may soil the carpet. One way of establishing a limit is to restrict the choice of play items to those that you can handle or tolerate. Clay, paint, sand, makeup, water, or noisemakers may not be given to children if you cannot tolerate their use.

Be cognizant of personal tolerance levels and have a reasonable idea of what you will or will not allow in the playroom. Differences among children and what may be therapeutic for a child requires you to be flexible in playroom rules. Once permission has been given to do something, you are stuck with the behavior in the name of consistency for the remainder of the play session. Having once allowed a child to toss a green sponge ball against a wall, the play therapist lived to regret the next 19 sessions, which consisted of 50 minutes of limited conversation and the constant thump of a sponge ball hitting the paneled wall. True, the child's ball placement did improve, but little was done to improve his behavior. The therapist allowed this to happen because she did not realize she could set a new limit in the following session. In retrospect, the limit setting would have improved the child's behavior by making him realize his behavior was not totally without limits.

Limits need to be set as soon as the behavior becomes bothersome or you see the potential for the behavior to become a hazard to the play therapy process. If you are not sure, it is better not to set the limit until you are assured of the direction of the child's intent.

The wording of the limit is especially important. State the limit in such a way as not to associate the child as a person with the behavior that must be stopped. You depersonalize the limit. The wording of limit setting is difficult at first but becomes more fluid with practice. Focus on the behavior and the receiver of that behavior. Here are some sample responses:

"The doll is not for throwing."

"The wall is not for painting."

"I am not for hitting."

"Your time is not up."

"You may leave when time is up."

The last three responses are a simple restatement of the rules you have already given. Rules sometimes need to be restated to lend reinforcement to their seriousness or as gentle reminders to a child with a short memory. You may also restate rules and give an alternative:

"Your time in not up, but I will tell you when you have only five more minutes."

"You may not hit me or the wall with the hammer, but you may hammer the nails into the board."

Because of the unusual language pattern of the limit-setting situation, children may be drawn to its uniqueness. A Latino male client found the limit-setting language very comforting. Juan found a popgun that fired a small yellow ball. He had seen a great deal of violence between his mother and father, which included the use of guns. He immediately pointed the gun at the therapist.

"I am not for shooting," the therapist stated without expression and in a matter-of-fact way.

Juan held the gun on the therapist briefly, then pointed it toward the lights, which would have broken and fallen on him had he shot them.

"The lights are not for shooting," the therapist stated in the same authoritative voice but without excitement or agitation.

Juan then smiled and progressed around the room, pointing the gun at every object except the obvious target placed on the wall.

This limit setting of the gun became a regular part of his pattern. In all the sessions that followed, he would begin the session with the gun pointing and the therapist would set the limit. He never fired the gun at any time. One day the play therapist arrived in the playroom a little after the child. Juan had the gun in his hand pointing at various items in the room saying, "The _____ is not for shooting." He continued with all the items where the play therapist had previously set limits. Then he turned to the target and said, "The target is for shooting." Even then he did not fire the gun.

On subsequent sessions, the play therapist never set limits about the gun because Juan would repeat the words himself each time he had the gun. What or why the gun and its limits were so important to him is only conjecture on the part of the therapist. However, the therapist assumed that because he had seen someone killed with a gun, the limits represented a form of security to him that a gun could be limited. A gun could be good if it had limits placed on it to prevent harm to oneself and to others.

When Limits Are Violated

Each new therapist wants to know what to do when limits are violated. If you present a limit in a firm, but gentle voice, it is seldom violated. You may find that children respond to women who lower their voice range or pitch, because children seem to interpret a higher pitched voice as not serious or unsure. Male therapists naturally lower their voices when assuming positions of authority, which can be problematic if it intimidates or makes the child feel unduly threatened.

Looking directly at the child with good steady eye contact seems to avert a lot of violated limits. The adult has to appear to enforce the violated limit if the child continues. You must develop the "I mean business" look, if the limit has any strength. You must not threaten but set a limit you intend to *enforce*.

If the child still challenges you, restate the limit and say that if the child continues the behavior, the child will be excused from the playroom for this session or restricted to a specific area of the playroom. If the violation involves a particular toy, the toy might be removed. If the child continues after the warning and consequence, remove the child from the playroom, kicking and screaming, if necessary. You and the child will see the limit through, once the limit is set.

A problem arises in public schools when the child must be removed from the playroom. It is not fair to the classroom teacher to send the child back early. Therefore, the child may be detained in some location that provides as little stimuli as possible. You may continue to reflect the child's anger from being removed and that these are the consequences of the violation of limits. Remain with the child until the time is up.

Manipulation

Manipulation is obvious when the child asks you to do something within his or her capability. A limit is set, although it may not appear to be a limit on first viewing. You might say, "That looks like something you can do for yourself."

A child that has been successful in what Dreikurs (1948) calls "inadequacy" will respond, "But I can't." You set the limit by repeating what has already been said. If the child repeats the complaint of inability to do this activity, do not respond, or say, "You would like for me to do that for you, but you can do it for yourself." Make no effort to move toward the child, and if the object is placed in your hands, set it down, refusing nonverbally to participate in the activity.

The play therapist maintains eye contact with the child and provides the child with undivided attention during the session.

When asked to do something for the child by the child that is obvious the child is competent to do, you do not do it. If the child is trying to manipulate you, the child will persist in demanding that you help. As stated earlier, if the child is asking about a jar lid or paint lid that could be stuck, wait until the child asks you for help and then only loosen the top so the child has the experience of removing it and experiencing self-competency.

Power Struggles

Power struggles exist in the playroom as in all parts of the life of the child. Very willful children can be a trial during the struggle period, but working with them in the long run is very rewarding.

In a power struggle, try not to overpower the child vocally or express any other obvious display of feelings inadequate to the child. Simply restate the limit and maintain the limit until the session is complete.

Some basic rules exist that you must establish with your colleagues before the first power struggle begins. One such ground rule is to advise others of the potential and what you expect in the way of support from outside people. This statement will become clearer with examples. Here are some basic rules to present to colleagues before working with a child of this nature:

1. Do not enter the playroom and make an effort to "help" the therapist "control" the child.
2. This is a test of wills between the child and the therapist; the therapist will win and there may be a lot of noise. Do not be concerned.
3. The therapist will contact outside people if he or she feels it is necessary.
4. This session may go on longer than expected; please do not interrupt.

In the power struggle, remember that the child intends to make you angry or get his or her own way. If the child is crying, allow the child to cry, but do not allow the child to leave or end the session early. Ending the session early or allowing the child to leave encourages him or her to engage in the same struggle in succeeding sessions. Rather, reflect the child's feelings, unless reflection escalates the misbehavior. If the behavior begins to escalate, remain silent and somewhat passive to the child's behavior but still protective of self and property.

The hardest part of an encounter with a powerful child is that you must maintain a detached attitude to the behavior while maintaining an accepting role toward the child. If the child is destructive, take the child's hand and allow him or her to continue the tantrum. If the child kicks, hold the child's hand, but place a desk or other object so you cannot be kicked.

In the worst case scenarios, hold the child with arms crossed in front and draw the child back so you are holding his hands under his arms. In the case of kicking, seat the child on the floor and cross your legs over the child's. For the record, most therapists have never had to do this last maneuver unless working with very disturbed children who are usually in residential treatment. If you anticipate having to restrain a child in this manner, explore the policy of the agency in depth and the laws in the state where you are practicing.

Another way to illustrate and clarify what is happening in a session is by using an interaction matrix that records both the actions of the therapist and the reactions of the client. Analysis of such a matrix can prove to be most valuable to the therapist (Carmichael, 1993).

The Good-Bye Session

Saying good-bye is as much a part of the therapeutic process as what happens in between. The last session should be special and a time of reflection. It is a good time to review the child's file with him or her. Talk about the progress made and what the future plans are for the child. At this time, a small celebration may take place. It is a unique time.

Different therapists have found many ways to make this a special relationship to be remembered. One therapist allows the child to select a pebble from a bowl of washed river stones in her office. Another provides the child with the closure bracelet. One completes a "Me" book or "Story About Me" in the last session for the child to take home. Nearly all provide the child with a business card, so the child and the child's parents can contact the therapist at a later date if necessary. Most important is to provide the child with a sense that the relationship exists even if the therapist and child are not actually seeing each other. The therapist is always available in the future if the child needs to return to therapy.

The Good-Bye Personal Note

Sometimes children are taken out of therapy unexpectedly before they are ready. When this happens, it is important to help the child with the feelings of abandonment that come from that experience. A personal note or phone call is appropriate, if the parent or guardian will not bring the child back in for a last session. Here is an example of a personal note:

> Dear Rebekah,
>
> I am sorry we did not get to say good-bye. I want you to know that I enjoyed getting to know you. Our time together was a very special time for me too. I hope things go well for you. I am enclosing my business card so you or your mom will know where to find me in the future.
>
> Your play therapist,

You do not want to imply that the child should call you without parental permission; however, you do not want the child to think you wanted the therapeutic relationship to end. The abandonment issue is a difficult one to work with when the parent has decided the child will terminate against your recommendations. However, it is not an issue that should be discussed with the child or implied in the letter to the child. Keep a file copy of the letter also, should the issue of abandonment ever surface concerning this child. Any premature termination should be thoroughly documented as to reasons and in writing from the party terminating where possible.

Summary

The beginning therapist must first select and secure the appropriate materials and setting for the practice of play therapy. Guidelines and philosophies for these materials vary greatly from theory to theory of play therapy, as we see in future chapters. In addition, the therapist must have a firm legal and ethical knowledge of the client's rights to informed consent, confidentiality, and due care. Due care is defined as the safeguards for the client's privacy, protection, and support through the therapeutic process.

Evidence of due care or competent treatment was the emphasis in the documentation section of this chapter. Although briefly presented, record keeping represents the area of least interest for the therapist. However, if a therapist has difficulties with the law, likely it will be because of inadequate record keeping or documentation of treatment. This area of competence demands special awareness and responsibility.

The suggested procedure for a first session in this chapter was based on a training model that is essentially child centered in theory. This model was selected because the work of authors like Axline has traditionally used it as a starting point in teaching the process of play therapy.

CHAPTER 3

PSYCHOANALYTIC PLAY THERAPY

Some psychoanalysts who follow Klein's example provide each child client with a box of toys that are selected especially for the child. Every child seen has his or her therapeutic toys in a private box or locked drawer.

Psychoanalytic play therapy remains a widely practiced form of play therapy throughout the world. From the historical beginnings of the psychoanalytic theory and child development, play therapy emerged as a method to work with what were termed nervous and neurotic children. Today, psychodynamic play therapy is identified more with object relations and attachment theory interventions.

INTRODUCTION

Psychoanalytic approaches are based on the work of Sigmund Freud (1909). Psychoanalytic play therapists include Anna Freud (Freud and Clark, 1928), Melanie Klein (1984a; Klein & Riviere, 1983), Erik Erikson (1950), Hiam Ginott (1994), and Otto Weininger (Weininger, 1982, 1984, 1989). These therapists view play much like Freud viewed free association. The therapist's role is to help the child recognize and interpret his or her unconscious motivation into the conscious. Through the process of transference with a therapist, the therapist becomes the "ideal parent" and interprets the child's play to the child. Analysis of the transference relationship becomes of great importance.

The goal of therapy is lessening suffering, trauma recovery, life adjustment, medical treatment compliance, phobia elimination, academic and learning progress, anger management, and disability acceptance (Bromfield, 2003). The purpose is to go beyond the present pain and difficulty to help children come to terms with who they are and to help them develop "more secure, adaptable, compensating and self-accepting ways and attitudes" (Bromfield, 2003, p. 2).

In order to give you a better understanding of the many interpretations of psychoanalytic play therapy, its foundational tenets are summarized here. Play therapy began as a phenomenon of psychoanalytic psychology and subsequent study of human development. The theories presented will help you develop a firm foundation and understanding of how work with children came to be. In addition, the theories of Klein, Anna Freud, and Lowenfeld are still practiced today and account for variations in the styles and diversity in the practice of psychoanalytic play therapy.

Freud and Little Hans

In the case that became known as "Little Hans," Sigmund Freud wrote about his observations in three publications (Jones, 1955). Little Hans was the first case of psychodynamic therapy process applied to a child. In *The Sexual Enlightenment of Children*, published in 1907, his initial foray into work with children, Freud explains the natural sexual curiosity of children. Little Hans is called Little Herbert in this paper, which describes the observations of the father, who wrote to Freud about the child's display of the Oedipal complex, castration fears, and preoccupation with the erotogenic zones of the body. The paper was the first direct observation of Freud's previously hypothesized ideas about infantile sexual development.

The second mention of Little Hans appeared in the paper *On the Sexual Theories of Children* (1908). Freud stated that the study of Little Hans was convincing evidence of the correctness of his belief that childhood experiences influence the adult development of neurosis.

Finally, Freud (1909) published the entire case study of Little Hans in his paper *Analysis of a Phobia in a Five-Year-Old Boy.* As a bit of background, Jones (1955) noted that before her marriage, Hans's mother had been a patient of Freud and Hans's father had attended many of Freud's early lectures. So history has led us to believe that both parents were known to Freud and adherents of his principles. Freud did not conduct the analysis but rather worked in consultation with the father. In research today, these facts would have made Freud's research biased and would probably have made his papers unacceptable to most professional journals.

The Little Hans case is considered the first play therapy session because the spontaneous play of Hans was often used to interpret and understand the child's conflicts and phobias. Many of the father's observations concern things Little Hans did and thought as a result of his Oedipal complex. For example, the boy enjoyed getting into bed with his mother, where they would hug and caress each other. He also asked her to touch his penis because "it's great fun." He would masturbate and have sexual fantasies about his mother and playmate as he did so. He described one such episode as reprinted here. (Note: His opening remark refers to masturbation. The events he describes as he masturbated were taking place in fantasy. Grete is a female playmate.)

> I put my finger to my widdler just a very little. I saw Mummy quite naked in her chemise, and she let me see her widdler. I showed Grete, my Grete, what Mummy was doing, and showed her my widdler. Then I took my hand away from my widdler quick . . . the chemise was so short that I saw her widdler. (Freud, 1909, p. 32)

Little Hans also enjoyed being in the bathroom with his mother when she went to the toilet. "He goes on pestering me till I let him," she said. He had fantasies that he would someday marry his mother and they would have children.

Little Hans's Oedipal jealousy and hostility took such forms as being inappropriately aggressive in roughhousing with his father, defying his father's occasional attempts to keep him from getting into bed with his mother, fantasizing that he, and not his father, was married to his mother, and wishing his father dead so he could have his mother all to himself.

Little Hans first developed general free-floating anxiety, which very rapidly changed into a phobia of horses, particularly the fear they would bite his fingers. These and other associations indicated that for Little Hans, horses were displacement substitutes for his parents and his fear of being bitten by a horse was a disguised fear his father would bite or cut off his penis. Hans's fear of being bitten by a horse was derived partly from an experience he had in the country, when he heard the father of a little girl say, "Don't put your finger to the white horse or it'll bite you" (Freud, 1909, p. 29).

Hans had been threatened that if he masturbated (that is, put his finger on his penis as in the description of his masturbation fantasy just presented), Dr. A would be called to cut his penis off. These experiences became the associative links between his father and biting horses. He used to play biting games with his father, and once when the boy and his father were talking about Hans's wish that his father was dead, Hans "accidentally" knocked over a toy horse he was playing with.

Little Hans was 3 years old when his sister Hanna was born. Previously his only rival for his mother's love had been his father. Now he had to share his mother's love with Hanna, too. He often witnessed many unpleasant sights that made him long for the "good old days." Often he watched Hanna being bathed, toileted, and caressed by his mother. Eventually he denied such distasteful sights by fantasizing he had many children all of his own, whom he cared for lovingly. In the fantasy he participated in the kind of pleasant experiences enjoyed by Hanna and his mother.

Because of his Oedipal love for his mother, Little Hans also found it very disagreeable to see reminders of his father's relationship to his mother. Hans denied this situation with a fantasy in which he was married to his mother, she was the mother of his children, and Hans's father was married to his own mother.

Important to this description of Little Hans's story are the three interpretations that Freud and the boy's father distilled, summarized here:

1. Little Hans's mother and nurse had made castration threats when Little Hans was engaged in erotic genital play.
2. Sometime later, the boy saw his sister's genitals. When he saw his sister naked, he denied she did not have a penis. He explained she had a small penis and it would grow larger as she grew.
3. Little Hans developed a thinly disguised castration complex.

The father used a technique that was considered unorthodox in the psychoanalytic method. He questioned Hans in detail and would help Hans by providing words to help Hans express his thoughts. Because the father's suggestions might influence the outcome of Hans's analysis, Freud refrained from sharing his insights into Hans's case with the father. Freud's reticence allowed the father to flounder and made Little Hans responsible for the clarification of the connections.

The father taking an active role in the interpretation of the child's fears and fantasies would have made Little Hans experience healthy transference to the father, in Freudian terms. This healthy transference would have resulted in the child identifying with the father and learning appropriate male roles for the Victorian society in which they lived. According to Freud, this would have resolved the Oedipal situation, resulting in the child developing an adequate male sexual role.

In 1922 Hans and Freud met again. Hans was 19 years old. Hans told Freud he had read the case of Little Hans and remembered none of the events related in the case. Hans did remember the time he and his father had visited Freud, which helped him realize the case was truly his own. Freud interviewed him and thought Hans was quite well and seemed to have no ill effects left from his earlier phobias. However, Hans had faced some very severe family problems for the early 1900s. His parents had divorced and each had married again. Because of the family breakup, Hans and his sister were separated and saw little of one another. According to Freud, Hans appeared to miss his sister greatly (Jones, 1955).

Jones (1955) wrote,

> Instead of perceiving that a new and most fruitful field for psychoanalytic therapy had been opened up, and that from its very prophylactic nature child analysis must hold out great possibilities, he [Freud] evidently regarded the case as a lucky exception, one from which no general therapeutic conclusions could be drawn. (p. 260)

As Jones (1955) declared, the use of play in the analysis would later be "seized" on by early child play therapists Hermine von Hug-Hellmuth and Melanie Klein.

Klein and the Berlin School

Klein, working in Berlin, developed a line of thought that became known as the Berlin school. Klein's (1955) earliest child client was "Fritz." Therapy consisted of going to the child's home and using the child's own toys to provide therapy. As the child expressed his anxieties and fantasies, Klein analyzed the meaning for the child. Additional material surfaced in the course of the analysis. To Klein, this psychoanalytic technique resembled free association.

Klein (1955) was guided in her work by two tenets of psychoanalysis that she credited to Freud. The first principle was that exploration of the unconscious is the main task of the psychoanalytic procedure. The second principle was that the analysis of transference is a way to achieve the first.

After Klein's work with a second child, Rita, she no longer conducted therapy in the child's home. Klein (1955) observed that the feeling within the home toward the therapist and therapy were not conducive to the therapeutic process:

> I found that the transference situation—the backbone of the psychoanalytic procedure—can only be established and maintained if the patient is able to feel that the consulting-room or play room, indeed the whole analysis, is something separate from his ordinary life. (p. 125)

Klein kept each child's set of especially chosen toys in a locked drawer. She believed the toys, like adult associations, should only be known to the child and the therapist. Each child had a set of small toys that would allow the child to express his or her fantasies or anxieties. Klein (1955) described the toys she selected as nonmechanical and specified that human figures should vary only in size and color. The human figures were not to indicate any particular occupation. She did allow the children to bring and use some of their own toys. Klein (1955) was quick to point out that therapy does not depend on toy selection.

Klein observed aggressiveness displayed in the child through attacks on toys or destruction of toys. She states that the therapist must know why in this moment of the transference relationship this aggression takes place. In cases in which the child's aggressiveness has led to physical attacks, Klein (1955) says,

> I have sometimes been asked by what method I prevented physical attacks, and I think the answer is that I was very careful not to inhibit the child's aggressive phantasies; in fact he was given opportunity to act them out in other ways, including verbal attacks on myself. The more I was able to interpret in time the motives of the child's aggressiveness, the more the situation could be kept under control. But with some psychotic children it has occasionally been difficult to protect myself against their aggressiveness. (p. 128)

Klein (1955) found that the child's attitude toward a damaged toy was most revealing. The toy the child was most likely to damage purposefully was the one that symbolized a significant other in the child's life who caused anxiety. She interpreted that when the child puts aside a damaged toy, it may indicate a dislike for the toy because of fear of retaliation or other danger. The child may experience persecution feelings covering feelings of guilt and depression. The feelings of guilt and depression could be so strong that the child may reinforce his or her feelings of persecution. When the child can again play with the toy, Klein (1975) interpreted this to mean the defenses of the child had been analyzed, releasing guilt and diminishing persecutory feelings. With this release, the child could make reparations.

Children were not castigated when a toy was damaged, but the analyst did not encourage the child to express aggressiveness by breaking toys. The child was allowed to experience his or her emotions and fantasies as they occurred in therapy.

Klein found that some children are inhibited in their play. Inhibitions to play could be caused by a number of things (Klein, 1955). In one case she discovered that the child was so overwhelmed by his fantasies, he needed to verbalize them before playing. Klein found that inhibitions of childhood could become the inhibitions of adulthood. She did not find this would preclude the child from playing out his or her difficulties. Klein (Monte, 1987) stated, "—[A] severe inhibition of the capacity to form and use symbols, and so to develop phantasy life, is a sign of serious disturbance" (p. 138).

Klein saw that play is a symbolic language of the child. She believed this primitive form of expression is also the language of dreams. By approaching play as a symbolic language similar to dream symbols, Klein found she could have access to the child's consciousness. She viewed each child as having a unique meaning for the play symbols, but that a generalized translation of symbols is meaningless.

In play analysis the symbolic language allowed the child to communicate not only interests, but also fantasies, fears, and guilt to nonthreatening objects rather than people. Through this symbolic expression, the child experiences a great deal of relief.

Klein saw play as the symbolic language of the child to resemble free association.

Anna Freud and the Vienna School

Anna Freud and the Vienna school of thought differed greatly from that of Melanie Klein. Anna Freud (Freud & Institute of Psycho-Analysis London [from old catalog], 1966) differed from her father, Sigmund Freud, in that she based her theory directly on her work with children and adolescents. Sigmund had based his theories of childhood psychosis on the memories of adults and the isolated case of Little Hans.

Beginning in 1922, Anna Freud devoted the next 60 years of her life to using psychoanalytic techniques in her work with children and adolescents. It would be incorrect to classify Anna Freud as a neo-Freudian because she was rather a Freud. She received her training directly from her father. She did not receive formal education in analysis except from Sigmund Freud. Anna Freud was her father's hand-picked choice to carry on his tradition and his ideas. Through her work with children, she expanded the works and concepts of her father.

Freud supported her father's concept of the id, ego, and the superego. However she differed from the Neo-Freudians in that she saw the defenses of the ego as attempts of the rational person to deal with an irrational world.

Early on in her work, Freud realized children were not good at free associations and other verbal techniques typical of the psychoanalysis of the time. A second realization was that the child comes to therapy without an awareness of what an adult has perceived as a problem. Thus child clients are chiefly presented to the analyst involuntarily.

The child client presents yet another problem for the analyst: When does the child need intervention? Freud answered this with the concept that a child needs therapy when the child's development has become fixated, preventing normal emotional development. This concept of Freudian psychology was unique to her.

In the process of child therapy, Freud undertook a period of "breaking the child in" for analysis by seeing (1) his or her need for treatment, (2) the therapist as a strong and powerful ally, and (3) the need for commitment to self-exploration. On a less abstract level, Freud used creative strategies to provide the child with small doses of insight into personal problems, demands for cooperation, and sincere interest in the child's self-management.

Stage 1:   Her first moves in therapy were to mirror the child's actions. She presented herself as slightly more competent than the child in order to establish she could be a powerful ally. If the child entered into some game, Anna Freud played the game, always being able to win by a small margin. In her winning, she demonstrated the superiority of her adult skill and wisdom. She followed the moods of the child. No topic or subject was too delicate or too mature to be discussed with the child.

Stage 2:   Anna Freud then made herself useful to the child. She could write letters, record daydreams, record stories, and create small toys. With one such child, Freud was reported to have crocheted and knitted during appointments with the child to clothe all the child's dolls and teddy bears. Through this stage the analyst gained access to the child's fantasy life.

Stage 3: In stage 3, Anna Freud made the child realize that being analyzed and having an adult as an ally was to the child's advantage. She pointed out to the child that she could intervene with the parents in matters of discipline and/or rewards for the child's behavior. However, she could only intervene if she knew the innermost secrets of the child's world. In exchange for the intervention, the child must tell her everything and hold nothing back. In this stage the analyst helps the child gain insight into the behaviors as a cause of difficulties and gain confidence that the analyst can help rid the child of these difficulties.

In this stage the analyst has become the child's ideal self, as it were, and has usurped the parents' authority with the child. If the parents are opposed to treatment, the therapist may actively work against the parents' influence with the child. Once the child and analyst have developed their attachment, the analytic treatment of the child begins.

Freud did not use toys in her analysis because she was not sure what was a fantasy and what was simply play. She differed greatly from Melanie Klein in that she did not believe play is the equivalent of adult verbalizations in analysis. She used two tools in her analysis of children.

The first tool was using the child's reported fantasies and dreams. Children's dreams, as with adult's dreams, were seen as a production of the unconscious and therefore material for interpretation. Children were often encouraged to produce fantasies. An example would be to have the child with eyes closed describe what images came to mind.

Freud believed the dreamer's state differs little from that of a patient in the analytic hour. During dreams and fantasies, the patient suspends the functions of the ego. The analyst listens for the censorships, distortions, condensations, displacements, reversals, and omissions in the material presented by the patient (Freud & Institute of Psycho-Analysis London. [from old catalog], 1966). Freud believed the symbols of dreams and fantasies (Bergmann & Freud, 1966) to be "constant and universally valid relations between particular id contents and specific word or thing representations" (p. 16). She believed the interpretation of these symbols is a "short cut" enabling the analyst to understand the unconscious without disrupting the defense mechanisms of the ego. However, the analyst's understandings of the symbols might not help with gaining a deeper understanding of the individual patient. *Parapraxes,* slips of the tongue or forgetting, are a related occurrence in which the analyst gains insights into the unconscious mind because the ego defenses are relaxed or diverted as in fantasies or dreams.

The second tool used by Anna Freud was the interpretation of *transference,* or relationship between herself and the child. In adult therapy, this analysis of transference is the backbone of the analytical work. Adult analysis contains all the unresolved and sometimes unrealistic demands of their love relationship of childhood. The child, instead, is still establishing these initial love relationships; therefore, the analyst provides those needs from adults that are unmet in the child's life. The child in therapy does not ever experience transference neurosis. The analyst shares the child's world as an active participant, whereas in adult therapy the analyst reconstructs the client's childhood world. Intervention includes working with parents and getting their point of view by actively seeking information about the child in the home (Freud, 1965).

The therapist must carefully free the child's instinct because the child is still in the process of learning appropriate social behaviors. The lack of a well-developed superego, or sense of right and wrong, must be dealt with by the analyst. Child analysis not only includes freeing the unconscious material but also an educational process of learning how that material could be transferred into behaviors.

Anna Freud (1965) provided these therapeutic principles for child analysis:

1. not to make use of authority and to eliminate thereby as far as possible suggestion as an element of treatment;
2. to discard abreaction as a therapeutic tool;
3. to keep manipulation (management) of the patient to a minimum, i.e., to interfere with the child's life situation only where demonstrably harmful or potentially traumatic (seductive) influences were at work;
4. to consider the analysis of resistance and transference, and interpretation of unconscious material as the legitimate tools of therapy." (p. 26)

Anna Freud (1965) did believe the child has curative tendencies. These tendencies can best be described as "the patient's innate urges to complete development, to reach drive satisfaction, and to repeat emotional experience" (p. 27). The child was believed to be driven toward being normal rather than abnormal. Because of the child's development, the child has the ability to assimilate and integrate experience and to externalize onto objects parts of his or her personality. The contradiction between child reactions to therapy and adult reactions to therapy is that adults are rewarded for becoming normal, so to speak. Children often have to give up highly pleasurable consequences to get well, adapting to undesirable reality and losing wish fulfillment and secondary gains. However, Anna Freud believed the most overpowering urge is to complete development. No matter how unpleasant the developmental process might be for the child, the child must be urged toward its completion (Freud, 1965).

Freud found that children cannot produce free associations. She found no remedy for this lack of free association over the years. She says, "Play with toys, drawing, painting, staging of fantasy games, acting in the transference have been introduced and accepted in place of free association and, *faute de mieux* (for lack of anything better), child analysts have tried to convince themselves that they are valid substitutes for it. In truth, they are nothing of the kind" (Freud, 1965, p. 29). Because of this inability to use free association, the child's verbalizations are fraught with doubt and uncertainty found in most symbolic interpretation.

Freud found it a disadvantage that the child would "act" rather than talk when under pressure. Verbal associations were considered virtually without limits; however, she was quick to point out that children cannot be allowed to act out their frustration physically.

She was quick to point out that children cannot be allowed to act out their frustrations behaviorally. She provided guidance that when a child endangers himself or herself or others, destroys or damages property, or acts in sexually inappropriate ways, the play therapists needs to intervene. Freud noted that while words, dreams, thoughts and fantasies had little impact on reality, behavior was different and to allow inappropriate actions was not in the best interest of the child's therapy. She further made it clear that the therapist should not promise or set up an expectation that the child may do anything that the child wishes in the playroom.

The role of the therapist was the same with children and with adults: to make the unconscious conscious. However, the child differs from the adult in that most concerns are centered in mastering the external world surrounding the child while also mastering the chaotic emotions that dwell within. The child enters analysis either delayed or incomplete in this basic task. The analyst uses insight to help the child develop a superego, engage in reality testing, and develop ego control over the id. The outcome of providing the child insight into his or her behavior is resistance. The child does not want to change, especially when the child cannot see how the change will improve life. Change is achieved through the 'working through' of these resistances.

Here are the basic tenets of child analysis:

1. Free associations, dream interpretations, and transference analysis cannot be used as traditionally used with adults.
2. Because the child's personality is still developing, the focus is to help the child develop good mental health, as opposed to remediation of a neurosis.
3. The period of time is longer in children than in adults because the child needs a lengthy preparation period to become analyzable, and the analyst needs time to evaluate and assess the needs of the child.
4. Some environmental and constitutional situations cannot be changed through analysis, no matter how early the interventions may be made.
5. A child's difficulties may not be the result of the child's internalized world but may simply reflect what is a reality in the child's actual surroundings.

The final tenet is that the ego masters those problems posed by the development or maturation of the child, leading the child from dependency to independence. Through this process the child's ego gains mastery over internal and external reality (Lowenfeld, 1935, 1949, 1954, 1979, 1991; Lowenfeld & Lowenfeld, 1923; Lowenfeld, Urwin, & Hood-Williams, 1988; Urwin & Hood-Williams, 1988).

These two schools of thought were presented in detail here because they still influence many current play therapists and how they approach the child. A play therapist may be more aware of these differences in European practice than in the United States. Not only did child therapy divide into two distinct schools of thought, but Margaret Lowenfeld, a third child development theorist, emerged during this time, who disagreed with Klein and Freud about the nature of children, their play, and their treatment.

Lowenfeld

Margaret Lowenfeld was a contemporary of Melanie Klein and Anna Freud. Her training was in the field of medicine, so her background would have been in the psychodynamic area of the time. The vocabulary of her writings reflects the terminology of the psychodynamic therapists of that era. She developed a form of psychotherapy that differed greatly in focus from her contemporaries, however. Lowenfeld not only espoused that play is the medium that children could work through to master emotional conflicts and confusions, but she claimed it is also a cognitive process. Play to

Lowenfeld developed the World Technique. The child is asked to build his or her world in the sand tray.

Lowenfeld was a concrete example of how children reason or think. She emphasized less of the relationship between the therapist and the child and focused more on the child's ability to organize and make sense of the world and personal experiences. When she interpreted symbolic material, she focused on the meaning from the point of view of the child producing the play. Lowenfeld did not adhere to the then popular universal symbolism and meanings (Urwin & Hood-Williams, 1988).

Lowenfeld believed the child has the capacity to work through his or her own problems if a theoretical base is not imposed. She did provide interpretations when the child seemed to be confused, blocked, or misinformed of the realities. She believed the concerns of the child would be self-evident in the observation of the child's play and creative endeavors. Based on this belief, she developed the world technique, which was later adapted to become the Erica method, sand play, sand tray, and sand play therapy. She also developed the mosaic test.

The world technique was developed using a sand tray filled with moist sand that could be easily molded. Her instruction to the child was to "build a world." The child had many miniatures to choose from to construct this world. Lowenfeld got the idea from reading H. G. Wells's *Floor Games* (1911), in which Wells described how he and his sons built cities on the floor with toys. Lowenfeld incorporated this idea with the memory of playing in sand to develop her world technique. She collected many miniature toys that represented objects, people, places, animals, and things from daily life for the children to use.

Her mosaic test consisted of using parquetry blocks to form pictures. Because she believed play and creative endeavors express the child's ability to organize and to express their experiences, she used the mosaic test to indicate how well the child could organize thoughts. The designs made are traced and then colored as the child places them on paper. As therapy progresses, the child does another mosaic test. As the child becomes more organized and more in control of his or her world, the designs become more organized.

Lowenfeld's contribution to the field was to initiate the basis for what would become two viable tools in working with children: attachment theory and object relations. She also contributed a great deal to the study of human growth and development through her many published papers of the time sharing her observations of developing children.

Out of this period of high interest in the development of children emerged the initial foray into what has become known as **attachment theory**. Of the three matriarchs of the time period, Klein (1984a, 1984b) believed the development of impulses, fantasies, and anxieties are traceable back to the child's feelings toward the mother's breast. This beginning of object relations (relationships of love) was related to the first feeding experiences of the child, whose importance was reflected in all aspects of mental life and bound up with object relations. The concept was that as the mother reacts to the child, sometimes loving and caressing the child during feeding, the child learned this is good breast. Other times when the child might be making undue demands on the mother, feeding was either nonexistent or hurried, which was identified as bad breast. This love-hatred experience caused the child to develop a split in personality.

Object relations remain an important concept in psychoanalytic play therapy. Primarily, **object relations** are the relationships of the child with its caregiver, usually the mother. If the primary caregiver is warm, nurturing, and available to the child, the child tends to view others the same way. If the primary caregiver is cold, aloof, and unavailable, the child tends to expect others to be also. The former relationship leads to attachment; and the latter, to unattachment.

Psychoanalytic play therapists are developing therapy based on expansions of theories of attachment and object relationships. The basis of the theory is the relationships a child experiences from the moment of birth through childhood and adolescence.

Winnicott (1965), Mahler (Columbia University. Oral History Research Office, et al.; Mahler, 1968, 1979a, 1979b, 1979c, 1994a, 1994b, 1994c; Mahler, Furer, & Institute of Psycho-analysis (Great Britain), 1969; Mahler, McDevitt, & Settlage, 1971; Mahler, Pine, & Bergman, 1975; Mahler & Stepansky, 1988), and others have expanded the concept and deepened the understanding of the theory of object relations. The idea is the child is in a symbiotic relationship with the mother (caretaker) and totally depends on her for more than just physical existence. Therefore, the child's earliest definition of self is a reaction to the mother's caregiving style. This initial stage is from birth to approximately 9 months of age.

Next, the child realizes he or she is not actually a part of the mother but a separate entity. During this stage the child exerts independence. The child moves away from the object (mother) but returns often to check the object is still available. The child demands a great deal of attention at this time. The child may become excited about everything that can be explored. The child sees self as the center of the universe. In the child's eyes, the world is truly created for personal enjoyment. This stage of development makes its appearance between 10 to 18 months of age.

The child then learns the object is not solely available for the child's whims. Thus the *rapprochement* [pronounced ra 'prosh ma.] has begun. This time becomes a battle of wills between the child and parents. The battle is focused mostly toward the mother from whom the child is trying to separate but whose constant attention the child wishes to continue to engage. The approximate age of rapprochement is about 15 to 22 months.

When the parents meet these challenges of the growing child with patience and loving care, the child develops into a healthy individual. When these object relations crisis periods are not navigated with understanding and support, the child suffers from a lack of attachment. Lack of attachment may be brought on by many situations beyond the object's ability to control. Children who have had to be separated from the mother because of extended illness of the child or the mother, death of the mother, or other causes of prolonged absence have been found to have difficulty in attachment. The leading cause of attachment problems has been found in early and prolonged child abuse. Benedict (2003) has developed extensive tables and descriptions of children's play to help identify concerns resulting from problematic object relations and attachment disorder. Benedict has developed an extensive catalog of the possible meanings of children's play themes and a method of recording a play session in process codes. Her work is much too extensive to summarize here. However, attachment theory has greatly influenced child development play therapy theories and is discussed more fully in Chapter 10.

Psychoanalytic play therapists share with therapists from other schools the view that children's play is their work (Weininger, 1989). Children use play to gain control over the events and situations in their lives. The Freudian play therapist believes the child should be allowed to play freely, which allows the child to express psychic health. The goal of play psychotherapy is to help the children grow and rid them of mechanisms that prevent growth. The play is the therapy.

TOY SELECTION

The psychoanalytic play therapist differs little in the materials chosen for play therapy. However, they do differ in that each child has his or her toys used only by the specific child. The materials used in psychotherapy play are little dolls representing mothers, fathers, and a variety of children. Other items included are transportation vehicles, domestic and wild animals, blocks, balls, small house, fences, paper, clay, string, pencils, paints, and crayons. The therapist looks for toys the child can use in many different situations and ways, both realistic and fantasy, according to the material generated through the child's play. With the flexibility of the toy items, children can present a symbolic form of what is occurring in their minds.

The toys are kept in a private box and brought to the session by the therapist. No other child is allowed to use these toys, thus protecting the child's work from intrusion by others. To the child this means the toys are safe from damage, the play is private, and the therapist considers the toys important enough to keep them safe for the child. Symbolically, the box becomes the container holding the child's feelings, and the therapist guards the child's feelings by keeping the box safe and private. The contents of the box, symbolically extended to include the child's emotional life, is shared only between the child and the therapist (Klein, 1964; Weininger, 1989).

Children are interested in what other children may have in their boxes and what other children do with their toys. Although the boxes and toys are not shared with the curious children, the therapist does explore what about the other boxes the children find of interest. The therapist encourages the children to explore events, situations, and thoughts that have aroused their curiosity within the safety of the therapeutic relationship (Weininger, 1982, 1989). Weininger (1984, 1989) emphasizes the sameness of the place, time of day, length of session, and process of therapy in working with children. This sameness adds to the security and safety that allows the transference relationship to be established. This transference cannot happen unless the child sees the relationship with the therapist as unique and separate from the child's home life (Klein, 1964; Weininger, 1989). The playroom should be easily cleaned and contain sturdy toys. The room needs to have a water supply, a table with at least two chairs, a small couch, and walls that can withstand aggressive behavior without being damaged (Weininger, 1989).

Toys represent the important objects in a child's life. The child's feelings and thoughts are transferred to these inanimate objects. Then the child uses the toys in the same way the child might want to use the original object. The child is free to use the toys in any way the child wishes and the therapist interprets the play. The interpretation is used to allay the child's anxiety, so the child can talk about and play out the concerns. The interpretation needs to be appropriate to the child's developmental understanding. The therapist uses the words the child uses for the toys, what the toy symbolizes to the child, and how the child talks about his or her own body and others. The interpretation is based on the concept that the play is a disguise and communicates the therapist's understanding of its meaning. The therapist may acknowledge the symbolic representation to the child, which Weininger (1989) believes greatly enhances the interpretation and transference between the child and the therapist. Klein (1964) also indicated that not only the interpretation, but the child's reaction to the interpretation helps reveal more of their fears and provides opportunities for the child to develop control over their fears.

Whereas Weininger (1982, 1984, 1989) sets apart the child's toys in separate boxes, Bromfield (2003) and Lee (1997) appear to use the playroom in much the same manner as other play therapy theorists. Chethik (2000) does not provide a description of his use of toys. Because he does not elaborate on this aspect of his therapy, the assumption is made that he displays the toys in a traditional playroom much like other theorists.

ROLE OF THERAPIST

The therapist creates a safe place to explore inner thoughts and feelings (Bromfield, 2003). The role of the therapist is to help children when the play becomes blocked or too frightening. The therapist learns from the play and interprets the play to the child (Weininger, 1989). The therapist is a special adult who is attentive to the child but does not allow the child to hurt self, others, or damage the toys or room. Through play, drawings, constructions, and verbalizations, the therapist begins to understand the conflicts, fantasies, and concerns of the child. These media allow the

During the play therapy session, the play therapist listens empathically, and responds to the underlying feelings and meanings the child expresses. The child is treated with patience, respect, and honesty.

therapist an opportunity to explore the child's unconscious. The role of the therapist may also extend to act and function as a nurturing parent to the troubled adult parents and to provide sustenance that allows the parents to give adequate parenting to their child (Chethik, 2000).

The play therapist listens empathically and responds to the child. The child is treated with patience, respect, and honesty. The therapist responds to the child with candor and in his or her best interest (Bromfield, 2003). Interpretation may be pointing out what the child is not in the child's awareness (Bromfield, 2003). Here is an example of an interpretation to a child whose mother has recently been the victim of a violent crime and is hospitalized:

> *Child:* "I know my mother is not going to come home from the hospital. She is too sick."
>
> *Therapist:* "Sounds like you are pretty sad about that."
>
> *Child:* "No, it doesn't make any difference. It could have happened to anyone." The child looks down and then breaks the crayon he is holding.
>
> *Therapist:* "Clayton, you say it doesn't matter, but you broke the crayon in anger. I am thinking you are angry with the person who did this to your mom."

The play therapist works from a premise that the child cannot change what the child does not acknowledge. Therefore the role of the therapist is to help the child know what is reality and what changes need to be made (Bromfield, 2003).

STRUCTURING THE SESSION

Assessment takes place in the initial referral during an extensive interview with the caregivers. According to Chethik (2000), the psychodynamic play therapy treatment process consists of four concepts: the therapeutic alliance, resistance, transference, and interventions.

The **therapeutic alliance** is the observing part of the relationship; nontransference is the focus of this part of the relationship. The therapeutic alliance allows the child to work and to share goals in treatment. Another example can be taken from therapy with Clayton. Clayton's grandmother has disclosed in the interview that Clayton's mother will not return home because of her injuries. Clayton's father has given custody to the boy's grandmother. Clayton has problems with soiling, sleeplessness, and emotional outbursts:

> *Therapist:* "Your grandmother told me about your mom and the hard time you have had over the last year."
>
> *Clayton:* "Yeah, I'm here so I can stop feeling so bad and messing my pants."
>
> *Therapist:* "That is what you want to work on most while we are together?"
>
> *Clayton:* "I think so. I cannot go to school as long as I mess my pants."

Resistance is the stalemate experienced when the child does not wish to change. Resistance impedes the ability to remember, gain, or assimilate insight. An example from Clayton's therapy is presented here. Clayton has refused to speak except in nonsense gibberish, a language that only Clayton claims to be able to understand.

> *Therapist* [making an interpretation of what she thought Clayton wanted to hear]: "Sounds like you would like for your dad to care for you while your mom is ill."
>
> *Clayton* [continues with nonsense language].
>
> *Therapist:* "I bet it really hurts to have him send you to foster care rather than take the responsibility for you."
>
> *Clayton* [continues nonsense language but looks at the therapist and gets even louder with language].
>
> *Therapist:* "I guess this is pretty hard to hear."
>
> *Clayton:* "I don't want to hear what you have to say."

Transference is the child's way of projecting unconscious feelings and wishes on the play therapist that the child feels or wishes toward significant adults in his or her life. These feelings, drives, attitudes, fantasies or defenses seem to be misplaced or inappropriate in the play therapist-child relationship as they are played out in the playroom. Transference may be experienced by the child as seeing characteristics in the therapist that are shared by significant adults in the past or present. The transference may be more generalized and the child act toward the therapist as the child does to all adults or others that share commonalities like race, gender, language, age or other observable characteristics. The child may also see the therapist as the child sees himself or herself (Chethik, 2000).

Another example from Clayton:

Clayton: "Cockle-doodle-doo doesn't want me. He keeps bothering me."

Therapist: "Tell me about him."

Clayton: "He just bothers me. He doesn't like me. He says that I am in the way."

Therapist: "Seems like you imagine him when your dad doesn't call. I wonder if he says what you think your dad is thinking."

Interventions are the techniques used in therapy to help the child improve the child's problems. The interventions are confrontation, clarification, interpretation, and working through. *Confrontation* is making the phenomenon undeniable to the child's ego. *Clarification* is the sharpening and defining of the phenomenon. *Interpretation* is making the unconscious meaning of the phenomenon conscious to the child. *Working through* is the complete exploring of the phenomenon through gaining additional insights, assessing resistances, examining symptoms, and looking at how this affects daily life for the child.

LIMITS

According to Weininger (1989), children need to be contained or restricted in what they can do to protect them physically and emotionally. The child who breaks or destroys something may fear retaliation from the therapist and become more aggressive or become fearful, thus creating in the playroom the danger the child sees in the outside world (Weininger, 1989). The re-creation of the outside world allows the therapist to set healthy limitations on the child and the child's activities with the therapist in the role of the ideal parent to the child.

Bromfield (2003) describes psychoanalytic play therapy limit setting as an important part of therapy to assure the child the therapist will not allow the child to hurt self or office. Bromfield (2003) believes allowing the child to lose control will frighten the child and leave the child "at the peril of his own uncontained aggressions and impulse" (p. 6). Limits set by the therapist guide the child toward expressing self in symbolic action. Through setting limits on the child's behavior, the therapist helps the child maintain a sense of safety and yet still extend the space for self-expression (Bromfield, 2003).

PARENT INVOLVEMENT

Chethik (2000) says no child can succeed in treatment without the parents' consent to engage in treatment. Through the support of the treatment, the parents allow the child to use the therapy experience for their growth. The therapy with the child can be greatly enhanced by an alliance between the parents and the therapist. The range of interventions with the parents may range from parent guidance, transference parenting, and treatment of the parent-child relationship.

Parent guidance usually falls into one of two categories: issues that affect the emotional balance in the family and issues that center on the child. Issues that affect the emotional balance include working with predicaments in either parent's life that may affect parenting skills; working on disparity between the parents' management of their children; and working with stresses that emerge in parents caused by the child's treatment. Issues that focus on the child include collecting intake information about the child and family; conveying to the parents a broad understanding of the child's development and internal emotional life; instructing the parents on a specific understanding of the child's symptoms or behavior changes that emerge; and clarifying the problematic interactions between the child and the parents (Chethik, 2000).

In transference parenting, the therapist acts and functions as the nurturing parent to a troubled adult. Through the role of nurturer, the therapist provides sustenance through interest, availability, and support of parenting of the parent. The therapist supports the parent in a way that allows the parent to be competent in his or her parenting role.

The treatment of the parent-child relationship is the process of helping the parents to understand what the child believes about himself or herself and what meanings the child may assign to his or her parents' words or behaviors. Through this process the parents are helped to understand and gain perspective on what the parents are reliving through the child.

Chethik (2000) respects the parents' request for the therapist to focus on the child's behavior, believing the parents are seeking to participate in the child's therapy to become better parents.

TERMINATION

The decision to terminate is made based on the observation of the child's play. Weininger (1989) provides guidelines for when to terminate therapy. Termination is approaching when the reported problem is no longer viewed as a problem. The child has developed the ability to be appropriately aggressive, dependent, and adaptive. The child can use his or her emotional energies in constructive ways to enhance growing developmental interests and curiosities. The child can internalize and identify without being overcome with anxiety and/or avoiding of people or events. The child can accept failure or success without splitting or denial. The child can incorporate parent's increasing demands with the child's developing needs. The child can envision the future with expectations of both good and bad. The child can take joy in his or her own efforts but still ask for help when it is needed. The child can make and keep friends and believe he or she has something to offer others. The child can sublimate and continue symbol formation.

The therapist and the child usually agree on a date for termination. Then Weininger (1989) suggests the therapist give the child a small gift that has a special meaning to the child at the end of therapy. This gift is a transitional object that allows the child to feel some connection to the therapist, although the child will not be attending sessions any longer. The gift becomes the symbol of the goodness of the therapist, and the child can now carry the goodness of the therapist and the therapy both inside and outside of himself or herself (Klein, 1958; Weininger, 1989).

Assessment and Techniques

The assessment begins with the initial contact with the parents. A phone conversation is used to screen the child and to determine if a full evaluation is needed. This initial contact is also a time when the therapist may have to clarify if the parents are seeking therapy for themselves or for the child. The therapist typically meets with the parents alone in the first meeting before a final determination of a full evaluation or not. If a full evaluation is recommended, this session also serves to guide the parents in how to prepare the child for the evaluation.

Information the therapist may ask the parent to share:

1. Describe your relationship with the child.
2. Describe your responses to the child's behavior and the results of your response.
3. Describe how and when the child's behaviors most affect you.
4. Describe the incident(s) that led to seeking therapy.
5. Describe any other worries you may have about this child.

Based on information from this type of interview information, the therapist may or may not recommend further evaluation. If a further evaluation is recommended, the therapist collects an extensive developmental history, history of the parents' relationship and marriage issues, parents' perception of parenting difficulties, current living context of the family, and any important events in the life of the family history and child's history. The therapist is trying to construct a perception of the emotional climate of the child (Chethik, 2000).

The assessment process may begin with the initial phone contact with the parent or significant person making the appointment for the therapy session.

The full evaluation consists of clarifying the presenting problem, its history, and the parents' attempts to remedy the presenting problem. Following this part of the interview, the parents are asked to give a detailed developmental history. Next each parent is interviewed about their own childhoods and experiences. The therapist asks the parents how they met, a history of their courtship, and description of their early marriage.

Through interviews and clinical observation, the therapist assesses the child in the following areas: drive assessment, ego assessment, superego assessment, and genetic-dynamic formulation. The *drive assessment* includes the psychosocial phase of development, phase level, and quality of object relations.

The *ego assessment* includes defense mechanisms preferred, their appropriateness, and the efficiency of their employment. The extent of the capacity to relate to others, the capacity to adapt to change, nature of cognitive processes, drive regulation, and control are examined in the ego assessment. Intelligence, memory, motor function, perception, and language are also assessed. The child's ability to integrate and organize experiences and whether the child's ego functioning is as expected for age and developmental stage is also considered.

In the *superego assessment,* the therapist looks at the nature and extent of guilt versus fear of external authorities. The superego is the area of rules, morals, and values that guides the child's behavior.

The *genetic-dynamic formation* is assessed through examining sources of conflict in regard to psychosexual state, external and internal conflicts, and major sources of identification for the child and their contributions to the child's adaptations. All of this information is usually gathered from the parent prior to seeing the child. The treatment recommendations are then formulated. The treatment recommendations usually include a regularly scheduled session for the child. The sessions for the child may be weekly or twice weekly. The parents are asked to attend a parent guidance session on a weekly basis. If the parenting problem seems to warrant more intensive intervention, the parents may be scheduled for individual, couple, or family therapy (Chethik, 2000).

SUMMARY

Psychodynamic play therapy represents the first of the theories developed from the initial work of Sigmund Freud. His early work with Little Hans represents the first attempt to analyze children.

Anna Freud and Melanie Klein further developed psychodynamic play therapy, although the literature attests to their conflicts about the nature of the process with children. In the early development of play therapy theory, Klein and Freud developed their theories along different lines of thought and with much disagreement as they tried to develop a therapy for children that paralleled the work with adults.

Today, psychodynamic play therapists generally select the toys for each child and reserve these toys in special containers for the exclusive use of a specific child. However, this model is not consistent for all current theorists. The role of the therapist is to help the child through resistances and frightening experiences. Attachment and object relations theory is an outcome of the work of these early therapists.

CHAPTER 4

ADLERIAN PLAY THERAPY

Terry Kottman engaging in cooperative play with a child in Adlerian play therapy.

This chapter presents the basic tenets of Adlerian play therapy. Alfred Adler (Ansbacher, 1974; Ansbacher & Ansbacher, 1956) posed a theory of individual psychology that diverged from Freud's psychoanalytic theory. Rudolf Dreikurs (1953, 1967, 1989, Dreikurs & Cassel, 1972; Dreikurs & Soltz, 1984) later operationalized Adler's theory for work with children. Several authors have proposed play therapy methodology, but Terry Kottman (1995, 2001a, 2001b, 2003; Kottman & Schaefer, 1993) has developed Adlerian play therapy into a unique approach to play therapy. The majority of this chapter is based on Kottman's writings, but contributions and variations by other authors are also presented.

INTRODUCTION

According to the Alfred Adler Institute (2004), classical Adlerian psychology is a completely integrated theory of personality that is value based and includes a model of maladjustment, a philosophy of life, an approach to preventive learning, and a therapeutic technique for the provision of therapy. The mission of individual psychology, also called Adlerian theory, is one that encourages people to become psychologically healthy, to live and relate to others in a cooperative manner. Adlerians believe that it is highly desirable for people in all relationships to seek a socially equal and democratic lifestyle for themselves and others. Because Adlerians are enthusiastically optimistic and inspiring in their approach to therapy, Adlerians emphasize that the most advantageous development and social responsibility occurs within the individual.

Adler believed the child's play reflects his or her characteristic manner of behaving or style of life. Based on these observations of play, the therapist could hypothesize how the child would behave as an adult, if no intervention took place. Because of their limited frame of reference and experience, children may misinterpret their experiences. However, the Adlerian does not view these deviations from actuality as "wrong." Adlerians view all reality as subjective and limited by the individual's perceptions of the situation. Therefore, the Adlerian play therapist helps the child explore alternative perceptions or perspectives of his or her experience.

According to Dinkmeyer, Dinkmeyer, and Sperry (1987), "The assumption underlying Adlerian counseling theory is that people are indivisible, social, decision-making beings whose actions and psychological movement have purpose. Each person is seen as an individual within a social setting, with the capacity to decide and to choose" (p. 9). Adler said that people are socially embedded, goal-directed, subjective, and creative organisms that must be viewed as a whole (Ansbacher & Ansbacher, 1956).

Kottman (2003) interpreted socially embedded to mean that individuals strive to belong. Without a positive sense of belonging, the child belongs in negative ways. The child's relationship to parents and siblings provides the therapist with some indication of the child's sense of positive or negative belonging in the family. How the child behaves in this original socializing unit determines how the child views himself or herself in other social contexts. Kottman described these contexts as "boxes," or categories. Examples of this concept of boxes are the smart child, the lazy child, the good child, the bad child, or the phobic child (Kottman, 1995).

To best understand the child's box, Kottman interviews both parents and the siblings, when possible. A guideline for whom to include in the interview is everyone living under the same roof with the child. One of the more important aspects of the interview is to assess the development of social interest, that is, a sense of belonging to the overall society (i.e., school, community, church, nation, etc.). The more positively socially embedded the child, the more social interest is indicated. The more connectedness the child experiences, the less the child feels inferior, alienated, and isolated (Griffith & Powers, 1984). In other words, the child with positive socially embedded experiences has high social interest and exhibits fewer maladaptive behaviors.

Adlerians believe all people are goal directed and behave in a purposeful manner. The individual's positive behavior is adopted in order to move the person toward the desired goal; however, if the person becomes discouraged, he or she will use negative behavior to advance toward the goal. The goal is always the antecedent of the behavior. Whether the behavior is positive or not depends on whether the individual can move toward the goal with positive behavior and avoid overwhelming frustration and discouragement.

Dreikurs and Soltz (1964) designated the goals of negative behavior or misbehavior into four categories: attention, power, revenge, and inadequacy. To help identify the goal of the misbehavior, the therapist must look at the child's behaviors, reactions to the child's behavior, and the child's reaction to correction. The attention-getting child irritates the parent. If the parent gives attention the behavior stops, but if the parent attempts to ignore the child, the behavior exacerbates, moving toward power. When the child's misbehavior is directed toward power, the parent is provoked to show the child who is in charge. The child responds by becoming more oppositional. The revenge goal of misbehavior is most often indicated by the phrases "I hate you," "You don't love me," "If you were my real parent you would . . . ," and other responses meant to hurt the parents. This behavior can resort to physical violence, if not stopped by the parent.

Dinkmeyer and McKay (1989) suggested four goals of positive behavior. The first is the goal of attention, involvement, and contribution. This child believes belonging comes from what the child can contribute to the family and social group. The second goal of positive behavior is that of autonomy and self-responsibility. This child believes he or she has appropriate power and can make responsible decisions. The third goal of positive behavior is that of justice and fairness. This child is cooperative and responds to cruelty or hurt with kindness and caring. The final goal of positive behavior is the child who avoids conflict and accepts others' opinions. This child is one that resolves conflict in a nonviolent manner, ignores provocations, withdraws from power struggles, and resists peer pressure. This child exhibits mature decision-making skills and responsible behavior. The role of the play therapist is to identify the goals of misbehavior and help the child attain goals with positive behavior.

Adlerian psychology is based in *phenomenology,* which means to Adlerians that all individuals base their decisions on a subjective perspective of reality. In other words, the individual has his or her own unique interpretation of reality based on previous experiences and life's teachings. The habitual way a person relates to the world and other people determines the individual's lifestyle, or style of life. Individuals have a discrepancy between how they perceive themselves to be and their ideal selves. Because of this discrepancy, people are always falling short of the ideal self, which creates feelings of inferiority. These feelings of inferiority serve as motivation to either strive toward perfection or to find it overwhelming and respond with discouragement.

The play therapist's role is to become aware of when the child is using this unique perspective of his or her reality in developing a private logic that is harmful or negative to the child's developing style of life. The play therapist may do this through offering alternative perspectives or different interpretations of the events to the child. This emphasis on many ways to interpret the same events helps the child develop an ability to change perspectives and to take responsibility for how he or she chooses to view a situation. The intervention strategies are designed to encourage the child and give the child a sense of personal power. The child may not be able to control the circumstances of his or her life, but the child does have control over whether to use events to inspire or dissuade the child's seeking personal significance.

Adlerians believe each person is endowed with an ability to create their own lives by the choices and perspectives they take. Each individual is self-determined in the ability to choose his or her own interpretation of situations, events, and relationships and to act as if these interpretations were true. This major deviation from psychodynamic determinism means an individual is free to make new interpretations and decisions about his or her life at any point in the lifetime. Because of this ability, every person expresses themselves in a creative way that is uniquely them. The play therapist's responsibility is to discover and appreciate these unique qualities and help the child channel these in a socially appropriate manner.

Toy Selection

According to Kottman (1995), the toys used in play therapy assist the child to (a) create rapport between the child and therapist, (b) convey a variety of emotions, (c) examine and role-play situations and relationships from the child's life, (d) provide a safe environment to test behavioral and emotional limits, (e) empower the child's sense of self, (f) advance self-understanding and (g) improve the child's self-control and personal responsibility for behavior and feelings. The toys are selected in five basic groupings of family/nurturing toys, scary toys, aggressive toys, expressive toys, and pretend/fantasy toys.

The family/nurturing toys, such as dolls, dollhouse, food, dishes, and blanket, are used to explore the family constellation and family atmosphere. The scary toys, like snakes, rats, alligator, dinosaurs and insects, help the child examine mistaken beliefs, perceived threats, and past traumas. Aggressive toys, resembling punching toys, toy soldiers, handcuffs, and weapons, are used to delve into control and trust issues. Expressive toys or craft/art supplies assist the child to open up feelings, family relationships, and to express creativity. The pretend/fantasy toys, for instance, masks, costumes, blocks, transportation toys, magic wands, telephones, and animals, aid in examining relationships and practicing new behaviors.

According to Kottman (2003), the most important element in the playroom is not the toy selection or the design of the room, but rather the attitude of the therapist. She claims that if the therapist feels safe, happy, and comfortable in the space, the child will also feel safe, happy, comfortable, and welcome. Through the use of creativity and flexibility, the therapist can create an environment the child can safely and comfortably explore in therapy.

Role of the Therapist

The role of the play therapist is to be a partner with the child, with equal power and responsibility in the therapeutic relationship (Kottman, 2003). The therapist treats the child with respect and gives the child appropriate power. The Adlerian play therapist treats the child client as the therapist would treat an adult client. The therapist makes sure the child understands the therapeutic relationship and its limitations in language appropriate to the child's level of understanding.

The therapist uses tracking, restatement, reflection, questioning, interaction, collaboration, encouragement, and limit setting to build an egalitarian relationship in therapy. The play therapist employs brainstorming, problem solving, and teaching to communicate skills the child may practice within the session and outside. The child is encouraged to practice these skills outside of the session and to report the outcome. The therapist utilizes encouragement to sustain the child during this crucial time. The therapist teaches the parent the skills of encouragement and other techniques to help sustain change and healthy development of the child.

A major goal in Adlerian play therapy is to motivate the child toward self-understanding and insight through therapy. The outcome of this understanding and insight is intended to result in permanent changes in the child's attitudes, cognitions, emotions, and actions (Kottman, 1995).

Kottman (1995) describes specific skills the therapist applies in the process of Adlerian play therapy: tracking, restating content, reflecting feelings, answering questions, asking questions, interacting with the child, role play, encouragement, setting limits, and cleaning up the room. Although many of these are therapeutic skills familiar to most therapists, Kottman (2003) puts her unique Adlerian interpretation on the use of them, which she believes builds an equal relationship with the child.

Tracking behavior is simply stating the action the child is performing. The purpose of the tracking behavior is to let the child know the therapist is paying attention to the child and wishes to engage in the play communication mode. An example of a tracking response might be "You are feeding the doll."

Restating the content is repeating what the child has said in a way that conveys the therapist understands what the child is saying. Through tone and inflection of the restatement, the therapist conveys an understanding of the nonverbal understanding of the child. The child may say, "I am going to draw a house on the chalkboard." The therapist might restate this with "So you have chosen to draw a house with the dry markers."

Reflecting feelings is articulating the feelings that the child appears to be experiencing in the play. The cues to the feelings may be seen in the nonverbal behavior and the intonation of the child's verbalizations. The therapist observes the child's pose, facial expressions, gestures, proximity, and interjections. The speed, volume, and tone of the speech provide additional cues. The child may lay his head down on the table and move a toy car lethargically. The therapist might respond, "You seem a little down today."

Answering the child's questions is an important aspect of Adlerian therapy. Adlerians believe children's questions serve a purpose and are worth exploration. The questions fall into the following categories: practical, personal, relationship, and process. The practical question is one that is asked because the child needs information. An example is "May I go to the bathroom?"

A personal question is believed to make a connection or to lower anxiety. An example might be "Do you live here?" The personal question is asked to determine the strength of the relationship with the therapist and to provide the child with protection from being too attached. In these cases, Kottman (1995) recommends the therapist reflect the motivating feeling and make a guess about the purpose of the question. The child may ask, "Do you wish we could be together more?" The therapist might respond, "You enjoy your time in the playroom, and you are wondering if I enjoy being with you as much as you enjoy being here?"

The process question asks about the therapeutic process. The purpose underlying these questions is the child trying to define the parameters of the play therapy process. The child may ask, "What should I do next?" Kottman (2003) suggests the therapist respond in a way that gives the responsibility and control to the child. An example of the therapist's response might be "In here, you can decide what you do next." Kottman cautions that the therapist should stop and think about the child's question before answering. The therapist needs to consider the underlying meaning and purpose of the question before answering.

The therapist may also wish to ask the child questions. Kottman (1995) reminds the therapist that Adlerians follow the common practice of asking open-ended questions and never "why" questions. The child will respond to the open-ended question with something more than "yes" or "no." The why question is not asked because children seldom actually know how to say, "I don't know." The Adlerian focuses questions on the present and does not delve into the historical background of the concern. Questions the Adlerian therapists ask fall into one of two categories. The first category is questions that obtain information about the presenting problem or the events in the child's daily life. The second category is questions asked to explore the child's style of life. Therefore, the questions asked by the therapist are always about the present situation or events in the child's life. The Adlerian does not force the child to answer a question. Kottman (2003) does acknowledge the child not answering by saying something to the effect that the child chose not to answer the question. Equally important to the verbal response or no response to the therapist questions is the nonverbal response. The therapist observes the child's reaction to the question or any clue to feelings preceding the response.

Kottman (2003) encourages the therapist to participate actively with the child. The therapist may choose to play with the child or not to play with the child. The important aspect is that the therapist does not play with the child as a response to the child's manipulation or to appease the child. The question the therapist must answer before choosing to play with the child or not is whether playing with the child will be therapeutic for the child or meet a therapeutic goal. If the therapist chooses not to play with the child, the therapist may respond with a straightforward response like "I choose not to play for now." Sometimes the therapist may wish to initiate playing with the child. When this happens, the Adlerian therapist has a clear goal in mind that will test a therapeutic hypothesis.

The therapist may choose to engage in role plays with the child. The child may initiate a role play by asking the therapist to take a part. Kottman (1995) suggests the "whisper" technique. In this technique, the therapist asks the child for direction in a whisper and then does what the child suggests to say or do in the role of the character the child desires. By asking for direction in a whisper, the child can direct the action and direction of the role play. The therapist may also choose not to engage in the role play or pretend play by saying, "I want to watch today; maybe you can show me with the puppets."

The therapist looks for occasions to provide the child with encouragement. The Adlerians believe most children come to therapy because they have become discouraged. Therefore, a major part of Adlerian play therapy is to provide encouragement. Here are some responses to the child that provide encouragement:

1. Convey unconditional acceptance by responding to the child's value without conveying need for change.
2. Show faith in the individual's abilities by recognizing the child's accomplishments and progress.
3. Recognize the child's efforts.
4. Focus on strengths and assets.
5. Emphasize the endeavor and the pleasure of the undertaking, not the achiever.
6. Acknowledge the positive aspects of the child's products or contributions, and ignore the negative aspects.
7. Demonstrate support for the child.
8. Model for the child that it is not necessary to be perfect.
9. Help the child learn from mistakes and not be devastated.
10. Direct the child, toward positive ways to gain significance.

According to Kottman (2003), Adlerian play therapy appears to be especially appropriate for the following kinds of childhood concerns:

1. Power and control issues, like those exhibited through temper tantrums, bullying, and oppositional behaviors with parents and teachers.
2. Traumatic experiences (e.g., sexual abuse, parental divorce, death of significant person, or natural disaster).
3. Poor self-concepts, as demonstrated through becoming easily frustrated by a task or making demeaning comments about self.
4. Family relationship concerns, for instance, sibling rivalry or conflicts with parents.
5. Poor social skills, as observed through having trouble making age-appropriate friends, not getting along with other children, or being isolated.

STRUCTURING THE SESSION

In Adlerian therapy, four phases are considered to form the process: building a relationship, exploring the client's lifestyle, helping the client gain insight into the chosen lifestyle, and reorienting and reeducating the client (Kottman, 2003). Kottman is less structured than Nystul (1980).

Nystul (1980, 1987) formulated a list of how to conduct an Adlerian play therapy session. His play therapy is based on the following seven assumptions:

1. The counselor attempts to establish a feeling of mutual respect with the child.
2. The counselor believes there are not maladjusted children, just discouraged ones. Encouragement, therefore, is the main tool.
3. The counselor allows the child to feel understood by identifying the hidden reasons for his or her behavior.

4. The counselor modifies the child's motivation for change by redirecting his or her teleogical movement (goal-directed movement).

5. A session starts with 15 to 30 minutes of the DUSO program (other therapists may use other types of psychoeducational materials, i.e., body safety, good touch, bad touch, etc.) and ends with 15 to 30 minutes of creative arts therapy.

6. The counselor uses logical and natural consequences to establish the limits necessary to anchor therapy to the world of reality.

7. The counselor recognizes that parent and teacher education are important adjuncts to therapy. Together they promote long-term positive outcomes for children.

Nystul (1980) provides a brief overview of his interpretation of an Adlerian play therapy session, but not all Adlerians are as structured. Kottman (2003) certainly adapted much of the child-centered work of Landreth (2002) into her structure of a play therapy session. Her guidelines are presented in this section as more indicative of today's Adlerian therapists.

The Adlerian therapist asks the child what the child was told or understood about coming to play therapy. The therapist answers questions the child may ask about the play therapy. In addition the therapist provides the child with information about the therapeutic process, consultation with parents and teachers, and confidentiality. The therapist may say something like this:

> You and I will be meeting in the playroom for 30 minutes once a week. In here you may say what you would like and do many of the things you would like to do. This is our time together. I will not tell your parents exactly what you say or do, but I will be talking to them about ways they may help you. I will meet with your parents either at the beginning of our session or at the end of our session; you may choose whether I see you first or not. You may be present when I talk to your parents. If I think you might be hurt, hurt yourself, or hurt someone else, I will take steps to keep you and others safe. I may share some of my guesses about you and new ways to talk to you with your teacher and your parents. When it is possible, I will talk to you about what I am going to say before I meet with your teacher or parents.

Indication of the child's lifestyle comes from observations of the child's habitual play themes and interactions with the therapist and others. The child's goals of behavior can be indicated through the collection of information from the parents, the child, and metaphors used in artwork and play. The family constellation, family atmosphere, and early recollections are usually gained through formal and informal questioning techniques. This information about the child's lifestyle is shared with the child in the third phase of therapy to help the child and parents gain insight into the child's behavior. The techniques used by the therapist include tentative hypotheses, interpretation, metaphors, art techniques, confrontation, immediacy, and humor. Through these techniques, the child scrutinizes attitudes, perceptions, feelings, thoughts, and actions to determine which of these are to be perpetuated and which are to be rejected for a more favorable choice.

Yura and Galassi (1974) provided direction in observing children in play therapy and determining their style of life and goals of behavior. If the child's misdirected goal was attention getting, the child would play in such a way as to get the attention of others. The child might take such roles as movie star, rock singer, or sports hero, who would perform before large audiences. The child, who sought power, might take the role of leadership or boss. These roles are reflected in the play themes of military commander, president of the United States, school principal, or sheriff. Children seeking revenge might beat or break toys. Destruction is often the theme of these children, who feel revengeful. The withdrawn child might be silent, play tentatively, or engage in solitary activity. The extremely defeated child's play expressed the child's fear of this being another unsuccessful experience (Yura & Galassi, 1974).

Adler believed that how a child plays is a rehearsal for what role the child will take in later life. If the child takes leadership roles, the child is preparing for leadership positions. If the child takes a teaching role, the child is preparing for a teaching position in society. Through the information obtained in the play session, the therapist can direct and redirect the child's behavior at an early age (Yura & Galassi 1974).

Observations of a child in play groups give an indication of social interest, the expression of giving and taking in a social situation. The child who has not developed social interest may play alone or behave aggressively toward other children (Yura & Galassi, 1974). Children who lack social interest may become antisocial.

Adlerian methods of play therapy would be considered structured play interventions, using puppets, dollhouses, and games. In the puppet play the therapist has a variety of puppets representing family, the child, and other children or animals. The therapist either structures the situation to be dramatized or allows the child to structure the situation with the therapist suggesting alternatives to misbehavior on the part of the child puppet. The therapist may have the child speak for all the characters, thus gaining insight into the feelings of others (Yura & Galassi, 1974).

The miniature house and doll family allows the therapist to have the child act out a typical day. Through this reenactment, the therapist gains information about how the child views his or her home environment. The therapist can then have the child try out new behaviors in the context of the doll play before actually doing so at home.

Yura and Galassi (1974) suggest group games can also be used to redirect useless games that are not in the child's best interest. The attention-getting child benefits from games that only allow attention if the child is quiet and willing to wait his or her turn. Such a game would be one in which only one child gets to choose or guess at a time; the next child chosen to be "it" is the child who is the quietest. Bossy children are often best put together with a single goal, such as a play or puppet show to present to the class or jumping rope. In working together, the children learn cooperation. The withdrawn child should be placed in charge of some highly desirable object or piece of equipment that will force the other children to interact with the withdrawn child in order to gain use of the object (Yura & Galassi, 1974).

The therapist generally takes note of the goals of behavior, degree of social interest, style of life, and other aspects of the child's free play during the first session. The therapist may set up structured activities, much like those described by Yura and Galassi (1974), to ascertain this kind of material.

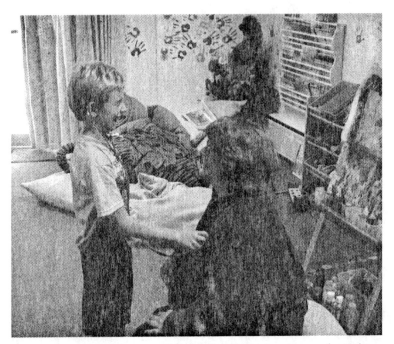

Adlerian therapists generally take note of the goals of behavior, degree of social interest, style of life, and other aspects of the child's free play during the first session.

Following this first session, the parents are given a brief report in the child's presence about the session. Usually a brief comment is sufficient because the parents have already been interviewed extensively. The comment might be something like "We had a really good session today. We decided that next week, I will see you (the parents) for the first 10 minutes (or for the last 10 minutes) of our session. We will always meet in my office for that time." The child is given a business card and told to call if he or she ever needs to talk to the therapist. The presentation of the business card is a subtle way to indicate the child is the primary client and the relationship is a professional one (Kottman, 2003).

Play therapy sessions that follow are goal directed, and treatment is based on the reason for referral. Adlerian play therapists intervene in free play to help direct the child toward needed skills by asking the child to reenact a play scene or engaging the child in specific activities they have chosen for the child to learn a particular skill or concept. Adlerian play therapists typically move in and out of the nondirective free play mode to a more directive activity-based mode. The therapist is attentive to every opportunity to move the child toward the agreed on goal of therapy.

LIMITS

Setting limits is an important part of the therapeutic process, creating an environment in which the child can safely explore new behaviors and feelings (Bixler, 1949; Ginott, 1994; Landreth, 2002; Moustakas, 1997). Thoughts, feelings, wishes, fantasies, or beliefs are all accepted in the play therapy room. However, behaviors that may be harmful physically or emotionally are limited by the therapist to make the child safe and to provide alternative forms of expression. The main goal of Adlerian limit setting is to help the child gain self-control and to teach responsibility in redirecting inappropriate behaviors to gain positive significance. Kottman (2003) describes that a limit needs to have the following components:

1. Stating the limit.
2. Reflecting the feelings or guessing about purposes of behavior.
3. Generating alternative behaviors.
4. Setting up logical consequences.

For example, "The lights are not for shooting [the limit] even though it looks like fun [the feeling or purpose]. You may shoot the target [alternative behavior] or choose not to play with the gun [logical consequences]."

In addition to creating a safe environment, limits are designed to help the child learn and assume personal responsibility. Limit setting is a natural extension of the function of teaching social and personal responsibility for the Adlerian play therapist. Through the choice of limits to set, alternative behaviors generated, and the logical consequences, the therapist teaches the child socially and personally responsible behaviors.

PARENT INVOLVEMENT

Adlerians do not underestimate the importance of the parents in the child's treatment. The parents are included in the treatment through consultation and parenting skills. Usually the parent is seen for 10 to 15 minutes at each session by the therapist. Because of a personal bias that says the child is the client, I have the child present at all of these meetings, then excuse myself and the child to the playroom for the rest of the time. The child need not be present for the intake as the therapist collects data about the family, child, siblings, and concerns. When possible, both parents benefit from being present and providing the therapist with their views.

During the initial parent interview, the Adlerian play therapist asks questions to gain extensive data about the child's family and the relationships within that family. Several Adlerian theorists (Dinkmeyer & Dinkmeyer, 1977; Eckstein, Baruth, & Mehrer, 1992; Kottman, 2003; Powers & Griffith, 1987; Shulman & Mosak, 1988) have developed structured interviews to provide guidance to the therapist in collecting the data from the parents. The general categories of questions include family atmosphere, family constellation, academic ability/concerns, social relationships, goals of behavior, sibling relationships, and emotional functioning. The questions are posed to each of the parents and to the child individually. A comparison of the questions provides the therapist with a more accurate picture of the family atmosphere and the child's lifestyle. Because the questions may overwhelm and limit rapport building, Kottman (2003) suggests the therapist ask a few questions at a time and not bring the form into the session. In addition to the traditional lifestyle questionnaire, Kottman asks the child to draw and to answer questions that call on the child's creativity. How the child answers questions about a drawing of his or her family and the creative questions provide more insights into the child's lifestyle.

The parents are included in other aspects of therapy beyond the initial interview. The parents are provided with suggestions to follow at home for helping the child. Improving parenting skills has always been a substantial part of Adlerian interventions with children. Some of these parenting skills improvement materials are *Children: The Challenge* (Dreikurs & Soltz, 1984); *Raising Kids Who Can* (Bettner & Lew, 1989); *Parenting Young Children* (Dinkmeyer, McKay, & Dinkmeyer, 1989); *Active Parenting* (Popkin, 1982), *Systematic Training for Effective Parenting (STEP)* (Dinkmeyer & McKay, 1989), and *The Effective Parent* (Dinkmeyer, McKay, Dinkmeyer, Dinkmeyer, & McKay, 1987). These books describe the parenting skills of reflective listening, problem ownership, goals of behavior, logical consequences, and encouragement.

Dinkmeyer and McKay (1989) and Kottman (2003) suggest parents be taught to do reflective listening. Reflective listening helps the child feel understood, which increases the child's sense of security and self-esteem. The parents are instructed to listen to the child, think about what the child is feeling, put that feeling into a single word, and then incorporate that feeling into a sentence. These specific directions help the parents learn reflective listening successfully without feeling they must completely change their communication pattern with the child.

Defining the problem ownership is simply helping to decide who actually has the problem or whose needs are not met. Three possibilities exist. First, the child's behavior is not bothersome, but the child's needs are not being met. In this situation, the child has the problem because the child has chosen not to make it known what his or her needs are. The parents do not have a problem, unless they decide to intervene and not allow the child to experience the consequences. An example might be that Daniel refuses to sign up for soccer because he is angry with his father. If the father insists Daniel play soccer, the problem shifts to the father.

The second possibility is there is no real problem. The child's needs are being met and the parents do not find the behavior troublesome. A case in point would be that Rachel did not want to join a girls' club and the parents thought she was already involved in too many activities.

The third possibility is that the child's needs are being met but the behavior is annoying for the parents. In this case, the parents have the problem. An illustration is that the child has begun a science project in the living room, but the parents are expecting guests and will be embarrassed by the disarray. If the child's needs are frustrated, the child is unlikely to engage cooperatively in problem solving. However, the parents can offer choices to provide an acceptable responsible alternative that is mutually satisfying to both the child and the parents. Such a solution might be that if the child will help clear the project from the living room, the parents will assist the child with the project when the guests go home or allow the child to move to another acceptable location.

The four goals of misbehavior are what the parents find to be most bothersome. The child may be unaware of the goals he or she is seeking. The child's behavior may appear illogical to others but is consistent with the child's interpretation of his or her place in the family group. These are the four goals of misbehavior:

1. Attention getting. The child wants attention and service. The parent can identify this goal by the behavior and their feeling of mild irritation with the child. The parent may feel a need to remind and coax the child. The parent is encouraged to withdraw attention when the behavior is inappropriate but to provide attention when the behavior is appropriate.

2. **Power.** The child wants to be in control. The parents feel they must take immediate steps to indicate their authority over the child. The child may have too little power; if that is so, the parent will want to provide more responsibilities and/or more choices. If the child has too much power, the parent will want to disengage from the power struggle with a statement of fact and no further discussion. The Adlerian concept of "taking your wind out of the child's sail" applies in this situation. More accurately put, the parent withdraws from the discussion emotionally and, if need be, physically.

3. **Revenge.** The child wants to hurt someone. The parent can recognize this goal by their feelings of hurt as a result of the child's behavior. The difficult task for the parent is to remain nurturing, patient, and consistent without showing frustration and hurt.

4. **Display of inadequacy.** The child wants to be left alone, with no demands made. The parents can intensify this goal by their own desire to give up with the child and by displaying a sense of discouragement. The parents' role to counter this behavior is to encourage and support the child. To help the child ensure success, the parent sometimes has to help the child break down a task into smaller, but easily executed steps.

Natural and logical consequences is a technique in which the parent allows a child to experience the consequences of his or her own behavior. In the case of natural consequences, the child will not be endangered but will feel discomfort. For example, if a child dawdles in the morning, the parent allows him to experience the unpleasantness of being tardy. In logical consequences, the parent and child agree what will happen if the rule or limit set on the child is violated. The consequence must be related to the behavior. For instance, if the child draws on the wall, the child must scrub the wall, a logical consequence. The child who cannot keep from playing in the street must play in the fenced-in yard. The logical consequence can be provided to the child as a choice. You may choose to stay at home with a babysitter or you may choose to spend the night at a friend's house. All choices provided to the child must be real choices in which the parents do not favor one choice over the other. Experiencing the consequences of choices and behaviors allows the child to develop a personal sense of responsibility for her behavior.

Encouragement implies unconditional faith in and respect for the child. The parents set age-appropriate standards and ambitions for the child. Lack of encouragement is the source of the child's misbehavior along with the belief that positive means will not be successful. The parent is taught to separate the child from what the child produces. In other words, if the child gets a bad grade, the child is not bad. The grade is unacceptable. The parent helps the child gain the skills needed to make an acceptable grade. The parent will have to set the expectation to meet the child's maturity and level of skill.

TERMINATION

The decision to terminate is based on the changes in the child's basic convictions and lifestyles. The therapist uses consultation with parents, teachers, and significant adults in the child's life to determine if the child's goals of behavior have changed from negative to positive goals. Kottman (2003) asked the parents and teachers to quantify their appraisals of the child's behavior on a scale of 1 to 10. A rating of 1 would be no observed change and 10 would be no problem. Although Kottman does not mention this technique, asking the same appraisal questions in the initial interview and then again at the end provides a comparison of how the person assessing has observed the change.

Kottman (2003) suggests the therapist begin to talk about termination 4 weeks before the last session. During these last sessions, the therapist talks to the child about how the child perceives the changes in his or her life. The therapist also shares that he or she has noticed a lot of improvement and feels it may be time to end their sessions. The therapist observes how the child reacts to this suggestion, trusting the child to provide indications as to readiness for termination. Negative reactions or regression are an indication that termination may be premature.

During the countdown to termination, the child may show some regression. Teachers and parents need to be warned to expect this behavior. The parents and teachers may need to be reminded not to respond by reverting to their old patterns of interactions with the child. The child is reminded that termination does not mean the child cannot come back. The child may return to talk to the therapist as needed. The therapist gives the child a business card and invites the child to call whenever the child may need to do so.

ASSESSMENT AND TECHNIQUES

Adlerians use both formal and informal instruments to assess the child. Formal assessments may include intelligence tests, learning disabilities screening instruments, and projective methods. Informal assessment may include various drawing tests, sentence completions, and questionnaires. The unique assessment used by the Adlerian play therapist is the lifestyle interview.

The style of life interview (Dinkmeyer, Dinkmeyer, & Sperry, 1987) presented here has two parts. The first interview is with each parent or the parent who brings the child into the therapy session. The more information gathered, the more clearly the therapist will understand the style of life. The therapist needs to remember that Adlerian psychology treats perceptions with the same respect as factual information. The following outline can be used to structure this interview.

Problem Statement
1. What is the presenting problem?

Family Constellation
2. List the name and ages of all the family members including parents, siblings, step siblings, stepparents, and any significant adults who may reside in the household.

Family Atmosphere
3. Which of the siblings is the child in most conflict with? How does that happen?
4. Who is Dad's favorite child? Why?
5. Who is Mom's favorite child? Why?

6. How would you describe yourself?
7. How would you describe your spouse? Your ex-spouse?
8. Which child is most like your spouse (and/or ex-spouse)? How?
9. Which child is most like you? How?
10. Describe the relationship between you and your current spouse. Ex-spouse? Stepparents? Who makes the decisions? Who is more ambitious for the children? In what way? Do you two disagree openly? About what? Do you agree on child-rearing methods?
11. Describe other environmental influences on the child. Who has been important to the child? Grandparents? In what way? Other relatives? In what way? Stepparents? In what way? Friends or neighbors? In what way?
12. Do any members of the family use alcohol or other drugs? To what extent? Is this a family problem? If so, how do you cope?

Parental Perception of the Child
13. How does the child stand out in the family? Positively? Negatively?
14. What does the child want to be when he or she grows up?
15. What are the child's responsibilities?
    - Getting self up in the morning?
    - Off to school?
    - Getting self to bed at night?
    - Household chores?
    - Pets?
    - Does he or she stay alone?
    - What is mealtime like?
16. Does this child have nightmares? Dreams? About what?

Ratings
17. List the highest and lowest (most > or least <) sibling for each attribute.
    - Intelligent
    - Hardest worker
    - Best grades
    - Follows rules
    - Helps around the house
    - Complains/finds faults
    - Does nice things for others
    - Selfish
    - Tries to please
    - Feelings easily hurt
    - Temper
    - Likes to get things
    - Friends
    - High standards (achievement and morals)
    - Athletic
    - Most spoiled
    - Best looking
    - Most punished

Functioning at Life Tasks

18. How does this child get along with adults? Who is the child's favorite adult to be with? Who is the child's least favorite adult to be with?
19. How does the child get along with children in the neighborhood? Who is his or her best friend in the neighborhood?
20. Does the child get along with peers at school? Who is the child's best friend at school? Describe the friend. Does the friend come over very often?
21. How do things go for the child at school? What do you know about how the child is at school?

Traumas

22. What traumatic events have occurred during this child's life (death, divorces, sexual molestation, physical abuse, moving, house fires, tornados, parental loss of job, loss of pet, etc.)?

Behaviors

23. If any, what are some of the behaviors the child engages in that are annoying to you or other family members?
24. What do you do in response to these annoying behaviors?
25. How do you feel if these annoying behaviors persist?

Dreams for the Child

26. What are your hopes for this child?
27. Is there anything else I should know about him or her?

The child is also interviewed without the presence of the parents.

The therapist will then be able to compare the child's perceptions of style of life with that of the parents. Although there may be some differences of perception, an examination of these differences can provide the therapist with important insights into the goals of behavior and the parental needs for change in the child. The following interview for the child is based on one by Dinkmeyer, Dinkmeyer, and Sperry (1987).

Family Atmosphere

1. What are the names and ages of your parents, brothers and sisters, and other people who live in your house?
2. Which sibling is most different from you? How?
3. Which sibling is most like you? How?
4. What kind of person is your father? Your stepfather?
5. What kind of person is your mother? Your stepmother?
6. Which of your siblings is most like your dad? How?
7. Which of your siblings is most like your mom? How?
8. Which of your parents are you most like? How?
9. What would you like to change about your family?

Ratings

10. List the highest and lowest (most or least) sibling for each attribute:
    - Intelligence
    - Hardest worker
    - Feelings easily hurt
    - Temper

- Best grades
- Follows rules
- Helps around the house
- Complains
- Considerate
- Selfish
- Tries to please

- Likes to get things
- Friends
- High standards
- Athletic
- Most spoiled
- Best looking
- Most punished

Functioning at Life Tasks

11. How do you get along with adults?
12. Who is your favorite adult to be with?
13. What do you like about him or her?
14. How do you get along with other children?
15. What would you change about your relationships with other kids?
16. Who is your best friend?
17. What is your best friend like? Describe him or her.
18. What do you like about your best friend?
19. How do things go for you at school?
20. What do you like best about school?
21. What do you like least about school?
22. What would you rather be doing?
23. What would you like to change about school?
24. What are your plans/hopes for the future?
25. What do you get into trouble for doing? At home? At school?
26. What happens when you get into trouble? At home? At school?

Techniques that Adlerian play therapists use to determine the goals of behavior are drawn from many sources, representing an eclectic approach to interventions.

The Adlerian play therapist uses metaphorical techniques to allow the child to communicate in a less stressful and anxiety-provoking manner about concerns in the child's life. Children use metaphors naturally for communication and for processing their concerns. A child's play can be viewed as a metaphor for the child's life or worldview (Kottman, 2003). Techniques the Adlerian play therapist uses to determine the goals of behavior and the style of life are drawn from many eclectic sources. The use of art (Kottman, 2001a); psychodrama (Carson-Sabellil, 1998; Guldner, 1991; Johnson & Ironsmith, 1994; Moreno, 1990a, 1990b, 1991); music (Carmichael, 2002, 2004); mutual storytelling (Gardner, 1970, 1971, 1972, 1974, 1975, 2003); and bibliotherapy (Hynes & Hynes-Berry, 1986; Shank, 1982) is incorporated into the play sessions to move the child toward the therapeutic goal.

SUMMARY

While Adlerian theory remains the most imitated and adapted of the psychotherapy theories, one major tenet remains unique to Adlerian and Individual psychology. The premise that good mental health depends on a sense of connectedness to others and the community remains fundamental to Adlerians. This sense of connectedness can be defined as "social interest" (Alfred Adler Institute, 2004).

Adler's individual psychology defines maladjustment as not having social interest. In other words, a person is considered to have problems when his or her behavior is harmful to self, to others, or to society as a whole. Adler stressed the importance of responsible behavior, which means an individual's behavior should add to the improvement of self and society. Maladjustment is also considered irresponsible behavior.

People are considered the sum and total of their choices. Although we cannot choose the circumstances of our existence, we can choose how we view the circumstances (e.g., a disability can be viewed as terrible tragedy or as an inconvenience that requires creativity). The pattern of the way a person views his or her life was described by Adler as the person's style of life. Although the style of life is established early on (0–6 years), Adlerian theory is optimistic, believing we can always change. Change is believed to take place when people change their early decisions and choose to behave in a responsible manner. Play therapy is one way the therapist uses the natural language of the child to develop this prosocial, goal-directed lifestyle espoused by Adlerian individual psychology.

CHAPTER 5

JUNGIAN ANALYTICAL PLAY THERAPY

The use of sand and miniatures in a tray allows the child to symbolically communicate difficulties and concerns to the play therapist.

In this chapter the essentials of Jungian analytical play therapy are presented. John Allan (1988, 1997; Allan & Bertoia, 1992) has described Jungian play therapy to its fullest extent. Jungian therapists such as Gisela de Domenico (1994) have expanded and further developed the concepts of Jungian therapy applied to play therapy. Jungian play therapy is not a particular set of techniques, but rather a way to conceptualize the nature of the psyche, the meaning of the play, and the goal of therapy in influencing the natural ability of the child to heal (de Domenico, 1994).

INTRODUCTION

Carl Gustav Jung was a Swiss psychiatrist and a contemporary of Freud and Adler. Freud viewed Jung as his heir apparent; however, the two men had fundamental disagreements over the nature of libido. To Jung, the central human drive is the individuation process, or the need to establish a unique personality and identity; Freud believed the central human drive is sexual, or toward pleasure (Allan, 1997). Ultimately, Jung's independent views led to an end to Freud's mentorship and friendship.

Because Jung never worked with children directly, most of Jungian play therapy is based on the analyst's reflections on the importance of play in his own childhood and later adult life. Jung's theoretical writings describe his personal play experiences and their resulting therapeutic value. Through spontaneous play, Jung found he could sustain, expand, and reform his inimitable individual cognitions, emotions, view, and nature. The time he spent in solitary play in private dialogue with his deeper self helped Jung calmly come to grips with the realities of his life. In the safe place of play, Jung strengthened his ego and prepared for his future as a writer, philosopher, and therapist (de Domenico, 1994).

Because of Jung's emphasis on curative play, paramount in work with children is the understanding that the psyche has a self-healing potential, that the archetypes assist in organizing the child's behavior, and that the creative processes of play, art, drama, and writing intervene and transform the child in the direction of healing. Although Jung never worked directly with children, he did analyze a child's series of dreams and concluded the child was reflecting the parent's unresolved struggles. Jung's work was primarily with adults; however, some of his concepts are incorporated into Jungian play therapy and bear exploration in relation to child therapy.

In Jungian theory, the *psyche* has three parts: ego, personal unconscious, and collective unconscious. The *ego* is the center of consciousness and includes awareness of reality, thoughts, feelings, fantasies, sensations, and emotions. The job of the ego is to mediate the demands of the personal and collective unconscious and the outer world of parents, teachers, peers, and culture. The *personal unconscious* is made up of the thoughts and feelings that are too painful to acknowledge or deal with. The personal unconscious also houses the undeveloped potential and new or different aspects of the child's personality. The *collective unconscious* contains the archetypes that are the "instincts coupled with images that direct and influence behavior and emotions" (Allan, 1997, p. 101).

The *archetypes* are methods of the psyche to perceive and respond. The central organizing principle is considered the archetype of the *self* (Allan & Bertoia, 1992). The archetypal world is expressed through fantasies and dreams. The symbols, rituals, and traditions around events like birth, marriage, motherhood, death, and separation are archetypes. The archetype of the self is the innate, unconscious psychological structures that direct psychological growth and development (Allan & Bertoia, 1992).

Throughout Jungian theory, we see the inner world of the psyche striving to reconcile experiences and meaning with external reality. Archetypes are illustrated by symbols, experiences, or images that hold shared meanings across cultures, such as birth, death, love, the divine child, the great mother, the trickster, God, and the devil. The archetypes may be positive or negative. Another way to view the archetype is to see it as the common understanding of symbols and experiences of all people. The most common sources for these archetypes are in the world's religions, myths, dreams, folklore, television programs, and advertising. The personal unconscious and the collective unconscious make up the archetype of the self.

In Jungian theory, the ego has the responsibility of mediating between the child's inner drives and the reality presented in the external world. In children's drawings, Allan and Bertoia (1992) say the ego is often depicted by land; the unconscious is symbolized by the sea or water.

Because the infant is very fragile, its ego is very easily threatened. The infant develops two types of ego defenses: biological and psychological. The biological ego defenses are associated with the perpetuation of the species and infant survival. These are present at birth or shortly thereafter. The psychological ego defenses include repression, projection, hallucinations, and the splitting of "good" and "bad." In either case, the purpose of the ego defenses is to allow the child to survive and adapt to the reality of his or her environment. The ego deintegrates under stress and reintegrates when the infant is calmed, fed, or receives pleasure. Allan and Bertoia (1992) explain that when the child is threatened and "deintegrates" too frequently, his or her defense mechanics become rigid and the child learns to avoid pain through escape behaviors.

Children seen in therapy seem to have two distinct patterns of defensive structures: rigid or nonexistent. In the rigid system the child seems very controlled, aloof, detached, or emotionally flat. The child appears quite passive but is given to outbursts of violence and temper. This child has a rigid and thick barrier between the ego (conscious) and the self (unconscious). On the contrary, when the child has a nonexistent defensive structure, he or she may appear to have low impulse control, be hyperactive, and/or be undersocialized. The defense structures between the ego and the self are so thin, the child cannot hold the impulses in check.

The healthy child has a wide range of emotional expression with an appropriate control and flexibility of impulses. The healthy child's emotional development stems from a good relationship and connection between the self and the ego. The ego needs to be nurtured in order to maintain its good health. The replenishment occurs through satisfying relationships, positive experiences, sleep, dreams, relaxation, and creative and artistic activities.

Psychopathology occurs when disturbances between the ego-self relationship cause innate striving toward individuation and socialization (de Domenico, 1994). These disturbances and resultant strivings are opportunities for growth. Because of the experiences and teachings of childhood, the child often loses his or her innate ability to experience, order, or transform these experiences symbolically. The child's self becomes untrustworthy. The child or adult may have lost the ability to play or to use and express emotions, cognitions, memories, sensations, and perceptions. Through the process of adjustment to family and societal demands, life becomes too painful or requires too much effort. The resultant behavior is acting out because the experience of the self or the external world cannot be utilized or trusted (de Domenico, 1994).

The healing process is initiated by opening the dialogue with the ego-self through the symbolic language of the self. This language of symbols is best explored through play, drawings, poetry, music, ritual, dreams, stories, and other creative forms of expression of the psyche. When the ego-self relationship is opened to this symbolic expression in a safe and supportive environment, the child regains this trust of the self and intuitively begins the healing process.

Allan (1997) declares that a central tenet in Jungian play therapy is the ego-self axis. The concept conveys the existence between the conscious (ego) and the unconscious mind (self). The healthy child's ego allows the child to express feelings and thoughts in appropriate ways while controlling inappropriate actions. The ability to express thoughts or feelings appropriately and to behave acceptably within the social cultural context is the goal of Jungian play therapy. Thus a healthy ego remains paramount to appropriate functioning and eventually to individualization and the fulfillment of the child's potential.

De Domenico (1994) explained that what sets Jungian play therapy apart from the other theories is not the set of play techniques used by the therapists, but rather "the way the therapist's understanding of the nature of the psyche, the meaning of the play, and the goal of the therapy influence the play therapy process" (p. 253).

TOY SELECTION

Jungians encourage the use of all types of symbolic expression. Art, play, sandtray, sculpting, drama, writing, and music are a few of the media employed in Jungian play therapy. The art materials are chosen on the basis of the sensual experience of the medium. The feel of the medium and how it appeals to the senses is most important to the Jungian therapist. The medium allows the child to access the self and to express symbolically the unconscious knowledge and healing ability of the psyche.

The traditional play therapy room used by Jungians (Allan & Levin, 1993) includes a dollhouse, doll family, art center with supplies, wet sand and dry sand in trays, collection of miniatures, water source, nursing bottle, telephones, puppets, small bed, construction toys, and areas designated for construction activities and for board games. According to Allan and Levin (1993), some play therapists use separate boxes to keep special or specific toys for clients. Allan and Levin do not provide guidance for what kind of toys might be in these special containers; however, the author has seen anatomically correct dolls, toys with special accommodations for children with disabilities, or uncompleted art projects kept in these boxes for the child client. One therapist allows children to keep one meaningful toy from the playroom or from home in the child's private box. Consistently, the therapists, who use the private storage boxes for the child clients, do so to extend the Jungian concept of the playroom as a "container" for the child's emotional experiences and a safe, protected place to express the self.

Allan and Levin's (1993) playroom was divided into two basic sections. One section provided a carpeted area with the emphasis on a soft and warm atmosphere with a dollhouse, stuffed animals, baby bottles, and a small bed. The other section of the playroom was set up with a vinyl tile floor with an atmosphere of hardness and coolness with sand play, water play, kitchen center, construction activities, and other centers for messy activities. The playroom setup subtly helped the child separate the ambivalent feelings and experience each separately, so the child's ego was not overwhelmed by chaos.

De Domenico (1994) includes use of costume play, drawing, sand play, and puppets and other toys that can offer the child interpretation of archetypes like the Shadow, Animus, Anima, Gods, Goddesses, Demons, and Helper. Other aspects of these archetypes or subpersonalities, such as the Demander, the Lady, the Critic, the Hero, the Protector, the Controller, and the Vulnerable Child, are provided in the assortment of media for the child's imaginative play. Other play materials for storytelling and story writing are included in the playroom array. Recorded music and simple musical instruments for dance, mime, rhythm, and song are available for the child. Art materials include paints, pastels, crayons, pencils, enamel, modeling clay, and different papers. Some therapists may include scissors, glue, or tape. Other toys that de Domenico (1994) includes are balls, puppets, dolls, stuffed animals, vehicles, blocks, guns, sand trays, miniatures, and other toys the child may enjoy. De Domenico (1994) suggests that ritual or exploratory play be addressed with earth (sand or mud), water, fire (e.g., candles, matches), and air (e.g., balloons, fans).

Jungian play therapy has been practiced in a variety of settings. Like other types of play therapy, Jungian play therapy is not limited to exclusive use of a formal playroom. The setting for the so-called playroom may be places like hospitals, schools, clinics, and office buildings, but additional places include the child's home, parks, playgrounds, and beaches (de Domenico, 1994). Jungian play therapy requires a child and an environment where the child can be assured of a private and emotionally secure environment.

Children often take on the role of various archetypes. Archetypes assist the child in organizing his or her behaviors, thoughts, and feelings.

Role of the Therapist

The Jungian play therapist purports that the individual psyche is able to heal itself when provided with a free and protected environment and while in a "transference relationship to a supportive therapist" (de Domenico, 1994, p. 253). This safe and protected place is what Jung called *temenos* (Allan & Bertoia, 1992). According to Allan (1988), the first priority after temenos is for the therapist to establish a therapeutic alliance and rapport in order for the healing potential embedded in the child's psyche to be activated. This healing potential is part of what Jung (Storr, 1983) termed the "archetype of the self," which leads the child to individuation or fulfillment of the child's potential.

According to Allan (1988), children frequently use spontaneous play with fantasy themes that have direct relevance to their psychological struggles, which indicates to the therapist what work the child wishes to do and needs to do during the course of therapy. Allan claims this is also true of the child's spontaneous drawings. Therefore, it becomes incumbent on the therapist to provide toys and art media for the child to use in a safe and protected environment to allow the archetype of self to lead the child toward growth and healing.

How therapists go about establishing temenos, according to de Domenico (1994), varies greatly from therapist to therapist. Often the therapist determines therapeutic behavior based on intuition and subjective experiences with the client. The behaviors of therapists may differ greatly in accordance with the developmental needs of the psyche and age demands of the child.

In addition to temenos, Allan (1988) maintains that the amount of emotional and symbolic material a child shares depends on how sensitive and skilled the therapist is in communication skills. Therefore, one of the roles of the therapist is to develop skills of communication. Allan (1988) has determined that the following skills in communication are useful:

1. The therapist believes talking with children about their concerns helps the child.
2. The therapist actively observes, listens, and perceives what the child is saying or doing.
3. The therapist restates or mirrors back the content of what the child has said to allow the child to know he or she has been heard.
4. The therapist uses questions selectively, preferring restatements or asking for descriptions of the child's experiences.
5. The therapist uses reflection of feeling that captures the underlying feelings, making the unconscious conscious and communicating understanding.
6. The therapist uses his or her own feelings, intuitions, and perceptions and verbalizes these to the child.
7. The therapist sets limits that are clearly defined with consequences that are immediate, of short duration, and designed not to reinforce the child's negative behavior.

Another important role of the therapist is to work within the frame of the child's symbolic meanings produced in the play session. When the therapist is working with images and symbols in play, expressive arts, or fantasy, the therapist addresses the symbol as if it were alive or real. Thus the therapist uses the symbol to focus the child's psyche or to provide a conduit for further growth. Sometimes the child may present many symbols at one time in the therapeutic interactions. The therapist then chooses one that seems to be most prominently used. When the therapist accurately focuses on a key symbolic area, the therapist is rewarded with the child continuing to explore the area. The role of the therapist is to help the child focus on key symbols and to advance toward growth using the experience of the symbol.

An additional role of the therapist may be to help the child develop a flexible persona. In Jungian theory, the psyche is made up of the child's ego, which stores his or her external and internal conscious knowledge or awareness, and the personal and collective unconscious, which represents knowledge from the child's experiences and culture. The *persona* is the facade or attitude the child uses in the external world. The persona is the social mask, with both negative and positive elements. The child with a flexible persona interacts effectively with others and still is able to maintain his or her identity and emotional spontaneity. Some children may develop an overly rigid persona, resulting in lack of identity and hiding behind a socially acceptable role or mask. Stereotypical behavior may be observed by the therapist. Other children may not develop a persona, resulting in undersocialized and impulsive behaviors. The role of the therapist is to help the child develop a flexible persona or social mask, resulting in individuation and healthy emotional expression.

The *anima,* those characteristics most stereotypically identified as feminine, and the *animus,* those characteristics most stereotypically identified as masculine, are two aspects of the *syzergy,* or contrasexual aspects of the individual. The therapist's role is to help the child find a psychological balance between the opposite side and the genetic structure. Allan (Allan & Bertoia, 1992) says the results would be "a person's ability to be both assertive and receptive, firm and caring at the same time" (p. 103). In other words, the child is helped to balance those roles and characteristics that were stereotypical and historically associated with males and females. The current politically correct term for masculinity is *agency* and for femininity, *communion.* Agency includes independence, self-confidence, and decisiveness; communion includes warmth, concern for others, and understanding (Fujita, Diener, & Sanvik, 1991). The healthy child shows a balance between agency and communion.

The therapist shows the same respect for the child's dreams and play work, observing without interference, judgment, giving directions, interpretations, or making interactional demands. The play therapist may help the child design rituals or ceremonies to mark the passing of one phase of therapy to another. Small gifts like a stone are sometimes given to mark these therapeutic events.

The role of the therapist is to ensure the child is not overwhelmed by the fantasies or physical harm. "The therapist's ego watches that the client's surrendering to unconscious impulses, archetypal images, and the accompanying emotions, creative plays, memories, and insights can occur in a constructive rather than hurtful way" (de Domenico, 1994, p. 269). What is meant by constructive is the eventual integration of these experiences into the self. When the child is integrated, the child understands the positive and negative parts of the child's personality are present and accepts that he or she is not all good or all evil. The child understands that what others may consider negative can serve as motivation toward positive or appropriate responsible behaviors. For example, a child may become very angry and can express that anger through creative endeavors, like an abstract drawing. The energy produced by the child's anger might also be redirected to cleaning his or her room, acquiring sports skills, or other positive outcomes.

The play therapist may join in the play activities with the child when it is deemed to be beneficial therapeutically or when the child has invited the therapist to do so. Jungians view this participation as a way to validate the child's experience and as a venue for cooperative sharing or play. During this play, the therapist encourages a transference relationship, which allows the therapist to be attuned to the personal symbolic, archetypal meaning of the child's play. From this shared play experience, the therapist interprets the meaning of the play in the context of the archetypal symbolism.

The therapist may contemplate "If this child were a character in a book, the child's character role would be described as . . . ?" The answer to this question—hero, victim, witch, scapegoat, or other character—may help identify the archetypal symbolism. These silent and personal interpretations of the shared experience help the therapist make the soft hypotheses or tentative guesses about the meanings of the symbolism, which are not shared with the child or others. The therapist participates in what de Domenico (1994) has termed the "silent knowing." Although the therapist may not interpret the play to the child, he or she may create a verbal link between the child's fantasy and the child's daily life. An example might be a child who is having problems adjusting to a new sibling and continues to attend to every need of the baby doll. The therapist might respond, "It would be nice to be taken care of like a baby again." If the baby doll fantasy appears to be a very demanding baby, the therapist might say something to this effect: "Babies need so much more attention than older boys or girls."

Another way the therapist may intervene is to tell the child a story or relate a custom that may have similar content to the theme the child is playing out. The idea behind this intervention is to provide cultural validation that will allow the child to understand what is natural and what is not natural in everyday life (de Domenico, 1994).

Amplification techniques are used by Jungian therapists. This technique is a post-play reflective sharing in which the child verbalizes or acts out what certain parts of the play were like for the child so the therapist can share the experience. For example; Jimmy's play was very chaotic and seemed to lack any kind of theme or organization.

The therapist said, "Jimmy, today seemed different. I wonder what that was like for you today. Is there something we can do that will help me feel like you did today?"

Jimmy went to the scarves in the corner and got as many as he could. Then he began to pile them on top of the therapist. "I am feeling like everything is on top of me. I cannot see a way out." Jimmy giggled and began taking the scarves off.

The therapist commented, "So today seemed like everything was just holding you down."

Jimmy sat cross-legged on the floor in front of the therapist. "Sometimes I'm the only one who gets into trouble. Today was bad."

"So sometimes it seems like you are the one who gets blamed for everything and it is too much to take."

"Yeah."

The therapist may photograph or draw a diagram of temporary works of expression, like a picture on a dry-erase board, a sand tray world, a toy configuration, or a construction the child has made. Some therapists photocopy artwork on the copy machine for the file. Still others have rules that no art project may leave the playroom. Whatever rule or method used, the therapist keeps a record of the child's created nonverbal expressions. These artifacts of the therapy sessions are used to review the play processes with the child. The review may take place at anytime, although some therapists only do so at termination (de Domenico, 1994).

To truly be a Jungian therapist, you must study at a Jungian training institute and undergo personal therapy exploring play and dream analysis. De Domenico (1994) lists other types of studies common to Jungian therapists: comparative religion, mysticism, esoteric teachings, mythology, folklore, rites, rituals, beliefs, art, literature, cultures, and symbolism. Beyond clinical practice, most therapists are well grounded in art, dance, and movement. However, you can use Jungian methods or espouse the theory without the training but may not legitimately be called a Jungian therapist without the requisite training and experiences.

Jungian therapists examine the symbolic representations in childrens' artwork. Jungians believe that the symbols reproduced in art have meaning that can be recognized by all people independent of their cultural differences.

STRUCTURING THE SESSION

Similar to other therapists, Jungians take a history of the child from a responsible adult. Jungians differ from other theorists in the exploration of more detail in religious beliefs, ethnic origin, cultural identity, cultural practices, and archetypes that the child seeks as ideals. The archetypes children identify as part of their psyche can be assessed by asking them and the parents about favorite stories, movies, fantasy figures, television programs, and similar sources of archetypical images. According to Allan (1997), the Jungian play therapist makes "soft hypotheses" or clinical guesses based on the information the therapist has gathered from the significant adults in the child's life. These soft hypotheses are either confirmed or discarded as the child moves through the stages of play therapy. The therapist learns to live and work with the uncertainty and the sense that nothing is absolute in the process of therapy.

The therapist provides an atmosphere in which the child can experience what Peery (2003) terms safety, welcome, and trust. Typically, the child is seen once per week but may be seen as frequently as five times per week. Other common schedules are also considered according to the needs of the child and the psyche (de Domenico, 1994). The counselor maintains flexibility in interactions with the child, respecting the child's uniqueness.

During the initial phases of therapy, the therapist follows the child's direction. If the child chooses to talk, the therapist responds, reflecting feelings when possible and sometimes answering questions posed by the child. When the child is very quiet and involved in activity, the counselor remains quiet, attends to the child's demeanor and the images created by the child, and monitors the therapist's own feelings or reactions to the child's symbolic communication (Allan, 1988). Quiet play often creates in the child a focus of attention similar to meditation, which manifests the images of the child's unconscious mind (de Domenico, 1994).

The sessions are predominantly nondirective with the therapist providing the materials (toys, music, art supplies), permissiveness, safety, and nonjudgmental environment, creating the safe vessel for the unconscious or temenos, wherein the child can explore the depths of the self. The therapist allows the child to move in the safety of the playroom toward healing, trusting the child's psyche knows what the child needs without pressure or confrontation from the therapist. Structure is provided by asking questions and providing an open-ended format (Allan & Bertoia, 1992).

However, Allan (1988) provides nondirective therapy, directive therapy, and partially directive therapy. The degree of direction the therapist uses in working with the child depends on the way the child enters therapy. If the child comes to the session and begins his or her psychological work readily, Allan (1988) provides a nondirective intervention. The therapist may serve as a witness to the child's exploration and natural healing process. These children appear to already be connected to the curative process and intuitively know what work needs to be done. The therapist does not need to provide any structure other than attentiveness and acceptance of the child.

Some children may approach the session withdrawn, stuck, confused, or uncertain of themselves. The therapist may provide a suggestion of what to do to help the child move toward initiating the child's own curative process. The therapist typically may ask the child to do one of many structured drawing activities or other directed play activity until the child may act independently, reject the therapist's suggestions, or substitute the child's own activities. The therapist's directives are not made randomly but are based on what is known about the child and the child's current struggles or based on the image or symbol that seems to have special meaning to the child at this point. The therapist may also change to a nondirective or partial directive approach when the directive approach does not seem appropriate.

In the partial directive approach, the therapist may ask the child to draw or participate in an activity meant to explore a particular scenario or image that the child gives special significance. Allan (1988) states that four to six weeks needs to transpire before change may be observed in the child's play. This change in the child's psyche can be witnessed through the emergence of a new attitude or relationship in the symbolism the child uses. By looking at changes in this image or scenario, the therapist may indicate change in the progress of the child toward wholeness and healing.

Jungian play therapists see play therapy as evolving in a series of stages. Although theorists agree that stages are present in the therapeutic process, they may label them slightly differently. Allan (1997) describes a rhythm or series of stages of play therapy. In the entrance stage, Allan reports that the child enters the play therapy session like one enters a ritual space, where the child's time within the playroom moves from the ego (reality) to the dominance of self (emotional and symbolic play themes). De Domenico (1994) describes the initial stage of therapy as the time for the therapeutic alliance, the creation of the protected space, learning to trust, and learning the limits of freedom. According to Allan (1997), the child is best described as engaging in avoidance in the entrance phase of the therapy session.

De Domenico (1994) terms the phase following the initial and orientation phase as the struggling phase and separates it from the working through phase. This phase is marked by the child's efforts to test the limits of the playroom and the acceptance of the therapist. The child is testing to see if the "bad self," or Shadow of the child's personality, is acceptable. The child who ascribes negative behaviors and projections onto the therapist is manifesting fragmentation, wounding, negative internalized past experiences, and unformulated and unusable empowerments of the true personality. Allan (1997) terms this stage the chaos phase and considers it part of the working phase. In the chaos stage of play therapy, the child may be overwhelmed with the flooding effect of many aspects of the self.

Allan (1997) indicates that as the child transitions to the working phase, he or she goes through the stages of chaos, struggle, reparation, and resolution, followed by the exit phase. De Domenico (1994) terms the working through phase as a period of integration, disintegration, and transformation followed by the termination phase. The working phase is characterized by the child experiencing cycles of disintegration, chaos, emergence, and then ultimately integration. Although the two theorists differ in terminology, they appear to agree on the child's experiences during the working phase. De Domenico (1994) provides some guidelines to the play themes characteristic of this phase: violence, disaster, destruction, isolation, and war followed by peace, reconstruction, rectification, and joining. Allan (1997) compares the working phase to the rebuilding or remodeling of a home. The child must tear down emotional and cognitive walls, experience frustration, and expend a great deal of energy to sort through the resultant chaos. The outcome of this phase is that the child will have an integrated self. The therapist may attempt with limited success to assist the child in the integration process of the inner and outer experiences, achieving balance between the ego and the self. De Domenico (1994) wrote that this is often the most difficult time for the therapist to do integrative work with the child; however, the outcome of this period of confusion and chaos is the experience of wholeness and balance.

The struggle between the desire to grow and the desire to regress is central to Jung's ideas about growth and development. For transformation and development to occur, children must struggle with these utterly different impulses inside themselves. That means the child must examine the opposite and often painful experiences and emotions. The child must contain these various impulses and not act them out in a destructive way to self or others. Through the containment of these impulses, an integration and transformation can occur, resulting in inner and outer development. The therapist allows the conflicting thoughts, feelings, and actions to be expressed safely with toys, paint, journaling, or a special notebook (Allan & Bertoia, 1992).

Change in Jungian play therapy is indicated when the key symbols the child introduces are no longer those of hurt, pain, or damage. They are replaced with the symbols of growth, new life, or renewal. De Domenico (1994) believes that play therapy reaches its pinnacle when the therapist provides support and enhancement to the child in such a way that the child may learn to trust personal resources and to maximize his or her growth throughout the lifespan. The therapist should not focus the sessions on just the play interpretation and direction.

In the termination phase of the session, the therapist may ask about anything observed as unusual. The therapist may ask probing open-ended questions to ascertain understanding for the therapist and for the self. Termination is a time of review and reflection. Therapist and child may reexamine the child's collection of creative works to clarify to the self what has transpired and what, if any, work is still needed.

LIMITS

Allan and Levin (1993) believe limitations on the child's behavior are not set until it becomes necessary to protect the child from physical injury. The therapist uses limits placed on the child's behavior according to what is deemed therapeutic. Allan and Levin (1993) used two guidelines in determining what limits are appropriate therapeutically: (1) the age and development of the child, and (2) the strength of the child's inner ability to find his or her way through and out of emotional turmoil.

PARENT INVOLVEMENT

According to Allan (1994), a child's concerns or problems are a result of acting out the parent's unfinished or undeveloped aspects. Because this view is somewhat commonplace among Jungian therapists, the parents are encouraged to enter into therapy themselves. The parents' work on their own issues allows the child to be free of parental projections, which permits the child to develop and live out his or her own individualization (Allan, 1994).

Even if the parents are divorced, it is important that both parents see the need for therapy. The parents are encouraged to talk to the therapist about their own issues, struggles, and difficulties with the child. Divorced parents may want to meet separately with the therapist, but they are encouraged to have a few joint sessions focused on what the parents can do to help the child (Allan, 1997).

Peery (2003) provides a little different slant on the involvement of parents. In the initial contact with the parents, he explains how important their input will be to the therapeutic process. He sets up a "parent consult" after every third or fourth session to compare the observations from the home to the observations of the playroom, to communicate the child's progress, and to coordinate the efforts of the parents and therapist in the treatment of the child. During this time the changes in the child's behavior and its effect on the parents becomes appropriate for sharing with the therapist. Because of these changes, the therapist may act as a resource for the parents in the changing dynamics of their parent-child relationship. The parents participate in deciding when termination is appropriate based on their observations outside of the playroom (Peery, 2003).

TERMINATION

Allan (1997) insists that the therapist prepare the child for the ending of individual therapy. The preparation time for the end of therapy should be proportional to the length of time the child has been in therapy. For children who have been in therapy a year or more, the preparation time may take 6 weeks or longer. For children in therapy for a shorter time, Allan indicates that a month may be sufficient time for preparation. He describes a "weaning away" of the child from therapy by reducing the child from weekly sessions to biweekly and ultimately to monthly sessions. Another approach is to move the child from individual therapy to filial therapy, in which the parents serve as play therapists to their own children. The Jungian therapist may continue to see the child in family therapy for a few sessions. Ideally, the Jungian sees the child for 6 months to a year. Allan (1997) says the time is essential to facilitate separation and activation of the individuation process.

ASSESSMENT AND TECHNIQUES

Jungian therapists tend to do their assessment of the child in the context of therapy. Certainly they collect the information available that helps describe the reason for the referral and gather necessary disclosures and permission forms. Treatment plans and goal setting is demanded by most agencies, which Jungians describe in the broadest acceptable terms. The primary goal is always to alleviate the child's suffering and free the child for normal emotional growth. However, formal assessment and interviews are not a matter of course in Jungian therapy or required as a precursor to therapy. During the therapeutic process, the Jungian therapist uses the growing knowledge of the child's symbolic world and reports from significant adults to determine the direction of therapy. The therapist, child, and significant adults are all continually assessing the therapy process and its effect on the primary goal of therapy.

One of the techniques Allan (1988) uses is the serial drawing. The therapist has the child draw every week in the presence of the therapist. The therapist tells the child to draw whatever the child wishes. Here is a paraphrase of the verbal instructions provided by Allan (1988):

> "You may talk, do, or draw many things you would like during our time together. What you say in here is private, which means that only you and I will know what you say in here. I will not tell anyone unless something is against the law or I am told by the judge that I must tell. I will keep all of your pictures in this private file that stays in my office where only you and I can see it. I will write your name, date, and a name for your picture and keep it safely in this file. After we have seen each other for a while, and things get better in your life, then I will see that you get the pictures back."

Allan (1988) then gives the child a sheet of white paper and a pencil. Crayons are reported to distract from the process. Rulers, erasers, and crayons are kept from view but can be provided to the child, if the child requests them. A new piece of paper is used each time the child draws. The child is not allowed to take the drawing away from the session.

The therapist's role is to sit quietly, not to initiate conversation or discussion with the child. Notes are not taken in the therapy room. If the child talks during the session, the counselor attempts to follow the child's direction. At the end of the session the counselor prompts the child to (Allan, 1988):

1. Tell me a story about your picture.
2. Tell me what has happened before this picture. What happens next?
3. Give the picture a title.
4. Tell me the moral or lesson that this picture can teach.

Serial drawings are one of many interventions that Jungian play therapists use to better understand the child's symbolism and inter-world.

Allan (1988) does advocate that the counselor may become more directive as the sessions progress: "The amount of directiveness and intervention depends on the needs of the child, not on the needs of the counselor." Allan may direct the child's drawings by telling the child to draw specific things. He may ask the child to draw his or her family doing something, to draw a house, to draw a tree, to draw a person, or even to draw a rose bush. Traditionally, these drawings can be interpreted to learn more about the child. These drawings are discussed elsewhere in the chapter and text.

Another Jungian technique to use with a group of acting-out children is creative drama. The therapist takes the role of facilitator and helps the children to

1. talk out the dramatic plays or scenes they wanted to do,
2. select one,
3. share the roles,
4. carry out a short rehearsal,
5. perform the dramatic play for videotaping and
6. then discuss what they saw. (Allan, 1988, p. 180)

Allan (1988) then played back the videotape of the drama. In the discussion that followed, three questions became the focus of the discussion:

1. What did you like about today's drama?
2. What did you not like? and
3. What would make it better next time? (p. 180)

A third technique often used by the Jungian therapist is serial story writing. The child is allowed to write whatever he or she wishes. Through the caring relationship established with the therapist, psychological growth occurs.

Parallel to this concept is that of the mutual storytelling technique of Robert Gardner (Gardner, 1968, 1970, 1971, 1972a, 1972b, 1972c, 1974, 1975). The therapist asks the child to pretend to be a guest on a television show where stories are told. The tape recorder is turned on if the child seems interested in the task. The therapist takes the role of the commentator and announces the show into the tape recorder.

The therapist listens to the child's story. Then the therapist retells a similar story, but the negative attributes of the child's story are changed into positive solutions, behaviors, or actions. If the child has difficulty beginning the interview, the therapist may start a generic story line to help the child get started. The story line may be something like this: "Long ago and far, far away in a place not unlike this place . . . "

Summary

Jungian play therapy works more within metaphor and symbolic areas than any other theory. The interventions are mostly those found in the creative arts that lend themselves to the expression of this inner symbolic world. By understanding the symbols, the therapist comes to understand the child and how to help the child.

Jungian therapy is based on the premise that all people share a common heritage and the internal human experience remains the same despite culture or environment. This commonality of human experience allows the child and the therapist to reach out to one another and draw understanding in shared symbols and metaphors expressed in play scenarios, artworks, drama, music, movement, and storytelling.

CHAPTER 6

CHILD-CENTERED PLAY THERAPY

Garry Landreth in the playroom engaged in child-centered play therapy. Child-centered play therapy was first called nondirective play therapy by its originator, Virginia Axline.

In this chapter, we look at child-centered play therapy, which grew out of the work of Carl Rogers (1942, 1951). Virginia Mae Axline (Axline & Carmichael, 1947) was the leading proponent of this type of play therapy with her classic book about play therapy and a popular book, Dibs: In Search of Self *(Axline, 1964). Although many play therapists espouse the child-centered approach, the most published single person to define the theory is Garry Landreth (1982, 2002), the founder of The Center for Play Therapy, which has promoted the development and training of play therapists nationally and internationally.*

INTRODUCTION

Child-centered play therapy (CCPT) was first called nondirective play therapy by its originator, Virginia Axline. Axline (Axline & Carmichael, 1947) first described the process and procedures for play therapy in her text *Play Therapy* in 1947, followed by a revision in 1969. Carl Rogers in the introduction wrote, "this book is more than this [practical book], much more than a cold analysis of a therapeutic process, much more than a body of practical suggestions . . . the doorway to the inner world of childhood about which so much has been written, but which is so rarely discovered." Between her original text and the revision, Axline gained national attention in her published case study of a little boy in *Dibs: In Search of Self* (1964). Dorfman (1951) included a section on play therapy in what is now Carl Rogers's classic text *Client-Centered Therapy* (1951). Axline dominated the play therapy field throughout the early 1950s and into the 1960s, as did Rogers's theory. Today Landreth (2002) and Guerney (2001) have assumed the leadership in this theoretical orientation to play therapy.

The early work of Carl Rogers (1942, 1951) was in the area of nondirective therapy, which later became known as client-centered therapy. In the 1980s the name was changed once again to *person-centered* to reflect the more humanistic aspect of the theory. Person-centered therapy forms the basis for child-centered play therapy. Person-centered therapy requires a therapeutic environment that provides the client with empathy, unconditional positive regard, and genuine concern and feedback. The feedback is provided to the client by reflecting or mirroring what the client is saying back to the client, conveying the therapist has understood the client. Reflective listening is more than a simple parroting of the client's words. It requires the therapist to give voice to the underlying feelings experienced by the client. These tenets of client-centered therapy were incorporated by Axline (Axline & Carmichael, 1947) into child therapy through play therapy.

Axline (1989; Axline & Carmichael, 1947) defined play therapy as "based upon the fact that play is the child's natural medium of self-expression" (Axline, 1947, p. 9). Play therapy to Axline (1949) is the opportunity provided to children to play out feelings and concerns, similar to the talk therapies provided to adult clients where the client talks out his or her difficulties.

Axline (Axline & Carmichael, 1947) indicated that the structure of personality is still very wide open, and attempts to test, predict, or analyze have not been adequate to explain satisfactorily what has been observed in regard to individual inner dynamics. She posed a tentative theory, "open to criticism and evaluation, but based upon observation and study of both children and adults during and after a nondirective therapeutic experience" (p. 10). She believed that within each person is a powerful force that continually strives for complete self-realization. The observable component of this striving is seen as forced movement to gain maturity, independence, and self-direction. The force driving the person forward is relentless, but there needs to be a fertile environment for a well-balanced personality to develop. She defined this fertile environment as one of permissiveness to be oneself, acceptance of oneself by the individual and others, and "the right to be an individual entitled to the dignity that is the birthright of every human being in order to achieve a direct satisfaction of this growth principle" (p. 10).

She saw growth as a spiraling process in which the child's experiences change the child's focus and perspective. She described life as a kaleidoscope of constant changing relationships in which the patterns fall apart and then rearrange themselves into something quite different but always maintain balance. "So it seems, is personality. The living organism has within it the bits of colored glass and the personality is structured by the organization of these bits" (Axline, 1969, p. 11). Hers was a dynamic theory, in which even habits give way when the individual no longer feels a need for them. Within the individual lies the ability to change for the better. She believed the child is motivated toward a positive solution of problems. This observable flexibility of personality and behavior of a child places the therapist at the open door to welcome hope and optimism for the child laden with difficulties. When the child is able to distinguish the power of self-direction and accept the responsibility of authority over self, the child gains the ability to determine the course of action needed more accurately. Given a permissive environment, the child seeks positive solutions to his or her problems. Play therapy is the invitation to growth in the most favorable environment.

Axline believed children are forgiving and do not hold grudges toward negative experiences. She believed it takes an extraordinary negative experience to interfere with the child's accepting of life and the people in his or her life. Axline saw children as enjoying growing up and wanting to seek new challenges with eagerness. She described the normal child as "both humble and proud, courageous and afraid, dominant and submissive, curious and satisfied, eager and indifferent" (Axline & Carmichael, 1947, p. 12). She said these dichotomies are more than reaction to the stimuli; they are reactions to growing up. The child integrates and assimilates all of these expressions into his or her unique configuration that becomes the child's personality.

Each child is considered to have basic needs, which the child strives to have met. When these needs are met straightforwardly, the child is considered well adjusted. When the child's efforts to meet required needs are blocked, the child often resorts to devious paths to have these needs met, resulting in maladjustment. Axline (Axline & Carmichael, 1947) states, "In fact, one is inclined to admire the 'maladjusted type of behavior' because it seems more complex, more ingenious, and more selective than that which is based on direct satisfaction of needs" (p. 13). How the maladjusted child behaves depends on past and present experiences, conditions and relationships that thwart or propel the child toward self-realization. The development of self-confidence helps bring the child's self-concept out of what Axline (Axline & Carmichael, 1947) termed the "shadow land" and into an existence directed by problem solving and self-realization. Ultimately, the well-adjusted child is the self-realized child. Child-centered therapy assumes that each child has within the ability to solve problems satisfactorily, and the need for growth makes the child more satisfied with mature behavior over immature behavior.

By playing out feelings, the child externalizes them in a form in which the child can deal with them, control them, or abandon them. Through emotional relaxation, the child recognizes personal power to make decisions, to have personal thoughts, to become mature, and to move toward selfhood. The child is free of the usual adult "suggestions, mandates, rebukes, restraints, criticisms, disapprovals, support, intrusions" (Axline & Carmichael, 1947, p. 16); rather the child encounters an adult who provides complete acceptance and permissiveness. Through the sensitivity of the therapist, the child learns to trust and develops a sense of security. The therapist expresses sensitivity to the child through the reflection of the child's emotions. The therapist conveys to the child the belief that the child is competent and has the ability to handle life's challenges.

In addition to helping the child gain a better understanding of the self through the reflection of emotional attitudes, the therapist also conveys to the child the feeling that the therapist has understood and accepted the child, regardless of what the child says or does. Thus the therapist gives the child the courage to go deeper and deeper into the innermost world and bring out into the open the real self (Axline & Carmichael, 1947, p. 17). Play is used to connect the child's concrete and abstract thoughts. Children are still in the concrete stage of reasoning until about 11; therefore, a child has to have concrete ways to express the internal world. Through play the child moves toward the child-centered goal of self-actualization or self-realization.

The child does not need to have a clearly defined problem to benefit from play therapy. The theory expounds the virtue that the child knows what business the child must be about and that given a warm, empathic, and positive feeling from the therapist, the child will heal. In fact, the intervention or direction of the therapist is considered detrimental to the child's growth in therapy. The focus of the therapy is on the child, not on the identified or reported problem. According to Guerney (2001), CCPT is based on the assumption that play therapy is most effective when the therapist does not direct the child and allows the child to take responsibility for the direction of the session. Toys help the play therapy process. Using toys allows the child to order his world and to use the toys as he *sees* fit (Axline, 1969). Through play, the child experiences independent thought and action; the child chooses which toys to accomplish which tasks.

Axline (1969) defined maladjustment of the child as a child who lacks the opportunity to be free and independent without a personal struggle. Adjusted children, according to Axline (1969), are those who have not encountered too many obstacles in the path toward this free and independent development of self. The adjusted child develops the capacity or self-confidence to direct his or her behavior toward self-realization. The maladjusted child lacks self-confidence and the ability to direct himself or herself directly toward this goal of self-realization. Instead, the child is incongruent between the picture of self and the experience as perceived by the child. The further apart these two perceptions are, the more maladapted the child.

Axline (1969) presented a summary of child-centered play therapy with her eight principles of nondirective play therapy. Those eight principles can be summarized as recommending that the play therapist provide the following conditions in the therapeutic session:

1. Establish a warm, friendly relationship with good rapport.
2. Establish acceptance as the child is.
3. Allow freedom to express feelings completely without fear reprisal.
4. Reflect the feelings the child expresses in a manner allowing the child to gain insight.

5. Respect the child's right and ability to solve his or her difficulties, leaving the responsibility for change to the child.
6. Allow the child to lead the way through therapy without directing the child's actions or verbal expressions.
7. Allow the child to progress through the therapeutic process at the child's own pace.
8. Set those limitations on the child that will provide an anchor to reality.

CCPT has been applied to multitudes of childhood problems and behaviors. Although other theories may advocate a more prescriptive approach to specific problems, CCPT remains focused on providing the core conditions of empathy, warmth, and genuineness with the assurance the child's natural tendency will move the child toward self-healing or self-realization. Over the last 50 years, research has supported the efficacy of the CCPT approach in working with a broad spectrum of childhood problems. Only severe autism or active schizophrenia appears to be contraindicated for CCPT (Guerney, 2001).

Landreth (2002) points out that CCPT is a philosophical stance that encompasses an orientation to life beyond the playroom. The therapist believes children have an innate capacity for growth and resiliency, which enables them to be capable of directing their own growth experiences. Landreth (2002) agrees with Guerney (2001) that the purpose of the playroom is to create an environment for the child to play out feelings and experiences. Given the permissive environment, the child will seek emotional growth and belief in self. As Landreth (1991) states, "Child-centered play therapy is an attitude, a philosophy, and a way of being" (p. 55). Landreth and Guerney are not alone in their beliefs about the power of CCPT.

West (1992), a British child-centered play therapy theorist, states that play therapy is based on proven theory and practice. She believes several major assumptions are requisite to the practice of CCPT:

1. Children in the majority of the white Western world use play like adults use language.
2. Children express themselves more freely in play than in formal conversation.
3. Children reveal their concerns, problems, and fears in their play.
4. Children can use fantasy play to express conflict-laden content and repressed primitive wishes that cannot be expressed through language.

CCPT differs from other forms of play in that it requires attending, caring, healing, serving, and being patient with the child's development in the process. Play therapy in the CCPT theory is a holistic methodology that provides the child with an intervention that is not invasive and does not avoid looking at the whole child. The physical, spiritual, emotional, unconscious and conscious characteristics of the child are considered in respect to the child's past, present, and future (West, 1992). Play therapy differs from other play interventions in that it is concerned with the child's feelings and not just behavior. The child in CCPT is a co-therapist to the adult therapist and the process in the playroom. The adult therapist provides the safe environment and boundaries; the child, the agenda.

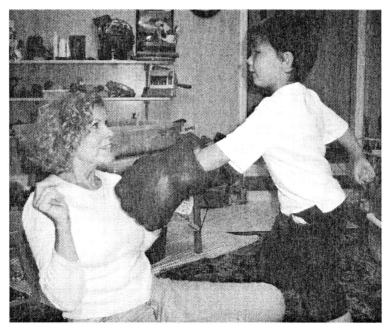

Children can use fantasy play to express conflict-laden content and repressed primitive wishes that cannot be expressed through language alone.

TOY SELECTION

Toys become facilitative materials that help a child fully communicate his or her inner and outer world with a caring, listening adult (Landreth, 1991). Therefore, toys need to be provided that allow the child to play out the child's real life. The child experiences all feelings—love, anger, sadness, fear, joy—and during the play with toys, the child utilizes independent thought and action to release feelings and attitudes (Axline, 1969). So that a child may experience personal power, the therapist carefully selects toys the child can use in a multitude of ways to enhance his or her own growth (Landreth, 2002; McCalla, 1994).

Landreth (2002) emphasizes that toys should be selected and not simply collected on a casual basis. According to Landreth (2002), the therapist should consider whether the toy has a wide range of creative and emotional expression. Does the toy engage the child's interest and facilitate expressive and exploratory play? Can the toy be used symbolically and not demand verbalizations from the child? Can the toy be used in a number of ways that are not committed to a prescribed structure or meaning? Finally, is this toy sturdy and will it withstand the active use in the playroom? The selected toys need to provide ways to explore real life, testing of limits, development of self-understanding, development of positive self-image, and provide an opportunity to gain self-control. The selected toys contribute to the positive relationship between the therapist and child and expression of both negative and positive emotions.

Landreth (2002) divides the playroom toys into three basic categories: real-life toys, acting out–aggressive toys, and creative expression–emotional release toys. The real-life toys are dolls, puppets, transportation toys, dollhouse, kitchen center items, toy store items, and dressup items. Acting out–aggressive toys are bop bag, toy soldiers, aggressive animal puppets, guns, knives, swords, pounding toys, and a log with nails and a hammer. Toys for creative expression–emotional release are water, sand, blocks, and art supplies. Items like a dry-erase board and other art supplies may fit into more than one category, depending on how the child uses the item. A dry-erase board may be part of the real-life toys when used as a schoolroom whiteboard, but when used to draw a picture, the board becomes a creative expression–emotional release toy.

Landreth (2002) provides an extensive list of suggested toys for what he calls a "tote bag playroom" for the practitioner who does not have a playroom. The tote bag of toys may be used in the corner of an office or other available space. A much longer list is provided than for the standard playroom. The basic list for the tote bag is crayons, paper, blunt scissors, rubber knife, doll, molding material, dart gun, handcuffs, toy soldiers, two play dishes and cups, spoons, small airplane, small car, black mask, sponge ball, craft sticks, pipe cleaners, cotton rope, telephone, aggressive hand puppet with a mouth, doll family, dollhouse furniture, transparent tape, and costume jewelry. He also suggests a cardboard box with rooms marked on the bottom and doors and windows cut into the sides. Today, many small inexpensive dollhouses can be purchased that easily fit into a tote bag. These were not available when Landreth (2002) was writing.

Guerney (2001) offers additional guidelines for selecting toys for the CCPT playroom. First, the toys need to convey to the child that a variety of behaviors are permitted in the therapy session. The toy selection should include toys of aggression, regression, independence, and mastery issues. Guerney (2001) includes games that can be played alone by the child or with the therapist. For younger children, Guerney (2001) includes dolls, baby bottles, stuffed animals; for older children, she includes board games, building materials, and a large come-back toy. Office equipment, science experiment materials, dressup costumes, puppets, cards, art materials, and clay are made available. When space permits, a mini-basketball hoop or other competitive games are included. Essential playroom equipment included by Guerney (2001) includes table, chairs, sandboxes, easels, and a water source. Guerney (2001) warns that some toys or activities may require the therapist to set too many limits; therefore, these can be eliminated without fear of jeopardizing therapy outcomes.

ROLE OF THE THERAPIST

Because the therapist believes the child has an innate sense to move toward health, he or she creates an environment in which this natural healing process can function without interference. The therapist refrains from directing the child in even the most subtle of ways. Guerney (2001) suggests that the therapist not quiz the child, even subtly, on what is happening in the child's life outside the playroom. The focus is on the child and the child's internal growth and development, as opposed to external behaviors and demands of significant others.

Landreth (2002) points out that the therapist and the relationship with the child is real. The therapist role in CCPT is a way of being, rather than a way of doing therapy. This genuineness is expressed through the therapist being congruent with the child in the therapeutic relationship, both inside and outside the playroom. The play therapist needs to be self-aware to the point of understanding and being to separate what the child is experiencing in the session and what the therapist is experiencing. An example would be the therapist who interprets the child's behavior as an expression of rejection or affection toward the therapist, rather than an expression of the child's experiences and emotions.

The therapist provides an environment of warm caring and acceptance of the child. All behaviors of the child are not acceptable, but the child, as a person, always has unconditional acceptance. However, the therapist conveys to the child a sense of respect and acceptance. The child is treated with dignity and worth, just as a therapist would treat an adult client. The therapist's behavior communicates to the child that the child is cared about and prized by the therapist. The child is just as prized and respected even when the child's behavior is not acceptable. The child is allowed to be fully a child in the playroom. The therapist avoids making judgmental comments. Most therapists easily refrain from negative comments, but the lack of judgmental comments involves both the negative and positive. The goal of this aspect of the therapist role is to have the child become self-reinforcing and critical in his or her exploration of experiences. Landreth (1991) believes that the therapist needs to provide an empathic, warm, and accepting attitude toward the child and the child's experiences of the world. Through this permissive atmosphere of the child being free to explore, learn, and grow, the child learns that the therapist is to be trusted to both allow experiences leading to resolution and to set limits to protect the child from emotional and physical harm.

Another important role of the therapist is that of what Landreth (2002) terms "sensitive understanding." The therapist strives to understand children's internal frame of reference of their subjective world. The therapist puts aside his or her own experiences, beliefs, and expectations in order to provide sensitive understanding of the child's personhood, activities, experiences, feelings, thoughts, and wishes. Rogers (1961) maintained that this ability to see the world through another's frame of reference is true empathy. The therapist does not protect the child from painful experiences but rather gives voice to what feelings these must have created in the child. Through this giving voice to the child's emotions, the child's feelings are reflected back to him or her as legitimate feelings. The development of empathy is crucial to the role of the therapist in providing the therapeutic environment for the child to experience and develop toward self-realization. Landreth (1991) makes the point that nowhere else does the child experience having the emotional part of his or her life accepted as being important and worthy of attention and respect.

The therapist reflects the observed emotional expressions of the child, trusting the child will correct spontaneously a misinterpretation of the therapist's reflections. The goal is not to interpret the play but to make the child aware of his or her emotions and to enhance the sharing of these feelings. Maladaptive behavior is seen as a lack of awareness of the child's feeling or a lack of understanding of his or her feelings. "After recognizing his feelings and having a label for those feelings, the child can determine for himself/herself how he/she wants to cope with them by experimentation within the playroom" (McCalla, 1994, p. 8).

Landreth (2002) reflects that trying to describe the therapeutic relationship that develops between the therapist and the child is not unlike trying to pick up mercury with your fingers. The therapeutic relationship, like mercury, is such that it defies understanding, just as mercury defies being picked up. The relationship is something that must be felt and experienced to be identified. The relationship focuses on the present and the reality shared between therapist and child. Landreth (2002) offers a series of dichotomies to help the therapist understand the emphasis of the relationship. Here is an adaptation of those dichotomies:

Person versus problem centered

Present versus past orientation

Feelings versus thoughts or acts

Understanding versus explaining

Accepting versus correcting

Child's direction versus therapist's instruction

Child's wisdom versus therapist's knowledge

An additional dichotomy that could be added is no preconceived agenda versus a planned agenda for the session. Although this is alluded to in much of Guerney's (1983, 2001) and Landreth's (1969, 1980, 1982, 1987, 1996, 2001, 2002) writings, the necessity of the therapist being completely open to what happens in the playroom and not being influenced by the demands of external sources is imperative to making child-centered therapy successful.

The therapist does have goals and objectives, but the goals and objectives are not specific to the session. Landreth (2002) describes these as broadly defined as opposed to prescriptive specific goals for the child and each session. The broad goal is for the child to gain self-understanding and to seek to resolve his or her personal issues that are inhibiting natural development toward positive growth. More specifically, Landreth (2002) offers objectives for the child engaged in CCPT. A summary of these objectives includes:

1. The child will develop an optimistic perception of self.
2. The child will take on greater responsibility for self.
3. The child will become capable of directing self.
4. The child will be able to accept his or her own strengths and weaknesses.
5. The child will become more self-reliant.
6. The child will demonstrate the ability to make personal decisions.
7. The child will express a sense of self-control.
8. The child will know when and how to cope with life's situations.
9. The child will develop an internalized sense of right and wrong.
10. The child will learn to trust his or her self.

STRUCTURING THE SESSION

Guerney (2001) makes a distinction between the tenets and the principles that guide CCPT as making the child-centered approach unique and distinct among the current theories of play therapy. According to Guerney, the first of these tenets is that the child directs the content of the therapy. In CCPT, the child has the personal responsibility without the therapist imposing an agenda of interventions. The second tenet is that CCPT is not specific to concern or symptom. The only concessions to this tenet are those that involve compliance on the part of the therapist to professional and insurance requirements. Even then, the minimal assessment, diagnosis, and intervention are imposed on the child's free exploration of the healing process. The third tenet concerns the acceptance of the child's sense of reality. The therapist accepts reality as the child presents it without correction or influence to the "accurate" perception. Guerney (2001) believes this acceptance of the child's reality and person is the heart of the child-centered theory. Fourth, CCPT cannot be partially followed or adopted; the theory must be followed completely if it is to be successful. Fifth, if the therapist does not trust the process and introduces other methods or techniques when progress is slow, CCPT will lose its effectiveness. These tenets coupled with Axline's (1947) principles define the approach and dictate the therapist's behaviors.

Stages of CCPT

Warm-up, aggressive, regressive, and *mastery* are the names Guerney used to describe the stages of CCPT (Guerney, 2001; Nordling & Guerney, 1999). The warm-up stage is characterized by testing limits, less focused and tentative play activities, and a growing trust toward the therapist. The aggressive stage is marked by a level of aggression relative to the child. An inhibited child may not put the toys away or let a little water spill on the floor. Less inhibited children are likely to express behaviors that most people would label as aggressive (e.g., hitting the bounce-back toy, stabbing stuffed animals, or shooting the army men). Some children may attempt to be aggressive toward the therapist, but Guerney considers this behavior a rare occurrence. The regressive stage is distinguished by a decrease or elimination of aggressive behavior. The child may regress to infantile behaviors, but more likely, the child will engage in play themes focused on dependence, attachment, and nurturance. Children often prepare "meals" for the therapist during this stage. A different theme is also common during this stage, one in which a traumatic event occurs followed by a rescue or restoration. This stage is not a consistent period for the child but exemplified by the pendulum swing from independent to dependent behaviors. During the final mastery stage, the child's play reflects a sense of competence and emotional control. The play theme tends to be scenes from everyday life.

The stages help the therapist to know where the child is in the therapeutic process. If the child seems stuck in the warm-up stage, the child may be struggling with trust issues centered within therapy and the therapist. When the child spends most of the time in the aggressive and regressive stages, the child has a great deal of work to do to cope with the underlying emotional concerns. Once the child appears

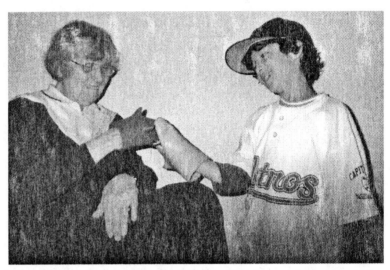

The child may appear to be shy and tentative during what Guerney terms the warm-up phase.

to be relatively consistent in the mastery stage, the child has completed the therapeutic work (Guerney, 2001).

West (1992) comments that work in play therapy seldom proceeds in an orderly fashion; rather, therapy progresses in a piecemeal way with tiny snippets of disclosures popping up spontaneously and dealt with in that moment. She has observed that the child's concerns are represented in the child's play themes in an unprocessed and sometimes disjointed manner. In what she calls the middle phase of therapy, play themes take on a more focused way with resolution and solutions to problems being demonstrated, but still in a fragmented, underdeveloped way. During the middle phase, the school and parents usually begin to report noticed changes in the child at home and school. The final phase is demonstrated by a constructive resolution of play themes. The child's relationship to the therapist and to other adults and children is more age appropriate. The child's behavior meets realistic expectations for his or her age group in social situations outside the playroom.

Guerney (2001) indicates that although it may seem that CCPT may take months or years to complete the stages, the process is typically completed in about 12 sessions or fewer. Landreth (2002) considers 10 to 12 or fewer sessions of play therapy to be short term. Short-term therapy may be most appropriate for developmental issues or a variety of childhood difficulties. Difficulties like chronic illness, learning disabilities, behavioral difficulties, emotional adjustment, violence witnesses, and low self-concept are some of the types of issues or difficulties that have been found to respond to CCPT in short-term therapy. Landreth (2002) recommends long-term therapy of more than 12 sessions with children having severe emotional problems or prolonged trauma.

CCPT may fail to reach the goals set by the therapist and child within the allotted time or financial means of the parents. West (1992) provides some insight into what may perpetrate this failure. Some children are not suited for play therapy. The child may be too old or too young or too disturbed to relate to the interaction that must take place. Another reason may be that the parent or caretaker does not really believe the child needs play therapy and does not actually want a change in the child's behavior. The caretaker may sabotage the sessions by continued lateness or simply not showing up for appointments. West (1992) points out that some parents are jealous of the attention the child is getting in therapy and develop ways to prevent the child from getting or valuing this time with the therapist. Because some behaviors may get worse before they get better, some parents lose patience with the process and withdraw the child from therapy prematurely. Parents may be fearful that the child's progress in therapy may demand they enter therapy to resolve issues they are not ready to resolve.

Sometimes, according to West (1992), the child may find the sessions too painful and express a desire not to see the therapist. Usually gentle encouragement restores the child to the playroom, but intervention by others or parents may cause therapy to be terminated prematurely. An improperly or poorly trained therapist can create sessions where the child's best interests are not served, resulting in the child and parent refusing to continue. For some children, play therapy may be found to be inappropriate and referral needs to be made elsewhere (e.g., residential care, hospitalization).

Children that West (1992) found to be unsuited for CCPT were those with severe learning deficits, problems separating fantasy from reality, and learned maladaptive behaviors from dysfunctional families. Children facing major life change and those whose safety or protection could not be assured are also unsuited. She found that children with the following specific disorders are not good candidates for CCPT: autism, childhood psychoses, hyperkinetic syndrome, and personality disorder.

Although the therapist may consider that CCPT failed, West (1992) cautions that the therapist needs to handle the termination carefully with an attitude that the failure was just an inappropriate choice of therapy, not a failure of the child. The therapist must treat the child with encouragement, compassion, and respect. West (1992) provides this admonishment to the therapist that "even in failed work, it is more than likely that something will have been gained from the sessions" (p. 16).

LIMITS

Guerney (2001) maintains that Axline's eight principles (Axline, 1969), which assert that the therapist only establish limits on the child's behavior as necessary to anchor the child in reality and to make the child responsible for the relationship, is second in importance only to the total acceptance of the individual. Therefore, the determination of when to set a limit or when not to do so is based on the idea that a limit is placed only on behavior and must not imply or be interpreted as rejection of the child. A major aspect of this limit setting is to help the child avoid dangerous behaviors. With the introduction of the child's responsibility to the relationship, Guerney (2001) includes that the child is not allowed to hurt the therapist or to destroy the therapist's possessions. The playroom contents are considered the possessions of the play therapist. The therapist does not generally allow the child to break a toy intentionally.

Guerney (2001) points out that Axline never actually wrote that an essential part of limit setting and enforcement is the use of empathic statements. However, Guerney (2001) observes that in Axline's illustrations, empathic statements about breaking the rules are paired with limit-setting statements. Through a combination of empathic acceptance of the child's wishes and the authoritative consistency of the therapist to maintain limits on the child's harmful or self-destructive behaviors, the therapist creates the therapeutic milieu that is the power behind CCPT. According to Guerney, this combination relates to the child that the therapist understands and accepts the child's feelings but does not actually allow the child to violate the limit or rule.

Limit setting is one of the most important interventions for the acting-out child. According to Guerney (2001), children who act out learn through limit setting to make a distinction between motivating emotions and negative behaviors. Over the course of therapy, the child learns self-control in the playroom, which later generalizes to the outside world. Guerney (2001) states that rarely do children not learn to conform to the limits of the playroom.

PARENT INVOLVEMENT

Simply because children depend on parents to bring them to therapy and make other financial arrangements, the parents or responsible adult must be involved to some degree in the therapeutic process. The foremost involvement of the parents and significant adults in the child's life is to access information about the child's situation and the context in which the child lives. This valuable information can help the therapist understand the child's play. However, the information is not used to effect change in the playroom (Landreth, 2002).

Landreth (2002) suggests that an ideal procedure would be for the parents to be interviewed and receive therapy from another therapist. If another therapist is not available for the parents, Landreth recommends the parents be scheduled at a different time than the child. Although acceptable, but not preferable, the child and parent may split the therapy hour. The therapist needs to make sure the child knows the parents are going to be seen also. One way to avoid problems for the child is to assure the child and parents that the child will not be discussed without the child present in the session and to limit the therapy with the parents to their marital and parenting concerns.

Landreth (2002) says the role of the parents in the child's life and in the child's difficulties cannot be denied. Therefore, working with the parents in developing parenting skills may be necessary and can accelerate the child's progress in therapy.

According to Guerney (2001), the CCPT therapist attempts to include parents, or others directly concerned with the child's welfare, in all aspects of the data gathering process and to keep them well informed throughout the therapeutic sequence as to how the child is progressing and how the significant people in the child's life may help. The details of the session are not shared with the parents, but the parents are given general information about the counseling goals, the child's progress, attitudes toward therapy, and issues the child is facing. Cooperative parents are offered parent education or parenting suggestions to become more effective in working with their own child.

TERMINATION

Determining when to end therapy with children has never been a question that is easily answered in CCPT or any other form of therapy. The changes in the child through the play therapy sessions are not always clear because the play may not change significantly over the period of therapy. Change in the child's behavior outside the session is often left to significant adults, who may have a difficult time recognizing changes in the child until the changes are dramatic. The child does not show a great deal of assistance either. Children seldom have insightful, dramatic revelations about changes in their lives or behavior. So the therapist cannot rely on the child suddenly being able to verbalize a major breakthrough, announcing the success of therapy and indicating time for termination.

Children change gradually because the growth process is protracted. The frustrating snail's pace of human development may take its toll on the therapist, who feels the pressure of outside forces of parents, school, or insurance demands for immediate results with the child. The therapist may begin to doubt the process of CCPT or even personal skill level when asked to quantify change in the child. CCPT therapists continue to insist that the therapist trust the process and ignore the pressures. However, with the advent of health maintenance organizations (HMOs), most practitioners' survival has come to depend on the capability of indicating progress in therapy and providing a prognosis of treatment.

Landreth (2002) provides some indication of what to look for in determining change. The therapist must have more extensive notes on the first few sessions, noting the repetitive patterns in the child's play. Sometimes it takes more than one session for a child to develop a play pattern. Landreth (2002) suggests the therapist look at "firsts." These firsts are those changes in the child's pattern of play. The first time a shy child begins to play close to the therapist is an indication of change. The first time a child who has witnessed violence does not surround himself with guns is an indication of change.

Firsts are not always positive behaviors. Negative behaviors can be just as important as indications of change or progress. The passive child, who suddenly begins to fight with the come-back toy, can be demonstrating an increased sense of competency. The sullen and silent child, who begins to beat on the drum and scream obscenities, may be expressing the pent-up anger within herself. Both negative and positive firsts are important in determining the prognosis for termination.

The CCPT therapist is likely to use some combination of the answers to the following questions to determine when the time for termination has arrived. The questions are based on those posed by Haworth (1964) and Landreth (2002).

1. Does the child appear to be less dependent?
2. Has the child ceased to ask about what other children are doing in the playroom?
3. Does the child's play indicate that the leading characters have both good and bad qualities?
4. Does the child seem to accept the therapy session as a time to work on personal issues?
5. Does the child accept self and own capabilities?
6. Does the child ask for help and express needs appropriately?

7. Does the child focus on self and provide appropriate self-evaluation of behavior?
8. Does the child express feelings and thoughts in appropriate ways?
9. Does the child channel and express strong emotions in a socially acceptable manner?
10. Does the child accept limits or rules and self-regulate behavior under daily stresses?
11. Does the child appear to have normal, creative emotional expressions in art, music, drama, and other creative forms of expression?
12. Does the child express age-appropriate and realistic fears?
13. Does the child seem less confused and assured when approaching novel situations?
14. Does the child have a spirit of cooperation without being conforming?
15. Does the child appear to be happier, self-directed, and competent?

When the child appears to meet most of these questions and the significant adults report the child's behavior has become manageable, the child is told the time has come to end the sessions. Landreth (2002) indicates that the actual termination needs to begin two or three sessions prior to the final session. These final sessions may be on a regular schedule or spread over several weeks or months. Some therapists prefer a weaning away technique to termination. The child is told how many more sessions there will be and allowed to explore the feelings about ending the therapeutic relationship. The final session, like the other sessions, is determined by the child's needs leading the way. The child may react with sentiment, as in drawings for the therapist, or with anger, as in trying to destroy the playroom. Whatever the child does, the therapist reflects the feelings in the context of the final good-bye to the child.

The major tenet of the theory is that if the child is provided with a warm, accepting, and safe environment, the child will naturally grow toward mental health and development.

ASSESSMENT AND TECHNIQUES

CCPT therapists are not known for taking extensive histories or formal assessments. The emphasis on the relationship and creating a safe environment for children to access their inner healing and movement toward self-realization is foremost in this theory. However, because integrity and honesty are paramount in the relationship with the client, CCPT therapists do provide informed consent, permission to disclose information, and other types of documents that are a sign of professional behavior in accordance with their individual professional ethics and standards of practice. When possible, these documents are secured by a therapist or other professional who will not be providing therapy for the child.

SUMMARY

CCPT has its theoretical basis in Rogers's person-centered therapy. The major tenet of the theory is that if provided a warm, accepting, and safe environment, the child will naturally move toward good mental health and development. The therapist provides the environment, reflects the child's meanings, and sets limitations that ensure the safety of the therapeutic session. The major challenges of CCPT for the therapist are to trust the child-centered process, let the child lead the way, and not to succumb to external pressures for change in the child's behavior.

CHAPTER 7

GESTALT PLAY THERAPY

Gestalt play therapists encourage children to express pent-up frustrations in a safe environment.

Violet Oaklander (1988, 2000, 2001) is considered the founder of the Gestalt theory of play therapy. Gestalt therapy is best described as a "humanistic, process-oriented mode of therapy that focuses attention on the healthy, integrated functioning of the total organism, comprised of the senses, the body, the emotions, and the intellect" (Oaklander, 2000, p. 28).

INTRODUCTION

The work and writings of husband and wife Frederick (Fritz) Perls and Laura Perls (1951, 1968a, 1968b, 1968c, 1969a, 1969b, 1973; L. Perls, 1973) are the origins of Gestalt therapy. Violet Oaklander adapted Gestalt theories and applied them to play therapy as described in her book *Windows to Our Children* (Oaklander, 1988). She emphasized that play for the young child is a form of improvisational dramatics, the way the child tries out his or her world and learns about the world. Through play the child achieves essential developmental health. Play is serious and purposeful, an imperative for mental, physical, and social development. Oaklander presented the goal of therapy as assisting the child in becoming aware of self and the child's existence in the world.

Oaklander suggests that therapy is a delicate balance between directing and guiding the session while determining whether to move with the child or to follow the child's lead in the therapeutic dance. She emphasizes that child therapy is a living, flowing relationship between the child and the therapist, challenging the creative communication process of each. The therapeutic process depends on the internal processing that takes place between the child's inner world and the therapist's inner world. In Gestalt therapy, the therapist and child join at the soul level.

Oaklander (2001) states that play offers the child the opportunity to learn about the world and to take safe risks. According to Oaklander (2001), play is serious work intended to develop the child cognitively, physically, and socially. Play is a way the child can access self-therapy and discover possible resolutions to his or her anxieties, confusions, and conflicts. Play allows the child a venue through fantasy to test new and different ways of being. The child is safe in this fantasy world to be antagonistic, tender, considerate, or dangerous. The popular studious wizard role is as possible as the martial arts champion; the beauty as possible as the medical examiner. All roles are available to the child in fantasy. Play is not the flippant pastime perceived by adults but rather serves as a language to children, expressed with tactile, manipulative symbols (Oaklander, 2001). Many times children may find what they are witnessing and perceiving in their field of awareness is difficult to express in the limited form of language or with their small vocabulary, and so they play to help inculcate the meaning of their experience. Through play, the imagination soars, encouraging freedom and expansion of the child's spirit while releasing the inhibitions and restrictions imposed in reality. Without play the child cannot develop in a healthy manner. Because Gestalt theory is a compilation of concepts from psychoanalysis, Gestalt psychology, humanistic theories, phenomenology, existentialism, and Reichian body therapy, a plethora of theoretical concepts and principles have developed in defining the tradition of Gestalt practice (Oaklander, 2001).

For the child, play is a kind of improvisational dramatics. Through play the child experiments with his world and learns about self in relation to the world. "For the child, play is serious, purposeful business through which he develops mentally, physically, and socially" (Oaklander, 1988, p. 160). Play is self-therapy for the child where the child works through confusions, anxieties, and conflicts. Play is also the symbolic language of the child, as opposed to being the frivolous, lighthearted, pleasurable activity that adults wish to believe it is (Oaklander, 1988).

During the play session, Oaklander (1988, 2000, 2001) attends to basic tenets of Gestalt therapy, specifically, figure-ground, organismic self-regulation, I/Thou relationships, and contact and resistance. By observing these relationships in the child's dramatic play, artwork, and other playroom experiences, the therapist grows to understand the child, the child's conflicts, and the child's personal ability for problem solving.

In every picture are the negative spaces, or those spaces that make up the background. The Gestalt play therapist looks and explores these spaces. Sometimes in Gestalt therapy what is missing or avoided is as important as the positive elements that represent the foreground of communication or representation. The foreground is what is obviously depicted either verbally or as an element in a creative project. The foreground is also those feelings or expressions within the conscious knowledge of the therapist and child. The background is those aspects of the individual that are less obvious and usually unknown to the therapist or child. The background may also be considered the context of the child.

Children have a tendency to respond too quickly to invitations and overtures from the therapist to form a tentative relationship. However, some children are not capable of quickly forming a relationship, especially those who have experienced early emotional injury. These children lack the ability to trust others. The formation of a relationship becomes the goal of therapy with children who may be lacking in this area. The therapist must find creative and nonthreatening ways to reach these special children (Oaklander, 2001).

Organismic self-regulation is another major tenet of Gestalt therapy. The organism seeks balance, or homeostasis, between good health and need satisfaction. The organism is constantly being forced out of balance because the demand to satisfy different needs is ever changing. Children are especially vulnerable to this imbalance because of developmental needs, which poses a critical and problematic time in the life of the child (Oaklander, 2001).

According to Carroll and Oaklander (1997), the emerging sense of self is affected by the biological predispositions of the child and interaction with the environment. In order to get his or her needs met, the child must move toward the environment or aggress. Aggression is considered necessary for the healthy growth and development of the child. Another way to state this concept is that the child must find ways to communicate needs to the environment if he or she is to thrive. If the child has a nurturing environment, the child has a clear picture, or Gestalt, of the "me" and "not-me" concept. The self-Gestalts result in children who have relative constant sets of attitudes and ethics about what is and is not true of themselves and others, as well as what capacity the children have to relate within and outside of themselves to others.

Children often engage in self-blame in reaction to family dysfunction, trauma, crisis, and loss. Children may become fearful of rejection, abandonment, or failure to have other basic needs met. In the struggle toward health and growth, children react any way they can to get these basic needs met. Their lack of cognitive and emotional maturation may cause children to select counterproductive ways to get their needs met, causing them additional difficulties. Oaklander (2001) gives the example of this counterproductive reaction in the expression of anger. The child may initially express anger, which is met with nonacceptance; the child suppresses the anger. The suppressed anger may manifest itself in emotional, physical, and social difficulties. One child may respond to this suppressed expression of anger with headaches, withdrawal, mutism, or self-injury; another, by hitting, kicking, striking. The first child is said to *retroflect* the experience; and the second, to *deflect* the experience. Hyperactivity and dissociation may also be ways to handle repressed emotions (Oaklander, 2001).

The purpose of these symptoms is to cover up or mask the authentic expressions. As a result, children bring into therapy their attempts to cope and survive the stress in their world and to regain homeostasis, or balance.

Contact and resistance are two more important tenets of Gestalt therapy. *Contact* is the ability to be fully aware and available for relationship. When healthy contact is made, all of the senses are engaged in awareness. The mind, the body, and the intellect are functioning optimally. When the mind, the body, or the intellect is inhibited, restricted, or blocked, contact diminishes. Fragmentation, as opposed to integration, occurs, resulting in a compromise of the child's sense of self. Troubled children armor and restrict themselves by turning emotionally and intellectually inward, inhibiting their expressions, and blocking healthy growth. Healthy contact results in a feeling of security for the child.

Some *resistance* is expected in working with children. The therapist recognizes this behavior as the child's protection and respects it. When the child becomes comfortable in the therapy session, the resistance decreases. However, resistance returns repeatedly throughout the treatment, an indication that the child has reached a limit to what he or she can disclose or experience for the time being. The therapist must respect this form of resistance. Resistance can be thought of as energy and as a barometer of contact with the child. A decline in energy results in lower contact, observed as resistance. Resistance may manifest by the child ignoring, being distracted, changing the subject, or not listening. A child may actively declare he or she does not wish to continue talking about the subject or asking to do something else (Oaklander, 2001).

Children who demonstrate inappropriate behaviors are experiencing resistance or contact-boundary disturbances. Inappropriate behaviors are used to help the child avoid healthy contact and to protect. Because of the child's lack of cognitive, physical, and emotional maturity, he or she cannot express deep feelings directly. Although the inappropriate behaviors are the child's way to achieve homeostasis, children are not generally aware of the linear relationship they use in coping, in getting needs met, and in protecting themselves (Oaklander, 2001). The edict is so strong within children for growth that children do what has to be done to limit, stop, block, or deny themselves (Oaklander, 2001). Children become desensitized, restricted, blocked, and inhibited in the body, emotions, and intellect.

The consequence of contact-boundary disturbances is increased diminishing of self and impaired contact abilities. Resistance helps the child take care of self. The child must not be pushed beyond his or her capabilities to cope with the disclosures or experiences. Resistance signals that this area of exploration has important material that needs to be disclosed and worked through.

The child may be referred to play therapy because of feelings of discomfort in the process of growing up. The child lacks the ability to take action, make contact, make choices, and behave authentically. These inabilities result in stasis, resistance, rigidity, and the need for control (Carroll & Oaklander, 1997).

Play therapy helps the child become more aware of what is "I" and what is "Thou." Through gaining awareness of the internal, external, and "intraternal," the child learns to form a relationship, select a different behavior, make better decisions, and behave in an authentic way (Carroll & Oaklander, 1997).

The therapist poses "experiments" in which the child creates a scenario. The therapist then asks the child to describe how each character in the scene feels, what motivated the character, and what other choices the character could have made. The therapist offers interpretation of the scene directly to the child for the child to identify as "me" or "not-me."

TOY SELECTION

The items included in the playroom should provide the child and the therapist with creative inspiration, motivation, and direction. The items are chosen on ability of the material to assist the child in creative and fantasy exploration.

Art materials included by Oaklander (1988) are all sizes of paper, felt-tip pens, crayons, pastels, colored pencils, finger paints, and similar art supplies. Oaklander includes various gadgets in her playroom (e.g., kitchen timer, stop watch, egg hourglass-type timer, counters, and beads) to be used in the children's creative projects.

Storytelling, poetry, and puppets materials are also included. Oaklander (1988, 2000, 2001) uses these materials for creative play projects: books, writing materials, tape recorder, pictures, projective tests, puppets, flannel board, sand tray, drawings, open-ended fantasies, videotape, walkie-talkies, toy microphone, and an imaginary television set. She uses an old box, but an old television set that has the interior removed could be used. Oaklander (1988) also recommends Gardner's series of therapeutic games.

Items placed in the playroom are selected for their ability to appeal to the child's sense of taste, touch, hearing, smelling, and seeing. A guitar, autoharp, or keyboard are useful. Oaklander (1988) also includes recorded music, especially folk songs and guided fantasies.

Clay is definitely one of Oaklander's favorite items for the therapy room. It provides a tactile experience for the child with its primitive appeal to the sense of touch, (Oaklander, 1988). Clay helps children get into touch with their feelings and unblock their emotional expressions. Children who may be having problems with anger can vent it by pounding and punching the clay. Clay appeals to children who fear making mistakes. It is easily erased and virtually mistake proof. Other substances can be used in place of clay (e.g., dough, plastic modeling compound, mud, or wet sand). Water is a playroom essential. A basin of water and a selection of pouring items is included in the playroom. These water sources can be used in sand play or in water play.

Plaster, wax, soap, wood, wire, metal, paper, pipe cleaners, straws, boxes, plastic foam, and other items can be used to construct and sculpt. In addition, nails, hammer, glue, staples, and tape are useful. Screws, nuts, bolts, and other items may be included. Consider the age of the children and their capabilities in selecting tools (e.g., hand drill, coping saw, or screwdriver). Spray paint may be useful for children who are unlikely to abuse paint.

Collage materials are also part of the toys selected. These supplies may include many types of paper, paints, string and yarn, fabric scraps, colored sand, beads, shells, or anything that might be appealing in texture or color. The Gestalt therapist is looking for materials that offer a sensory experience and aid in the expression of the child.

ROLE OF THE THERAPIST

Gestalt play therapists use play as a stimulus for their therapeutic interventions with children. The therapist supplies the setting and resources that help children work through problematic events, situations, and issues in their life. Oaklander (2001) says the therapist must have a willingness and the experience of enjoying playfulness.

Gestalt therapy is a process therapy, which means the play therapist attends to the "what" and "how" of behavior as opposed to the "why." The therapist assists change by helping the client become aware of what is causing the difficulties. Armed with this awareness, the child can decide what changes to make.

According to Oaklander (2001), the relationship itself can be therapeutic and forms the basis for the therapeutic process. Initially, the therapist and child meet as equal but separate individuals. The therapist is responsible for maintaining this equal and separate stance. He or she enters the relationship with authenticity and genuineness, without manipulation, patronization, or judgment. The therapist maintains an optimistic attitude about the child's potential for health. The child is accepted as the child appears to be. The therapist remains fully present with the child and not distracted in thought or deed, no matter how the child may behave. He or she respects the child and attempts to move at the same speed as the child in forming the relationship (Oaklander, 2001).

Although the child may perceive the therapist as a parent, this aspect of the relationship is not encouraged. The therapist has a unique point of view, personal limits and boundaries, and his or her own mode of response. Because the child is envisioned as separate and unique, the child has the opportunity to face the self with its limits and boundaries in a new way. The therapist does not have the same involvement with the child a parent does, so he or she retains the therapeutic distance that allows the therapist to keep personal issues separate from the child's issues. The therapist must be aware of any experiences that could cause him or her to respond in an inappropriate manner to the circumstances the child presents and to examine these responses for possible countertransference. Without self-examination and exploration, the therapist may respond in ways detrimental to the child client. The therapist provides services with integrity to self, courage to face personal feelings and responses, and knowing and respecting personal limitations. The therapist respects personal commitments and convictions, for example, beginning sessions on time (Oaklander, 2001).

The I/Thou relationship is an important tenet in Gestalt play therapy. One role of the therapist is to help the child make these discriminations between figure and ground perceptions, or I/Thou. The therapist helps the child determine what is true of the child and what is true of the context within which the child lives. A child may live with neglectful parents who compose a "ground" of lack of nurturing, but the figure is that the child is still lovable. The figure-ground perception relates directly to the Gestalt concept of "I" and "Thou" with "I" being the figure and "Thou" being the ground. The Gestalt therapy is a perception of both the figure and the ground composing the child's perception of the world. A basic premise of Gestalt play therapy is that the child will concretize this Gestalt, figure and ground, symbolically in art, drama, music, movement, fantasy, or other creative products.

Gestalt experiments can be guided fantasies followed by drawings or storytelling, sand tray reproductions, or dramas.

The therapist is directive, providing the child with a specific exercise, or "experiment" as it is called in Gestalt therapy. These experiments can be guided fantasies followed by drawings or storytelling, sand tray reproductions, or dramas. The therapist sets up the creative activity to tap into the child's inner world and assist the child in gaining awareness of self and understanding his or her existence in the world. Therapy follows an activity or experiment in a structured process termed *Gestalting* the activity. Any fantasy, dream, or wish is considered fertile material for the Gestalt process and resultant awareness.

Here are some of the experiments, or activities, a Gestalt play therapist might use in helping children explore their Gestalt:

1. Using a visualization exercise, children draw how they feel.
2. Children draw themselves how they would like to be. Then they draw what they believe they will look like when they are older or what they looked like much younger.
3. Children look at an object (e.g., flower, picture, small toy). Then they draw how the object made them feel. The children draw an emotional response to a story, dream, fantasy, poem, or piece of music.
4. The children draw opposites (e.g., happy/sad, crazy/sane, angry/calm, serious/silly, good/bad, love/hate, etc.).

5. The children draw a road map of their life, showing all the bumps, dips, mountains, and so on.
6. The children show where they believe the road will be going and what that will be like. Then they draw themselves on the road.

These experiments represent a small portion of the type of activities described by Oaklander (1988). A therapist is limited only by personal creativity in developing ways to tap into the child's Gestalt symbolism in the use of experiments.

The therapist focuses on the process of the child's play. In observing how the child approaches the materials, what toys the child chooses, and what toys the child avoids, the therapist gains insight into the child's worldview. Other clues to the child's general style are gained through observing how the child can transition from one activity to another and the organization or lack of organization to play themes. The therapist also focuses on the content of the play. Of particular interest are the themes of loneliness, aggression, nurturance, and tragedies.

Oaklander (2000) selects the concepts of the relationship, contact and resistance, sense of self, and awareness and experience as salient Gestalt concepts that apply to children. The relationship between the therapist and the child is one of equality despite the differences in age, experience, and education. The relationship is determined to be a dialogical stance between two equally entitled people. The therapist is without value judgment and honors and respects the child. The therapist is congruent and genuine while respecting personal limitations and boundaries.

Oaklander (1988) describes the importance of making contact. *Contact* in a Gestalt sense is made through the five senses and physical movement. Effective contact means the child can interact with nature and other people without losing a sense of individuality or self (Corey, 1991). In order to have good contact, the child needs a clear awareness, full energy, and the ability for self-expression. Without this contact, there can be no growth and change for the child.

In Gestalt therapy, the therapist must also look at resistances to contact. Defense mechanisms prevent the child from contact and from being authentic. The Gestalt therapist focuses on the interruption of contact with the environment when the child is not aware of the loss of contact. Contact or awareness of environment and self is considered normal and healthy, but to ignore or purposely choose not to be aware of the self or environment is considered unhealthy (Corey, 1991).

The Gestalt therapist believes if people are not aware of what is going on inside and outside of them, they experience a need to control their environment and make themselves safe. The Gestalt therapist looks at these resistances to contact or boundary disturbances to indicate the degree of discomfort the child may be experiencing. The greater the loss of contact, the more distress the child exhibits.

STRUCTURING THE SESSION

The therapeutic process is described by Oaklander (1988). The therapist provides the child with a creative activity, such as drawing a picture, creating a story, performing a drama, or sculpting a clay image. For clarification of the process, let us assume the child has been instructed to draw a picture of the child's world in shapes, lines, and colors.

The process begins with the therapist asking the child to verbalize the process of approaching the task, feelings about and during the task, and determining the ending of the task. The therapist might say, "I'm wondering what you are feeling right now."

Then the child is asked to share the activity by describing the drawing in the child's own words: "Tell me about this in your own words."

The therapist helps the child explore further by asking him or her to elaborate on the individual aspects of the drawing like colors, shapes, forms, representations, people, and objects: "I'm wondering about this blank space over here. Tell me about that."

The next step in processing the drawing is to ask the child to pretend to be different parts of the picture or design. The therapist might prompt the child with the words, "I am this picture, and I have a lot of bright yellow circles and tiny red triangles."

The therapist may ask the child to describe some parts of the drawing in more detail by saying, "Be the red triangle in the top corner, and tell me more about you. What do you do? What is it like to be in this picture? What is your job in this picture? What does it feel like in your corner?"

The therapist may explore the element of the drawing further by asking even more questions about the "triangle" and its purpose, existence, and relationship to the other elements in the drawing. The therapist might ask, "What if the little red triangle were made larger or moved to another part of the drawing? What would change?"

Each element of the drawing is processed by these probing questions and extensions of the child's awareness. If the child answers that he or she does not know, it is time to move to another element of the drawing. The process continues with each element until the sense of energy or excitement seems exhausted.

Sometimes the child may show a lack of interest or excitement. When this happens the therapist may provide an answer and move on to another part of the drawing.

"I'm guessing this blank space is something you are not sure about right now. Maybe some feelings of emptiness that were left after your grandfather died."

Because some aspects may be more threatening than others to the child, the therapist may come back to elements that seem to pose an exceptional lack of response from the child to see if after other awareness the child is better ready to discuss this element.

A particularly rich venue in the Gestalting of a drawing is the dialoguing between two elements of the drawing, story, drama, sculpture, dream, or sand tray. "Tell me what the little triangle would like to tell the large yellow circle in the middle." "I am wondering what the yellow circle would say back to the little triangle."

The therapist encourages the child to pay attention to the colors used in the drawing. The therapist may want to begin the drawing by asking the child to close their eyes and think about the colors he or she would like to use. The therapist might guide this part of the process by asking focusing questions to help the child. Here are some examples of focusing questions:

1. What do bright colors mean to you? What colors are those?
2. What do dark colors mean to you? What colors are those?
3. What do dull colors mean to you? What colors are those?
4. What do exciting colors mean to you? What colors are those?
5. Which colors will you use on this drawing? Will you use bright colors or dark colors, or will you use dull colors or exciting colors? Will you use just one kind of color or different colors in your picture?

Oaklander (1988) says that she talks about how much pressure the child may apply to certain colors or the amount of certain colors used in the drawings. She says, "I want the child to be as aware as she can of what she did, even if she's not willing to talk about it" (p. 54).

Whether a drawing, sand tray scene, toy play, or other expressive mode, the therapist asks the child about each of the elements and how these are perceived emotionally. Then the child is asked to take the role of each of the elements and to retell a story from that element's point of view. The child is then challenged through the therapist's interpretations to see what part of the interpretation is the "me" (what fits or is true of myself) and "not-me" (what is not something the child acknowledges about self or does not fit). Each session is structured so the child recognizes that cleaning up is the signal for closure of the session (Oaklander, 2001).

LIMITS

Although Oaklander (1988) allows the child a permissive atmosphere, focusing on acceptance of the child as he or she is, she does not imply the child is allowed to play without limits in the therapeutic session. She usually sees children for 45-minute sessions with a definite limit on the time the child is in the session. Children are not allowed to abuse equipment or the playroom. She does not allow children to abuse her or themselves. Children are not allowed to take toys from the playroom. Oaklander (1988) gives a warning that the session is ending. She might alert the child to the impending end of the session by saying, "Our time is about up" or "You have five more minutes until time to go."

The child may wish to ignore the limit or to violate the limit. Oaklander (1988) acknowledges the child's desire and accepts this desire but holds firmly to the limit. She might say, "You would like to play a while longer, but it is time to go join your mom."

PARENT INVOLVEMENT

Oaklander (1988) finds that most parents contact her by phone initially and try to discuss the child's difficulties during this first conversation when they make the first appointment. She explains that the parents will bring the child with them to the first session, and she will ask them to tell her again about their concerns in the presence of the child. Oaklander (1988) believes the child's presence in the discussion alleviates the child's worst fears about what is wrong. The child is very much aware that something is wrong but may not have had it explained in a direct manner.

Oaklander (1988) does not ask the child to sit in the waiting room while she interviews the parents. She believes whatever the parents have to say needs to be said in front of the child. During the discussion, Oaklander can observe the child and the child's reactions to the parents' dialogue about the concern. In addition, she can see the dynamics of the parent-child relationship. Including the child helps establish a trusting relationship with the child. The child will see the therapist is impartial and respectful of the child as a client.

When the family comes into the office, Oaklander asks someone to tell her what encouraged the parents to seek help for the child. She finds that the mother is most likely the one who describes the situation. After a few sentences, Oaklander asks the child for his or her point of view. Some parents may try to use adult language that is hard for the child to comprehend easily; Oaklander stops the parent from doing this and requests that the parent speak so the child can understand. She may ask the child if he or she knows what the parent is saying, and then ask the parent to restate the comments more simply.

During this initial interview, Oaklander makes it clear that while understanding what the parent is concerned about, she does not necessarily take the presented problem as fact. She may make it very clear who has the problem in the concern. Oaklander may tell the parents or the school they have the problem, not the child.

Oaklander models talking to the parent at the close of a session in the video *A Boy and His Anger* (1987). She meets with the mother and the boy together. She asks the mother about the child's behavior at home. Oaklander solicits information about the home situation and any changes that may be taking place in the child's environment. She appears to be getting a feel for how the child's life has gone within the child's home and school since the last session. After she has a clear picture of the current home situation and explores the child's progress, Oaklander provides the parent with an experiment to try at home.

She offers her experiment to the parent as a possible suggestion, careful not to pressure the parent into doing or allowing something the parent finds uncomfortable. Oaklander gets a commitment from the parent to try the suggestion. She might say, "Is this something you might try at home?" If the parent seems hesitant, Oaklander makes adjustments to the suggestion until it is something that seems agreeable to the parent. Once the parent has agreed, Oaklander directs her attention to the child.

The child is allowed to choose a closing activity. Then the child decides whether he or she wishes to do the closing activity with the mother or the therapist.

A kind of termination interview is held to discuss with the parents and the child the possibility of stopping therapy. The child's progress and concerns are discussed openly and a decision is reached. The therapist asks for at least two more sessions to say good-bye over the next month, meeting on alternate weeks. The parent, as well as the child, is assured the child can return to therapy if needed.

TERMINATION

Oaklander (1988) believes the child should not be in therapy for long periods of time. She relates that children do not have a lot of unfinished business or "old tapes" typical of adults in therapy. Therefore, children can show some results within three or four sessions. Three to 6 months is enough time to warrant termination. Oaklander is suspicious of therapy that takes a year or more when the child's life has not had unusual circumstances.

She looks for natural stopping places in therapy. One such place is when the child reaches a plateau; the child is not getting worse or better. The child may need some time to integrate and assimilate the changes taking place because of therapy. The child has gone as far as possible at this point, given the child's developmental level and inner strength. The child seems to reach a stalemate which exhibits the child's inability to break through this psychological wall at this time. The child seems to have an inner barometer of what is developmentally appropriate. The therapist must learn to recognize this phase of therapy as a stopping place as opposed to another stumbling block in therapy.

Clues to ending therapy are changes reported by the parents and school. If the child suddenly becomes more involved in sports, organizations, or other forms of children's social life, therapy may get in the way of the child's movement toward growth. When the child does not want to come to therapy anymore, the time for termination needs to be evaluated.

Improved behavior is not the sole reason to terminate the child from therapy. The therapist needs to look at the work in the therapy session. If the child appears to be able to come to resolution in his or her play or the child expresses an understanding of the situation in a healthy manner, termination may be at hand.

Termination can also be premature. These children may revert to previous behaviors if terminated too soon. The child will be reluctant to terminate or will regress to a previous stage in therapy. Children can be terminated prematurely in two ways: either the child is not ready to terminate or the child is poorly prepared for termination. Oaklander (1988) says of the time to terminate, "Children tell us what we need to know" (p. 201).

Preparing the child for termination is very important. Once that termination has been determined, the child is told how many more sessions remain. Then the therapist focuses on dealing with the good-bye and the child's feelings about saying good-bye. This phase of therapy becomes an evaluation of what has happened and remembering the together times. The child is told they have come to a stopping place for now. If there is a time when the child needs to come back, the therapist will allow the child to return. The child is given the address and phone number of the therapist, who gives the child permission to call or write, if the child wishes.

When a child calls, Oaklander (1988) has found these conversations are much like old friends renewing their relationship. Some children actually do write. Oaklander responds with short notes or cards. She finds that most children do not continue to keep in touch after a few exchanges.

Termination to Oaklander (1988) seems to always be difficult, as the child may have more that he or she may want to share and the therapist may have more issues that he or she may have wanted to explore with the child. Because termination is difficult for both the therapist and the child, it is important to be honest about the difficulty and the sadness that results from the sense of loss and celebration at this time of separation.

ASSESSMENT AND TECHNIQUES

Oaklander (1988) prefers not to do an intake but rather to learn about the child as the relationship grows during therapy. She does interview the parents with the child present and then asks them to wait outside. She talks to the child about trying to make things better, doing some things that will be fun, getting to know the child better, and confidentiality. The child is then invited to look around the office and examine the toys and equipment. Oaklander asks the child to draw a picture or series of pictures. At the end of this initial interview, she explains that the child will be asked to use some of the things in the office and she and the child will be talking about feelings.

Oaklander does sometimes use tests or assessment instruments. She finds them helpful when she is not sure about the most useful direction for the child. The assessment is a delaying technique used "when I don't know what else to do" (Oaklander, 1988, p. 188).

She uses several assessment instruments as therapeutic aids. Oaklander has found that many projective tests are useful as what she terms an "expressive" medium. She does not consider her use of them to have diagnostic accuracy and does not intend them for the purpose of diagnosis. She says that being familiar with the interpretative notes is helpful. She uses the instruments much like she would any other story, drawing, or sand tray scene.

Oaklander (1988) describes the techniques she uses in detail in her text *Window to Our Children*. The first of these techniques is the use of drawing and fantasy activities. She encourages children to draw their world and family and to make free drawings. She uses guided imagery followed with drawings to make physical and emotional contact. Anger pictures, squiggle drawings, abstract drawings, finger painting, and foot painting are some the vehicles she uses.

Children are often encouraged to use clay, plastic modeling clay, dough, wood and tools, and collage to design artifacts that can become springboards to the Gestalt process. The child or the therapist may choose one or several tarot cards that appeal to them. Then the child weaves a fantasy story about the selected cards.

The empty chair technique is sometimes used to help children close unfinished Gestalts in their lives. The child imagines the person in the empty chair. With the ther-

Gestalt play therapists may have the child portray a dream or fantasy in a sand tray picture.

apist's assistance, the child says to the empty chair what he or she needs to say to the parent. This technique is used anytime it is either unsafe to give the message to the person directly, the child is not ready to tell the person what he or she wishes, or the person is not available because of death or absence.

Children are asked to share dreams. Oaklander (1988) has the child address characters in the dream as if they were puppets. The child speaks from the perspective of the character as well as from a personal perspective. The meaning of the dream is brought into the awareness of the child through this technique.

Oaklander uses many techniques to help children bring abstract feelings into awareness. Her techniques take children's nebulous experiences and emotions into defined expression through the five senses. Once children are aware of the experiences, they can better cope with the trauma or discomfort.

SUMMARY

Gestalt play therapy with children is one of the more directive types of play therapy. The therapist affects the selection of pertinent activities, remaining sensitive to the child's wishes and commitment. The therapy session has been likened to a dance, with therapist and child moving in rhythm with first one and then the other leading. This special relationship is the most important facet of the therapeutic session with the therapist helping the child gain awareness and resolving what changes need to be made. The therapist is active and fully present in the session. Ultimately, the therapeutic partnership moves the therapist and the child toward new growth and greater health.

CHAPTER 8

RELATIONSHIP PLAY THERAPY

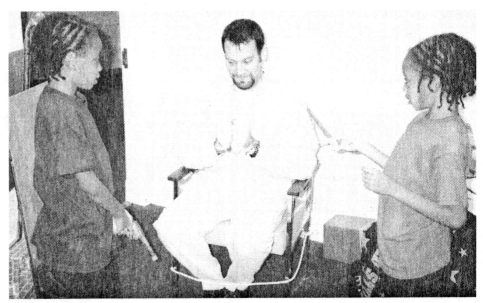

The relationship is paramount in relationship therapy.

In this chapter we examine the work of Clark Moustakas (Moustakas, 1953, 1955, 1959, 1973, 1997; Moustakas & Schalock, 1955) and existential play therapy. In 1997 Moustakas published a new perspective on his existential play therapy theory, which he renamed relationship play therapy.

INTRODUCTION

Moustakas (Moustakas, 1959; Moustakas & Schalock, 1955) is probably the most representative of the existential play therapists. He sees the relatedness of one person to another as an essential part of growth. In the relationship, the individual must feel free to express the personal self rather than be what Moustakas (1959) terms "the helpless victim of neurosis which can be cured only through a dependency relationship" (p. 1). Through self-growth the individual resolves the internal struggle of dependency versus autonomy, with the resultant feeling of freedom to face self. In order to gain this personal freedom to be, the therapist must believe and cherish the child's ability to resolve issues, and the therapist is obliged to extend acceptance and love to the child.

A major tenet that separates relationship play therapy from other play therapy theories is the belief that the therapist actively enters the child's world by the child's invitation. Without imposing a specific theory or method directed at intentionally changing the child's behavior or directing the play, the process of the creative experience and interactive communication is shared between the therapist and the child. Through this shared experience and interactive communication, the child experiences new ways of being and relating. The process is one of learning from the therapist to the child and from the child to the therapist. The relationship unfolds with the active participation between the partnership of therapist and child in play.

Through faith, acceptance, and respect in the shared experiences of the playroom, the relationship grows and develops. Through these shared essential conditions, the child moves toward resolution of his or her challenges or issues. The essential ingredient of change lies within the interactions between the therapist and child that lead to the development of the relationship.

An essential belief of relationship play therapy is the commitment of the therapist to the idea that each child, when treated with consistent acceptance, respect, and faith by the play therapist, will develop personal will, exercise initiative, and become a self-starter (Moustakas, 1997). The existential belief is that all persons have within themselves a desire to seek the highest state of good mental health they are capable of achieving, and given a conducive atmosphere and environment, the goal of good mental health will be attained.

TOY SELECTION

The number of toys in a playroom is not important to Moustakas (1997). The most important aspect of the toy selection is that the children do not feel pressured to use them in a certain way. Children need to feel they can project their feelings onto the toys and use the toys as they wish with few limits.

The room selected needs to be cheerful with pleasant colors for children and must convey this is a child's place to be free to play. The toys are not displayed in a specific way to identify their use or context. Usually toys like trucks, cars, guns, knives, airplanes, hot-water bottles, telephones, boats, and tractors are placed on child-level shelves. Hand puppets, stuffed animals, shovels, bowls, spoons, dolls, and jump rope are placed within the child's view. Crayons, clay, finger paint, paper, scissors, steel vises, tools, and plastic aprons are made available. A large dollhouse, doll furniture, and a number of doll figures are placed in a corner. Nursing bottles, soldiers, sand, water, easel paints, masks, blocks, balloons, and a bop toy are placed on the shelves (Moustakas, 1997).

Moustakas uses sand, water, paints, and clay, which he believes allows the child to express tension and pent-up feelings. He terms these *unstructured items*. In the category of *structured items* he includes guns, knives, swords, darts, and a punch toy, which he believes allows the child to express hostility. To express direct feelings, Moustakas recommends family dolls, puppets, and other items representing human figures. Noncommittal activities can be expressed through cars, trucks, tractors, checkers, paper, pencils, and boats.

The materials are not as important as the attitude of the therapist. However, Moustakas (1959) does insist the toys be organized and remain consistent to this organization as a subtle message to the child that the therapist and the playroom are unchanging and constant. Each child lives in an ever evolving world outside the playroom that is filled with change and inconsistencies. The child may feel out of control and victimized by the changes that are forced on the child by the significant adults and society's influence on his or her life circumstance. However, in the playroom the child is the leader and makes the changes that are to be made (Moustakas, 1959).

ROLE OF THE THERAPIST

The role of the therapist is to wait for the child. Through waiting, not pushing, the therapist allows the child to explore his or her issues within the child's own growth time frame. In the process of waiting, the therapist actively expresses a commitment of faith in the child's ability. This process differs from psychoanalysis in that it fosters independence rather than dependency (Moustakas, 1959).

The respect shown to the child expresses the therapist's recognition of the child as distinct and possessing integrity. Through this mutually respectful relationship, the child discovers and affirms who the child really is and comes to value the personal interests, thoughts, feelings, and internal directions toward identity, self-expression, and self-understanding (Moustakas, 1997).

Through the acceptance and caring environment created by the therapist, the child learns to trust and regard himself or herself as worthwhile. The child can then make active decisions about who he is and what he wishes to do. The child comes to recognize personal feelings as real, not mere whims or reactions to real or imagined situations. This growth toward positive self-worth allows the child to move toward self-actualization.

The therapist is fully present with the child throughout the therapy process. To do this, the therapist must enter the child's world by focusing directly on the child's feelings, thoughts, and wishes. The therapist responds to the child in a way that encourages exploration of the self and others. The therapist concretely indicates presence by participating in the child's play and plans but only when invited to do so by the child. The therapist provides comments, guidelines, and suggestions to assist the child in growth and development. However, the therapist's comments are delivered with respect, tenderness, and concern for the child.

The therapist is expected to begin where the child is, dealing with his or her immediate feelings. The child's symptoms or problems are secondary to the therapeutic process. Instead, the therapist focuses on creating an environment with unconditional positive respect and acceptance for the child, and a deep conviction that the child has the potential and ability to know and reach resolution of his or her own problems.

The therapist encourages the child to make choices, to talk freely, and to direct the activities of the playroom, thus regaining self-resources and self-esteem. According to Moustakas (1959), the therapist may provide the child information, suggest alternatives, or offer help. However, the therapist maintains an attitude that the child is competent to take responsibility for his or her own actions and decisions. The therapist's statements are aimed at assisting the child in awareness of self, confronting inner conflicts, and working through self-destructive attitudes.

Moustakas (1997) found that children who express hostility in play often became privately tranquil. He hypothesized that in owning their fears the child may come to feel safe and fearless. Through the admission of inadequacy, the child may experience an openness that leads to a renewal of confidence and courage. When the child is free to attack and destroy in play, the child becomes free to love in reality. Moustakas (1997) believes that the child's perceptions are the the only meaning of the situation that is valid for the purposes of therapy. Although the emotions may be intense and extreme, the therapist remains in the full presence of the child with acceptance and encouragement.

Listening is a major role of the therapist in relationship play therapy. The therapist communicates presence in the session by listening and hearing the child's expressions of point of view, thoughts, feelings, and the child's meanings of his or her experiences. An example of this type of reflection, which assures the child the therapist has heard the child's meaning as well as content, might be something like this:

"I am going to shoot you," Mark says with the gun poised in the direction of the therapist's foot.

"You want to shoot me," the therapist repeats. "Let's try that to see if it is OK to shoot my foot."

"Yes, I am going to kill you." The child shoots the gun at the therapist's foot.

"Looks like you shot me, all right," the therapist reflects. "Now, I have been killed?"

"Yes, you can't hurt anyone now," the child responds.

"So you have killed me, and now I cannot hurt you anymore."

Moustakas emphasized the importance of listening to the child. He wrote that the therapist attempts to be aware of the child as he or she is, and the therapist respects the child as the therapist observes him or her. In effect, the therapist conveys to the child, through words and feelings that the emotions that the child is expressing are accepted and honored. The child's feelings are sacred to the child, and because the therapist holds the relationship with the child as singular and reveres the child's being, the personal attributes of the child are accorded importance and value in the play therapy session.

STRUCTURING THE SESSION

Before the session begins, the therapist sets the climate. Four challenges exist for the therapist in establishing the setting for the therapeutic climate: accessibility of materials, atmosphere of freedom, atmosphere of tranquility, and communication of caring (Moustakas, 1981, 1997).

The accessibility of materials is created through open arrangement of the playroom and the therapist's inviting attitude, which encourages the child to experiment, explore, direct, and take charge of the child's world. The atmosphere of freedom is created when the child is encouraged to make choices and to express interests, wishes, and preferences. The therapist communicates this by allowing the child to manipulate the physical environment within the playroom, as long as moving things about does not endanger the child. Tranquility is communicated through the consistency of having the child meet in the same room, at the same time, with the same toys, and with the same therapist. The therapist behaves in a consistent way. The toys are always located in approximately the same place. The sessions are private between the therapist and the child. The final dimension is the communication of caring. The body language and the verbal responses of the therapist clearly signal the child that the therapist has only interest in the child and the child's well-being for the duration of the session (Moustakas, 1981, 1997).

The number of sessions and the length of the individual sessions vary with the individual child and the areas of concern. When therapy is initiated because of a situation like a new sibling, recent move, school changes, physical illness, or other temporary disturbances, therapy is usually brief. However, when there has been significant trauma or long-term stress, therapy may be much longer. How long therapy continues is determined by the child's response. Moustakas (1997) does not provide any definitive answer to what the expected timeline of therapy might be. Consistent with existential beliefs, Moustakas (1997) provides the suggestion that

Part of the process of therapy is to structure the sessions in such a way that the permissiveness of the situation is conveyed to the child.

therapy cannot be governed by the dictates of external rules without losing the essential freedom of the child to determine his or her own pace toward becoming the authentic being that is so important in the process of therapy. The child who is snatched from the therapeutic process prematurely suffers from a completed experience of self-determination and self-affirmation.

Part of the process of therapy is to structure the sessions so the permissiveness of the situation is conveyed to the child. Moustakas (1959) might use the following beginnings to structure for the child what is expected in the playroom experience:

> In the playroom you are allowed to do many things that you would want to do.

> I would like to hear what you believe.

> Your time in here is to be used as your time and special place.

> What you say in here is just between you and me. No one else needs to know.

> That is something that you will need to decide. It is important that you decide for yourself.

> You would like for me to tell you what to do, but in here, you can decide what is best.

> You want me to do that for you, but I know that it is better for you to try to do it yourself first.

> This is your task. I cannot do it for you. You will need to complete it as best you can.

> I can see that you are having trouble with that, would you like for me to give you a little start? After I start it, I think you will be able to finish it.

These phrases suggest the structuring of the session. Notice that the child is given the responsibility for the direction of therapy and self-direction. Some children may do things that are harmful to themselves or to others. Because of their age and experience, it would not be in the child's best interest to be allowed to work in the playroom with wild abandon; therefore limits are necessary. Setting limits on the child's playroom work is discussed later in this chapter.

In the process of therapy, the child is always seen as an individual with the ability to choose what is best for the child and to make decisions that will help the child meet his or her goals. Children who may have behavior problems are believed to be children who have been severed from their internal resources through criticism, ostracism, and rejection. In a relationship of acceptance and appreciation, the child can and will recover these internal resources.

The actual setting of therapy is influenced by the age, gender, and presenting problem of the child. Gender is most often seen influencing the choice of play items and how the child approaches and arranges them. Children of both genders usually begin play with items that are not gender specific, like paints, sand, clay, or water. Male children have been observed to be more attracted to trucks, cars, games, and books. The boys often move to family figures and then to community figures (e.g., police, firemen, etc.).

Moustakas (1959) introduces the idea that children considered "normal" and those considered "disturbed" differ only in their negative expressions and the intensity of these expressions. The so-called normal child usually expresses fewer negative attitudes less frequently with a clear focus and direction, whereas the disturbed child may simply lash out indiscriminately with more frequent, intense negative attitudes. Without the directness and focus, the outburst of emotion is less satisfying and more frustrating; therefore the intensity of the need for expression builds. Because of the unfocused feelings of anger and fear that result from the frustration building inside the child, the disturbed child is motivated to express hostility toward people and things. Conversely, the child may express these unfocused feelings through withdrawal and fearfulness of everything.

Therapy for the disturbed child helps the child regain the real self. Because of the unfocused feelings, the child has lost touch with the real self and the inner knowledge of problem resolution.

In the process of the therapeutic relationship, the therapist and child come to clarify and strengthen the child's focus on specific situations or issues. The child is allowed to express anger and actively play out fantasies toward events and even specific persons with the toys and verbalizations. As the child expresses these feelings and releases the negative attitudes, the therapist accepts the child and helps him or her channel and focus these feelings in nondestructive ways. The child gains control over the emotions and begins to feel a growing self-worth. He or she then begins a new phase of therapy with the growing knowledge that people and things can be both good and bad. The child may vary with great intensity in this ambivalent reaction to the new understanding about the self. Finally, the child will resolve the issues and not be overcome with negative emotions and hostility toward others. What emerges is a child confident and courageous, accepting himself or herself for who he or she really is.

Whatever the child's problems and symptoms, they reflect the child's attitudes; the problems and symptoms disappear as the child's attitudes change. One problem for the novice therapist is these changes in attitudes are not always observable. The changes are not necessarily sequential, but rather vary from individual child to individual child. Therapy does not automatically happen when a child plays in the presence of an adult. The therapeutic process demands that the therapist responds "in constant sensitivity to the child's feelings, accepts the child's attitudes, and conveys a consistent and sincere belief in the child and a respect for him" (Moustakas, 1959, p. 33).

Some children approach the therapeutic play session with great anxiety. The anxious child may be withdrawn, fearful, or shy. This child may be overly neat in the playroom and express distress over messy or disorderly play. The child can become immobilized without the ability to begin or complete a play activity. The child may appear to be unable to think clearly or to reach a solution in the fantasy play. The child seems not to know what he or she wants to do or how to accomplish a task. The parents or child may report night terrors or unrealistic fears. The pattern of play usually moves from the inability to get started in the session to a fear of a specific person or event. Following the focused fear or anxiety event, the child becomes more confident and courageous but experiences vacillation between confidence and inadequacy, courage and fearfulness. Eventually, the child will be very specific about the fear or anxiety to an appropriate degree warranted by the event. The child will have an understanding of the event but will not let it handicap other aspects of the self or the child's life (Moustakas, 1959).

In contrast, Moustakas describes the normal child in the therapeutic environment. The normal child presents himself or herself in the relationship as open, direct, and spontaneous about personal views and experiences. The child talks about people in his or her life who are important. The child shares interests, wishes, fantasies, and attitudes with the therapist. Entrance into the playroom is marked with immediate examination of the room, challenging the boundaries of the limitations. The child is capable of very concentrated play. The child will finish projects and use a wide variety of playroom materials. The child will discard stereotypical play for that of creative and individual approaches to the playroom. Negative feelings are expressed clearly and directly with little to moderate hostility. The demand for orderliness and cleanliness is not usually present in the child; neither is he or she excessively messy or disorganized. Fears that may be expressed are realistic and appropriate to the actual threat.

Moustakas (1959) makes the observation that the normal child often sings or hums during play. The child appears happy and content, whether playing alone or working with others. The child does not seek the support or help from the therapist for things he or she is capable of doing. However, the child can and may play with the therapist comfortably without dependency or clingy behavior. The normal child is not usually intense, but rather has a wonderful sense of humor. The child may disagree with the therapist or question the therapist, especially if the child perceives the therapist's perspective as different from his or her own view.

The normal child can establish a concentrated relationship with the therapist. Although the normal child may not have problems within his or her ability to build a relationship with others, normal children still benefit from play therapy as a preventive mental health intervention. The therapeutic relationship allows the child to explore feelings and conflicts that may not be expressed appropriately in school or at home. In three or four sessions, normal children can usually resolve temporarily disturbing experiences or troubling feelings. Moustakas (1959) suggests that play therapy be included in preschool education programs.

LIMITS

Although relationship therapy may accept some of the most permissive behaviors toward the child, allowing the child to be free to be and to express the inner self, limits remain an essential ingredient for effective therapy. Moustakas (1959) says that if limits did not exist there would be no therapy. Limits define the boundaries of the relationship and help the child tie the experience to the world of reality. Limits remind the child of the child's responsibility to self, the therapist, and the playroom. Through limits the child gains security but still has the freedom to move and play safely.

Limits provide the child with the experience of coping with boundaries and reconciliation of what the child may see as conflicting roles of the therapist to encourage freedom, and yet to set limits on the types of behavior that are acceptable. Moustakas (1997) said the therapist must hold to the limits while affirming the child's right to make decisions and to express his or her will. One way he suggests is to present alternative behaviors that are safe and acceptable as possible solutions for the expression of the child's will or desires.

Moustakas (1981, 1997) expressed a concern when a child is too compliant with other children or with adults by having sacrificed impulse, energy, and spontaneity for so-called good behavior. He was especially concerned about children who are unable to express anger appropriately when the expression of anger is a valid protector for the child. Another serious concern about anger that Moustakas voiced was the child who is cold, methodical, and devious in expression. Moustakas (1997) believed when children are subjected to too much control, the child's expression of will is impaired, resulting in serious maladjustments to normal expression of a protective emotion. Therefore the therapist's limits are set not to break the child's will, but rather to protect the child's safety, resulting in a strengthening of the child's will.

These limits provide for the child's emotional and physical safety. Moustakas (1997) might say to a child who was intent on breaking a toy against the wall, "It would be fun to throw the truck against the wall, but I cannot let you do that." With more than one child in the playroom, the possibilities of doing something that might jeopardize the health of either child is greater. In a sand-throwing attempt, Moustakas might respond with the limit, "You may play with the sand, but I cannot allow you to throw it at one another."

In addition to the limits imposed for safety reasons, a time limit is placed on the child. The therapist tells the child the amount of time allotted to him or her in the playroom. When only a few minutes remain in the session, the therapist gives the child a warning, by saying how many minutes are left to play. In order to end the session, the therapist may comment, "I see that our time is up for today. We'll have to stop now" (Moustakas, 1959, p. 11). Sometimes a child asks or insists on leaving the playroom before the therapy session is complete. Moustakas (1959, 1997) handles this situation by setting the limit that the child may not return to the session until the next scheduled appointment.

Moustakas (1959) does not allow a child to damage the therapist's clothing or to abuse the therapist's person physically. He does acknowledge the child's desire to do harm to the therapist but states a clear limit to the child. His limit might sound something like this: "You would really like to cut my jacket, but that is something I cannot let you do." An important point that Moustakas (1959) makes about limits on physical aggression is that the child who is allowed to hurt another not only suffers inwardly, but the act of aggression may be the child's way to avoid loving another. The act of aggression may in reality be the child's way of expressing his or her fear of being loved or loving. The aggression is a distancing of others to avoid personal pain.

Physical aggression against the therapist is not tolerated in the playroom, but verbal aggression is not restricted. However, when Moustakas (1959, 1997) reflects on the underlying meaning of the child's aggression, the verbal attack loses its momentum and stops rather quickly. Moustakas looks at verbal aggression as an effort to communicate the child's extreme emotion about a situation and treats it as such.

Another type of limit is on materials. Moustakas only allows the child to use the toys in the playroom and not to take them home. Expensive or irreplaceable items may not be destroyed by the child. Moustakas might respond to this situation by saying, "I know you would like to stomp that flat, but I cannot let you do that."

Limits to Moustakas are part of the realities of therapy. Without limitations placed on the child's behavior, the child could venture into frightening areas that might arouse guilt and anxiety. The therapist would in turn feel discomfort and anxiety. These kinds of externally induced emotions have the potential for creating a barrier that could seriously threaten the relationship between the child and therapist. A guideline would be to set limits on those activities that interfere with the total acceptance of the child and threaten the therapeutic relationship.

Most children accept the limit placed on their activities in the playroom. However, there are children who do not accept limits and may insist on continuing an activity. When a limit is broken, the therapist must enforce the limit. Moustakas (1959) provides three ways to enforce the limit in relationship play therapy: (1) place the object or area out of bounds to the child, (2) stand by the child and repeat the limit, or (3) restrain the child for a few minutes. Restraining can be as simple as holding the child's hand and not allowing him or her to continue to play. More severely disturbed children, especially those in residential care, may require more restraint. Therapists should not use restraint methods they have not been trained to provide. The possibility of restraint needs to be discussed with the parents or guardians in cases of children with more severe disorders. Signed releases need to be secured before the therapist restrains the child beyond holding the child's hands. Having to restrain a child outside of residential treatment is rare. Moustakas (1959) does not advocate the removal of the child from the playroom when a limit has been broken.

He reminds the therapist that limits exist in every relationship. The therapeutic limit provides the boundaries for growth and meaning in the playroom. With every child the playroom experience is different because the child is different. The uniqueness of the child, the therapist, and the situation makes each session a singular, matchless experience for the child and therapist. Both the child and the therapist grow in each session because each are becoming. Because the experience of the session cannot be repeated, each session becomes a challenge for the therapist and the child. Each child and session is different from another, so the therapist may set a limit with one child but not with another. This apparent unequal application is not a reflection of the inconsistencies of the therapist but rather a reflection of the unique relationship of the therapist with each child.

The broken limit provides an opportunity for therapeutic growth that is not present in the compliant child. The struggle between the therapist and the child can hurl the relationship into hostility or despair, which creates new issues and controversies. Without the struggle, the relationship cannot result in the emergence of some final limit that can be maintained. Both the therapist and the child continue in a living relationship fraught with conflict and, ultimately, resolution. The child learns that conflict is not rejection; we are not unloved when we do not get our wishes. Conflict is treated with respect for the child and for the child's opportunity for growth. The therapist shares the experience, may suffer somewhat with the child, while continuing to express acceptance and caring for the child.

The therapist may find it easier to give in to the child or to remove the child from the playroom. These alternatives represent what Moustakas (1959) would consider the "safe" approaches to conflict. However, the safe approach cuts short

The broken limit provides an opportunity for therapeutic growth that is not present in the compliant child.

the learning and relationship experience for both the child and the therapist. Without moving into the struggle and exploration of new behaviors on the part of both the child and the therapist, a real relationship remains beyond the grasp of either. Moustakas maintains it is the willingness to plunge into the unknown therapeutic journey that provides the pain and complexity that emerges into a true relationship between the child and therapist. To allow the child to enter fully into his or her rage long enough for the child to discover what resources lie within for positive relatedness, for love and tenderness, and for self-examination and self-growth is both complex and painful for both the child and the therapist. In the final analysis, the boundary is set, the limit is maintained, and the bond of trust and respect is established between therapist and child.

PARENT INVOLVEMENT

Moustakas (1997) definitely believes in meeting with the parents and providing them with skills and knowledge about how best to help the child. Moustakas (1975) sometimes uses group therapy for the parents of children he is seeing, especially if the parents have similar problems or concerns about their children.

Moustakas (1959) indicates to the parent when he schedules the appointment that the first appointment is with the parent alone. The invitation is extended in an open manner that allows one or both parents to participate in the initial interview. If both parents wish to come to the first session, the therapist allows the parents to decide whether they will be interviewed separately or together. The goal of the first meeting with the parents is to gain an understanding of the presenting problem. After the intake interview, the therapist and parents can make a decision about whether to see the child or to refer the child to another agency or therapist. At this time the therapist can make recommendations about evaluation by the pediatrician, child psychiatrist, or other specialist, if appropriate.

Moustakas (1997) might initiate the parent interview by saying, "Please feel free to tell me what you feel is important." The discussion usually centers around the parents' concerns about the child's behavior. The focus of the initial interview is on the child with the parents discussing how the child's behavior is affecting the parent, family living, and school relations. Sharing that another family member is the source of the child's problem is not unusual. Following the description of the parents' concerns, Moustakas (1997) schedules the child's play therapy time. He invites the parents to participate in the child's experience of therapy. He might say, "Perhaps you would like to tell me about what is happening with the child from time to time or weekly. If you wish to talk to me, please feel free to contact me."

The parents are asked to sign various permission forms including permission to audiotape or videotape sessions. The one-way observation mirror is explained and who may or may not be in the room. Moustakas (1997) may have students or a person recording the interview in the observation room. The parents are told that observation by the parents without the child's knowledge would be unfair and violate the child's privacy.

Moustakas (1959, 1997) believes setting the tone of the parent interview is important. The therapist treats the parents with acceptance, respect, concern, and trust, establishing an attitude of belief in the abilities of the parents for self-exploration and growth. The therapist pays undivided attention to the parents and accepts the parents' statements without doubt. He or she attempts to see the child and the child's behavior through the parents' perceptions and experiences. The therapist displays an attitude of concern for the parents' suffering, anger, or fears. The parents' expressions of disappointment, defeat, and helplessness are met with empathy. The therapist tries to share the parenting dilemma and the process of growth toward a healthy relationship with the parents. The therapist's attentions and empathy encourage the parents to continue with open expression about feelings surrounding the child without guilt or remorse.

Parents are not forced to participate in therapy for themselves. However, the therapist does assure the parents that he or she is willing to meet with them regularly or on an as needed basis in conjunction with the child therapy. Moustakas (1959) poses the invitation like this: "If you'd like to come in to discuss further your experiences and relationships, I would be very much interested in exploring them with you" (p. 253). If the parents do not seem interested, they are asked to come in occasionally to discuss the child's progress and experience in the playroom.

Parents are allowed to join the child in the playroom, if the child insists a parent be present. The parent may remain throughout the first session or as long as the child deems the parent's presence necessary. Moustakas (1997) has found that the presence of the parent does not appear to obstruct the therapy process. For some children the presence of the parent may assist the play therapy process. A plus for the parent's presence is that the parent has the opportunity to gain knowledge and skills in communication with the child through the direct observation of the therapist with the child.

When parents make a request for information about therapy, Moustakas (1997) provides them with a brief review of the course of therapy. The child's fantasies, stories, or other specific activities are not shared because this would be considered a violation of the child's privacy. The therapist focuses on the feelings of the parents and may provide child development information when indicated. Family therapy is advocated when it suits the needs and desires of the child in therapy.

Moustakas (1959) makes an observation about the classical case of Little Hans (Freud, 1907, 1908, 1909), which was presented in more detail in Chapter 3. He saw the case of Little Hans as teaching parents and others with significant relationships with the child about the damage of encouraging a child to sleep with the mother, engaging in excessive caresses and fondling. The classic case study shows the devastating effects of inconsistent and contradictory parenting. In addition, the case substantiates that parents or others in a close relationship with the child are inappropriate to provide therapy to their own troubled children.

Moustakas (1959) believes children can benefit from therapy without the parents concurrently entering into therapy. He indicates it is desirable for at least one parent to be available for interviews at each session. The parents' participation in at least the weekly feedback session with the therapist helps achieve therapeutic goals more quickly.

Most parents, according to Moustakas (1959), usually see the importance of their inclusion in the therapeutic process. These parents may seek to understand and improve their relationship with the child, to have a sounding board for their interests and concerns, and to look at new ways to work with their child. Although parents are influential in the child's life, the parents are not blamed for the child's emotional difficulties. Many problems arise for the child in the course of living and in engaging in significant relationships. Problems grow out of the challenges faced by the family. Many difficulties are beyond the control of the parents. Therefore the therapist approaches the parents with the attitude that each and every parent does the best he or she can to parent the child.

When a parent brings a child to therapy, the parent is conveying concern and love for the child at some level. Moustakas (1959) recognizes that other factors may motivate the parent to bring the child to therapy, but even so, most parents of children needing therapy are struggling and searching for a way to cope with their child. Moustakas believes it is rare to find a parent who actually feels rejection and hatred for the child. Many parents tend to identify the child's difficulties as their fault and personal failure. The parents often communicate they have made every effort to help the child using the parenting skills they possess. The parents are often overwhelmed with the child's problems, resulting in feeling confused, uncertain, and bewildered about what to do. The parent may articulate that the child hates them.

Parents were found by Moustakas (1959) to respond best to suggestions and advice, as opposed to being told what to do and what not to do with the child. The

Parents were found by Moustakas (1959) to respond best to suggestions and advice, as opposed to being told what to do and what not to do with the child.

therapist needs to realize the parents may be struggling with facing their own issues, exploring the nature of their experiences, and reaching a solution through their insight and self-examination. The parents need to be encouraged to share their experiences in parenting the child. This feeling includes not only their frustrations, feelings of inadequacy, parenting fears, and resentments toward the child, but the joys and rewards of being parents. The therapist encourages the parents to share their own experiences as children with their parents, the child's grandparents. Through these discussions, the therapist can understand what kind of parenting skills were modeled for the parents.

TERMINATION

Termination is determined by three factors: child terminates, parent terminates, or therapeutic goal becomes obvious. Moustakas (1997) elicits information about desired changes from parents, school, or other significant others, as well as the child's play. His case studies indicate that a lengthy or ritual good-bye session is not part of his procedure. The child may simply decide he or she no longer needs therapy and choose not to continue. The parent may become satisfied with the changes and not bring the child back. Moustakas appears to decide with the child when it is time to end sessions, when possible. He terminates the sessions by saying something like "I have enjoyed working with you. It has been a pleasure getting to know you. Good-bye."

ASSESSMENT AND TECHNIQUES

Moustakas (1997) does not use any assessment or diagnosis in the process of therapy. He believes the use of assessment and diagnosis undermines the concepts basic to relationship therapy. He values observation of how the child sees and directs his or her life. He looks for the unique qualities and the potentials that become apparent during the course of therapy. Moustakas regards the assessment and diagnosis part of therapy to be relationship focused, paying special attention to what is observed in therapy with regard to the relationship toward the therapist and adults that are naturally part of the child's life. The observation is not formal, but more a series of impressions and reflections by the therapist of the living relationship and experiences in therapy.

Although certainly not within the definitions or descriptions of relationship therapy provided by Moustakas (1959, 1997), the therapist wishing to ascribe to this theory of play therapy may find it becomes necessary to deal with third-party payments by offering some type of diagnosis. Moustakas uses the parent interview described earlier. He collects necessary professional documents including informed consent and permission to consult and to release information from the legal guardians. Structured techniques or assessments, however, are not part of relationship play therapy.

SUMMARY

Relationship or existential play therapy represents the most permissive of the play therapies. Moustakas is less focused on limits on children's behaviors than other theorists. He allows the child to do anything that does not hurt the therapist or destroy expensive property. Although relationship play therapy shares many tenets with other humanistic theories, it sees the relationship as the most important contributor to the growth and healing of the child in therapy. In order to assure this relationship, the therapeutic environment must have minimal restrictions on exploration of the self and the relationship between the child and the therapists.

CHAPTER 9

COGNITIVE-BEHAVIORAL PLAY THERAPY

The child is writing emotion words on the feeling wall with the therapist.

In this chapter we examine cognitive-behavioral play therapy (CBPT). Susan Knell (1993, 1998; Knell & Moore, 1990) is considered the founder of this theory of play therapy. Cognitive-behavior play therapy features goal-directed interventions, relying heavily on the theoretical framework of both cognitive and behavioral therapies while remaining sensitive to the developmental needs of children. Using play, cognitive change is indirectly imparted to the child, so positive behaviors can be taught. CBPT uses modeling, generalization, and response prevention as interventions.

INTRODUCTION

Cognitive-behavioral play therapy (CBPT) is based on behavioral and cognitive theories of emotional development and psychopathology and on the interventions derived from these theories. It incorporates cognitive and behavioral interventions within a play therapy paradigm. Play activities, as well as verbal and nonverbal communication, are used. CBPT provides a theoretical framework based on cognitive-behavioral principles. In addition, CBPT integrates principles in a developmentally sensitive manner (Knell, 1997).

Cognitive therapy, as founded by Aaron Beck (1976; Beck, Freeman, & Davis, 2003), has been applied to a broad range of adult populations but was not appropriate for use with adolescents or children without some modifications. Beck's theory lacked the necessary developmental aspects needed for working with children and adolescents. Young children lack the verbal skills required for cognitive therapy. Therefore the more traditional form of play therapy was incorporated into cognitive and behavioral concepts. CBPT was developed specifically for use with children between the ages of 2 1/2 and 6 years of age. Knell and Moore (1990) first published the use of this integrated model of cognitive, behavioral, and play therapy.

CBPT therapists understand the young child does not have the experiences or the cognitive processing ability of an adult. Therefore what is normal in a child would be considered cognitive distortions in an adult. The preoperational child is egocentric and developmentally limited in his or her ability to conceptualize a situation from another's point of view. These perceptions can be modified, however, through increasing experiences. Hence a child who may fear taking a bath for fear of going down the drain can be taught through repeated experiences that the fear is irrational. Although the child's fear is a developmentally appropriate cognitive distortion, the same type of cognitive distortion can become problematic if experiences do not counter the cognition and restructure cognition.

Because of their developmental stage and lack of experience, children may not attach a set of beliefs or meanings to an event or situation. The result of this lack of associated meaning or beliefs is that the child may fail to develop adaptive beliefs to aid his or her coping behaviors.

The three major premises of cognitive therapy are that (1) thoughts influence a child's response to events; (2) perceptions and interpretations of events are based on the child's beliefs; and (3) the child who experiences problems has errors in logic. The child is likely to make assumptions that are unspoken and erroneous. For example, "My parents are divorcing because I was bad."

Cognitive-behavioral therapy, as implied in its name, incorporates both tenets from cognitive therapy and behavioral therapy through the venue of play. CBPT uses play activities to help the child resolve problems. The emphasis on the child's involvement in treatment is unique to behavioral approaches, which either act on the child or instruct others in ways to act on the child without regard to the child's feelings or cognitions. In CBPT the child is active in the therapy and shares his or her thoughts or feelings with the therapist. Issues of control, mastery, and responsibility for personal behavior and the need for change are focused on with the child in the playroom environment. Knell (1993) has identified six specific properties that she believes effect the efficacy of CBPT:

1. involves the child in treatment via play;
2. focuses on the child's thoughts, feelings, fantasies, and environment;
3. provides a strategy or strategies for developing more adaptive thoughts and behaviors;
4. is structured, directive, and goal-oriented, rather than open-ended;
5. incorporates empirically demonstrated techniques; and
6. allows for an empirical examination of treatment (Knell, 1993).

CBPT is similar to other forms of play therapy in several ways. Like other forms of play therapy, CBPT sees the development of a relationship as crucial to therapy. Establishing contact with the child, engaging the child's cooperation in treatment, and gaining the child's trust is imperative for the success of therapy. Another similarity between CBPT and other forms of play therapy is the use of play therapy as a treatment modality and means of communication. CBPT therapists create a sense of safety and security in the therapeutic session, a highly valued concept in all forms of play therapy. As in other kinds of play therapy, CBPT therapists acquire clues to understanding how the child views himself or herself and others. In addition, conflicts, fantasies, and problem-solving approaches are expressed in the play therapy session in all its forms.

Although CBPT may share many tenets of play therapy with other forms, it differs significantly in many ways. Knell (1993) says that CBPT differs from other play therapy along these lines:

1. Therapeutic goals are established; direction toward goals is the basis of intervention.
2. Both the child and the therapist select materials and activities.
3. Play is used to teach skills and alternative behaviors.
4. Therapist verbalizes the conflicts and irrational logic to the child.
5. Praise is a crucial component. Praise communicates to the child which behaviors are appropriate and reinforces the child (social reward system).

Behavioral interventions used are systematic desensitization, time-out, positive reinforcement, shaping, extinction, and differential reinforcement of other behaviors. Cognitive interventions used are self-monitoring, activity scheduling, recording dysfunctional thoughts, bibliotherapy (Kircher & Catholic University of America, 1944; Lenkowsky, 1987; Scogin, 2003; Taylor, 2004; Vare & Norton, 2004; Warren, 2002), and coping self-statements. These interventions are described later in the chapter.

TOY SELECTION

The types of toys or materials offered to the child in CBPT include books, stories, structured workbooks, drawing and art materials, sculpting materials, puppets, and doll play. The therapy room includes a large assortment of materials. Dolls, puppets, action figures, art materials, and other toys are available. The CBPT therapist may also use board games, card games, and charts that address specific types of problem behaviors.

Bibliotherapy is the use of books, stories, recordings, and structured workbooks that address specific topics. The CBPT therapist believes the merits of reading and sharing stories with children are numerous. The first is the understanding that other children have experienced similar circumstances or events. The stories help normalize the feelings the child is experiencing. The child may wish to write a book about his or her own experiences to be shared with other children. So the CBPT therapist may have commercially prepared books, stories, recordings, or workbooks, as well as child-prepared stories and books. The selected books need to have a positive resolution to the problem and model expression of the child's feelings. The stories must present the solution in an indirect way that leaves the child audience the freedom to apply the theme and develop their own resolution to their personal situation without judgment. Davis's (1990, 1996) *Once Upon a Time* story series provides a collection of short stories aimed at specific child problems and concerns. Books and workbooks designed around a special topic may also be used. An example is *Red Flag, Green Flag* (Freed, 1985), a workbook developed to help children identify different types of touching. Many such books are available from play therapy equipment suppliers, which can be located through the Association for Play Therapy Web site: www.a4pt.org. A search by topic of the major book sellers online can quickly help the therapist locate some excellent children's books. Librarians have special training in selecting and locating such books and are a valuable resource.

ROLE OF THE THERAPIST

The initial task of the cognitive-behavioral play therapist is to conduct a thorough assessment of the child. Assessment does not differ greatly from other assessments procedures used by other theorists. The assessment information is couched in relationship to normal development, making it imperative for the CBPT therapist to be knowledgeable in human growth and development. Of particular interest to the assessment process are the child's "self-statements, attributions, beliefs, and assumptions" (Knell, 1998, p. 30). The information is gathered through observation, parent/ guardian reports, interviews, play assessment, standardized assessment instruments, and tasks the therapist may ask the child to provide. The therapist focuses on the cognitive distortions of deficiencies of the child. Throughout the process of assessment, the CBPT therapist is sensitive to the criticalness of the child's developmental issues.

The assessment is followed by interventions intended to increase the child's competence, change the child's thinking, or to teach the child adaptive behaviors (Knell, 1998). In planning the intervention, the therapist examines and capitalizes on the child's strengths as opposed to the child's weaknesses. The interventions are designed to be experiential rather than complex verbal activities. The therapist uses art, music, toys, and other nonverbal media to help the child with expression. Even though CBPT emphasizes less verbal expression, the CBPT therapist encourages language development, making connections between behaviors and feelings and learning to express maladjusted behaviors and cognitions with more adjusted cognitions and behaviors.

The CBPT therapist is guided by measurable objectives and designs interventions to meet these objectives. The therapist is very directive in interventions. The child is allowed choices within the structured environment the therapist provides. As with other types of play therapy, rapport building is essential for the child to feel trust for the therapist to provide effective interventions. The therapist works to make the child feel he or she is in a safe, secure environment to explore and express the child's behaviors and cognitions.

The therapist must be familiar with the behavioral techniques of modeling, systematic desensitization, contingency management, shaping, and other forms of behavioral modification. The therapist must also know how to challenge maladaptive ideas, cognitive restructuring, and other cognitive strategies. Beyond the basic concepts and their application, the therapist must be able to develop creative ways to assist the child in using these techniques. The therapist uses the toys, puppets, games, books, or other concrete objects to take these concepts and make them understandable to the child.

The role of the cognitive-behavioral therapist differs from other play therapists in that the therapy sessions are used to educate the child about appropriate behavior and cognitions about events or situations the child faces. The therapist chooses and directs the play activities to achieve goals established through the assessment. The therapist is very active in the child's activities, using praise and interpretations to educate the child in appropriate behaviors.

The therapist is very active in the child's activities, using praise and interpretations to educate the child in appropriate behaviors. This child is dealing with loss of a loved one and constructing a memorial stone.

STRUCTURING THE SESSION

The session starts with a comprehensive assessment. Following assessment and the development of measurable behavioral goals, the CBPT therapist looks at appropriate behavioral techniques: modeling, systematic desensitization, bibliotherapy, rehearsal, identifying and correcting maladaptive beliefs, and positive self-statements. The techniques and interventions are described later in this chapter. The therapist develops a series of scenarios or vignettes that would be helpful in providing modeling and learning of prosocial behaviors the therapist might use with the child.

The therapist may provide the parents with a picture book or other age-appropriate book that addresses play therapy. *A Child's First Book about Play Therapy* (Nemiroff, Annunziata, & Scott, 1990) is one book Knell recommends. Several books have been published since Nemiroff et al. (1990) that may be more age appropriate or provide a slightly different orientation to play therapy. Other books that may be related to the play therapy experience or the child's specific problem may be used in early treatment by the therapist or the parents. Knell (1997) prefers to work collaboratively with the parents and the child in preparation for therapy.

The first few sessions are usually observations of the child's spontaneous play, and verbalizations are used to continue the evaluation procedure. During this time the therapist may use puppets to gather information on an incomplete sentence form or do various drawing assessments to infer how the child may feel about the situation or event. The vignettes tied to specific goals are then used with the child to model the desired behavior. An example might be:

[Goal 1: Increase expression of feelings related to moving to father's house.]

Puppet: I used to live with my mom, then she got sick and now I live with my dad.

Child: I have to go live with my dad, now that my mom is sick.

Puppet: I was a little afraid that my dad wouldn't want me at first. He has other kids now. (A fear the child has expressed to his guardian.)

Child: Me, too.

Puppet: I was afraid I wouldn't like my stepmother.

Child: My stepmother is pretty, but she will never be my mother.

Puppet: It was a little hard at first. The other kids are younger than me. I am a big brother. I call my stepmother Mary. Mary said I could call her Mother someday, but not until I am ready.

The middle stages of treatment focus on helping the child learn adaptive ways to respond to individual situations, problems, or stressors. By this time, the therapist has a more definitive perspective on what toys or activities are most therapeutic. The therapist is also aware of what types of activities and toys have been met with indifference. The therapist sets additional goals, as needed, for the middle stage of treatment. The activities and vignettes are created or selected to accomplish these new goals. Two key concerns emerge during this time: are the adaptive behaviors in therapy generalizing to other settings, and are the adaptive behaviors reinforced enough to be maintained and to avoid relapse after the termination of treatment? Treatment goals in the middle therapy process are designed to move the child into mastery of adaptive behavior. Because children are not always able to maintain new behaviors on their own, involving the parents is very necessary. The attitudes the parents display for the child and the support they provide have a great impact on whether the child has a relapse or not.

In order for the child to generalize the behaviors to another setting, the therapist must provide specific training. The significant individuals in the child's life need to be included in the treatment plan and provided with instruction on how and when to reinforce the child's adaptive behavior. The therapist encourages procedures that further self-control and interventions that will continue past the first demonstration of the adaptive behavior to ensure mastery of the adaptive behavior. As in most behavioral change programs, the therapist needs to warn the significant adults that the child may indeed get worse before he or she gets better. Even after the initial setbacks, further setbacks may occur in the subsequent or new situations. The significant others should not consider these setbacks a failure of the child, the adults, or the program; but rather part of the learning process.

LIMITS

In her book, Knell (1993) addresses limits as a form of directive therapy. She points out that the importance of limit setting was first emphasized as an intervention by Bixler (1949). Subsequent play therapy theorists (Allen, 1942; Axline, 1989) have discussed that some children do not accept limits on their behavior and limits are often broken. Bixler (1949) is credited with giving direction to the therapist on how to handle the therapy session when limits are broken. According to Knell (1993), Bixler (1949) indicated that limits are essential but should be minimal and determined by the therapist's comfort level. Generally, Bixler (1949) recommended that children should not be allowed to hurt the therapist, destroy property, violate time restraints, or take toys from the playroom.

Ginott (1959, 1994; Ginott, Ginott, & Goddard, 2003) was also acknowledged by Knell (1993) as having established that children need clear guidelines about therapy and everyday life. Ginott said that children need to understand which behaviors are acceptable and which are not. Through limit setting, adults communicate to children a sense of security and protection. Further, Ginott indicated that acting-out children can experience negative feelings without negative consequences in the therapy session. This experience in therapy allows the child to gain control over his or her emotions.

The history of play therapy took a new critical direction with the introduction of limit setting (Knell, 1993). Knell believes that limit setting, as described by Bixler (1949) and Ginott (1994), might be the first example of the therapist taking the stance of a directive, structured, and goal-directed intervention with the child. The cognitive-behavioral therapist takes Bixler's (1949) article title as a mantra: "limits are therapy."

Cognitive-behavioral therapy, in summary, uses reinforcement, social or other, to stop problematic behaviors. Where Bixler (1949) would have reflected feelings, the CBPT therapist poses hypotheses of the child's cognitions. Where Bixler (1949) would have set a limit or said no, the CBPT therapist does not acknowledge the bad behavior and reinforces the good behavior. Where Bixler (1949) might have provided alternative behaviors, CBPT therapists model alternative behaviors through activities.

PARENT INVOLVEMENT

The parents are extensively involved in the support of therapy. They complete the Child Behavioral Checklist (Achenbach & Edelbrock, 1982), followed by an extensive interview to describe specifically the problematic behavior. Both parents are interviewed and complete the checklist. The discrepancies are examined and the perceptions of the parents are compared. The parents' perceptions indicate which parent may be experiencing the greatest stress from the problematic behavior of the child.

Parents are often asked to assist the child by recording information the child is not able to record. The parent may be asked to record when the problematic behavior occurs and how often.

The therapist may set goals for the parents in conjunction with the therapeutic goals for the child. These goals usually involve helping the parents structure the child's home life and develop contingency management plans to reward good behavior. Parenting skills and suggestions are made as needed to assist the parents in the ongoing monitoring and reinforcement of the child's behavioral changes.

The parents may receive instruction on how to help the child make positive, adaptive self-statements to improve self-esteem. Parent education may be advised to help the child with appropriate emotional expression and problem solving. Parents may be referred to another therapist for marital or individual therapy.

TERMINATION

Termination is introduced to the child over several sessions. Children, parents, and therapists usually have mixed feelings about termination. The therapist may broach the subject by reminding the child how many sessions are left until the final session. The therapist may also begin to space the appointments at wider intervals. Using naturally occurring events, like school starting, the child's birthday, vacation times, or holidays, may be meaningful ways to communicate the time of the final appointment to the child. The purpose of talking about termination with the child is to assure the child that he or she is ready to manage the adaptive behavior(s) apart from the therapist. Extending the time between the appointments allows the child to experience this independence from the therapist and allows the therapist to gauge the strength of the adaptive behavior. If the child maintains the adaptive behavior well between appointments, termination is indicated. If the behavior is not maintained, the therapist and significant adults need to reexamine what is happening and take corrective actions.

Knell (1997) cautions that children who find it difficult to part with the therapist may think all they have to do is to revert to their old behaviors to resume seeing the therapist. Knell suggests that to avoid this possibility the therapist provide the child with more positive ways to connect. Telephone calls from the parent, cards from the child, or brief visits from the child may be allowable. The therapist has to decide what is appropriate for the therapeutic setting and the child's situation.

ASSESSMENT AND TECHNIQUES

Assessment figures importantly in the CBPT and is approached from a normal development perspective. Behavior problems are considered normal development that has been interrupted or derailed by events, individual differences, or trauma. Extensive information is gathered from the parents concerning the child's problematic behaviors. The parent is asked to be very specific in describing concerns and to provide examples. Additional assessment information is sought from other sources, especially the day care provider, school, babysitter, or other persons with whom the child spends a great deal of time. The child is also interviewed to learn his or her perceptions of the problem. And finally, the therapist evaluates the parent's and child's readiness to enter into and commit to treatment. In addition to interviews, specific standardized assessment tools are used to collect data.

Parent-Report Measures

The *Child Behavior Checklist (CBCL)* (Achenbach & Edelbrock, 1982) is a standardized checklist the parents complete for children ages 4 to 16. A special form is available for 2- to 3-year-old children. The instrument measures social competence and behavior problems. The behavioral problems scale is compared to normal children's scores. The summative scores indicate internalizing and externalizing problems in the parent's perception. The instrument allows for both screening pretreatment and measuring treatment effectiveness posttreatment.

The *Minnesota Child Development Inventory (MCDI)* (Ireton & Thwing, 1972) provides a 320-item instrument that parents or other significant adults answer with yes or no to each item. The instrument is designed to be used with 1- to 6-year-old children. The MCDI provides a developmental status on six different scales.

Intelligence and Personality Measures

The *Thematic Apperception Test (TAT)* (Murray, 1943) and *Children's Apperception Test (CAT)* (Bellak & Bellak, 1949) are critiqued by Knell (1993). The TAT has stimulus pictures intended for adults, which may cause problems for children. The CAT, although designed for children, in one form has pictures using animals in human situations. Knell (1993) found that children do not always take the pictures seriously. Because of the problematic nature of the pictures used in the instrument, Knell (1993) supports McArthur's (1976) belief that children's responses may be more of a reaction to the stimulus pictures than indications of their unique personality characteristics. The scoring and interpretation of these instruments are subjective, require specialized training, and lack standardized scoring.

Robert's Apperception Test for Children (McArthur & Roberts, 1982) is designed for school-aged children from 6 to 15 years of age. The pictures used depict children in different activities. Sixteen stimulus cards are presented to the child. Gender-specific cards are used in some of the situations. Stimulus cards show parent-child, sibling, and peer relationships in the home and school. The cards have issues and situations in which aggression and mastery are represented. Separate cards are available for racial minority children; however, the racial minority cards are not normed.

The therapist and child are conducting a puppet sentence completion.

The *Sentence Completion Test* is a projective technique used to gain information about the child's thoughts, perceptions, assumptions, and underlying beliefs, in essence, the child's cognitions. The sentence completion can be written by the therapist for a specific child or a commercial one can be purchased. Several commercial sentence completions are available. Usually, the sentence completion is a set of 10 to 20 sentence stems and the child writes the completed sentences. Young children under the age of 5 or 6 are not developmentally ready to respond to the sentence completion in a coherent manner (Knell, 1993). Here are some examples of the type of sentence stems used in sentence completion:

My mother _____.

At school, I _____.

I am most upset by _____.

My favorite thing is _____.

I want _____.

The *Puppet Sentence Completion Task* (Knell, 1993) was modeled after the Sentence Completion Test. Knell's (1993) instructions for conducting the puppet sentence completion test suggest that the therapist first provides a model for answering the test with two puppets. One of the puppets reads the question and the second puppet completes the sentence. The first puppet writes down the answer for the second puppet. An example:

Therapist's first puppet, a dragon, says: I will read the beginning of a sentence and then you will finish it with the first thought that you have. I like _____.

The second puppet, a turtle, says: ice cream.

Therapist's dragon puppet responds: Very good. Now, finish this one. My mom always _____.

The examples that the therapist uses with his or her puppets should not be the same ones that are on the sentence completion, as this will provide the child with a set response.

Then the therapist lets the child choose a puppet to finish sentences that the therapist will write down. The therapist may continue to use one of the puppets to "read" the incomplete sentences to the child. One foreseeable problem with allowing the child to use a puppet to answer is that the child may provide only fantasy answers. The method could also allow the child to answer more honestly through the puppet providing the answers. The therapist will have to use his or her own judgment as to which is the best methodology. Here are examples of the type of sentences to be completed:

I like to _____.

My dad is _____.

The thing that scares me is _____.

My parents are _____.

The therapist's puppet reads the stem and the child's puppet fills in the blank. If the child gives two responses, one for the puppet and one for himself or herself, both responses are recorded in the blank.

Feeling Scales/Drawings uses a feeling chart with pictures of people's faces or drawings of faces. Children are asked to choose the face that indicates how they are feeling at this time. They may be asked to indicate how they feel following a particular activity. Children can also be asked to tell a story about a face and then asked to share a time they felt the same way. Feeling charts, feeling cards, and even small magnetic cards are available from many sources. Most teacher supply stores have a wide selection of feeling charts.

Play Assessments

Play assessments are not generally formal or standardized measures. However, the CBPT uses free play to make some tentative hypotheses about the developmental level of the child.

Behavioral Techniques

System desensitization is based on the premise that a child cannot have two responses at once; therefore, the child is taught an adaptive response to replace the fear or anxiety response. Because the body cannot be relaxed and anxious or afraid at the same time, the fear or anxiety-provoking stimulus is paired or presented with a relaxing event. In CBPT, the child is engaged in a relaxing and enjoyable activity in the playroom and the provoking stimulus is moved closer to the child until it no longer creates fear or anxiety in the child. The child is given positive statements to make to himself or herself that are aimed at self-encouragement and self-affirmation to keep anxiety or fear low. The therapist provides positive feedback in verbal responses like, "You are doing well" "Great job." "I knew you could do it."

Knell (1993) gives an example of a child fearful of being in a room with a closed door. The child begins by playing with the toys in a room with the therapist and the door open, which has never created the fear response. The door is slowly closed over several sessions. Then the child is moved to a smaller room with the door open, and gradually the door is closed over five or so sessions. Ultimately, the child is left to play alone with the door open, and slowly the door is closed over 10 or so sessions. The child finally can play alone in a small room with the door closed for 2 minutes or more and can ride in an elevator from one floor to another. The key to the success of this technique is to make the increments toward the desired behavior small enough that the child does not become overwhelmed with fear or anxiety. Knell's (1993) case example took 23 steps to go from play with toys in a large room with the door open to riding in an elevator to the next floor.

Contingency management is a behavioral term for controlling when, how, and who will reinforce desired responses to modify behavior and to structure the consequences (Knell, 1993). The contingency management programs are set up in the play therapy session to reward the child for specific behaviors. The child may be placed on a token economy, where the child is given stars or points for specific behaviors exhibited in the playroom. The tokens (e.g., stars, tally marks) may be cashed in for time with a special toy or activity.

However, the most common type of contingency management is positive reinforcement, which is often used without intentionality on the part of most play therapists. When the therapist pays more attention to a particular play behavior or may compliment a child on his or her achievement, the therapist is positively reinforcing the child. Any indication to the child that his or her behavior is appropriate or pleasing is positive social reinforcement. Social reinforcement is one of the strongest forms of positive reinforcement. The CBPT uses positive reinforcement with intentionality, targeting specific behaviors that will be socially reinforced and those that will not receive any reaction, verbal or nonverbal. The therapist might decide to say, "You really did that well" any time the child can complete a self-chosen task in the playroom.

Shaping, or **successive approximations,** is a special application of positive reinforcement. Positive reinforcement is a reward that increases the frequency of the desired response. Successive approximation is giving the child rewards when the child's behavior is almost what the therapist is seeking (Knell, 1993). The therapist may encourage the child toward a given behavior by making statements like "I like it when you help pick up the toys." Then when the child picks up even one toy and puts it on the shelf, the therapist responds, "I like the way you put that up." The same technique can be applied to emotions. When the therapist gives voice to hypothesized emotions, he or she is helping the child learn to express feelings and encouraging the verbalization of feelings in the session. When the child verbalizes an emotion, the therapist socially reinforces that expression by repeating it or expanding on it.

Discriminative stimulus describes what happens when a child behaves appropriately with a specific person or in a specific setting but not in other settings.

Sometimes children have learned to behave an appropriate way in the therapy hour, but appropriate behavior may not be observed in another setting. The therapist may need to see the child in the other setting to help transfer the learning to the new site. The therapist gradually ceases to participate with the child at school. This weaning away is termed *stimulus fading*. The behavior has transferred to the new setting but is no longer associated with the presence of the therapist.

Extinction occurs when the reward is not given for a behavior. When the behavior is no longer getting rewarded, the child will stop the behavior (Knell, 1993). Extinction is a method used with a reinforcement program. Through *differential reinforcement of other behavior (DRO)*, a incompatible and different behavior is reinforced as opposed to the maladaptive behavior.

Time-out is a technique whereby the child is stopped from an undesirable behavior and must wait a period of time before returning to a desired activity (Knell, 1993). The time-out may have the child sitting in a chair facing the therapist for a few minutes, may be taking the child outside the playroom for a few minutes, or similar activities. Classroom teacher interventions for bad behavior of sitting in the corner or sitting in the hall are familiar forms of time-out. Whatever form the therapist chooses, it is important that the time-out location does not offer reward in its self. One reason that placing a child in a busy hallway does not work is because of the attention the child gets from passersby may be more rewarding than being in the playroom. A short period of time is as effective as a longer period of time in time-out. Time-out needs to be used sparingly in therapy because it has the disadvantage of removing the child from the therapeutic interaction with the therapist.

Modeling is a social learning concept in which the child learns by observing the behavior of others. The therapist may use puppets, dolls, or stuffed animals to show the desired behavior to the child. The therapist directs a story or activity in which the puppet models the proper behavior with the therapist, encouraging and verbally rewarding the puppet for its appropriate behavior. A disadvantage to this technique is that the child may ignore the model or choose not to imitate the model. The therapist may introduce the modeling activity while acting out a story line incorporating the child's problematic behavior. Modeling allows the therapist to provide the child indirectly with an example of appropriate behavior without directly confronting the child's behavior.

Behavioral rehearsal allows the child to practice a new skill until he or she has mastered the skill. The goal of behavioral rehearsal is to teach a child a variety of acceptable responses through role playing that will replace the unacceptable behaviors the child has learned. Puppets or other toys may be used to practice new behaviors in a variety of situations.

Cognitive Techniques

Self-monitoring is a technique in which the child is asked to record instances of certain types of behaviors. Activities or events can be easily monitored by young children with the use of charts. Older children may be able to journal or to use simple rating scales from 1 to 10. A child may be given a Likert scale to rate feelings of anger from 0 to 10 with 0 being no anger and 10 being the desire to hit someone.

Activity scheduling is useful with children who are depressed, withdrawn, or very anxious. Activities are scheduled for the child to attempt to do. The pressure of being successful at the activity is removed and the child is more likely to respond to the activity with enjoyment. If the child does the activity without enjoying it, the child is still reinforced for attempting the activity. Knell (1992) presents what she terms "no-choice choices" in which a child is not given a choice of a behavior but is given a choice of how it is executed. An example might be "Do you want to dance to the fast music or to the slow music?" The child must dance but has a choice about the music.

Cognitive change strategies are often referred to as challenging irrational beliefs. The process for challenging these underlying faulty beliefs involves examining the evidence, exploring the alternatives, and determining the consequences of the beliefs. Because of the child's limited experience and cognitive development, play allows the child or therapist to enact the scenario, pose alternative scenarios, and demonstrate possible consequences for the child. The play scenarios may occur naturally within the play session or be posed by the therapist.

Coping self-statements are based on the idea that a child is not disturbed by the event but rather by the way the child interprets the event. How the child interprets the event results in self-statements about the event and its meaning to the child. Young children may need adults to repeat affirmations for them or model using coping self-statements until they reach a higher level of cognitive development.

Bibliotherapy is used when the child is read a story that is similar to his or her own difficulties, but the main characters of the story provide an appropriate solution to the situation.

Bibliotherapy (Kircher & Catholic University of America, 1944; Lenkowsky, 1987; Scogin, 2003; Taylor, 2004; Vare & Norton, 2004; Warren, 2002) is the use of books and stories to help children with specific problems. The stories can be created especially for the child by the therapist. The story will have a similar situation or the exact situation that is problematic for the child. In the story, alternatives to the problematic behaviors are provided and illustrated with consequences. A large market exists for commercially prepared stories, and many are available through various publishers of therapeutic play therapy supplies.

SUMMARY

Cognitive-behavioral play therapy (CBPT) is a form of play therapy based on the tenets of traditional cognitive and behavioral therapies adapted for children. From cognitive and behavioral therapy CBPT takes the concepts of emotional development and psychopathology. CBPT uses interventions from both cognitive and behavioral therapies in a play therapy paradigm. The developmentally sensitive application of play therapy grounded in the theoretical framework of cognitive-behavioral principles provides the therapist with an active and directive methodology to intervene in the lives of troubled children.

CHAPTER 10

CHILD DEVELOPMENTAL PLAY THERAPIES

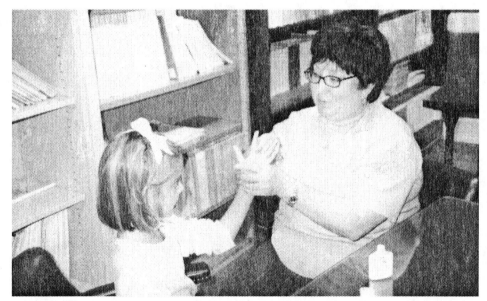

Hills and Valleys is an activity that Brody used in the dialogue of touch, a developmental play therapy technique.

In this chapter we explore two prevalent developmental theories of play therapy as espoused by their respective founders, Viola A. Brody (1997), Ann M. Jernberg, and Phyllis B. Booth (1999b). Brody has called her theory developmental play therapy. She is most famous for her text The Dialogue of Touch *(1997). Theraplay was developed by Jernberg and Booth (1999a) to help parents and children improve their relationship through play activities. Both of these theories are strongly identified with attachment theory and draw heavily from Bowlby and Ainsworth's (1991) work on attachment theory. The chapter begins with an overview of attachment theories.*

INTRODUCTION

The theoretical framework for child developmental play theories is attachment theory, which as we know it today is primarily the results of the joint work of John Bowlby and Mary Salter Ainsworth (Ainsworth & Bowlby, 1991). Bowlby conceptualized the theory, and Ainsworth developed innovative methodology to test and expand his hypotheses (Bretherton, 1992).

Bowlby studied with Melanie Klein in his postgraduate work at the London Child Guidance Clinic. Because of his experience in both pre- and postgraduate work, Bowlby began to doubt that the child's difficulties are separate from the relationship with the parents, especially the primary caregiver. One of his first discoveries was that the mother's experiences and feelings as a child in an atmosphere of acceptance and tolerance transfers to the mother, providing acceptance and tolerance in her offspring. This transgenerational transmission of attachment intrigued Bowlby as a possible method to treat maladjusted children (Bretherton, 1992). Related, but not the same, were the psychoanalytic object-relations theories of Fairbain (1952) and Winnicott (1958, 1965).

Mary Salter Ainsworth developed one of the major tenets of security theory when she indicated that young children need a secure dependence on their parents before encountering unfamiliar situations (Salter, 1940). After her marriage to Ainsworth, she moved to London from Toronto in 1950. Through a newspaper advertisement she accepted a position as a research assistant to John Bowlby. The initial research project under Bowlby's direction was examining the effect on the child's personality of separation from the mother. In the 1950s research unit, Ainsworth worked with James Robertson, Mary Boston, Dian Rosenbluth, Rudolph Schaffer, and later with Christoph Heinicke and Tony Ambrose, all contributors to attachment theory research.

During this time Bowlby was commissioned by the World Health Organization (WHO) to write a report on the mental health status of homeless and displaced children in Europe after World War II. The report was first published by WHO as *Maternal Care and Mental Health* (1951). Mary Ainsworth printed a revision in 1965 entitled *Child Care and the Growth of Love*. Both books concluded the infant needs to experience a warm, intimate, and continuous relationship with the primary caregiver if the child is to be healthy. The text pleaded that society provide economic and emotional support for the primary caregiver.

"The Nature of the Child's Tie to His Mother" (Bowlby, 1958), "Separation Anxiety" (Bowlby, 1959), "Grief and Mourning in Infancy and Early Childhood" (Bowlby, 1960), and two unpublished papers (Bowlby, 1962a, 1962b) represent the basis of attachment theory (Bretherton, 1992). The first three were presented to the British Psychoanalytic Society in London and represent Bowlby's first formal statement of attachment theory. Bowlby theorized that the nature of the child's tie to his mother is not the survival dependency described by the Freudians and Neo-Freudians, but rather a form of attachment. Bowlby was clear that the attachment is not a type of regression. Attachment is a natural and healthy function that extends into adult life. Bowlby's divergence from traditional views created a stir within the British Psychoanalytic Society (Bretherton, 1992).

Separation anxiety was the topic of the second seminal paper Bowlby presented. Bowlby claimed that traditional theory could not explain the intense attachment of babies to their primary caregivers or their powerful response to being separated from their caregivers. Robertson and Bowlby (1952) researched separation anxiety and found three phases of responses: protest, despair, and denial or detachment. Bowlby maintained that babies experience separation anxiety when the circumstances conjure both the desire to escape and to be attached but the primary caregiver is not available.

The excessive separation anxiety experienced by some children might also have its roots in negative experiences like threats of abandonment or rejection. Other contributing factors could be actual abandonment due to a sibling's or parent's illness. The separation anxiety level can be low or very high. Some children appear not to experience distress. Bowlby indicated that this pseudo independence is probably a defense mechanism. He claimed that the well-loved child is likely to protest at separation from parent but later becomes more self-reliant. Bowlby turned his attention to the primary caregiver with the thought that pseudo affection and overprotection might be the result of the mother's unconscious hostility toward the child (Bretherton, 1992).

In his third paper, Bowlby (1960) claimed that grief and mourning processes are presented by children when the attachment need is activated but the primary caregiver continues to be unavailable. Bowlby suggested that a child experiences this kind of grief and mourning too frequently; although substitute caregivers are present, they might not be able to form deep relationships. Working with Colin Parkes (Bowlby & Parkes, 1970), who was investigating adult bereavement, the separation response phases hypothesized by Robertson for children were expanded into the adult grief responses: numbness, yearning and protest, disorganization and despair, and reorganization. Kubler-Ross (1970) was influenced by this work in her influential book *On Death and Dying*.

Ainsworth left the research team to move to Uganda with her husband in 1953. This move allowed her to collect data on mother-child attachment from 26 families from 1953 through 1955, when she moved to the United States. Her data was not analyzed for several years because she took on teaching responsibilities at Johns Hopkins University. However, Bowlby sent her a preprint of his first paper on attachment theory. This incident rekindled their intellectual collaboration.

Ainsworth (1963, 1967) analyzed her Uganda data and discovered specific patterns in mother-child attachment. Infants who appeared to be securely attached to the mother cried little and appeared content to explore with the mother present. Infants who appeared insecurely attached cried frequently even when they were being held by the mothers. Infants that appeared not to be attached seemed to ignore the mother. The higher the sensitivity of the mother to the infant, Ainsworth observed, the more securely attached the infants appeared to be. This study laid the foundation for her Baltimore Project, for which she recruited 26 families expecting babies. She made arrangements to make 18 home visits to the families beginning at the baby's first month and ending at 54 weeks of age. Each visit was 4 hours long. She made observations every 5 minutes and recorded them.

Ainsworth also made observations of the children in the Strange Situation (1978; Ainsworth, Bell, & Strayton, 1971, 1974; Ainsworth, Blehar, Waters, & Wall, 1978; Ainsworth & Wittig, 1969). The child was placed in a playroom with his or her mother. Then a stranger came into the playroom and the parent left, but returned shortly. Then the mother left, which left the child alone. The stranger returned and left; and then, the mother returned. Her findings supported Bowlby's findings of the child being angry or ambivalent when the mother returned. Those children displaying this anger or rejection of affection from the mother were found to be those who had a less amicable relationship with the mother in the home.

Two methods of play therapy based on these theories are developmental play therapy (DP) and theraplay. Ecosystems play therapy also incorporates aspects of attachment theory, through the importance placed on the developmental stages of children and attachment. Benedict's work (2003) helps to codify much of the child's play therapy experience in relation to attachment theory.

DEVELOPMENTAL PLAY THERAPY

Developmental play (DP) therapy uses the dialogue of touch. The therapy is based on the ideology that touching is essential to the development of the healthy child. According to DP founder Viola Brody (1993), "The intent of touching the child is to bring about a fruitful dialogue between an adult therapist and the child she touches" (p. 13). Brody describes the DP therapist as a "midwife birthing the child's self" (p. 13).

Toy Selection

Brody (1997) suggests the following items be included in the therapy room: a rug large enough for an adult and a child to sit comfortably, a rocking chair, and a table and chair. She also has available paper, crayons, pencils, and a bottle of skin lotion. Brody does not recommend hypoallergic lotion, but the therapist might consider it for liability reasons. Brody stresses that the room needs to be private with a door that shuts.

Toys are not available in the room where the developmental play therapy is conducted. Toys would distract the child from the relationship with the therapist, which Brody considers essential to the child's healing.

Role of the Therapist

Although the therapist structures each session so the child will be touched, specific goals are not the focus during the session. The therapist is fully present with the child, experiencing and responding to him or her during the session. The therapist must remain aware of the child's response to being touched, which determines what the therapist will do next to promote the therapeutic goals.

During the therapy time, the child goes through specific stages in the relationship with the therapist: introduction/orientation stage, working-through stage, baby stage, intersubjective stage, and termination stage. The introduction stage involves getting to know one another and learning what is expected in the therapeutic session. During this stage the therapist's role is to gain the child's trust and respect. This stage is traditionally called establishing rapport. The message is given to the child that the therapist will not go away and will be there to touch, hold, comfort, and encourage throughout the therapy.

The working-through stage is distinguished by the child reliving the negative experience or situation in the presence of the therapist. The therapist becomes a container for the child's negative feelings. Regardless of the child's behavior, the therapist remains physically and emotionally with the child sustaining the contact. The therapist may set limits as needed while holding and helping the child focus on his or her body. The therapist maintains an activity level in which the child is aware of the therapist's presence and responds to the therapist.

During the baby stage, the child relives infancy. The child is not pretending to be a baby at this time but rather is actually infantile, still with the awareness of his or her present age. The therapist plays baby games like This Little Piggy or similar games played with infants. The child may appear not to be paying attention or appear to be sleeping. The therapist may simply allow the child to lie quietly on the floor or in his or her arms while the child enjoys the silence and warmth of being close. The therapist may become frustrated during this time because the action and progress appear to have slowed to a standstill. The seeming lack of evident progress is because the child has turned inward in his or her work.

In the intersubjective stage, the child begins to talk more to the therapist. The child has begun to clarify a separation between self and the therapist. This stage may be marked with limit testing, followed with desires to be cuddled or touched. The child can express his or her feelings and begins to deal with problems outside of the session. The child is ready for termination when the therapeutic goal is achieved.

Structuring the Session

Brody (1997) indicates that touch is an organizer of behavior. Through touch the child comes to define what is *you* and what is *I*, or the child's core self. Through the sense of touch the child is stimulated to move, feel, think, and relate to the DP therapist. Each session has three distinct parts: hello time, middle time, and ending time, or cradling. The hello time is marked by the therapist greeting the child and letting the child know the therapist is attending to the child. The middle time is indicated by play activities either initiated by the child or the therapist. The ending time, or cradling, is the relaxation and reflective time for both the child and the therapist.

The hello time of the session begins with the therapist talking to the child, reflecting what the child is doing in the room. The therapist conveys respect and caring for the child through the use of voice tone before touching the child. The therapist touches the child when the child approaches the therapist. Contact is maintained only as long as the child appears comfortable with touching.

During the middle time, different types of touch are used: nonsexual touching, hugging, kissing, speaking, chanting, and singing. DP therapy touching and holding differ greatly from the forced holding techniques used in therapies described by Welch (1988), Magid and McKelvey (1988), and Jernberg (1979).

DP therapy provides cradling to make the child aware of his or her body, to experience the pleasure of contact, and to enjoy the feeling of being alive. If a child resists cradling, the therapist stops the holding and may touch the child in a less intrusive manner that is acceptable to the child. The child in DP does not have to comply with the desires of the therapist for a specific activity. However, the therapist does make his or her presence known by being persistent in contact with the child. This contact can be eye contact or verbal contact in place of the physical contact of

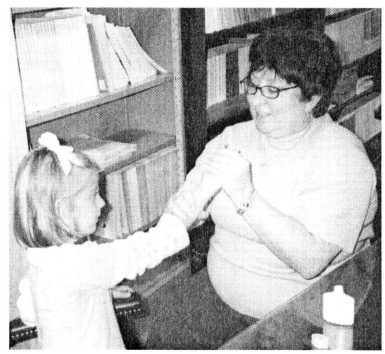

The therapist is giving the child a hand massage. Through touch the child comes to define what is *you* and what is *I*, or the child's core self.

touching. The therapist is in charge of the session, not through force, but through attending to the child and through nurturing touches. The holding therapies described by Welch (1988), Magid and McKelvey (1988), and Jernberg (1979) do not allow the child to say no, resulting in one-way communication from the therapist to the child. Developmental play allows the child to accept or reject the holding, thus establishing a two-way communication between therapist and child.

Touching and chanting body parts is another touching activity that is part of DP therapy. The therapist touches a nonsexual body part with fingertips or hands. The therapist may touch the child's hands, arms, and face. If the child is wearing shorts, the therapist may touch the child's legs to the knee. The child may remove shoes and socks and the therapist will touch the child's feet and toes. The therapist says the body part or may sing the body part to accompany the touch. The therapist may sustain the contact by holding the arm, leg, face, hand, toe, or finger for a short period of time or by playing a game with the child. Brody (1997) believes this type of touch focuses the child on himself or herself, turning the focus of the child inward and toward those experiences.

Brody (1997) will ask a child if there is a place that is kissable. This question invites the child to indicate an acceptable place. According to Brody (1993), "a kiss can help a child recognize and place a high value on a part of her body, a first step toward knowing herself as valuable" (p. 33). The kiss allows the child to give and receive unconditional affection. The same thing can be said of hugging. Kissing may be more appropriate for the younger children; hugging is often more acceptable to older children.

The voice is also a way to touch a child. Singing, especially while cradling, allows the child to feel the vibrations of the adult's voice. The child may choose to join in and add his or her own vibrations to the moment. The combination of rhythm, vibration, words, touch, and gaze has a powerful effect in communicating love and acceptance to the child.

During this middle time, developmental play games may be shared with the child. The following two games illustrate the type of games the therapist employs during this middle time. One of these games is the slippery hand game. The therapist puts lotion on his or her hands and holds it until it warms slightly. Then the therapist invites the child to put his or her hand between the therapist's hands. The therapist rubs the lotion on the child's hand and arm up to the shoulder with a circular motion, stopping at the upper arm, lightly encircling the child's arm. The therapist instructs the child to pull. Because the arm, hand, and fingers are slippery with lotion, the therapist's hands slip all the way to the fingertips, massaging the long muscles of the arm. This activity is called the Slippery Hand game. The same type of game can be played by putting lotion on the child's toes, feet, and legs.

In the Hills and Valleys game, the therapist asks the child if she is aware she has hills and valleys on her hands. The therapist starts by putting a finger on the outside of the child's thumb and moving the therapist's finger up, over, and down on the other side to show the first hill and valley. The therapist continues this for all five fingers saying, "You go up a little hill and down the hill, and up a big hill and down the hill" (Brody, 1993, p. 358) until you get to the outside of the small finger. These are two of the many games that Brody (1993) has developed for the middle time.

The ending time is the cradling time. Cradling is done by holding the child much like a mother holds a baby in the nursing position. In this position, the therapist can easily make eye contact and speak softly to the child. The therapist may sing a lullaby or even a song made up especially for the child. The therapist may touch parts of the child's body while chanting the names of the body parts. The child may be rocked during this time in the rocking chair or by the therapist swaying while sitting on the floor. Brody (1993) believes that cradling helps calm the child and makes him feel safe.

The DP therapist is not allowed to tickle the child. According to Brody (1997), tickling is the most hostile, invasive, and intrusive way to relate to a child. The child has no defense against the tickling. Brody does not say the child can experience pain or even experience tickling as torture, but the writer has had children report they were tortured by being held down and tickled or that tickling was painful.

Limits

A method used in DP is limit setting, which serves two purposes: (1) to inform the child of what behaviors are not permitted, and (2) to clarify for the child that the therapist is not controlled by the child. Brody (1993) believes there is no useful learning taking place when a child is allowed to be purposely destructive; therefore, she may restrain the child during tantrums. She helps the child focus. She may say something to the effect, "When you stop hitting me, I will let you go" or "It's very nice to be held." She may also call attention to the holding process by directing the child's attention to the body part she is holding; "Look at the hand I am holding."

Brody (1997) believes that experiencing limits is essential to maturity. No person is able always to do exactly what he or she wants to do, and the child needs to realize this is the reality of the world. The child needs to understand that he or she cannot control the world, other people, or some events. Limits need to be set that are realistic and help the child understand the necessity of and the desire for limits. When the child learns to respond to limits, the child experiences the capacity to set limits on his or her own behavior. Through limit setting, the child is enabled to separate from the adult and experience the dimensions and qualities of the self. Because the adult is not manipulated and takes responsibility, the child comes to recognize that adults can take care of themselves, alleviating the child of the responsibility of caring for adults.

Parent Involvement

Brody (1997) reported that she worked with the parents in separate and individual sessions. She taught the parent(s) how to touch the child and how to set age-appropriate limits on the child's behavior. In the process of demonstration, she touched the parents like she would the child, which helped them become aware of childhood experiences with their own parents, the child's grandparents. Brody (1997) claimed that after the training sessions the parents become more effective in touching the child and in setting appropriate limits for the child. When parents could not set appropriate limits, they were subtly communicating to the child that he or she must take care of the parent. Therefore limit setting by the parent is essential to therapy.

Termination

Once the child has demonstrated the desired changes outside of the therapeutic session, the therapist sets a termination date. The child does not participate in the termination decision. When the therapist decides the child is ready for termination, the child is given three more sessions for the termination process. During these three sessions, the child can express the pain of separation and positive feelings about having gained the requisite criteria for leaving therapy. The child is allowed to review what he or she has enjoyed.

According to Brody (1997), the most moving part of the therapy is the final session. The therapist and child review the whole therapeutic time in one session. The final session is a private celebration between the child and the therapist in which they celebrate the child's growth. In one example (Brody, 1997), she carries a little boy out to his mother and places him in the mother's arms. Then they say good-bye. In another example, the child asks to be carried out of the room. Brody carries the child out and puts the child down so the child can walk out. Exactly how the session terminates appears to be based more on the intuition of the therapist and the needs of the child at the time.

Assessment and Techniques

Brody (1978, 1993, 1997) does not include any formal or informal assessment instruments in her text. She relies on informal interviews and reports from significant adults in the child's life. Many of the children she describes having used DP were diagnosed by others as autistic and psychotic. Brody does not attempt to perform this type of diagnosis or assessment herself, however, or describe its process in her writings.

The techniques she uses are described in her book *Dialogue of Touch* (Brody, 1997). Many of these touching games are based on traditional nursery and kindergarten action and touching games. However, Brody indicates that the games are left to the creativity of the therapist and according to the needs of the child to be touched.

THERAPLAY

Theraplay is described as "a playful, engaging, short-term treatment method that is intimate, physical, personal focused and fun" (Jernberg & Booth, 1999a, p. 3). The Theraplay treatment takes its cues after the ideal natural and healthy parent-infant relationship. The parents are included in the treatment, first as observers and then as co-therapists. The focus of the treatment is to address the causal disturbance in the parent-child bonding experience. The treatment goal is "to enhance attachment, self-esteem, trust, and joyful engagement and to empower parents to continue on their own the health-promoting interactions learned during the treatment sessions" (Jernberg & Booth, 1999, p. 3).

Historically, Theraplay is presented second because it has grown out of the work of Austin DesLauriers (1962; DesLauriers & Carlson, 1969) and Viola Brody (1978, 1993, 1997), according to Jernberg and Booth (1999a). Jernberg borrowed from DesLauriers the vigorous intrusiveness and intimacy produced between the child and the therapist using direct body and eye contact. DesLauriers differed from other popular theorists of the time by his focus on the here-and-now and ignoring of fantasy, a tenet Jernberg adopted as part of her own theory. From Brody, Jernberg borrowed the aspects of nurturing and the therapeutic qualities of touch (Jennings, 1999; Koller & Booth, 1997; Perry & Gerretsen, 2002).

Theraplay began in 1967, when Jernberg became the director of psychological services for the entire Chicago Head Start program. Developing a model adapted from Brody's and DesLauriers's models, Jernberg collected a diverse group of experienced child workers with a talent for engaging children and committed to helping children reach their full potential to move the theorized model to its application with the Head Start program. This model was perceived as an unorthodox method of working with children (Jernberg & Booth, 1999a, 1999b; Koller & Booth, 1997; Perry & Gerretsen, 2002). To meet the resistance and criticism, two films were developed, *Here I Am* (Jernberg, Hurst, & Lyman, 1969) and *There He Goes* (Jernberg, Hurst, & Lyman, 1975). Through these films, the entire Head Start network was introduced to the Theraplay method. Lyman, one of the filmmakers on *Here I Am*, suggested the name *Theraplay*.

The Marschak Interaction Method (MIM) is an early assessment instrument used to form the treatment plan. In this scene the child is feeding the parent a piece of candy.

The first Theraplay classes were taught in 1971 and the Theraplay Institute was founded the same year. Because of imitators, Theraplay was registered as a service mark in 1976. The Theraplay Institute is currently a not-for-profit treatment, training, and consulting center (Jernberg & Booth, 1999b). The method has been used with infants through geriatric settings with success; however, Theraplay has been most often used with children 18 months to 12 years old.

Toy Selection

Theraplay does not use toys. However, the session room contains large floor pillows, beanbag chairs, and smaller throw pillows. The atmosphere is one of relaxation and fun. An observation room with a one-way viewing mirror is highly desirable but not necessary.

The room needs an enclosed storage unit to hold the following materials: lotion, baby powder, baby bottles, pretzels, small candies, raisins, water pistols, plastic garbage bags, bandage strips, straws, beans, crepe paper strips, newspapers, dressup hats, necklaces, and shaving cream. Foods like doughnuts, popsicles, milk or juice cartons, and watermelon chunks with seeds for spitting are made available (Jernberg & Booth, 1999a, 1999b; Koller & Booth, 1997; Munns, 2000; Perry & Gerretsen, 2002).

Role of the Therapist

The therapist is responsible for planning and structuring the sessions to meet the needs of the child. The child is not encouraged to engage in fantasy or to lead the way in the therapeutic process. The therapist is in charge and focused on the present relationship between the child and the therapist. The therapist coaxes the child into creating a relationship, even if the therapist must be intrusive to engage the child. The therapist is concerned in treatment with the interactional relationship as opposed to the conflicts within the child's psyche. The therapist maintains contact through resistance, even if the child is active or passive in the resistance. The therapist is active, directive, physical, and interactive in the play with the child. Symbolic play with toys or discussion of problems is not part of the therapeutic session. The therapist includes the parents in the sessions and initially models the behaviors for the parents to use in relating to their children (Jernberg & Booth, 1999a, 1999b; Koller & Booth, 1997; Perry & Gerretsen, 2002).

The therapist's threefold treatment goal is to substitute inappropriate solutions and behaviors with those that are healthy and creative, to increase the child's self-esteem, and to improve the child's relationship with caretakers. Through using focused eye contact, nurturing touch, and playful interactions, the Theraplay therapist models the "good enough" parent, who helps children discover who they are, what the world is like, who the significant people are in their lives, and how they feel about those significant others. The emphasis of the activities and interactions are on the child's good health and strength. The therapist's optimism helps the child feel accepted in the therapy session, even if the child is not accepted outside of the session by others. The role of the therapist is to help the child see himself or herself as loved by the significant adults in the child's life. After the child realizes that he or she is loved, the child can then experience the feeling of being lovable and of being an enjoyable companion (Jernberg & Booth, 1999a, 1999b).

Structuring the Session

The focus of the therapeutic session is the underlying disturbance between the child and significant adults. The goal of the therapeutic session is to enable the child to become more securely attached, to experience higher self-esteem, to learn to trust self and others, to learn to enjoy engagement with others, and to affirm the parents' ability to provide the conditions and experiences necessary for the child's continued healthy interactions and education (Jernberg & Booth, 1999a, 1999b).

Assessment forms the first part of the Theraplay therapeutic procedures. Theraplay begins with an intake interview with the child's caretakers only to gather information about the child's developmental history, the family background, and the current functioning of the family. This interview is followed by a directed observation technique, the Marschak Interaction Method (MIM) (Jernberg, Booth, Koller, & Allert, 1991), conducted with each parent, if both are available. At the conclusion of the interview and observation, the parents or caretakers are given feedback that provides a description of the perceived problems supported with video selections from the observations. When Theraplay is recommended, the parents are asked to commit to the treatment plan, an agreement is negotiated, and the number of sessions is contracted (Jernberg & Booth, 1999a, 1999b; Koller & Booth, 1997; Perry & Gerretsen, 2002).

The Theraplay session is structured with an opening, the session proper, and a closing. The opening consists of greeting and checkup activities. During the session proper, the child and therapist engage in structuring, engaging, nurturing, and challenging activities. At the closing, the parting and transition to the outside world take place.

The greeting is meant to communicate to the child the excitement and joy of meeting or reuniting with a friend. It is forceful, joyful, and extremely individual, communicating to the child appreciation of his or her uniqueness and lovability. The greeting is never prescribed or mechanical and does not include the impersonal, patterned responses often used in greeting children (Jernberg & Booth, 1999a, 1999b; Koller & Booth, 1997; Perry & Gerretsen, 2002), like the following:

How are you today?

We are going to have a good day playing today.

Follow me to the playroom.

How was your trip in to the center?

Greetings more in keeping with the unique manner in which the Theraplay therapist greets the child are based on the pure joy parents exhibit in their adored child (Jernberg & Booth, 1999a, 1999b; Koller & Booth, 1997; Perry & Gerretsen, 2002). Here are some sample greetings:

It's my friend Tristan with the big blue eyes.

Is that Madison behind that big smile?

Jon Evan, I do believe you brought the sunshine to my day.

Hunter, I bet there is a lot of energy in those hiking boots today.

The greeting is followed by the checkup activities, whose purpose is to reconnect after the week's separation, provide consistency of the therapist, reassure the child that his or her uniqueness is remembered, and convey to the child that growth is taking place. This part of the session may include an inventory of the child's unique physical qualities, measuring height and weight, measuring strength, muscle size, number of teeth, and length of hair. The therapist may also assess and record such information as the distance a child can jump, height of kick, or distance of a throw. These statistics are kept and recorded for weekly comparisons (Jernberg & Booth, 1999a, 1999b; Koller & Booth, 1997; Perry & Gerretsen, 2002).

The session proper is organized around four activity dimensions: structuring, engaging, nurturing, and challenging. The Theraplay Institute provides the Theraplay Activities Flip Book and Group Activity Cards through the publications part of their Web site (http://www.theraplay.org) as a resource for Theraplay activities. Based on the assessment of the child's needs, the therapist chooses activities that are appropriate from each of the four Theraplay dimensions. Some activities may cross over more than one dimension. To help the therapist determine which activities and which dimension they belong in for a particular child, the therapist asks himself or herself the question, "What is the primary goal to be accomplished?" The answer to this question helps the therapist clarify the appropriateness of the activity and the dimension in which it is used (Jernberg & Booth, 1999a, 1999b; Koller & Booth, 1997).

The structuring activities are meant to separate the time and space distinctly and to help the child internalize rules. Common types of games that the therapist may play with the child are Mother May I, Simon Says, or other games in which the child takes direction. During the structuring activities (Rubin, Tregay, & DaCosse, 1989), the therapist may have the child draw around her foot or hand, jump on the count of three, walk on specifically colored squares placed on the floor, or wrap the child in toilet paper and have her tear through the paper to escape. These activities have at their core the intention of setting and helping children understand boundaries or rules (Jernberg & Booth, 1999a, 1999b; Koller & Booth, 1997).

Engaging activities are intended to bring the child into engagement with the caretaker, to keep him interested and excited, to help him differentiate between himself and the rest of the world, and to increase his experience as a unique individual. The element of surprise and novelty to the child is highly desirable in this dimension. This Little Piggy, freckle counting, clapping games, and games that involve hiding stickers or cotton balls on the child's body are played. The therapist may use aluminum foil to make a print of the child's hand, foot, elbow, ear, or other body part by pressing the body part into the foil. The thinner the foil, which often means less expensive, the better the foil prints work (Jernberg & Booth, 1999a, 1999b; Koller & Booth, 1997).

Nurturing activities are meant to communicate to the child that her needs can be met without having to work for, deny the existence, or be rejected for expressing a need. The nurturing activities are usually those that provide a calming, soothing, reassuring, and quieting effect on the child. These activities may include feeding, applying lotion or powder, sitting close together in silence, singing a lullaby, rocking, face painting, or manicures with clear polish. Making wet footprints on a warm cement sidewalk or patio is another way to enjoy a gentle footbath. Indoors this can be done with baby powder or paint on paper, followed by the footbath (Jernberg & Booth, 1999a, 1999b; Koller & Booth, 1997).

Challenging activities help the child gain competence, arouse some frustration, and teach playful combat, competition, and confrontation. The purpose of these activities is to provide a release and focus for pent-up tension and anger in a safe, controlled manner. These activities include different types of balancing challenges, tug-of-war games, pillow fights, wrestling (thumb, arm, or leg), and water pistol fights. Target games, physical skill games, and tricks that require flexibility are appropriate in this dimension. Jernberg and Booth (1999a, 1999b) offer many suggestions in their text; however, for school-aged children, an elementary physical education text on games and skills training can offer additional ideas or resources for challenging age-appropriate activities.

The closing has two aspects. The first is the parting. The object is to indicate clearly that the session has come to an end but the relationship with the therapist continues beyond this time. This aspect may have some ritual attached to it to signal the ending, like putting on one's shoes or putting away materials. During this parting time, the child and therapist review the high points of the session and the therapist may suggest something for the child to try during the week (Jernberg & Booth, 1999a, 1999b; Koller & Booth, 1997).

The second aspect is the transition to the outside world from the session. The therapist may help the child straighten clothing, put on a sweater, comb hair, or other preparation to return to the caretaker. The therapist then takes the child directly to the caretaker. The child is not left alone or allowed to return to the adult without being accompanied by the therapist. The child is usually led by the hand and the child is delivered when the child's hand is placed in the caregiver's hand. The therapist then

The mother is teaching a song to the child. This song teaching activity is one drawn from Theraplay activities.

addresses the adult with some message that provides a continuation of the session into the realm of the caretaker and the child's world (Jernberg & Booth, 1999a, 1999b; Koller & Booth, 1997). For example, "Ms. Elliott, has Sheila shown you how she can snap her fingers on both hands?"

The session proper has approximately 12 activities that are chosen to meet the specific child's treatment goals. The hello and good-bye song are typically replaced with a special handshake or ritual for older children. The structure has a clear beginning and an ending to each session. The sample agenda here is adapted from Perry and Gerretsen (2002):

1. Hello song
2. Checkup
3. Putting lotion on minor scratches and hurts
4. Push-and-pull game (child pushes sitting therapist over and then pulls him or her up)
5. Three-legged walk
6. Mother May I?
7. Toilet paper bust-out
8. Stack of hands

9. Shave (The therapist puts shaving cream on the child and then shaves it off with a wooden craft stick)
10. Back writing or drawing game
11. Feeding or snack
12. Good-bye song

These activities are meant to provide playful interaction between the therapist and the child. Because the sessions are highly structured, the therapist can constantly assess the child's needs and maintain awareness of the child's responses to treatment (Booth & Koller, 1998).

The process of Theraplay treatment tentatively follows six phases: introduction, exploration, tentative acceptance, negative reaction, growing and trusting, and termination. In the introduction phase of treatment, the therapist establishes that the sessions will be fun, directed by the therapist, action oriented without disclosures or insight orientation, and delineated as to time, space, and therapist-child roles. The sessions are very therapist in charge and upbeat. The goal, purpose, or expectations are not introduced verbally. Some children may try to direct the sessions toward discussion or their choice of activities, but the therapist mostly ignores this and continues with his or her plan. If the child resists or refuses to participate, the therapist continues with the set activity agenda (Jernberg & Booth, 1999a, 1999b; Koller & Booth, 1997).

The exploration phase begins as the therapist and child get to know one another. During this time, the therapist learns the unique qualities of the child. The child is also learning about the therapist. The child and therapist may take inventory of who has the longest fingers, whose knuckle bones are longest, whose hair is the straightest, and other general kinds of observations. Negative behaviors may emerge during this time. The therapist treats these resistances by using paradox to make the behavior positive. The example given by Jernberg and Booth (1999) is of the child who resists by going limp to be complimented on her ability to be a "rag doll." Another example from the Jernberg and Booth text is the child who refuses to look at the therapist and is told, "Don't look at me." The resistance is treated in a spirit of love and acceptance. The successful maneuvering of the exploratory phase should result in the child having a clear picture of the therapist by facial features, voice, and physical strength. The therapist is known by the child in a crystal-clear image. The child is aware the therapist has this same clarity of the child's image (Jernberg & Booth, 1999a, 1999b; Koller & Booth, 1997).

The tentative acceptance phase starts when the child attempts to comply with the direction but does so apprehensively or tentatively. The child may behave with uncertainty, reserve, bewilderment, or excitement. The therapist must realize the child who seems to be fully involved too early in treatment may be doing so as a defensive apprehensive tactic to keep the therapist at bay and to avoid intimacy. The therapist continues to be engaging and insistent, nurturing or challenging, surprising, appealing, and fun no matter what the reaction or child's level of acceptance may be. When this phase is negotiated successfully, a more genuine and trusting relationship is the outcome (Jernberg & Booth, 1999a, 1999b; Koller & Booth, 1997).

The negative reaction phase is marked by the resistance to any further intimacy. The child who may have appeared to be so accepting and cooperative in earlier phases of treatment may abruptly become uncooperative, oppositional, and resistant. This sudden change in demeanor and attitude is considered indicative of the child testing the therapist's commitment to the relationship. The therapist's role during this phase is to continue being insistent and matter of fact that he or she will continue to support the child and the games will be fun. Emotional displays on the child's part are ignored and the treatment progresses as planned. The struggle that the child experiences is important to the outcome of therapy because without the struggle, the child and therapist cannot move to a deeper level of intimacy in their relationship (Jernberg & Booth, 1999a, 1999b; Koller & Booth, 1997).

The growing and trusting phase is distinguished by the child's pleasurable experience in interacting with another person in an acceptable way that is reciprocally satisfying. Once the trust relationship is firmly established, the time has come to introduce other members into the sessions. Through these experiences the child learns that others can respond with as much pleasure and support as the therapist. The extension of the child's world to incorporate other loving, involved, and encouraging people marks the time to prepare for termination of treatment (Jernberg & Booth, 1999a, 1999b; Koller & Booth, 1997).

The treatment is structured in generally 10 half-hour sessions. In sessions 1 through 4, the parent or parents observe the sessions from behind a one-way glass while another therapist sits with them interpreting what the child and therapist are doing. In sessions 5 through 10, the parents join the child in the Theraplay room for the second half of each session. The final session is usually marked by a party with light snacks and activities the child would like to do (Jernberg & Booth, 1999a, 1999b; Koller & Booth, 1997).

Limits

Because the therapist is in charge and the activities are planned, limit setting as first described by Bixler (1949) is not used in the Theraplay session. The therapist basically ignores resistances and continues with the planned activities, thus engaging the child. The therapist is instructed by Jernberg and Booth (1999a, 1999b) to remain firm in the face of the child's resistance. Children do become angry and many will have a temper tantrum. During these times, the authors describe a holding technique to assure the child is not hurt and does not hurt the therapist or property. The technique is aptly called *cradling*.

The therapist cradles the child on his or her lap so the therapist is looking into the face of the child. One of the child's arms is tucked behind the therapist's back, leaving one of the therapist's hands free to wipe tears or bathe the face gently with a cool cloth. The therapist's arm that cradles the child's head can also hold the child tightly and hold the child's other arm or hand. If the child kicks, the therapist can place a leg over the child's legs (Jernberg & Booth, 1999a, 1999b).

Larger children cannot always be contained with cradling. The child is placed face up on the floor, straddled, and the child's hands are held in order to maintain safety. The therapist does not straddle the child in such a way that the child supports the therapist's weight (Jernberg & Booth, 1999a, 1999b).

During either of these holding techniques, the therapist must remain self-assured and calm. The therapist must communicate to the child that even this behavior does not make the child unlovable; therefore the therapist reassures the child that he or she will stay with the child until the child feels better (Jernberg & Booth, 1999a, 1999b). The therapist soothes the child by saying, "I know you are angry and upset. I will stay with you until you feel better. I want to keep you safe. I will hold you until you feel better." The child may continue, and the therapist can reassure the child by saying, "I can see how angry you are. It is OK to be angry. We can go back to playing when you are ready."

The therapist monitors the child's body tension, releasing the hold on the child as the child relaxes. The therapist can respond to the relaxed child with "I think you are ready now." Some children may react with a renewed struggle or by hitting. The therapist responds with "I see you were not quite ready yet." If the child wants to bargain with the therapist by saying something to the effect that if he surrenders will the therapist let him go, the therapist responds with a statement conveying that all the child has to do is relax and then the therapist will let go (Jernberg & Booth, 1999a, 1999b).

Jernberg and Booth (1999a, 1999b) believe that holding has positive benefits for the child. The child will learn that the therapist can and will keep the child safe when the child is out of control. The child learns that anger does not drive the therapist away, and the child is not rejected or condemned because of the anger. The therapist remains fully with the child and accepting of the child throughout the ordeal and returns to the same caring, fun person following the tantrum. The child and therapist return to the planned activities.

An important distinction exists in Theraplay therapy. Jernberg and Booth (1999a, 1999b) caution that the therapist must recognize the difference between a child who is fearful because of previous trauma and the child who is being resistant or defiant. In the case of the frightened child, or a child with a trauma history for abuse, the therapist is asked not to restrain the child. Restraining might create further trauma for the child. Instead of restraining the child, the therapist is encouraged to work harder at engaging the child with interesting activities.

Crying is another behavior that occurs in Theraplay. The therapist must first determine the cause of the tears. The child may cry because of emotional pain or it could be an overt attempt to manipulate the therapist. In the latter case, the child's tears are treated like any other form of resistance. In the former, the child is comforted by the therapist in a nurturing way.

Parent Involvement

During the first four sessions, the parents are allowed to observe the child's sessions with the therapist. A second therapist, the interpreting therapist, sits with the parents in an observation room, where the interactions between the therapist and child can be viewed. If no one-way mirror is available, the interpreting therapist may sit with the parents off to one side of the room.

The interpreting therapist explains what the child's therapist is doing and provides tentative hypotheses about the child's responses. Beyond the simple explanation of the session, the interpreting therapist helps the parents see how what they are observing can be applied in their home environment. In addition to interpreting the session, the interpreting therapist discusses Theraplay principles with the parents, explores family dynamics, examines intrapsychic conflicts, appraises infant temperament, and reviews historical determinants. The therapist must have many talents and a broad experiential base to work with parents in Theraplay. The therapist must be able to help the parents in all aspects of the child development spectrum including parenting skills, educational decisions, family counseling, nutritional referrals, pediatric referrals, and other important information that the parents may need to support the child (Jernberg & Booth, 1999a, 1999b).

In addition to child development training, the interpreting therapist must have familiarity with the work of child rearing, psychological sensitivity, personal wisdom and maturity, sound judgment, and the ability to multitask between meeting the parents' needs and interpreting the session. The interpreting therapist remains with the parents to provide support and guidance during sessions 6 through 10, when the parents take an active role in the sessions. When the parents begin to take part in the latter half of the session in sessions 5 through 10, the interpreting therapist observes the parents and is alert to any concerns or problem areas. The interpreting therapist shares his or her knowledge and observations of the parents with the child's therapist so the two therapists coordinate the session with clear goals (Jernberg & Booth, 1999a, 1999b).

If a second therapist is not available to interpret, the child's therapist allows the parents to observe and then discusses what happened in the session with the parents afterward. An alternative is not to allow the parents to observe the session live, but rather to review a videotape of the session with the parents while the child's therapist serves as the interpreting therapist.

During the initial sessions, the interpreting therapist guides the parents' observations by calling attention to specific responses and behaviors in the session. Focusing questions about how the parent perceives the child to feel at a given moment or commenting on the child's demeanor helps the therapist emphasize crucial aspects for the parents. Some of the focusing comments and questions might be:

"How do you think Mary is feeling at this moment?"

"Look at that smile Austin has as his hands are rubbed with lotion."

Some parents will not be able readily to see positives in their child's interactions with the therapist. Parents may respond that when the child is the center of attention, there is no need to misbehave. The parents may disclose that the child is selfish and manipulative and having all this attention is undeserved and undesirable to remediate the problem behaviors. The interpreting therapist responds to these criticisms with a focused question such as "Does a baby have to earn the special attention that makes him feel good?" The therapist further explains that the process of Theraplay is to help the child be filled with good feelings, so she will have those feelings to hold on to and comfort her when the parents or other significant adults are not present.

The interpreting therapist may have the parents look critically at the incongruencies between the child's language and the child's behavior. A child may say he does not want to do baby stuff but seems engaged in the activity.

In the latter six sessions, the parents participate with the child in the activities that both therapists have chosen. The parents are coached through role playing and

Parents and therapist are reviewing a tape of the child's session focusing on the parent's empathic understanding of the child.

observation about how to participate within the session. The parent may be asked to do a role reversal, or take the child's part, in the practice sessions with the two therapists without the child present. Parents learn how to be successful in the session. The therapists prepare the parents for the possible resistances that may occur and for the phases of treatment. The parents are well informed of the structured plan and guided by the therapist, who is in charge.

The goal of these sessions is to help the parents see the child in a new way and to develop an empathic understanding. The therapists may assign the parent homework to be done between sessions with the child's therapist and the interpreting therapist. Usually the child's therapist takes less and less of an active role in the session and the parent takes more charge of the session. Usually by the end of eight or so sessions, the parents are directing the sessions. By the tenth session, the parents are ready to use what they have learned in Theraplay sessions in their own home.

Termination

The termination plan is built into the structure of the sessions. If the contract with the parents has been for 10 sessions, the termination session formally begins in session 7. The termination of Theraplay treatment has three distinct phases: preparation, announcement, and parting.

The preparation phase begins when the child's problematic behaviors have decreased or disappeared. The child appears to be happy and coping well with life circumstances. Although the relationship has become meaningful for both the child and the therapist, termination is not a time to be less upbeat or nostalgic, or to malinger. This therapeutic decision phase is followed by the announcement phase. The therapist announces to the child that termination is at hand (Jernberg & Booth, 1999a, 1999b). The therapist might phrase the announcement like this: "You and your parents are having so much fun together that you don't need to come to see me as much." When the therapist is sure the child understands, the therapist adds, "We'll have our sessions this week and next week, and then the week after that, we will have our good-bye party."

The focus of the next two sessions is on skills the child has learned, which may include balancing games, physical stunts, or similar activities that illustrate to the child the competency gained. At the end of each session, the child is reminded how many sessions are left until the termination party.

The termination party has light refreshments served to all the friends and family who have been part of the treatment. Jernberg and Booth (1999a, 1999b) suggest party hats, games, and party treats that capitalize on the child's strengths. Small favors or remembrances may be given. A T-shirt, poster, or scrapbook can be made at the child's party with everyone who attended having signed their name, drawn a meaningful picture, or stamped their handprint on the item for the child to remember them and this time.

The therapist is expected to model a healthy way of closing a meaningful relationship. The therapist may give the child a hug, tell her how much the therapist has enjoyed playing with such a special child, and convey to her that from now on she will be having fun with her friends and family. The therapist then reunites the child with the parents and makes sure the child is incorporated into a favorite activity. The session ends with a reminder to the parents of a checkup visit and contact information (Jernberg & Booth, 1999a, 1999b).

Assessment and Techniques

Theraplay assessment usually dominates the first three to four sessions with the child. The assessment process includes the following: an intake interview, the Marschak Interaction Method (Jernberg et al., 1991), and a feedback session with the caretakers who observed the sessions.

The *initial intake interview* is designed to gather information about the history and current functioning of the family. The child is not included in the interview. The intake interview includes the reason for the referral, developmental history, summary of parents' expectations and attitudes, parents' experience within their own families, and the parents' relationship with each other.

The *Marschak Interaction Method (MIM)* (Jernberg et al., 1991) is an assessment profile that guides the observer to the interaction between the child and the parents. The MIM examines patterns between the child and parent, indicating what works and what does not work in the relationship. The MIM consists of a large number of tasks. Eight to ten tasks are chosen based on the child's age. The tasks help evaluate the family on the following dimensions: giving affection, giving direction, alerting to the environment, and playfulness. These dimensions have been revised for Theraplay treatment planning to correspond with the Theraplay dimensions of structure, engagement, nurture, challenge, and playfulness (Jernberg & Booth, 1999).

Throughout the MIM session, the parent and child work alone in the session room with a selection of seven to ten activity cards (DiPasquale, 2000). The cards describe activities from each of four dimensions of Theraplay: structure, nurture, challenge, and engagement. The tasks are selected to represent a balance of structured activities from each dimension (Booth & Koller, 1998). Activity cards have activities like those listed here (Jernberg & Booth, 1999a, 1999b):

1. Adult teaches the child something the child doesn't know.
2. Adult and child each take one squeaky animal. Make the two animals play together.
3. Adult leaves the room for 1 minute without the child.
4. Adult and child put hats on each other.
5. Adult and child feed each other.

The materials and supplies needed for the child and parent to engage in each activity are provided either in a cupboard or envelopes. The parents are told there is no time limit and they may spend as much time as they wish on each activity.

The therapist observes the interactions, noting both verbal and nonverbal exchanges between the child and the parent at the beginning and during each task. The observation may be made either while observing the interactions through a one-way mirror or a postobservation using a videotape of the session. A kind of shorthand for recording the interactions has been developed (Jernberg, Booth, Koller, & Allert, 1991). A series of symbols are used to indicate who started the interchange, what the interaction was, and what kind of response it got from either the parent or the child. These symbols are recorded on an eight-column record form with the four left columns devoted to the adult and the four right columns devoted to the child. The observation headings (from left to right for each column) are feedback, inference, verbal, and nonverbal. The columns for verbal and nonverbal are completed during the observation time. The inferences column may be filled out during the observation session or postsession. The feedback column is used to enter cues for the observer of things to be discussed in the feedback interview (DiPasquale, 2000).

If more than one parent participates in the assessment, the parents are assessed separately. The parents each have time alone with the child to do five to six activities. The interview is further expanded by having the child and both parents engage in three activities for assessment.

After the activities are completed, the therapist conducts a debriefing interview, affording the opportunity for the parents to discuss reactions to the session (DiPasquale, 2000). The parents are asked to identify a favorite activity for both themselves and the child. This part of the assessment provides the therapist with insight into the level of the parent's awareness of the child. The MIM is always given at the beginning of treatment. It can also be given at the close of treatment to assess the effectiveness of the sessions. Using the same order of tasks, the MIM administered pre- and posttreatment provides a comparison, assisting the therapist in determining change over the period of treatment (DiPasquale, 2000).

The feedback session provides the parents with information and recommendations for treatment. The parents are usually shown portions of the videotaped MIM that illustrate cogent aspects of the parent-child relationship and the therapist's analysis of the problem. The therapist highlights and focuses on the strengths of the relationship between the parent and child. If treatment is recommended, the therapist describes the upcoming sessions and expectations of the parents' involvement (DiPasquale, 2000).

SUMMARY

Because of the intrusiveness and directness of these two theories, the author must insist these methods only be used by trained persons. The potential for misuse and harmful outcomes is great with theories in which the child's choices and willing participation is restricted. However, the author recognizes the importance of these methods and their power for work with identified populations of children suffering from attachment related issues. The author believes that touch can be therapeutic when provided by a well-trained, nurturing therapist, grounded in either Developmental Play Therapy or Theraplay theory. However, as with all powerful interventions, the technique can be equally destructive, if used by an inadequately trained and unsupervised person.

These two theories provide the most highly directive of the play therapy theories. Their contribution to the field of attachment disordered children cannot be overstated. The two theories provide a mode of reaching very difficult children with serious behavioral and developmental disorders, as well as the child and parent who need a little help in learning to enjoy one another in a healthy environment.

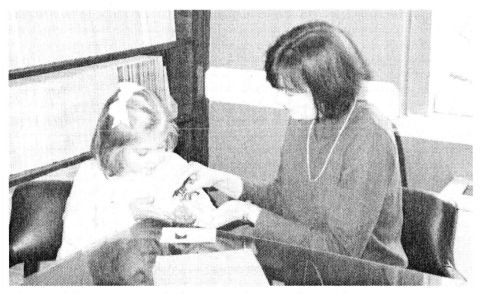

The Marschak Interaction Method (MIM) is administered pre- and posttreatment.

CHAPTER 11

ECOSYSTEMS PLAY THERAPY

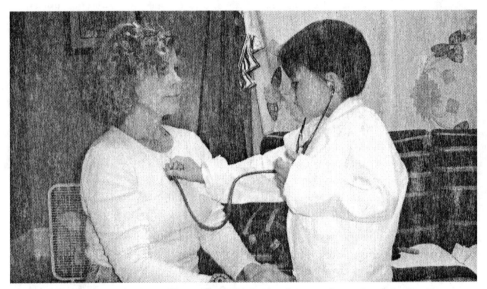

Ecosystemic therapist chooses a few toys to use in the therapeutic session. Ideally, the toys are chosen to represent developmental level slightly above and below the child's developmental level with one toy on the child's developmental level.

This chapter discusses those theories of play therapy that look not only at the child in the playroom but also at the child in relationship to the external world. The child influences the environment or family and vice versa. If any element in the relationships is changed, all of the elements or people must change to bring balance back to the environment or family.

INTRODUCTION

The founder of ecosystemic play therapy (EPT) is Kevin O'Connor (O'Connor & Ammen, 1997). He describes the model as a hybrid that blends biological science concepts, multiple models of child psychotherapy, and developmental aspects into a single theory. The model first made an appearance in 1994 (O'Connor, 1994a).

186

EPT focuses on optimizing the child's functioning within the context of the child's world or ecosystem. Although many aspects are drawn from other theories, ecosystemic play therapy is not considered an eclectic theory, but rather a "free-standing" model within itself (O'Connor, 1994a).

The biological term *ecosystem* means the entire community and environment that influences the subject being studied or observed. EPT looks at the child as the child is embedded in overlays of other systems. The concept goes beyond the *Gestalt,* or whole, to encompass any influence that may be acting or has acted on the child and the child's development. The initial work with the child involves exploration of these multiple layers, their influence, and their implications for the child in the context of the child's present living environment. The theory draws both from the perspective of sociology that people are the result of their society, and from the perspective of psychology that people are the product of how they interpret their world (O'Connor, 1994a).

In simpler terms, the play therapist focuses on the individual within many systems, a view that differentiates EPT from other systems models. The EPT model conceptualizes the layered systems of home, school, place of worship, and other external systems, as well as the internal systems of the mind and body. The orientation is not only to the here and now but to the child's past and future.

EPT's overall goal is to allow the child to resume his or her normal development and to enhance the child's ability to get needs satisfied without interfering with the needs of others. In order to help children reach this goal, they are assisted in developing new problem-solving methods that recognize all of the systems impinging on the problem. To this end, the therapist must help the child become unstuck in his or her attempts to get needs met. The process of becoming unstuck is accomplished by providing the child with alternative perspectives and an understanding of the child's life situation or problem.

TOY SELECTION

The therapist selects toys that seem best to address the kind of goals the child has established for the sessions. O'Connor (1994a) suggests about five toys at a time. He bases his choice on these guidelines: three of those are picked below the child's current developmental level, one is clearly at the child's current developmental level, and one demands higher functioning. An additional two or more toys are selected for their potential symbolic value relative to the kinds of problems the child is presenting. The child may not find just the right toy, but the therapist gains focus. Although some therapists may be uncomfortable with this limitation of toys, O'Connor (1993, 1994a) finds the focused outcome is worth the adjustment that many therapists may have to make.

O'Connor (1991) recommends the playroom be a minimum of 10 feet by 10 feet and no larger than 16 feet by 16 feet. He suggests the room be half carpeted and half linoleum tile. The tiled side is for messy activities and the carpeted side for quiet activities. He indicates that a lavatory or half bath adjoining the playroom is an advantage that allows the child to use the rest room in privacy without leaving the playroom area. Any windows need to be made of either safety glass or plastic.

Children and windows make for some unpredictable problem scenarios. O'Connor relates a story of a child almost falling from a third-story window in an office. Another alternative is to move to an interior room that does not have windows.

Equipment in the playroom should be at least a table and a few chairs. O'Connor suggests the chairs not be "baby-sized" but rather full-sized chairs and table. In addition, he recommends a cupboard, walk-in closet, or metal cabinet that can be locked, and a sand tray with a wooden top.

O'Connor (1991) presents his toys in four levels. Level-I toys are for children between the developmental age of 0 to 2 years. He includes the following toys in the Level-I category: baby bottle (one for each client), baby blanket, baby powder, baby lotion, stuffed animals, and "attention getters." O'Connor describes these as colorful balls, blocks, noisemakers, and musical instruments. One ball should be large enough to put the child on and rock the child. Empty boxes are included. Art materials like molding dough and finger paints are appropriate to this age group.

Level-II toys encourage pretend play. Level II generally addresses the developmental play needs of children from 3 to 6 years old. O'Connor suggests interactive toys, costumes, and miniatures for this age group. He considers interactive toys to be toy telephones, dishes, pretend food, appliances, and toy replicas of equipment from office, preschool, school, hospital, and other places common to the child's experience.

Art materials suggested at Level II are ruler, easel, felt-tipped pens, crayons, large sheets of paper, tempera paints and medium-sized brushes, molding materials, and items similar to those provided in the school setting. Coloring books used to introduce information about physical abuse, sexual abuse, or alcoholism can be available, but generally color and activity books are avoided.

Costumes or dressup items are recommended, although O'Connor indicates that therapists disagree on the value of costumes in the playroom. He recommends items to help the child rehearse for roles in life. Those items might include adult clothing, hats, a briefcase, stethoscope, jewelry, necktie or similar attire. In the arena of costumes, he recommends those items that allow the child to be a prince, princess, monster, angel, animal, astronaut, or superhero.

Level-III toys are usually for those children between the ages of 6 and 11. Children at this stage need toys that allow them to maintain distance from their fantasies. The toy selection recommended allows the child to project thoughts and fantasies into a miniature world. O'Connor suggests small people, animals, houses, cars, dolls, dollhouses, doll family, school-related miniatures, hospital- or doctor-related miniatures, and other miniatures of the child's fantasy. He does not suggest any type of military miniatures; however, this type of miniature might be useful during a period of time when military action is taking place or useful for children living in military-dominated environments. Soldiers or wartype miniatures are controversial, and many therapists prefer to avoid them in the playroom unless a child has a special need for their inclusion.

Level-III art materials include the addition of a self-hardening clay, plastic connecting construction toys, and simple crafts. Children of this age like to make and build things that are within their range of capability. Many models and crafts need to be carefully selected for level of expertise, if they are to be included in the playroom offerings.

O'Connor suggests board games that help children learn to follow rules and take turns. The games need to be simple. Games like The Talking, Feeling and Doing Game (Gardner, 1973); Imagine (Burks, 1978); The Ungame (Zakich, 1975); or Re-union (Zakich & Monroe, 1979) are provided as examples of the type of games recommended. O'Connor suggests the therapist not purposely allow the child to win or to allow the child to cheat at the game.

Level-IV play materials are a choice for children of 11 or 12. This age child may not want to be in the babyish atmosphere of a playroom. However, this stage of children may still wish to have materials to manipulate while they express themselves. O'Connor (1991) suggests art materials, construction toys, or a model kit. He does not mention the use of a sand tray and miniatures; however, this age group through adolescence does seem to respond to sand tray techniques. The therapist may find it most helpful to ask the child what kind of thing the child likes to do and then structure the time around that type of activity.

ROLE OF THE THERAPIST

According to O'Connor (1997; O'Connor & Ammen, 1997; O'Connor & Braverman, 1997), the work of the EPT therapist has two characteristics. The first is to maintain a commitment to the ecosystemic perspective at all times by focusing on the impact of the various systems on the child. The second characteristic is to adopt a clear and consistent personal theory, resulting in clarity and consistency in practice.

The EPT therapist seeks to facilitate the child becoming unstuck in her attempts to have her needs met within the multilayered system that forms the child's environment. The therapist accomplishes this goal by providing the child with new experiences and by helping the child understand the problem cognitively. Through the new experiences, the child comes to learn that life can be very different from what he has learned in the past. The child draws the natural conclusion that change is possible from these new experiences. These experiences may be provided in the session or in other system settings.

The therapist may effect change in the systems through consultation with the significant adults in that system to provide the child with alternative experiences. An example would be to consult with the child's teacher and ask that the child's assignments be broken down into smaller units, so the child can experience success. In addition, the therapist discusses with the child the problem, explaining in some detail that the child's perception of it may not be accurate. Then the therapist suggests other possible solutions to the problem that may be more effective for the child. O'Connor (1997) offers an illustration concerning a child who needed help overcoming fear of monsters in the dark. In his example the child is told that when monsters are hit by a flashlight beam, the monsters disintegrate. The child is then armed with his flashlight as a weapon to obliterate the monster hoard in his dark room.

O'Connor (1997) states that in addition to the minimal qualifications established by the Association for Play Therapy for the registered play therapist and specialized training in EPT, the therapist must be able to do the following:

1. Place the child's needs above the needs of the therapist.
2. Identify and sustain personal and systemic boundaries.

3. Strive to preserve the child's cultural and ethnic views and values in the acquisition of needs without violating others' needs.
4. Motivate the child to have confidence in the efficacy of ecosystemic play therapy, in the ability of the child's own skills, and in the ability to keep both the client and the therapist safe.
5. Accept the child's indecisiveness and developmental regression.
6. Develop flexibility in thought and in behavior in creative and therapeutic interventions.

Ultimately, the primary goal of the EPT therapist is to help the child change core beliefs that are creating difficulties. The therapist works to change these core beliefs either through providing the child with experiences or by using cognitive interventions that can include challenging logic, interpretation, education, and problem-solving models. The child's consideration of new beliefs creates a cognitive shift, which can lead to the solution of the problem (O'Connor, 2001).

STRUCTURING THE SESSION

Ecosystemic play is unique from many other play therapy models in that a specific and explicit treatment contract is negotiated. The contract is discussed in terms that the child can understand. This understanding and acceptance of the treatment contract is necessary to maintain the treatment alliance, according to O'Connor (1997).

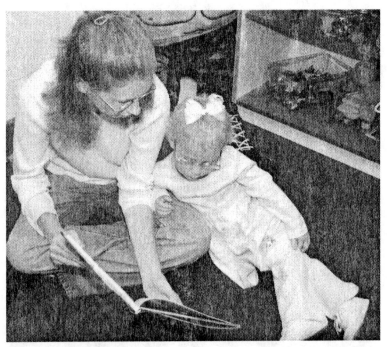

The ecosystemic play therapist is primarily focused on keeping the child optimally involved so that the child may learn and change.

The EPT therapist is focused primarily on keeping the child optimally involved so the child may learn and change. The therapist uses structuring, challenging, intruding, and nurturing behaviors, much like those advocated by Jernberg (1979a, 1979b). The therapist tries structuring behaviors to reduce the level of the child's excitement and to retain a safe environment. In the therapy session, structuring behaviors include all directed activities like selecting the toys and setting limits. Challenging behaviors are meant to stimulate the child and to push him a little beyond his developmental level. Problem solving and interpretations usually fall into this category. When the therapist discusses specific conduct or difficulties for the child or physically moves into his personal space, intrusion has taken place. Nurturing behaviors encourage the child and tend to help maintain whatever state of involvement he has achieved. When optimal involvement has been accomplished, the child is ready to engage in problem solving or change.

Once the child is involved to an age-appropriate level of understanding, the therapist engages her in the problem-solving modality by providing alternatives or corrective experiences. The therapist may also provide new cognitive understanding for the child at this point in therapy. The alternative or corrective experiences may be presented symbolically in the play session through the use of puppets or other materials. As in a case where the child and therapist may develop a puppet play to provide guidance on making new friends, the therapist and child pretend that one of the puppets has a similar problem to the child and then a solution or alternative behaviors are presented. Actual corrective experiences may be experienced through interactions with the therapist or as a part of a homework assignment for the child outside the session. The example that O'Connor (1997) gives is that an angry child may experience anger and intolerance outside the playroom but has the corrective experience with the therapist of her anger being met with acceptance and encouragement.

The alternative cognitive understanding of the difficulty is approached through O'Connor's (1991) five-stage model of interpretation. He describes the five levels of interpretation as reflection, pattern, simple dynamic, generalized dynamic, and genetic. *Reflection* requires the therapist to express a thought, motive, or feeling to the child that the child has not expressed directly. *Pattern interpretations* are those that identify similarities or consistencies in the child's behavior. The *simple dynamic interpretation* connects the child's unexpressed thoughts, feelings, or motives and the patterns in his or her behavior.

A *generalized interpretation* is recognition of a pattern across different settings and the strength of the pattern observed in each setting. The *genetic interpretation* is based on a historical antecedent of the pattern with a discrepancy between the original event and the current event that triggered the pattern of response or responses.

The therapist is also an advocate for the child. The therapist may assist the child in the external world by consultation with parents, teachers, physicians, social workers, or other caretakers.

Therapy begins with extensive interviews with the parents, guardians, or caretakers of the child, followed by an intake interview with the child. The first few sessions are marked by extensive assessment, discussed later in the chapter.

The assessment is followed up with a formalized list of treatment goals. The comprehensive list of case goals is then prioritized and assigned a context in which they might best be addressed. These are summarized and the primary hypotheses to be addressed in the treatment process are listed. The child and parents then enter into a treatment contract that spells out the treatment goal so the child can understand. The treatment contract is also provided to the parents, including ways that the care-givers are to participate in the therapy.

Because EPT casts a wide net, the goals and subsequent contractual commitments are broad, reaching beyond the treatment in the playroom. In setting the priorities for the goals, O'Connor and Ammen (1997) consider issues of safety or crisis, provision of a security base, developmental issues, problem or content, ability to cope, and systemic impact. Once these systematic goals are hypothesized, the goals addressed in therapy are designated and prioritized. Some possible contexts include individual, family, peer, school, medical setting, mental health setting, or community. Inside these contexts possible interventions to be used in the course of therapy could include referral, individual play therapy, family therapy, peer group therapy, filial therapy, consultation, education, evaluation, or advocacy. The contexts and possible interventions are presented to help understand the comprehensive conceptualization of the treatment and by no means are indicative of the possible interventions or contexts EPT would consider or use.

LIMITS

According to O'Connor (1991), the value of limit setting lies in its ability to teach children the acceptable boundaries of behavior, demonstrates the therapist's desire to maintain the child's safety, and helps develop interpersonal responsibility.

O'Connor (1991) believes much of the limit setting used in play therapy is unintentional. He points out that as the child is engaged in play the therapist attends to some behaviors and ignores others. Those behaviors that receive the most attention are the behaviors that are reinforced and become more frequent. The behaviors that are ignored are not reinforced. Because the child experiences the attending behaviors of the therapist as very reinforcing, O'Connor (1991) says the therapist ought to use this to a therapeutic advantage in changing the behavior of the child. Therefore the therapist must respond with intentionality and not talk just to be talking or to fill the silence. Through conceptualization of responses, actions, and verbal responses, the therapist can and does structure the play therapy session. Limitations on behavior are communicated indirectly through what is or is not rewarded with attention from the therapist.

When children act out, the session is continued and not cut short. The therapist focuses on helping the child learn how to handle his uncontrolled behavior. Limits communicate to the child that the therapist can control the situation and keep the child safe. Limits and staying with the child through the acting out communicates to the child that the therapist wants to be with the child and is willing to accept him, even though the behavior is not acceptable (O'Connor, 1991).

O'Connor emphasizes that early termination of a session is potentially detrimental to the child. Not only because of the child's sense of abandonment and the subtle message that the therapist feels the child cannot structure the session or stay safe, but because the child receives the message that only appropriate behavior will be tolerated. If only appropriate and positive behavior is tolerated in therapy, the child experiences a contradiction. O'Connor (1991) states, "If the child could behave appropriately all the time, she would not need the therapy, yet she cannot come to therapy if she does not behave appropriately" (p. 223). Finally, some children may learn to use negative acting-out behavior to avoid an uncomfortable session.

PARENT INVOLVEMENT

Parents are part of the extensive interview and assessment process. In addition, O'Connor (1991) emphasizes collateral work with the parents. The term *collateral* is used to describe work done with the parents and by the parents during the course of therapy. He insists that work with the parents is essential if the child's needs are to be met successfully.

O'Connor (1991) provides three venues for how parents may be engaged in collateral therapeutic work. The first is to press the parents into service as therapists for their child with the clinician becoming the clinical supervisor to the parents. The second venue is to secure the parents' participation in joint or family sessions with the child. And finally, the parents may become involved in couples or individual treatment paralleling the therapeutic treatment goals of the child. According to O'Connor, this takes the collateral work beyond the traditional alliance expected in play therapy and expands it to meet the needs and conflicts of the parents in working with the child.

O'Connor suggests splitting the therapeutic hour into 20 minutes for the parents and 30 minutes for the child. He argues the advantages and disadvantages of seeing the parents before the child and the advantages and disadvantages of seeing the parents after the child. He concludes that whichever format the therapist selects, it needs to allow for the best formation and maintenance of a positive working relationship and support of the child in therapy. Parent inclusion in the process is imperative if the parents are expected to support the treatment over time.

Parents need to be told that the child's behavior often gets much worse before it gets better. Therefore it becomes important for the parents to give the therapist feedback about the child's behavior at home, in school, and throughout the ecosystem. Beyond the exchange of this vital information, the therapist reassures the parents that part of the treatment is to help with problem solving of behaviors. O'Connor (1991) uses a four-step model to engage the parents in the problem-solving sessions. First, the parents have described the problem behaviorally that is to be resolved. Second, the parents are encouraged to brainstorm creative, not necessarily practical, solutions to the problem. Third, the parents are encouraged to evaluate the solutions they generated and determine which might be implemented. Finally, the parents are to implement and evaluate the effectiveness of their chosen intervention.

During the parent sessions, the therapist may become aware that the parent or parents do not have the knowledge base to initiate problem-solving or behavioral management approaches with the child. Therefore the therapist may provide psychoeducational interventions with the parents in the areas of the treatment process, the child's current level of functioning, the prognosis, normal development, and parenting interventions. These educational interventions are intended to provide the parents with knowledge and skills that may be lacking from their repertoire. O'Connor suggests bibliotherapy to convey large amounts of practical knowledge to the parents.

TERMINATION

When considering termination, O'Connor (1997) believes the ideal time is when the goals developed at intake are accomplished. Although the answer to termination may appear simplistic, the process is not so clear cut. During the course of therapy, the treatment goals may have changed significantly as new material emerged that needed therapeutic attention. Given the nature of children to be unable to discuss or explore verbally all of the aspects of their problems at the time treatment was initiated, the child may simply not know what is wrong or why it is wrong.

A second issue in establishing when the goals of therapy are met is the continued development of the child. The child is still growing and developing during therapy; therefore the child may have advanced to another level. The change in developmental level can result in new aspects of an old problem needing to be explored and new skills needing to be learned. O'Connor (1991) warns that changes in development do not mean the therapist can keep the child in therapy until adulthood, but it does mean the therapist needs to be sensitive to the growth and development of the child and the child's changing needs.

Another method for deciding when termination will occur is to establish a pre-planned termination date. O'Connor (1991) favors this method when the treatment goals are clear, when a brief intervention is optimal, or when the caretaker's commitment to follow through is low. A contract can be developed for 8 to 12 sessions. The number of sessions, rather than a termination date, is considered practical because children miss sessions due to illnesses and other events beyond the child's control.

Unplanned terminations are difficult. When the therapist or client is relocating, changing jobs, or experiencing other life-altering changes occurring in the systemic environment, termination must occur without the completion of the child's work (O'Connor, 1994a). These abrupt endings can be very disconcerting for both the child and the therapist; however, referrals can be made, and sometimes a farewell visit can be arranged to reduce the lack of closure. In his videotape *Interpreting Children's Verbalizations in Play Therapy*, O'Connor says this about termination: "If the therapy actually gets to finish, I generally find endings are more fun" (O'Connor, 1994b).

Termination of therapy is an important part of the therapeutic process. Once the termination date is set, therapy continues to the last minute of contact with the child. The therapist may have to work with the child on ending the relationship and the child's anxiety over this ending. However, the therapist relaxes the boundaries or expectations in the treatment as termination approaches. The therapist-client role is maintained until the end, avoiding a shift to a friend-child role. Although some therapists may wish to ease the child out of the anxiety of ending a relationship by

While some therapists may wish to ease the child out of the anxiety of ending a relationship through allowing the child to call, write, or otherwise contact the therapist, O'Connor (1991) recommends that the end of therapy be the end of contact.

allowing the child to call, write, or otherwise make contact, O'Connor (1991) recommends the end of therapy be the end of contact. However, he does leave the door open for the child to return to therapy by providing the child with a business card with contact information should the child need the therapist in the future.

ASSESSMENT AND TECHNIQUES

According to O'Connor and Ammen (1997), the process to collect assessment data may take many forms in order to meet the needs of the client, the therapist, and the agency or system where the treatment is being provided. O'Connor and Ammen provide these key components of the EPT intake process:

1. Describing the present problem from the child's point of view and from the point of view of significant adults in the child's life.
2. Taking developmental history emphasizing the history of the child and family experiences.
3. Examining the child's past and present functioning in relevant systems that affect the child.
4. Investigating the sociocultural and metasystemic variables influencing the child's functioning and experiences.

The *interview with the caregivers* begins with open-ended questions similar to "Tell me how life in your family was when . . . " Both parents are asked this question, and the question is repeated for each stage of development: prepregnancy, pregnancy, birth, birth to 12 months, 1 to 3 years, 3 to 5 years, 5 to 11 years, and 12 to 18 years. O'Connor and Ammen (1997) offer an extensive outline for the structured interview of the caretakers focusing on key developmental tasks and aspects for each age.

An example of the type of information sought at the 5- to 11-year-level is the child's social and academic competency assessed by asking questions that are directed to ascertain information about school history, social history, and family relationships. The authors are concerned about how the child adjusted to changing grades, academic expectations, and conduct requirements. The caregivers or parents are also asked about the child's close friends and relationships with peers, especially those that might be problematic. How the child relates to the family and any family changes are discussed with the parents during this time. If family secrets are disclosed during this interview, O'Connor and Ammen caution that the therapist does not agree to maintain secrecy without knowing the impact of the secret on the therapeutic process.

The interview is usually followed with the use of the Developmental Therapy Objectives Rating Form (DTOF-R) (Developmental Therapy Institute, 1992; Wood, 1992a, 1992b).

The *child interview* follows the parents' interview. Its purpose is to ascertain what the child knows about the presenting problem and the child's perceptions of the problem. The therapist may review some of the more salient events from the history given by the parents to see if the child's perceptions match those of the parents or what the parents have reported. Again, O'Connor and Ammen (1997) provide an extensive intake form for this purpose. Some guidelines they suggest include speaking deliberately and slowly to the child, posing questions in the subjunctive case, and using exaggerated statements. An example of the subjunctive case might be "Suppose you could become invisible, what do you think you would overhear your parents say about . . . ?" The exaggerated responses would be something like "When you get angry, are you more like a tornado or a dust devil?" (Dust devils in the Southwest are small circular winds that pick up dust and are usually harmless.)

The *family interview* combines the parents and children to focus on observing the interactions between and among the family members in relation to the child client or identified patient (O'Connor & Ammen, 1997). The family interview is a time to collect different family members' perspectives on the problem and to generate possible and plausible solutions for this family. The final aspect of the interview is to understand the strengths and weaknesses of the family, as well as the family's support, resistance, and compliance regarding the treatment of the child.

The family interview consists of the following stages: greeting/engagement, problem definition, systems analysis, goal setting, and closure. The greeting/engagement period of the interview introduces the family, sets the parameters for the treatment sessions, reduces surface anxiety, and builds trust. Problem definition allows each member of the family to provide a perspective on the problem and how the problem affects them. Systems analysis is collected from the therapist's observations of the family's interactions and reactions to the discussion. This data can help the therapist see the family in the context of the enmeshment-disengagement contin-uum, power hierarchies, and emotional atmosphere. At the end of the interview the therapist negotiates with the family about the goals of treatment and course of treat-ment. The therapist usually closes the meeting with an agreement about future meet-ings or further treatment.

Standardized instruments are used to collect information about how the child functions in comparison to a normative group. The information collected from stan-dardized tests provides not only a comparison to the normative group but also a sys-tematic way to compare the child to other children the therapist may have experienced in past therapeutic sessions. Standardized measures provide a quick be-havioral snapshot of the child that may reduce the amount of time required in ther-apy to gain the same information.

The *Wechsler Intelligence Scales for Children—Third Edition (WISC—III)* (Wechsler, 1991a, 1991b) is one of the most widely used individual assessment in-struments for gathering information on cognitive functioning, prediction of school success, and strengths and weaknesses of cognitive understanding. The instruments provide two indicators of cognitive functioning: performance and verbal. Discrep-ancies between these two scores are often used to determine special cognitive inter-ventions. The subtests can also form patterns that are indicative of how a child might process information or have problems processing some types of information. The WISC—III requires specific training for its administration and interpretation and should not be administered or interpreted by individuals without special training. Even those clinicians who have had extensive training often need to refresh their skills when new versions of the instrument are published.

The *Personality Inventory for Children (PIC)* (Wirt, Lachar, Klinedinst, Seat, & Broen, 2001) is a test used to assess young children. The assessment is completed by the caregiver. Three validity scales and a further assessment scale provide a general screening of level of functioning. Cognitive functioning dimensions are Achievement, Intellectual Screening, and Development. Clinical dimensions reported are Depres-sion, Somatic Concern, Delinquency, Withdrawal, Anxiety, Psychosis, and Hyperac-tivity. The PIC provides indications of family functioning and peer functioning.

The *Developmental Teaching Objectives Rating Form (DTORF—R)* (Develop-mental Therapy Institute, 1992; Wood, 1992a, 1992b) is an instrument that O'Con-nor and Ammen (1997) use in treatment planning. The instrument provides information about social-emotional functioning. The social-emotional development is indicated by several domains, which include Behavior, Communication, Socializa-tion, and Academics. O'Connor and Ammen (1997) limit their use of the instrument to the first three domains, preferring to use other instruments to assess academic functioning. The instrument provides an inventory of developmental tasks the child has not accomplished at the appropriate developmental stages. The instrument al-lows the examiner to indicate a normative age-level designation for the child's social-emotional functioning. In O'Connor and Ammen's (1997) example, the client was 12 years old and the instrument indicated the child was functioning at a 4- to 6-year-old child's level of social-emotional development.

The Connors Rating Scales (CRS) (Connors, 1996; Connors & Barkley, 1955; Connors, Sitarenios, Parker, & Epstein, 1998) assesses a broad range of behavior problems. The CRS is most recognized for its ability to assess attention-deficit/ hyperactivity disorder. The instrument comes in both a long and short form for each possible respondent. The respondents include parent, teacher, and adolescent self-report forms. The instrument is recommended for routine screening in schools, mental health clinics, agencies, private practice, and other settings. The age range is from 3 to 17 years of age. The assessment instrument is individually administered in approximately 45 minutes for the long form and 15 minutes for the short form. O'Connor and Ammen (1997) indicate use of the 1985 version, but since the publication of their book, a revision is now available. The revision includes an index to identify children at risk for attention-deficit/hyperactivity disorder (ADHD), scales directly linked to the DSM-IV criteria for ADHD, and the Conners' Global Index, consisting of two parts identifying Restless/Impulsive and Emotional Liability. The 1996 version has several types of feedback forms the clinician might find helpful.

The *Dean Behavioral Checklist for Child and Adolescent Multiple Personality Disorder* was discussed by James (1989) as an instrument to assess dissociation on the basis of children's behavior in multiple settings and the child's drawings. O'Conner and Ammen (1997) report using the Dean Behavioral Checklist to assist in the recognition of dissociative phenomena among child clients who may have experienced trauma and abuse.

Functional behavioral assessment is a problem-solving process for addressing child problem behavior. A variety of techniques and strategies are used to identify the purposes of specific behavior and to help select interventions that address the problem behavior directly. A functional behavioral assessment examines behavior beyond the obvious. When conducting a functional behavioral assessment, the clinician focuses on identifying significant child-specific social, affective, cognitive, and/or environmental factors associated with the occurrence (and nonoccurrence) of specific behaviors. Using this broader perspective, the clinician is offered an enhanced understanding of the function or purpose behind the behavior. Behavioral intervention plans based on an understanding of why a child misbehaves is useful in addressing the range of presenting problems encountered in play therapy.

The *Cipani Behavioral Assessment and Diagnostic System (C-Bad)* (Cipani, 1993) uses four categories to prescribe behavioral interventions based on the child's behavior. The instrument helps the clinician identify the function of each of the child's behaviors and the contingency or contingencies that lead to their maintenance. Once the functions of the behaviors and the contingencies that maintain them have been identified, interventions can be designed to disrupt the problem behaviors.

Projective instruments are restricted to specialized training when used for the purpose of diagnosis. A person not specifically trained to use certain projective tests or projective techniques is in violation of the ethical codes to do so for the purposes of diagnosis. The basic requirement for most publishers is that the clinician seeking the purchase of projective instruments document having had a course in administration of projective instruments and projective techniques. Clinicians without this special training may wish to have these assessments done by other qualified persons or seek the specialized training and supervision to become qualified in this area. Be sure to check the laws in the state where you are working about the legality of using these tests with your licensure or certification and the limitations of use. The two projective tests suggested by O'Connor and Ammen (1997) are the Children's Projective Drawing Battery and Roberts Apperception Test for Children (RAT-C) (McArthur & Roberts, 1982).

The *Children's Projective Drawing Battery* (Sullivan, 1996) includes these exercises: the Draw-A-Person, Mother-Child and Father-Child Drawing, Kinetic Family Drawing, and Draw-A-House. The Draw-A-Person is intended to elicit perceptions of the child's self. The Mother-Child and Father-Child Drawing indicate the child's perception of relationships with caregivers. Family relationships are examined by the Kinetic Family Drawing. The child's perception of the environment is illustrated by the Draw-A-House. The battery provides a view of the child's perceptions across different systems that are significant to the child.

The *Roberts Apperception Test for Children (RAT-C)* (McArthur & Roberts, 1982) uses cards depicting various black-and-white scenes. The child is asked to tell a story with a beginning, middle, and an end. The test comes with a matrix for analysis of the story's content. Some cards are for both boys and girls; some are designated for only boys or only girls. The difference in the gender-specific cards is the gender of the main character in the picture. The instrument is appropriate for children between the ages of 6 and 16. The administrator needs to have specialized training in projective techniques. O'Connor and Ammen (1997) believe this assessment technique can help the therapist understand the way a child organizes his or her perceptual world and the relationships within that world.

O'Connor and Ammen (1997) suggest that other projective instruments might be helpful in gathering information to help understand the child's unique organization of experiences, perceptions, and relationships. Other projective techniques and instruments suggested are projective drawing (Cantlay, 1996), the Rorschach inkblot test (Exner, 1993; Exner & Weiner, 1994), storytelling techniques (Teglasi, 1993), and puppet play interviews (Irwin, 1991).

The Westby Symbolic Play Scale (Westby, 1991) is used to evaluate the child's level of representational play, defined as the child's ability to enter into symbolic or pretend play. O'Connor and Ammen (1997) find that three of the five scales are most helpful in play therapy: decontextualization, play themes, and organization of play themes.

Decontextualization is the ability to shift from life-size realistic props to miniatures or no props. Play themes are considered any play activities, from the use of everyday scenarios to complete fantasy depictions in the child's play. Organization of play themes examines limited symbolic play to sequentially organized play. The instrument helps the therapist determine the developmental level of the child's play.

The *Marschak Interaction Method (MIM)* (Jernberg, Booth, Koller, & Allert, 1991) was discussed in Chapter 10. However, the MIM is mentioned here as it is used by O'Connor and Ammen (1997) in their assessment tableau.

SUMMARY

Ecosystemic play therapy (EPT) was developed to examine the child, the child's problem and the therapeutic process systematically within the context of the child's complete ecosystem. EPT is an integrated theory that incorporates theoretical aspects from analytic psychology (Freud & Clark, 1928; Klein, 1975a, 1975b); child-centered theories (Axline, 1964, 1969, 1989; Axline & Carmichael, 1947; Landreth, 2002); and cognitive-behavioral theories (Knell, 1993, 1997, 1998; Knell & Moore, 1990), according to O'Connor (2001). O'Connor has also drawn from Theraplay (Jernberg & Booth, 1999; Jernberg et al., 1991; Jernberg, 1979a, 1979b) and reality therapy (Glasser, 1975). Through extensive assessment, parent involvement, and directed play activities, a prescribed set of therapeutic goals are accomplished that are developmentally appropriate for the child.

CHAPTER 12

FAMILY AND FILIAL PLAY THERAPY

Working with parents of children in play therapy has always been considered to be important in the process of therapy. Parental contact may take the form of parenting classes, or even a few informal moments following or preceding a child's session. Parent contact can take many forms and the length of contact varies greatly.

This chapter explores the emerging group of family play therapies and filial play therapy. The identified patient (IP) or the person who manifests the problem that brings the family to therapy is viewed as symptomatic of the interactions and context of the family unit. Family therapy focuses and directs treatment to this context, or environment. This chapter examines strategic family play therapy (Ariel, 1992, 1997); dynamic family play therapy (Harvey, 1994c, 1997); filial play therapy (B. Guerney, 1964; L. Guerney, 1976a, 1983a, 1987, 1988, 1991, 2000; Guerney & Guerney, 1987, 1994; Van Fleet, 1994, 2004); and a general overview of including parents or caretakers in the therapy process (Hardaway, 2000; McGuire & McGuire, 2001; Schaefer & Carey, 1994). Of necessity, this and the following chapters use a different format because of the nature of the content.

INTRODUCTION

Miller (1994) recognizes that working with the parents and family of children in therapy has always been considered by therapists. Common ground for all theories of family therapy is the idea that the therapy focuses on the family rather than on the individual. The problematic behavior of one or more family members is seen as a function of the family and the stress the family organization or system places on the individual. Because the individual's behavior is a result of the family organization or system, the focus of diagnosis, treatment, and intervention is essentially on the family organization or system rather than the individual.

According to Miller (1994), there has been a shift from the either-or concept of family therapy or play therapy. This shift has resulted in an integrated theory of family play therapy. A major factor of this shift is that family play therapy does not give up the comprehensive understanding of the symptom-bearing child; family play therapy allows the child to explore his or her emotional difficulties and includes the child's emotional environment in the therapeutic process.

Family play therapy, according to Griff (1983), is an "electic technique, combining elements from play and family therapies in addition to the methods of adult education" (p. 65). Play therapists have always included the parents to some extent in the therapy process, whether with parenting education support or allowing passive observation in the playroom. "Children only" has remained the philosophical stance in the bulk of the play therapy treatment scenarios. Parents have historically been encouraged to seek parenting skills training or marital or individual counseling as an ancillary to the child's therapy. In contrast, when family therapy has been recommended, play therapy has been used as a subordinate or secondary strategy for the young children in assessing the family's problems (Griff, 1983).

PLAY THERAPY PARADIGM FOR FAMILY THERAPY

Any discussion of family therapy must include one of the masters of family theory, Carl Whitaker (Keith & Whitaker, 1994). Whittaker connects play therapy and family therapy through Bateson (1972), an early family therapy theorist, who said that in some ways therapy is not the reality, but rather is play. Bateson (1972) believed play has the characteristic of allowing acts that would not have the same relevance and organization in nonplay. Hostility, aggression, and even combat that would be intolerable in another situation are dismissed in play, which allows an individual the ability to express unacceptable feelings in an acceptable way. The benefit from the expression is the same, whether in play or reality.

Whittaker (Keith & Whitaker, 1994) points out that in play the parents may be more loving because of the unique situation of the playroom. The playroom and toys allow for freedom of expression that transcends the normal limits of expression within the home and society for child and adults. At the same time, the therapist is also freed of the restraints of professional distance and may enter into the situation with mocking shock, fear, or teasing distance. Scenes of child horror or aggression can be depicted in creative art projects. The most gross, crude, and distorted fantasies of everyday life can be acted out. No topic is taboo in the playroom fantasy. The child is freed through play to be as crazy, infantile, or exotic as he or she may wish to be.

Keith and Whittaker (1994) have taken play therapy as the model for family therapy and developed a list of how play therapy and family therapy blend:

1. Although both play therapy and family therapy are theory based, they remain learned mostly through experience with families and children.
2. Both are structured by rules and by the boundaries of the relationship with the therapist. The therapist must be clear as to where the therapist ceases to exist and where the person begins.
3. The scope of the session allows the participants to transcend the moment and experience an intensified experience within the confines of time and the safety of the therapy room.
4. Symbolic and real, primary and secondary processes, are mixed. These mixes manifest themselves in metaphors or slips of the tongue.
5. A metaphorical reality exists in which participants are free to express themselves through symbols or stories on multiple meaning levels with the safety of emotional distance.
6. Shifts continually occur between the metaphor and the reality with both acceptable.
7. The interpersonal experience is projected or reflected on the therapist in both play therapy and family therapy.
8. The poses and attitudes of the body carry special meaning within the session.
9. Both family and play therapy use symbolic cueing to decide the course of therapy. A child will often signal time to cease therapy by suggesting another child for therapy; a family may begin to put less priority on the sessions and cancel for other family events.

These points of comparison support the idea that family functioning is fundamentally at the nonverbal level. Like a television drama, the family comes into therapy with set lines, roles, and affects that determine how they act in the family drama. The family drama revolves around a central theme. Through therapy, the family has the opportunity to rewrite their roles and move their characters toward self-actualization (Keith & Whitaker, 1994).

The methods of the family therapist may include having the children and toys available at all the family meetings. These meetings are nonconventional with the therapists and parents sitting on the floor playing with the children as they talk. The therapist may actually talk through the children to make a point with one of the parents. Problems of jealousy or flirtations may be exposed in pseudo education, where the therapist gives voice to the desire but also sets boundaries. The therapist may exaggerate the problem to the point of humor. Through encouraging bad behavior, talking in a silly way, absurdity, switching places, or fantasy (delusions), the therapist may exaggerate behaviors, ideas, rules, or other symptoms that are getting in the way of family functioning. These exaggerations are playful but call attention to the difficulties in the family.

Keith and Whitaker (1994) indicate that family play therapy is contraindicated when the family is very rigid or if the family is experiencing trauma or grief. The therapist should avoid initiating family play therapy if the therapist is anxious about his or her skill level or gets exuberant or sadistic in therapy. Family play therapy should not be used to reduce the family's anxiety, but rather to increase the anxiety sufficiently to provide motivation for change.

CONJOINT PLAY THERAPY

Safer (1965) is one of the first to include the parents and child in a therapeutic session. He calls this technique *conjoint play therapy*. He requires the parents, child, and himself to engage in the play activities that the child chooses. The role of the therapist is both active and directive during the therapeutic session. During the session, Safer provides demonstrations, educational information, and interpretation to the parents. The therapy session moves in a spontaneous and random fashion through a fluid and ongoing process.

FAMILY PLAY THERAPY

According to Griff (1983), her concept of family therapy expands the ideas used in goal-oriented play or activity sessions to include the child and his or her family and the therapist. The development of family play therapy grew out the frustration of working with children with emotional disorders. When parents were not included in the therapy, the parents were less likely to incorporate suggestions made by the therapist in the home. When the parents took part in a directed activity with the child and therapist, the parents sessions were designed around the premise of parenting skill development and assimilation. Parents who had not been able to implement the suggestions prior to participation in the session were able to demonstrate and maintain positive changes in the child to a greater degree than previously.

Griff (1983) developed a contract for family play therapy session that would encompass 8 to 10 sessions. The therapist determined the goals for the sessions in accordance with the treatment goals and the allotted time for treatment. A new contract was devised for additional sessions if needed. Griff would break down a long-term goal into smaller more manageable goals, which would assure the success of the child and the parent(s).

In the first session, all family members are invited to participate in the session, which allows the therapist to observe which family members need to be included in subsequent sessions. Griff (1983) discussed a situation in which a father had the greater skill in playing with the child and overshadowed the mother's abilities. The father was asked not to attend a future session, so the mother could further develop her skills with the child. The father later returned to the sessions when the mother could parent with more confidence.

Planning the activities may appear more challenging than it really is. Parents and children are asked about their favorite games, play activities, and pastimes. The interactions of the family during the activity, rather than the activity itself, is actually the focus of therapy. The activities chosen need to be close to the family's style and preferences for play. The activity needs to be one that the family can succeed in accomplishing and enjoying (Griff, 1983).

The therapist's role in family play therapy has many functions: educator, play facilitator, role model, and player. The therapist needs a background in marital and family therapy, child development, play therapy, and clinical therapeutic skills. A therapist with experience and confidence in both play therapy and family therapy has a distinct advantage in using this model. Both active and directive involvement is required, if the therapist is to also serve as a role model to the parents during the session.

Griff (1983) describes the treatment process as having three major stages. In sessions 1 and 2 (stage 1), the therapist takes on the role of introducing and directing the play activities. During this time the therapist can observe the family to get a better assessment of the family's interactions while establishing rapport with the family. In the next three sessions (stage 2), the therapist usually takes a more active role in directing, modeling, and teaching skills to help parents with interactions with children. The final three sessions (stage 3) are used to encourage the parents and the child or children in using the skills they have learned. The therapist moves into a role of coach, providing feedback and supporting and encouraging the family's efforts to change.

DYNAMIC FAMILY PLAY THERAPY

Dynamic family play therapy (DFPT), whose leading proponent is Steve Harvey (Harvey, 1990, 1991, 1993, 1994a, 1994b, 1994c, 1997; Harvey & Kelly, 1993), engages the family members in natural, creative, and expressive play activities. The session may include all the family members, a subset of the family, or an individual in the session. The aim of the therapist is to help the family become more spontaneous and to create playful metaphors to address relationship problems. The therapist may use art, drama, movement, videomaking, or other play therapy modalities to assist the family. Using more than one mode of expression encourages the family to engage in a creative, expressive project that reflects the dynamics of their family.

As the family engages in creative and expressive play, the therapist guides them into interactive play that may be very different from the family's status quo of relationship interactions. Through the experience of joining in the creative and expressive play, the family is provided with the power of change inherent in this intervention process. Harvey (1997) says the essential goal of dynamic play therapy is to help the family member "rechoreograph" the quality of their emotional relationships and intimacy. This theory draws on the theoretical models of "creative problem solving (Getzel & Csikszentmihalyi, 1976), those humanistic approaches to family therapy (Satir, 1967, 1972), attachment theory (Bowlby, 1982), and the curative powers of the play experience (Schaefer, 1993)" (Harvey, 1997, p. 342).

Through the use of creative arts therapies, Harvey (1994) provides tangible illustrations of the problematic themes within the family. Problems such as ineffective power relationships, continuing conflict, and attachment difficulties are seen when the family is asked to engage in simple games like Simon Says or Follow the Leader. Once a theme is identified in one play modality, the theme is extended to other modalities, which are used to lead through the difficult process of metaphor making. Harvey (1994) gives an example in which the family is asked to dramatize a family argument without using any words but may use facial expressions to express their intense feelings. This dramatization is followed with an art activity where the family has a "scribble" argument on paper. Both of these activities are videotaped for the family to review at home, work out ways to alter their behavior, add lines, and even develop additional scenes. The basic premise is that the family will use these metaphors of symbolic play; they may find solutions to their daily interactions.

An important concept is that of choice making. The therapeutic environment promotes the development of conscious choice making in the activities. The degree and type of participation is open to each family member. The illustration is given of a power struggle between a parent and a child. The power struggle is played out as a race. Each family member is included in the race, but each may choose how fast or slow to take part in the race.

During the activities, family members are encouraged to examine the patterns, breaks, and cures in the family interactions. At first the therapist may guide the family, calling attention to the patterns of interaction used by the family members in the activity and making parallels to the family's experiences at home. Gradually, the family becomes apt at this examination and metaphor building. Once the family accomplishes the metaphor making, the family is coached to pose solutions in the session that can be used at home. Creative problem solving taken in small intentional steps leads to family members enjoying and negotiating their daily challenges. Toward the end of therapy, a core theme emerges that lends itself to drama and play images. The enactment of this core theme, or drama, constitutes the family's greatest creative challenge. The solutions that the family generates for this core scene usually have a profound effect on the family, offering insight for changes in emotional expression and intimacy.

As the family engages in creative and expressive play, the therapist guides the family into interactive play that may be very different from the family's status quo of relationship interactions.

Harvey (1994) suggests the therapist have a background in family systems, attachment, and expressive arts therapy. Play therapy is considered an expressive therapy in Harvey's definition. He encourages the therapist to observe normal healthy families in a playroom, park, or playground. He suggests the nuances of interaction in healthy families focus on creative, playful, and flexible solutions to challenges presented in their relationship. "Humor, catharsis, security, and support, as well as individual choice making and expressive exploration, are present" (Harvey, 1994).

Harvey indicates that families with concerns of sexual abuse, physical violence, attachment difficulties, or developmental crisis experience frustration and pain during the simplest forms of play, like storytelling or a game of tag. The therapist needs to have a familiarity with what is normal play and expression so he or she can intentionally encourage the family stuck in conflict toward a creative, imaginative solution.

The therapist's own creativity is much in demand in effective dynamic play therapy. The therapist may be required to model the expressive-creative process to set up and reframe tricky family interactions in playful scenarios for the family without knowing the outcome. This strategy demands a secure therapist who must trust his or her ability to participate with the family in moments when strong feelings are being expressed, defended, and negotiated, even through the guise of playfulness. The therapist's trust in the process and professional skills allow him or her to permit the process to continue without interference. The process must be allowed to continue in spite of the temptation to redirect, stop, or offer boundaries during the family's exploration of creative options.

The logistics of the setting require a playroom location where the uninhibited play of a child will not disturb others. The sessions can be very noisy with banging, laughing, and screaming. An important element is the freedom to engage in free, spontaneous play between children and adults without fear of reprisal from others. The room should be large enough to accommodate adult and child play. A 15- by 20-foot carpeted room is probably large enough. The room is most useful if divided into a talking center with a couch and chairs and a play area with play props. If the location permits, two rooms are recommended: one as the playroom and the other as an office or talking room.

Harvey (1997) suggests the following types of play props for dynamic family play therapy: large pillows, stuffed animals, long scarves, stretch ropes, gymnastic balls, a parachute, butcher paper, crayons, colored pencils, markers, and sculpting clay. The props need to be large enough to accommodate an adult or be used by the entire family at once. A video camera and monitor are helpful to record the session for review by the family and therapist. When the family is court ordered or a court case is pending, the therapist needs to take special precautions in using videotaping so the confidentiality of the family is maintained.

Harvey (1997) typically sees the family weekly; however, not all family members are included in every session. The children are usually seen alone and the parents are seen alone, followed by being seen together in a small group. When the parents are divorced, each parent may be seen with the children on alternating weeks. Sessions may include both divorced parents, if the parents are tolerant of each other. The time allotted for sessions, frequency of sessions, and composition of sessions depends on the needs of the family members and the degree of loss or pain within the family.

STRATEGIC FAMILY PLAY THERAPY

Ariel (1997) describes strategic family play therapy (SFPT) as a genre where "all the family members, together with the therapist, are engaged in free, imaginative, make-believe play, with or without toys, costumes, and props" (p. 368). In the conjoint sessions, play is used to diagnose, communicate, and change the family relationship. The process of strategic family play therapy is based on the concepts and methods drawn from both play and family theories. Much of the integrated theoretical framework is extracted from structural, strategic, systems, symbolic-representative, and narrative family theories. Family studies and play theory distilled from information-processing, semiotics, ethological, and anthropological theories are also a part of the theoretical base of strategic family play therapy. Psychoanalytic play therapy serves as the point of departure for a theory of play therapy.

SFPT makes it possible for young children to participate fully, actively, and meaningfully in the therapeutic process. Through the rich and expressive medium of make-believe play, the family can communicate and express themselves to one another and to the therapist. Covert and unconscious thoughts, emotions, and relationships are projected through make-believe play. Play is used as a precision instrument that has the ability to deflect defenses and create an intense and condensed experience, resulting in immediate change. Using play as a direct, semiconscious, cognitive-emotional experience, SFPT has been used across varied concerns, cultural backgrounds, and social levels (Ariel, 1992, 1997).

Ariel (1997) describes "make-believe" behavior in three propositional attitudes: realification, identification, and playfulness. *Realification* occurs when the child or adult pretends something or someone is not just a figment of the imagination but is really present. An example would be that Batman is in the playroom with the child or family. *Identification* describes the kind of imaginative play where the child or adult takes the role of a character. Drawing on the previous example, the person pretends to be Batman. The final propositional attitude is that of *playfulness,* where the child or adult neither believes he or she is the object or person nor believes the person is present, but is only claiming to be the person or object for amusement (Ariel, 1992, 1997).

Ariel (1997), uses the word *emotive* to mean something akin to the psychoanalytic term *complex*. Therefore, an *emotive* would be "a group or system of related ideas or impulses that have a common emotional tone and exert a strong but usually unconscious influence on attitudes and behavior" (Corsini, 2002). He believes a person can process information better through sensation, perception, memory, divergent and convergent thinking, motor activity, and other processing channels, if the information is related to the person's emotives. Contrary to this assumption, he also says that if the emotive becomes too aroused, the individual blocks or delays processing. This information-processing model functions as a mechanism for controlling the level of arousal around an individual emotive. Those students of family systems theory will recognize Ariel's (1997) description as similar to the analogy of a thermostat. A thermostat controls the heat and cooling so the temperature remains balanced within a few degrees and the room never gets too hot or too cold. This balance of temperature, whether of air or emotional temperature, is called *homeostasis.*

According to Ariel (1992, 1997), the way the family maintains the balance or homeostatic state is observable in make-believe play. Make-believe play is primarily mental activity. Pretending requires retrieving information from memory and then creating mental associations. The individual must then transform these associations and present them in an external form. Therefore, Ariel (1997) hypothesizes that the individual's emotives will be overrepresented in make-believe play. The converse of underrepresentation would be true if the emotives present too much arousal. To reduce arousal the threatening theme can be replaced with a less threatening theme. Ariel offers the example of substituting a fishing boat for a submarine about to be sunk. With the selection of those representations that create arousal and those that reduce arousal, Ariel believes the individuals will demonstrate a homeostatic feedback loop.

Another concept introduced by Ariel (1992, 1997) is family programs. *Program* in this sense is analogous to a computer program or operating system. The family program represents the routine plan for how the family faces issues and meets goals. The program is developed by the family members over time to achieve their individual goals within the family unit. Because this program runs in any setting, make-believe play supplies a symbolic, imaginary disguise of the family program. The process of using make-believe play reframes the family program. Reframing is the changing of perspectives on behaviors or communications (Ariel, 1992). The family can be observed in make-believe play to demonstrate the relationships, conflicts, and interpersonal transactions in the choices of their fantasy play.

The therapist in this setting observes and identifies the dysfunctional interactions between and among the family members. Once these have been identified, the therapist joins in the play, initiating new play themes that combine with the family's play but directing the play into well-chosen functional directions. The family is then stimulated "to play in ways that automatically activate well-defined curative structural and psychosocial properties of play" (Ariel, 1997, p. 373). Ariel calls these play interventions "bug-busters" because they debug or weaken the family's program.

The make-believe play takes the family program out of the conscious and intentional behavior of the family, resulting in family members providing an uninhibited and uncensored view of their program. The more the play stays within the realm of the unconscious and nonrational, the more likely the emotional change will occur. The use of the play allows each member of the family to both own and alienate themselves from the content of the play, which greatly frees up the emotives underlying the family's dysfunction. The play provides the therapist with insight into each family member's convictions about self and about other family members.

The basic duality of the play allows the player to be both inside the fantasy experiencing the fantasy and outside the fantasy judging the experience and self. Because of this duality, the therapist can work inside the fantasy to help the individual understand errors in the way he or she has interpreted information or information processing. The dysfunctional information processing leads to contradictory messages among the family members. These contradictory messages occur when the content of what is said is not congruent with the tone or behavior of the speaker. The object in the therapy is to clarify these contradictory messages and make them congruent. How Ariel (1992) does this is not clear from the literature. We can only guess that he directs the players or the play theme toward a more congruent scenario.

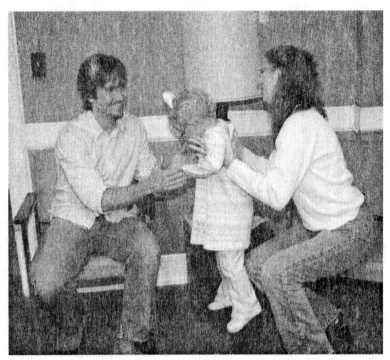

Play provides the therapist with insight into family members' convictions about themselves and about other family members.

Another aspect of this duality is cognitive dissonance or the experience of tension when the individual becomes aware of the contradictions between what he or she does or feels and the denial of what he or she does or feels.

Ariel poses the concept of the *signifier* (word or symbol) and *signified* (thing designated by the word or symbol). The terms come from the work of the linguist De Saussure (1993), who is credited with introducing the terms *signifier* and *signified*, which could be either arbitrary or motivated signification. Ariel provides the example of motivated signification as a child representing a baby with a doll; thus the signifier (doll) is similar to the signified (a real baby). His example of an arbitrary signifier is the use of a stone (signifier) by a child to represent a baby (signified). An arbitrary signification is indicated by dissimilarity between the signified and the signifier.

The participants in the family sessions may be different combinations of family members in each session or series of sessions. The sessions take place in a family play therapy room stocked with toys, puppets, containers, props, costumes, musical instruments, tools, art supplies, miscellaneous items, sports, and movement aids. The sessions are usually 50 minutes long, once a week, for a maximum of 10 sessions. Some sessions may require more than 10 sessions, but this is not the norm.

The therapist engages the family in make-believe play by participating in the play. The therapist may assign roles to the other adults if they are reluctant to participate with the children. A series of objectives and subobjectives have been established during an assessment period completed during the intake process. The activities to implement the specific interventions are termed *tactics:*

> A tactic includes the specific target of the interventions (e.g., a special bug or particular emotive), expected change (e.g., making the players aware of the bug; making the defenses associated with the emotive less rigid), bug-busters by which the change can be effected, and expected resistance or undesirable side effects and how to deal with them. (Ariel, 1997, p. 387)

To carry out the tactics the therapist must follow four basic steps: observation, planning, preparatory moves, and main or auxiliary moves.

Observation occurs when the therapist watches the family's free play and formulates some understanding of the dynamics. Although observation may be time consuming, the themes and actions that indicate the targeted changes needed emerge naturally.

Planning involves the therapist setting goals, developing possible scenarios, and anticipating where the family will likely move in a given activity. Once the therapist plans some moves ahead of where the family is currently operating, the therapist joins the play.

Preparatory moves are those the therapist may use to set up the intervention before the main and auxiliary moves are made. The *main and auxiliary moves* are those in which the therapist directs the play in such a way that the intervention is made. The result is that in a subtle way it unbalances the family system of functioning and makes it reorganize in a more positive manner. If the intervention is successful, the family will transfer the learning from the world of make-believe to the family's reality.

FILIAL THERAPY

Filial therapy was developed by Louise and Bernard Guerney (B. Guerney, 1964; L. Guerney, 1976a, 1976b, 1983a, 1983b, 1987; Guerney & Guerney, 1987) as a treatment for children experiencing social, emotional, and behavioral difficulties. According to Van Fleet (Van Fleet, 1994, 2004), filial therapy has been renamed child relationship enhancement family therapy (CREFT).

CREFT (Guerney & Guerney, 1994) therapists train parents to provide child-centered play therapy with their own children. Using a psychoeducational basis that is competency oriented, the therapist takes several roles. The therapist teaches the parents how to conduct specialized play sessions and supervises the parents during the play sessions. After competency has been reached, the therapist helps the parents provide play sessions in their own home and further develop parenting skills.

Filial therapy is most appropriate for children between the ages of 3 and 12. However, Van Fleet (1994) believes a designated time to focus on the child and his or her concerns and interests can extend into adolescence. She suggests the activities may be selected by the adolescent with the parents employing many of the skills they learned in the play sessions. The sessions in the home are usually conducted with one parent and one child at a time. The one-on-one format allows for the most advantageous relationship development and attention to the child. Van Fleet recommends that all the children in the family have a "special time" or play session with their parents.

CREFT is based on the belief that play is a medium for children to express themselves, learn new skills, incorporate new experiences, and develop better problem-solving and coping abilities. Filial therapists consider play a major contributor to a child's healthy development and self-understanding. Another tenet underlying filial therapy is the belief that parents can be taught the skills necessary to provide child-centered play therapy session with their own children. Because the parents are the most significant adults in the children's world, they are likely to have greater influence on the children than an outside adult (e.g., the therapist). When parents improve their parenting and communication skills, the results are longer lasting and permanent.

Through the filial therapy training, the family becomes empowered to achieve higher levels of functioning. The final tenet is a preference for an educational model in evaluating and intervening with the family. The filial therapist views the difficulties within the family as based on lack of skill or knowledge about child rearing. Through the process of learning therapeutic techniques and related parenting skills, the parents are encouraged to assume the responsibility of assuaging the difficulty and providing the therapeutic environment for growth.

The goals of filial therapy for the child participant, paraphrased from Van Fleet (1994), include the following:

1. Recognize and express feelings fully and constructively.
2. Provide an opportunity to be heard.
3. Develop effective problem solving and coping.
4. Increase self-confidence and self-esteem.
5. Increase trust and confidence in the parents.
6. Reduce or eliminate problematic behaviors.
7. Develop desirable behaviors.
8. Promote a functional family climate.

Goals for the parents in filial therapy, as paraphrased from Van Fleet (1994), include the following:

1. Increase understanding of child development.
2. Increase understanding of own child.
3. Recognize importance of play for healthy emotions for themselves and their children.
4. Decrease parental frustration.
5. Improve parenting skills.
6. Increase parenting confidence.
7. Facilitate communication.
8. Enable teamwork.
9. Increase parental warmth and trust toward children.
10. Provide a safe place to work on issues related to their children.

Research on filial therapy has indicated that CREFT is effective in reducing child-related problems and in amplifying parental acceptance of their children (Van Fleet, 1994).

CREFT follows a prescribed agenda for training the parents to provide play sessions. The training, according to Van Fleet (1994, 2004), is presented in the following order: assessment, training, initial play sessions, therapist-supervised sessions, home sessions, skills review, and closing. Child-centered play therapy, which forms the basic theory for the play sessions and the playroom setup, was discussed in Chapter 6.

In the first meeting with the parents, the filial therapist takes the traditional intake information about reason for referral, developmental history, and family social history. Questionnaires, behavioral rating scales, or pretests may be administered as needed. The therapist, with the help of the parents, develops a comprehensive description of the child and the history of the difficulties. The therapist summaries the concerns, shares initial reactions, suggests immediate interventions, and recommends a family play observation.

The second visit is the family play observation. The therapist visits briefly with the children before taking the entire family into the playroom. The therapist observes behind a one-way mirror if possible, or selects an unobtrusive position in the room for the observation. The therapist focuses on the family's patterns, strengths, and possible problems.

In the third meeting the therapist meets once again with the parents alone. The therapist attempts to gain a perspective of how the observations in the playroom compare with the child's behavior in the home. If the child's behavior demands immediate intervention, the therapist makes recommendations. The therapist will recommend filial therapy at this point if the family seems to be appropriate for such an intervention. The parents must be able to make a commitment for 4 to 6 months of weekly or biweekly therapy sessions in the clinic or office and weekly sessions at home. This recommendation is followed up with addressing any of the parents' questions or expressions of doubt. The therapist clarifies the parents' concerns with additional explanations or rationales. If the parents agree to filial therapy, specific goals are identified and prioritized for the filial therapy treatment plan.

The parents observe a play therapy session done by the filial therapist with each of their children between the ages of 3 and 12. These demonstrations usually take one session to provide 15- to 20-minute play sessions with each child. After the observation, the therapist meets alone with the parents to discuss their questions, concerns, observations, and reactions to the session.

The parent training consists of teaching the basic skills of filial therapy. Guerney (1988) provides detailed information about the parenting skills given to the parents, which is only alluded to here. Van Fleet (1994) provides a detailed description of the training that is only sketched out here for your understanding of the process.

Based on the theory of child-centered play therapy, the parents are taught to structure the session by how to enter the playroom, how to handle bathroom breaks, and how to leave the playroom. The therapist provides the parents with strategies for working with the child, who may not want to enter or exit the playroom. The parents are then taught the skill of empathic listening and responding. They learn how to conduct a session in a nondirective manner, allowing the child to lead the way in the playroom. Child-centered limit setting is the next skill taught. The limits-setting skills specifically address stating the limit, giving a warning, and enforcing the consequence. Once the skills have been presented to the parents through lectures, demonstrations, modeling, role playing, skills exercises, feedback, and reinforcement, the parents are ready to move on to the play session demonstration. This training is usually completed in a single session.

The next training session involves mock play sessions. The filial therapist takes the role of the child; the parent practices his or her role in the treatment. The therapist chooses the content of the series of approximately four sessions of 15 to 20 minutes. The four or more role plays begin with a well-behaved child and advance in demand of skill level to a difficult child. The final role play may have content that parallels the problems the parents are having with their own child. At the conclusion of each role play, the parent is given extensive feedback and encouragement. The parent is allowed to replay a part that may have been difficult or was not thoroughly understood. The parents are given one area for improvement with each role play. Once the parents appear to have the basic skills, they are ready to move on to the supervised session with their own children. Basic skills training takes only a few sessions with one or both parents; however, basic skills taught to a group of six to eight can take at least 2 months (Van Fleet, 1994).

The parents are ready for their supervised play therapy sessions with their own children when the therapist and the parents feel they are ready. The first session is planned for 20 minutes with following sessions of 30 minutes. Each parent plays with the children one at a time with the therapist observing from behind a mirror. If possible, the other parent may be included in the observation room. If an observation room is not available, the parent and therapist may observe from just outside the room. Supervision following the sessions follows a pattern of asking the parent to share reactions, reinforcing what the parent did well, and making suggestions of one or two things the parent may improve in the next session. The supervision session

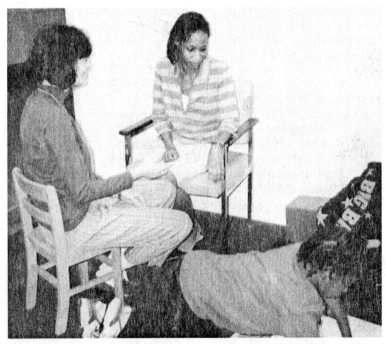

The therapist supervises the mother in the playroom as she works with her child.

closes with discussion of the child's play themes. When the parents and therapist believe the parents are ready, the play sessions are transferred to the home setting (Van Fleet, 1994).

The parents, during the direct supervision with the therapist, have been acquiring a set of toys for their special time or play sessions at home. The minimal list includes a come back toy, dart gun and darts, doll family, dollhouse, puppet family, baby bottle, bowl of water, container with water, crayons or markers, kitchen dishes, writing board, blocks, plastic soldiers, dinosaurs, molding clay, 6-foot piece of rope, deck of cards, and play money. These items do not have to be new or expensive. The therapist can discuss sources and creative alternatives to purchased toys. The parents need to select a place for the sessions that provides enough privacy and room for active play. A clear space of about 8 by 10 feet is recommended (Van Fleet, 1994). The parents also prepare for the transition to the home setting by discussing how they will schedule the play sessions and handle interruptions. They renew their commitment to the process and changes they anticipate taking place.

Once the parents are conducting their sessions at home, they meet either weekly or biweekly with the therapist for supervision. Every 6 to 8 weeks the therapist might ask the parents to come in for direct observation and supervision, especially if the case is difficult. The skills training continues during supervision time with more and more emphasis on generalization of skills to daily life. Discharge or termination is determined by the progress the parents and therapist feel is being made. The parents are encouraged to return to therapy in the future if they feel they need to do so. However, the final session is usually one in which the parents have a final direct observation and supervision with the therapist. The therapist and parents review their progress and make plans for their future sessions without the therapist. Parents are encouraged to continue the "special time" with their children into adolescence, although the special time will no longer be a play session (Van Fleet, 1994).

Louise Guerney (2000) writes that filial therapy (FT) was introduced to the clinical field in 1964 by the originator, Bernard Guerney. FT became popular in the 1960s but declined with the emphasis on behavioral methods. FT has experienced a resurgence in the last 15 years, due in part to the growth of play therapy and demand for parenting programs. Filial therapy melds the two into a smooth seam of treatment. The professional research is expanding on the populations and applications of FT. In 2000 filial therapy commanded a special issue of the *International Journal of Play Therapy*. "Basically, FT was too far ahead of the times. The times and proficient advocates have come together to offer to practitioners and parents a method that is robust, empirically valid, pleasant to swallow and rewarding" (L. Guerney, 2000).

LINKING PARENTS TO PLAY THERAPY

After the therapist has listened to the parent's description of concerns, the therapist may realize the parent's concern about the child is not appropriate for his or her practice and experience. A child may have a specific disability, disorder, behavior, or challenge that is beyond the capabilities of the therapist's qualifications or facilities. An example of this kind of limitation is working in a nonmedical private practice and a child may need residential treatment or medication. You may be aware of your own limitations in working with particular populations. Some therapists are uncomfortable working with populations that are culturally different from themselves. Some clients require special or advanced training, for example, forensic interviews for child sexual abuse or custody issues. In these cases, you must take the ethical action and refer the parent to an appropriate source and treatment. You must be familiar with the professional community and the resources available (McGuire & McGuire, 2001).

If the concern that the parent is expressing is appropriate for the therapist, the first appointment is scheduled and usually attended by the primary caregiver. Having both parents present, however, can provide a great deal of additional information about the child and the family environment. During the first appointment, the purpose is to listen further to the parent concerning the child and to gather background information. Specific data about the reason for referral, the presenting problem, changes in the presenting problem, what other course of action the parents have tried, and a general medical and developmental history of the child are collected to a greater or lesser degree. During this time you explain about the play therapy process and the expectations of the child and parents in the treatment. The goal is to have the session flow in such a way that the parents do not feel interrogated or resentful, but rather supported, reaffirmed, assured, and empowered in their choice of bringing the child to play therapy. Information is important in the course of treatment, but being responsive and sensitive to the parents' concerns and emotions is paramount. Information can be gathered as needed, but trust in you and treatment cannot be established too soon in the treatment process (McGuire & McGuire, 2001).

McGuire and McGuire (2001) offer some tips on how to talk to parents during the interview. Reflect and acknowledge the feelings that parents are experiencing about the child. Clarify any expressions the parents may use to describe the child or the family situation to assure understanding of the meaning. When gathering information, be sure to reflect and clarify the meaning of what is being said. If a comment or answer seems important, but unclear, ask the parent to tell you more about the answer. Sometimes the development of a client questionnaire is beneficial, especially if the parent can take it home and answer in a relaxed atmosphere. Discuss the legal parameters of confidentiality with the parents. Define the goals of therapy and how play therapy helps meet these goals. Explain how the parents can support the treatment and your expectations of their role (McGuire & McGuire, 2001).

When you meet with the child, part of that session is set aside for the parent, usually the first or last 15 minutes of the hour. McGuire and McGuire (2001) recommend the child not be present for these conversations but be allowed to choose whether the therapist meets before or after the session. The child may be in an adjacent room with the door ajar, so the parents and therapist can see the child and the child can see inside the room but cannot hear the conversation. The parent meeting is focused on three topics: the highlights of this session, sharing session themes, and homework. The homework outcome is discussed and new homework may be given for the parents and child.

Parents are encouraged to make contact before the session if they are unhappy, sad, angry, or frustrated with the child concerning something that has happened during the week. This precaution is seen as a way to protect the child from hearing or seeing the parent upset about what the child has done (McGuire & McGuire, 2000, 2001). Although the parents may contact you between sessions and see you without the child present, the parents' meeting "is not intended to be a time to punish the child by 'tattling' or reporting about them in a negative way" (McGuire & McGuire, 2001). If 15 minutes to meet with the parent is not sufficient, reevaluate the situation and see if a recommendation for a separate appointment or a referral is indicated for the parents' concerns (McGuire & McGuire, 2001).

SUMMARY

Family play therapy is difficult to discuss as play therapy or family therapy because of the prevailing professional view that treatment must be either family or individual therapy (Hardaway, 2000). Hardaway points out that this polarization of viewpoints is as logical as insisting that one medication will cure all ailments. Decision making in therapeutic interventions is based on the problem and often requires an eclectic treatment. The therapist must remain flexible in making the best choice in treatment mode for the presenting problem.

Family play therapy allows small children to take an important role in the treatment of the family. This modality of treatment benefits those older family members who may have difficulty expressing their views and issues as they affect the strengths and deficits of the family's functioning. Although this material may be accessible in traditional family therapy, family play therapy exacerbates the issues in a dramatic behavioral form that is readily observable and difficult to deny (Hardaway, 2000).

Family play therapy allows small children to take an important role in the treatment of the entire family.

CHAPTER 13

ASSESSING CHILDREN IN PLAY THERAPY

Therapists use drawing tests like the House-Tree-Person during play therapy to provide insight into the child's world and experiences.

This chapter reviews the methods that play therapists generally use in the course of therapy to gain more information about the child and generate insights in the therapeutic relationship to clarify the child's world. The assessments described here are commonly reviewed in the literature as used by play therapists and are generally organized into four categories: drawing assessments, interview assessments, storytelling assessments, and structured assessments.

INTRODUCTION

The length of the assessment phase and its degree of formality depend on the training and theoretical background of the play therapist. For example, psychologists are more apt to use extensive assessment techniques than social workers or counselors; directive or systemic theories are more prone than nondirective theories to favor extensive assessment. Other influences on the degree of commitment to assessment are determined by the population and the treatment setting. Children in residential treatment for severe behavior or developmental disorders naturally require more assessment than children referred to a private play therapist for adjustment to a new sibling.

The time commitment on the part of the individual therapist differs depending on the setting. Residential treatment usually employs a team approach for assessment and treatment, whereas the private practitioner does the assessment or refers the client to someone else for the assessment. Play therapists working in public schools may need formal assessments for those children receiving special services such as gifted programs or special education. The emphasis need not be on what type of assessment but rather on the appropriateness of the assessment for the child client.

If you suspect a need for assessment beyond your scope of training, make a referral to a qualified examiner. You should have a ready list of possible referral sources or collaborative arrangements to meet the needs of those clients you cannot serve personally.

Specialized training in assessment is required in most states for the administration and interpretation of individual intelligence tests and certain types of projective tests. The latter are restricted in most states when used for diagnosis. However, projective techniques are frequently used by play therapists in informal assessment for the purpose of understanding the child's concerns and gaining insight into the child's interpsychic world. These techniques should be used in formal diagnosis only by those who are specially trained. When relying on the techniques for therapeutic insight, approach any interpretation as tentative and simply as a possible hypothesis for exploration with the child. Examine any interpretation in light of what you know of the child and the child's situation. Methods for informal interpretation of projective techniques abound. The most commonly used are drawing techniques. They have no or little established validity or reliability. However, a familiarity with the essence of the technique will provide you with a background for exploring the child's spontaneous and directed artwork as an informal assessment.

DRAWING ASSESSMENTS

Drawing methods include such techniques as the *House-Tree-Person, Kinetic Family Drawing, Human Figure Drawing,* and many others. Burns (1987) indicates that the use of projective drawings to add to the understanding of people is a relatively new concept in the mental health field. Goodenough (1926), and later Harris (1963), attempted to norm figure drawing for the purpose of indicating intellectual development and maturity.

House-Tree-Person (HTP) drawings were introduced by Buck and then extended by Hammer (Buck, 1948; Buck & Hammer, 1969; Hammer, 1971). The HTP was used both projectively and developmentally to learn more about children and adults. Jolles (1964) developed an interpretation guide, which he termed a catalog, for the HTP. Other catalogs exist, but generally, Jolles's model (1964) is the standard; albeit a highly psychodynamic interpretation orientation. Machover (1949) examined and provided a thorough interpretation of children's human figure drawings. The human figure drawings of children were further studied and developed into a developmental scoring system by Koppitz (1968, 1984).

You need to be aware that some religions for example, Islam, do not allow a child to draw the human figure. However, Islam does allow the drawing of geometric shapes. An instrument like the Lowenfeld Mosaic Test might be an adequate substitute for an assessment.

The Draw-A-Family (DAF) technique was developed by Hulse (1951). The DAF provided a obdurate representation of the family. Because of this lack of emotional portraiture of the family, Burns and Kaufman (1970, 1972) developed the *Kinetic Family Drawing (KFD)*. Burns (1987) expanded the kinetic principle to be used with the House-Tree-Person into the *Kinetic-House-Tree-Person (KHTP)*.

The Draw-A-Person (Goodenough, 1926) was developed initially to estimate nonverbal intellectual functioning. This development was quickly followed by Machover's (1949, 1951) projective *Draw-A-Person (DAP)* instrument. The DAP remains a popular instrument in clinical assessment. In 1963 the Goodenough Draw-A-Man became the *Goodenough-Harris Drawing Test* (Harris, 1963). The Goodenough-Harris has been found to correlate with other intelligence tests as slightly above a guess (Anastasi & Urbina, 1997). The Goodenough-Harris may

A typical draw-a-family drawing.

prove to be a good instrument to support other intelligence testing for other-culture-dominated children, however (Anastasi & Urbina, 1997).

A blank sheet of paper and a pencil with an eraser is provided to the child. The instructions are to "draw a person." Most therapists ask the child to draw a second person of the other sex from the original drawing or first figure. The child is then asked to make up a story about the person as if the child were a character in a storybook (Machover, 1949).

Interpretation is based on psychodynamic premises of the unconscious mind projecting into the drawing the true feelings of the artist. The interpretation is what Gregory (2000) terms a "clinically-intuitive manner." Machover (1949) paid attention to size, line, and placement, which she considered more stable than body detail, clothing, and accessories.

Gregory (2000), in his review of Machover (1949, 1951), finds her to be "colorful, interesting, and plausible" (p. 509). However, the instrument lacks validity and reliability. Gregory is harsh in his criticism of the test except in the instance of its use for screening children assumed to be behavior problems or emotionally disturbed. He recommends the *Draw-A-Person: Screening Procedure for Emotional Disturbance (DAP:SPED)* (Naglieri, McNeish, & Barbos, 1991), which has been found to improve significantly the prediction of emotional problems in children.

Koppitz (1968, 1984) developed two scoring systems for the Human Figure Drawings (HFD). One is based on the Goodenough-Harris (Harris, 1963) and the other on the work of Machover (1949). Koppitz's (1984) instructions are "Draw one whole person. You can draw any kind of person you want to draw, but not a stick figure" (p. 10). After the child has drawn the figure, Koppitz (1984) asks three questions:

> Is the person you drew someone you know or someone you made up?
> How old is the person you drew?
> What is this person doing or thinking, and how does he (she) feel? (p. 12)

Koppitz (1984) provides the therapist with a description and figure examples to aid in scoring the drawings for mental maturity and for emotional indicators. Koppitz (1984) has distinguished 30 emotional indicators that were found to separate children with emotional problems from "normal" children. The emotional indicators include the face shading, transparencies, grotesque figures, and omissions of expected features like eyes, neck, or mouth. Both Gregory (2000) and Anastasi and Urbina (1997) caution that these instruments are only used to generate hypotheses about the children and are not meant to be used out of context or for diagnosis.

The HTP can be administered by providing the child with three sheets of 8.5 × 11-inch white paper and a pencil. The child is given one sheet of paper in the horizontal position and asked to draw a house. Then the child is presented with a new sheet of paper, presented vertically, and asked to draw a tree. Finally, the child is asked to draw a person on a vertically positioned sheet. The child is reminded that this drawing should be a person, not a stick figure, but a whole person (Buck, 1948, 1981; Buck & Hammer, 1969).

The interpretation guides are based on Freudian psychodynamic principles (Burns, 1987). According to Ogdon (1982), artistic training or ability does not affect the outcome of drawing tests such as the HTP. Young children have higher correlations to the detail, proportion, use of shading, and expression and intelligence. The more detailed the drawing, the more intelligent the child is thought to be (Goodenough, 1926; Harris, 1963). Although the literature seems to be replete with negative inferences from drawings, the impression may be assumed that a "normal HTP does not exist. However, a 'normal' HTP should have essential details and a few details that are not essential" (Ogdon, 1982). A so-called 'normal' HTP will have the following characteristics (Ogdon, 1982):

1. Figures will be about 6 or 7 inches tall and centrally placed or placed slightly below the center line.
2. Details will be on the head and face, which will be drawn first.
3. Proportions will be normal for the size of the drawing and will look as though they could move. Drawings will be relatively pleasant and appear balanced.
4. Improvements to the drawing will be made with minimal erasing.
5. Lines will be drawn with a steady pressure and consistent manner.
6. The self-sex person is usually drawn first.
7. Male figures will have larger shoulders, shorter hair, flatter hips, and reflect the fashion of men's apparel for the time.
8. Clothing will be present.
9. Some missing details like pupils in the eyes, neck, correct number of fingers, and so on, are clues to developmental stage.

The interpretation of the HTP is based on three major assumptions about the subject. The first is that the house drawing provides an indication of the subject's home life and family relationships. The second is that the tree indicates how the child experiences the environment. The third is that the person indicates the child's interpersonal relationships (Gregory, 2000).

Landreth (1980) provided a broad interpretation of the HTP in his advanced play therapy class. According to him, the child either spontaneously draws a house, tree, and person on a single sheet of paper or is instructed to draw the three items on a single sheet. He indicated that the house represents the mother, the tree represents the father, and the person represents the child. Kottman (2001a) has an interpretation of the House-Tree-Person drawings that are based in her Adlerian play therapy theory.

Many interpretation schemes exist for interpreting the HTP (Gregory, 2000). Unusual HTPs are readily identified by the experienced child therapist. Broken windows in the house, missing or broken limbs on the tree, or a person that has an aggressive demeanor is readily recognized by the least experienced as not a "normal" drawing. The context of these drawings needs to be explored by the therapist. These drawings need to be followed up by asking the child to tell a story or to talk about the picture.

The culture of the child may affect the type of drawings the child makes. Because the HTP and all drawing projective tests lack reliability and validity, reliance on interpretation needs to be cautious and tentative.

Buck (1981), the technique originator, criticizes the HTP's validity and reliability. He has written that the technique cannot be validated because of major research blocks. Some of his points are that the technique does not have a single infallible indication of a strength or weakness in the subject. The meanings of the HTP are based on an overall impression, not specific element or sign. The technique is greatly influ-

The person drawing from a House-Tree-Person drawing.

enced by the interest of the subject and the mood of the subject. Colors that may be used do not have any universal meaning across all cultures (Buck, 1981). The interpretation is left mainly to the intuition and experience of the therapist. Both Anastasi and Urbina (1997) and Gregory (2000) warn that the HTP, despite its continued popularity for the last 40 years, has failed to provide a valid and reliable instrument for assessment of personality. Gregory (2000) goes so far as to say that "reviewers have repeatedly recommended the abandonment of the H-T-P and similar figure-drawing approaches to personality assessment" (p. 511).

The *Kinetic House-Tree-Person (KHTP)* was developed by Burns (1987). The child is given a 8.5 × 11-inch piece of paper presented to the child in the horizontal position. The directions are "Draw a house, a tree, and a person on this paper with some kind of action. Try to draw a whole person, not a cartoon or stick person."

In interpreting the picture, Burns offers many questions to help guide the interpretation. Does the picture tell a story? What first impressions does the figure give? What kind of action is taking place? What is the emotional experience of viewing this picture? Are the elements in the picture safe or hostile? What are the distances between the figures? What kind of symbols are used in the picture? These questions represent only a limited number of observations used in the interpretation of the KHTP.

Burns provides an interpretation based on a modification of Maslow's (1987) hierarchy of needs. He divides the drawing interpretation from lowest to highest, including belonging to life, belonging to body, belonging to society, belonging to self and not-self, and belonging to all living things. He further divides each of these into approach and avoidance or aggressive and passive types at each level. He provides many examples and clear representations of interpretation of the figures.

The KHTP has received the same criticism as all the other drawing tests. It has little or no reliability or validity. Burns does have a unique interpretation with the Maslow's Modified Model and a practical appendix that summarizes general and individual characteristics of the KHTP.

The *Draw-A-Family (DAF)* was developed by Hulse (1951). Hulse asks the children, "Will you draw your family?" When the child finished drawing his or her family, the child was asked to name the people and to comment on the drawing. Hulse examined the drawings for spacing, size of figures, and distribution over the paper. He was most concerned about the pressure the child used in drawing the family, shading and coloring, and the sequence in which the family members were drawn.

Through looking at the family drawings, Hulse (1951) believed he would have a snapshot of the child's perception of the family constellation. He thought that children project their perceptions, attitudes, and feelings about different family members in their drawings. The placement of the child in the family helps indicate alliances or perceived closeness to specific family members.

Several studies have been conducted to validate the DAF. Deren (1975) studied 239 family drawings of both children and adults. His sample included African American, Puerto Rican, and Anglo American subjects. His findings supported the validity of the DAF technique. Reznikoff and Reznikoff (1956) studied the family drawings of black and white children. Their findings indicated that gender differences are more prominent than racial differences. Males placed themselves centrally and omitted the mother significantly more often than females. Black children were more likely to omit siblings. In low-income families, the oldest child was often drawn in a more dominant position; the mother was often omitted. The families were often drawn as if hanging in midair. The father was sometimes drawn without arms.

Di Leo (1973) used family drawings to indicate the sources of behavior disorders. When examining the drawings, he looked for omissions of significant family members, the omission of the child, who the child placed himself or herself closest to, who the child indicated dressed alike, and spatial relationships between and among the family members.

An illustration of unusual experiences with this technique was experienced by a beginning school psychologist. A first-grade child was referred for behavior problems and inattention in the classroom. As was the custom, the child took the battery of screening tests used to assess learning disabilities and behavior concerns. Included in this battery was the DAF. The child drew himself, his mother, grandmother, and 16 siblings. When asked to name the siblings and give their ages, the child provided all the names and ages. The drawing was not of high quality and appeared to be developmentally less than expected, but the child had done the drawing in a hurry. Both the school psychologist and a more experienced associate examined the drawing and felt the child was simply getting lost in the family with so many children. The next step was to interview the mother to see what might be done to make the child feel not so lost in the shuffle of the family.

The mother agreed to come in and talk to the school psychologist, who had administered the instrument. When the mother had left, the school psychologist came to the associates' office holding out the picture and reported the child was an only child. Both realized how far they had been led astray by the child. As time passed, they learned the child in his loneliness had created the 16 imaginary siblings from neighborhood children and cousins. He was not lost; he was lonely.

The *Kinetic Family Drawing (KFD)* (Burns & Kaufman, 1970) instructions ask the child to draw everyone in the family, including themselves, doing something. Children are reminded not to draw cartoon or stick people. When the child is finished, the therapist asks the child to tell who each person is and their age. Rather quickly the therapist can see by the proximity and shared activities which family members are united or distanced from each other. The interpretation is focused on the action. Using the ages, the therapist can see if the alignments are based on age, gender, or other shared designation in the family. The proximity to the parents may indicate either a desired relationship or the actual relationship.

Klepsch and Logie (1982) indicate that a mother engaging in nurturing activities is positive, as is a father relaxing. However, a mother cleaning or ironing is considered negative, as is a father mowing the lawn or driving to work. Ball throwing or other competitive activities are viewed as rivalry between the players. Klepsch and Logie (1982) provide references to several scoring schemes. Several researchers have tried to simplify or clarify the scoring procedure. However, although many new correlations were found, no formal reliability or validity was established (Klepsch & Logie, 1982)

The *Draw-a-Group (DAG), Kinetic School Drawing (KSD),* and *Akinetic School Drawing Technique (ASDT)* are some of the other attempts to use human figure drawings to gain insight into children's perceptions of others and their place within groups.

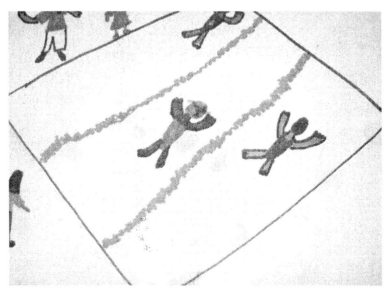

The child has drawn a Kinetic Family Drawing. The instructions are that the child is to draw his or her family doing something.

The DAG instructions ask the child to think about who he plays with on the playground and then to draw them in an activity the child likes best. When the child has finished the drawing, the examiner writes down a description of what is happening as the child dictates the action.

The KSD was developed by Prout and Phillips (1974) to ascertain how the child saw herself in school. The child was instructed to draw a school picture with herself, her teacher, and a friend or two in the picture. Everyone should be doing something, and the child was asked to make the best drawing she could. The technique was found to have potential, but whether it actually indicated how the child saw herself in school has not been established.

The ASDT was developed by Kutnick (1978), who asked the children "to draw a classroom with people in it." The drawings were found to be better indicators of the teacher's social position in the school than an indication of how children perceived themselves in the classroom.

Klepsch and Logia (1982) provide practical guidance and interpretation of all the techniques discussed in this section. Their work represents a classic in the field of drawing assessment techniques. Many other techniques, like Draw a Person in the Rain, Draw an Animal, and Draw a Car, are described as techniques providing the clinician with many drawing assessment alternatives.

The Rosebush, described by Allan (1988), is a visualization strategy for identifying possible child abuse. The technique consists of three parts. The first part is a structured relaxation and visualization exercise in which the child is asked to picture himself as a rosebush. Following the structured visualization, the child is asked to draw the rosebush. The child is given a standard 8.5 × 11-inch sheet of paper, number 2 pencil, and a box of 12 colored crayons. A postdrawing inquiry is conducted. The questions encourage the child to describe how the rosebush looks. The child is asked specific questions about the rosebush's blossoms, stem, roots, thorns, and branches. The child is asked who takes care of the rosebush. The complete interpretation, visualization transcript, and postdrawing inquiry are recorded by Allan (1988).

The *Color-Your-Life* technique (O'Connor, 1983) was developed to provide a graphic description of the child's emotional life. The child is given a standard sheet of 8.5 × 11-inch white paper. The eight colors provided are in a box with red, orange, yellow, green, blue, brown, black, and purple. The child is asked to pair each color crayon with a feeling. Ammen et al. (1996) selected the following standardized emotional-color pairings: red—mad, orange—excited, yellow—happy, green—lonely, blue—sad, brown—bored, black—scared, and purple—choice. These are the standardized instructions:

> Pretend the sheet of paper is your whole life. Fill up the paper with the colors that show what feelings you have had. If you have felt mostly happiness, then use mostly yellow. Color the paper in any way you want, but use the colors and feelings I have written on the blackboard (or chart). (Ammen et al., 1996)

Through the CYL, the therapist can see a visual representation of the child's perceptions of his or her emotional life and emotional history. The technique has been used with child cancer patients (Boley, Peterson, Miller, & Ammen, 1996) and with the siblings of pediatric cancer patients (Boley, Ammen, O'Connor, & Miller, 1996).

Bird's Nest Drawing (Gil, 1998) is a metaphor for birth, home, and nurturing, according to Gil. The placement of the bird's nest provides a metaphorical representation of how the child sees his or her security and safety. The presence or absence of the mother bird represents the child's perception of the nurturance or lack of nurturance from the mother figure.

Draw-A-Volcano (Gil, 1998) was developed by Carol Cox to indicate the level of affective tension. Volcanoes may be drawn with lava flows, explosions, and flying ash or may be peaceful, barren, and silent. The concept of the volcano provides the child with a vivid expressive tool to describe the child's emotional tension.

Draw a Picture of a Person Picking an Apple from a Tree represents the child's view of the his or her ability to secure nurturance. Some children may not be able to draw how to pick an apple; others may draw the apples close to the ground and easily reached. Still other children may draw themselves climbing into the tree or using a ladder to get an apple. Some trees may even have spoiled fruit or show the apples being stolen by birds. The drawing provides the therapist with a perspective of the child's accessibility to nurturance and the quality of that nurturance (Gil, 1998).

The Bender-Gestalt Visual Motor Test, commonly called the Bender-Gestalt Test (BGT) (Bender, 1938), consists of nine figures, each on a 4 by 5 card, presented individually to the child. The child has been given two pieces of clean, lineless paper, 8.5 by 11 inches and a number 2 pencil with an eraser. Additional paper and pencil is available for the child on the uncluttered table. The child is shown the stack of nine cards and provided with these instructions: "I have nine cards here with designs on them for you to copy. Here is the first one. Now go ahead and make one just like it" (Koppitz, 1964). No attempt is made to let the child know that all the figures should be on the same page or additional pages are available. The paper is placed vertically in front of the child and the cards are placed and aligned carefully. The examiner is instructed to answer any questions the child may ask in a noncommittal manner.

Bender's scoring criteria is based on 12 indexes. If 5 of the 12 indexes are scored positively, the child is considered to have minimal brain damage, a potential sign of a learning disability. However, the Bender is not frequently used by play therapists to detect cognitive functioning, but rather developmental indicators.

The Koppitz Developmental Scoring System (Koppitz, 1964) is composed of two phases: developmental scoring and emotional indicators. The developmental score provides a visual-motor perception score that indicates a developmental age for the child. The percentile norms are for children between the ages of 5 years, 0 months, and 11 years, 11 months. The emotional indicators overlap other disabilities on the test and are not considered except for further investigation. The Bender Gestalt is a good screening device but lacks the rigor used for diagnosis (Anastasi & Urbina, 1997; Gregory, 2000).

INTERVIEW ASSESSMENTS

Interviewing has been a time-honored method used to gather important information from the client (Anastasi & Urbina, 1997). Interviews may be structured, unstructured, quantitative, qualitative, written, verbal, or observational. The form of the interview does not matter if the interview provides the information being sought. The interview offers two distinct advantages: (1) a direct observation of the behavior, and (2) a view of what the client has done in the past as a good indicator of what will be done in the future (Anastasi & Urbina, 1997).

Major drawbacks exist in the interview, especially the less structured ones. The inexperienced interviewer may lack the necessary skills to elicit information, resulting in the incorrect collection and interpretation of data. The interviewer may lack interview experience and not correctly identify those topics that need to be probed further. The interviewer may lack observations skills and miss important cues in the client's behavior that may need to be probed and verified further through other methods (Anastasi & Urbina, 1997).

The Puppet Interview

The Puppet Interview (Ross, 1991) is a family puppet interview technique for the family. Ross explains that in order to get a clear picture of the family's concerns, she would like them to act out a recent situation with the puppets. She allows one parent and the child to choose a puppet each and then decide which recent scene they want to reenact using the puppets. If the other parent is present, he or she serves as observer and takes a turn later with the child in another scenario.

The parent and child are asked to do exactly what happened as closely as they remember it: the other parent and the therapist watch. The therapist disengages from the process by taking notes and pulling the child's chair slightly away from the parent and child. After the parent and child have portrayed the scene as they remember it, the therapist asks them to replay the scene, but this time to switch puppets and roles in the scene. Finally, the parent and child assume their original characters and play the scene as they would have liked to have had the scene play out. A discussion may take place following the final scene. If the other parent is present, he or she and the child now select a different scene and follow the same process.

Usually the scenes are very accurate descriptions of what is going on in the home. The interview allows the therapist to observe the dynamics and interaction with the safe barrier of the puppets doing the action, not the child and parent. The model provides one method to observe the parent-child interaction directly when the child is very young (Ross, 1991).

Irwin (1991) uses puppets in yet another way to gain understanding of the child. She introduces the puppets by presenting them in a large collection or heap for the child to explore. Then Irwin encourages the child to choose several puppets for a puppet play. She represents herself as the audience for the child's puppet performance. Her prompts to the child may be something along the line of "And now, we have our first character. This is . . . " (Irwin, 1991, p. 622). Once all the characters are introduced and named, she may ask the characters questions about their role in the play that is about to take place. She will then cue the child to start the play with something like "Let the play begin . . . " If the child seems stuck, she will ask the characters about the setting and what might take place. Then she will watch as the child acts out the scene. After the play is over, she may ask questions about how the puppets feel, what made them want to do what they did, and other open-ended questions.

The child and therapist are doing a dollhouse interview.

Once the puppets have been interviewed, Irwin may interview the child about what the puppet play experience felt like. She may ask, "What part of the play did you like best? Were there parts you would like to change? What kind of title would you like to give the play? What kind of moral would you guess the play taught?" Answers from the child and the puppets help the therapist understand the child's worries and wishes.

The Dollhouse Interview

The *Dollhouse Interview* is a useful tool in the practice of play therapy. The assessment technique presented here is not original with the author; however, review of the literature could not locate a source. The furniture is placed off to one side for the child's selection. Furniture for two bedrooms, a bathroom, kitchen, and a living room is the minimum. The house may be a box with lined-off rooms or a formal wooden dollhouse.

The child needs a selection of dollhouse dolls to select the family. Typically, the selection may include a grandfather, grandmother, mother, father, male child, female child, baby, and several other children of varying sizes. Dolls representing different races are most important, especially if the family may be racially mixed. Racially different dolls are often hard to find, so animal families may be substituted for human families.

The child is asked to place all the furniture in the house and to select a family that has the same number of people and family roles as in the child's family. A child from a single-parent home would only choose a single parent and children. Some children might choose a grandparent, a parent, uncles, aunts, and then siblings. Each family member is given a name and approximate age. The child is asked to place all the people in the house as if it were nighttime and everyone was at home asleep. Then the therapist says, "It's time to get up. Show me who gets up first and what happens."

The therapist then follows the home routine throughout the day until it is night-time again. Following a description of a normal day, the therapist asks the child to show what would happen when the child does something wrong.

If the child sometimes lives with another parent or other significant adult, a second dollhouse, furniture, and characters may be employed to illustrate what living in the alternate residence is like for the child. The same process can take place with the use of other props. Other types of play stages available to the child may be a schoolroom, ambulance, operating room, court room, and a barn. For fantasy or what the child might wish, a castle and a fort might be available.

STORYTELLING ASSESSMENTS

Storytelling assessments are based on the concept that in response to a stimulus the child will tell a story, usually with a beginning, middle, and end. The child's response is a reflection of fundamental aspects of his or her personality. Storytelling techniques provide the performance test of personality (Teglasi, 2001). Through the story told by the child, thought processes, problem-solving strategies, and inroads into the child's "schemas for organizing the inner world in relation to the external environment" (Teglasi, 2001) is narrated to the therapist/examiner. The story told helps clarify the child's thoughts about self and the world that differs greatly from forms of self-report and checklists.

The child is expected to produce a logical, coherent, and stimulus-related story with a resolution of the conflict in a socially acceptable manner. Because of the ambiguous nature of the technique, storytelling indicates the child's adjustment to new, stressful, or complicated life situations, which challenges the child's inner resources to respond. The story format allows the children to show how they understand the world to be and how they perceive their role in that world in a less threatening manner. Without the usual social restraints, the child reveals the underlying moral development, cognitive development, and social awareness by the intentions, actions, and outcomes of the story characters. Although the storytelling method supplies a rich and fertile ground for insight into the child's problems, the one step away from reality that permits the expression of these inner thoughts, feelings, and moral development can also be its downfall (Teglasi, 2001).

According to Teglasi (2001), there are some pitfalls in assuming or predicting aggressive behavior from the stories. One of the first is that children who exhibit aggressive behavior may not do so in storytelling methods. The stimulus may not access the necessary social stimulus that precedes the aggressive behavior. Of main importance is that a nonaggressive child may be pulled toward an aggressive response because of the aggressive nature of the stimulus. Therefore, the influence of the stimulus content and the context in which the child lives must be taken into account (Teglasi, 2001).

In the clinical use of storytelling methods, you need to develop a system for organizing the information into logical concepts. You must have a thorough comprehension of the developmental stage of the child and the expectations of the child's storytelling ability. Use a theoretical framework in the interpretation to indicate what may be relevant in development, psychopathology, and personality. All of the material generated in the storytelling method needs to be viewed in light of the information gained through other informational sources. An overall consideration is how the information gathered from the method allows you to gain understanding, plan for further interventions, and unravel the complexities of the presenting problem (Teglasi, 2001).

Reliability and validity studies on storytelling methods show low reliability and validity. Those methods that are standardized are often restricted and require special training to administer and to use for diagnosis. Review the state law in your state and determine whether your practice license allows for the use of such techniques and what the limits of practice are on projective tests. Generally speaking, the restriction does not apply when the method is used for generating material for discussion or in the course of an intervention, but does apply if it is to be included in a formal psychological report or the basis for a diagnostic label. Most codes of ethics for professional mental health workers do not allow the use of any assessment instrument that the person has not been trained to use. Before using any assessment instrument, check your professional code of ethics for limitations of practice.

Storytelling methods are intriguing, but they may not be helpful to ongoing therapy. Children from cultures, especially the culture of poverty, may live in a very concrete world where reality is emphasized. These children often give what is called a *poverty of response* or simply tell what is happening in a picture or refuse to cooperate with the task. This experience is very frustrating to both the child and the therapist. Therefore, like children who must be taught to play before they can be successful at play therapy, some children must be told stories and have experience with storytelling before they can participate in storytelling methods.

Make A Picture Story (MAPS) is a projective technique developed for adolescents and adults. The instrument has 22 picture background 8.5 × 11-inch cards showing both structured and ambiguous scenes. Examples of the structured scenes include bedroom, baby's room, bathroom, schoolroom, or a park. Examples of the ambiguous scenes include a forest, cemetery, doorway, and cave. A blank card is included for creating the background the client may choose. In addition, 67 cutouts of figures are included. These figures include men, women, children, law enforcement officers, fantasy figures, animals, people with disabilities, nudes, ghosts, and other characters for creating a story. The backgrounds and the figures are all in gray-and-white drawings, reminiscent of charcoal drawings.

The therapist asks the client to choose a background card and cut out figures. The examinee is then asked to dramatize a story using the background and figures he or she selects.

Although the MAPS is the forerunner of many similar tests, it does not offer any kind of standardized interpretation for children. The gray-and-white qualities of the backgrounds and figures appear dated. The clothing on the figures looks dated.

The *Scenotest* has a 50-year history of use in Europe. The test is recommended to help assess emotional difficulties in children. The Scenotest grew out of the play therapy tradition (Anastasi & Urbina, 1997). The test consists of a standardized selection of toys, which include human figures, animals, vehicles, fantasy figures, trees, flower beds, fruits, building blocks, and various household objects. These items are displayed in a large carrying case that has specific compartments for the various objects and figures. The top or lid of the case can be used as the stage for the human figures and the prop objects. The manual (von Staabs, 1991) provides a complete listing of all of the items, an observation sheet, and helpful guides for interpretation. Several case illustrations are provided with photographs to aid in the understanding of the concept.

The items are rather primitive in design featuring wooden toys that are common in European toys but less common in the United States. Some items might be problematic across cultures (e.g., carpet sweeper, milk bottle, chamber pot, and slate). The human figures are small, much like small dollhouse figures, dressed in clothing that is more European than American. The Scenotest seems to have great possibilities but needs to have more updated figures for American culture.

Gardner Children's Projective Battery (GCPB) Gardner (2003) is a "comprehensive psychodynamic evaluation of the child" (p. 1). Gardner recommends a token chip reinforcement to ensure the child's cooperation in the many activities he includes in the battery. An examination of the companion book's table of contents reveals the content of the battery to include freely drawn pictures, bag of faces, storytelling cards, draw-a-person, and draw-a-family. He uses wish questions and verbal projective questions about people, animals, and objects. The battery includes asking the child for descriptions of animals that would suit each parent. He explores the best and worst experiences of life, dreams, and family life. Free play with human figures, self-change questions, and created stories are included. The companion book has a chapter in working with parents to attain input in the assessment. The manual that comes with the battery provides detailed instructions (Gardner, 2003) but does not provide clinical examples. The companion book does provide clinical examples to guide the therapist in interpretation of the battery.

According to Gardner (2003), the Gardner Battery is intended to take about 3 to 4 hours or three to four sessions to complete. He developed the battery after more than 40 years of experience with traditional instruments (i.e., Children's Apperception Test [CAT], Thematic Apperception Test [TAT], and the Rorschach test). The intent of the GCPB is to overcome Gardner's perceived complications and limitations of these methods in assessing children. The battery is designed to maintain the child's interest and not to tire the child by asking for self-created material. The battery lacks the reliability and validity of most projective techniques, but Gardner has this to say about the clinical illustrations from the GCPB:

> The clinical examples provided in this companion volume to the GCPB provides the author'[s] interpretations of material elicited from his patients and evaluatees and should only be considered reasonably accurate interpretations for the particular children who were examined by him. This caveat notwithstanding, the volume (Gardner, 2003) provides a rich compendium of clinical examples that should serve as valuable guidelines for the therapist utilizing the GCPB. (p. 2)

The Storytelling Card Game is based on the assumption that children's made-up stories can provide the therapist with an inroad into the child's problems. However,

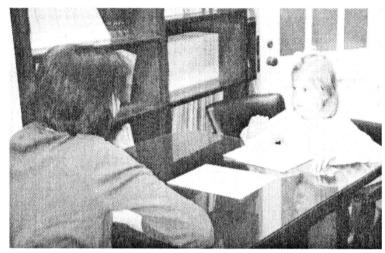

The child and play therapist are using the Storytelling Game.

Gardner (1968, 1970, 1971, 1972a, 1972b, 1975) found that children are sometimes reluctant to reveal themselves in self-created stories and developed The Storytelling Card Game to make the process easier for the child and the therapist.

To start the game, the child spins a spinner with 10 possible outcomes of gaining or losing green tokens. Six of the positions on the spinner direct the child to select 4 specific cards from the 24 available scenes. A total of 24 cards exist, with 20 depicting a setting void of animals or humans and 4 that are blank cards. The 24 scenic cards have scenes of classrooms, parks, forests, children's rooms, and so on. After using the spinner to select the cards, the child then throws a die to choose the tagboard cutout people. The selection of characters includes 15 Caucasian, 6 African American, 6 Hispanic, and 3 Asian adults and children.

When the child places these characters on the scenic background, a chip is awarded. The child may earn more chips by creating a story with a beginning, middle, and end. The child may earn an additional chip by providing a moral to the story or a title.

The instruction manual comes with alternative ways to play the game and ways to use the materials as an intervention. One method includes using the game for a mutual storytelling experience. Gardner's mutual storytelling allows the child to tell the story first. Then the therapist retells the story in a way that improves the problem solving of the main character (Gardner, 1968, 1970, 1971, 1972a, 1972b, 1975).

The Storytelling Card Game is listed here with other assessments, although it requires less formal evaluation training than the MAPS or Scenotest. Many of the techniques described in Gardner's Projective Children's Battery are used in The Storytelling Card Game. The game has the added appeal of not being restricted in its use; although the more you know about projectives, the more you can learn from the game.

Other materials by Gardner (2003) that you might find helpful for use in planning interventions or providing interventions include The Talking, Feeling, Doing Game; The Helping, Sharing, and Caring Game; Pick and Tell Games; and the Adoption Card Game.

Projective Questions

Projective questions are commonly used in social work to discover how the child may feel about the child's family and life (Webb, 1996). Here are some examples of these questions:

> If you had three wishes, what would you wish for?
> If a baby bird fell out of the nest, what might happen?
> If you were going on a rocket trip to the moon, and you could take only one person with you, who would you take? (Webb, 1996)

The child is encouraged to answer in an unhurried manner. The child may be reminded there are no right or wrong answers to the questions. The questions provide the therapist with clues to the child's altruism, moral development, attachments, and ability to foresee consequences of behaviors.

STRUCTURED INTERVIEWS

The clinical interview is usually unstructured or open ended. When the child is interviewed, the clinical interview is often an observation of the child at play or in an interaction with the primary caregiver. The clinical interview may take place without the child present when the information is gathered from the caregiver. Usually the clinical interview is directed toward gathering the nature of the problem, the past and present history of the problem, information about the environment of the home or school, feelings and perceptions of the significant adults, attempts at solving the problem, outcomes of attempts, and what the expectations are concerning treatment (Wicks-Nelson & Israel, 2003).

The structured interview has developed to gather specific information, which may be considered more reliable. The development of the structured interview has a limited purpose of helping make a diagnosis based on specific criteria, as in providing a Diagnostic and Statistical Manual of Mental Disorders classification. The structured interview represents a standardized procedure with exact guidelines and scoring and recording procedures (Wicks-Nelson & Israel, 2003). Some of the more common ones are briefly reviewed here.

Anxiety Disorders Interview for Children (ADIS-IV) (Silverman & Albano, 1997) is both a child and a parent interview to help diagnose childhood emotional disorders when anxiety is a major component. The problem behaviors the interview addresses include are school refusal behavior, separation anxiety, social phobia, specific phobia, panic disorder, agoraphobia, obsessive-compulsive disorder, and post-traumatic stress disorder (PTSD). The structured interview assesses attention-deficit/hyperactivity disorder (ADHD) and allows for differentiation of inattentive type, hyperactive-impulsive type, and combined type. The interview questions in the child interview are meant to be easily understood by a broad range of age levels.

Other child and adolescent structured interviews recommended by Wicks-Nelson and Israel (2003) include *Child Assessment Schedule (CAS)* (Hodges, Cool, & McKnew, 1989); *Child and Adolescent Psychiatric Assessment (CAPA)* (Angold, Costello, & Erkanli, 1999); *Children's Interview for Psychiatric Syndromes (ChIPS)* (Weller, Weller, Fristad, Rooney, & Schecter, 2000); *Diagnostic Interview for Children and Adolescents (DICA)* (Reich, 2000); *Interview Schedule for Children and Adolescents (ISCA)* (Sherril & Kovacs, 2000); *NIMH Diagnostic Interview Schedule for Children Version IV (NIMH DISC-IV)* (Shaffer, Fisher, Lucas, Dulcan, & Schwab-Stone, 2000); and *Schedule for Affective Disorders and Schizophrenia for School-Age Children (K-SADS)* (Ambrosini, 2000). These structured interviews are available from various psychological assessment catalogs, and many of them are restricted by the therapist's training and practice. These structured interviews are presented as a reference for the play therapist who might be seeking a special instrument for forensic or development assessment.

SUMMARY

Many techniques can be used to assess the inter- and intrapsychic world of the child. Most of the techniques are within the scope and training of clinically trained mental health therapists. Special training and supervision greatly adds to the competency of the individual therapist in using these tools. The assessments in this chapter should be viewed as tools to indicate areas of investigation, but total reliance on tools in any craft is not complete. The therapist must use adequate therapeutic skills and training to ensure a quality experience for the child.

CHAPTER 14

DIAGNOSIS AND TREATMENT

The parent and play therapist complete various checklists and interview forms.

This chapter reviews the disorders most commonly seen in children along with a brief description of treatment. Certain treatments appear to have a better fit with some theories of play therapy than others. The suggestions of play therapy theories are based merely on a survey of the theory and not on any empirical data or present literature.

INTRODUCTION

One of the most difficult tasks a novice play therapist must learn is how to take the observations in the playroom and transfer that information into an explanation of what might be happening with the child. Because of the pressure of managed care, more and more play therapists are being asked to provide DSM (*Diagnostic and Statistical Manual of Mental Disorders*) designations for the children seen in play therapy. No matter how many years you practice, this part of play therapy is an on-going learning process. The names of old diagnoses change and new diagnoses appear in the literature. The criteria for a disorder changes as the mental health community moves more toward standardization and greater sophistication of diagnosis.

ANXIETY DISORDERS

Anxiety or fear is a complex pattern of reactions to what the child perceives as a threat. The child may react in ways that can be observed (e.g., running away, voice tremor, squinting eyes shut). The child may also have physiological responses (e.g., rapid pulse, breathing difficulties, muscle tension, upset stomach). The subjective responses are harder to identify but are usually reported by the child to include thoughts of being scared, images of being hurt, or thoughts of dying (Wicks-Nelson & Israel, 2003). The Fear Survey Schedule for Children II that is currently in the norming process is showing great promise in helping identify children's fears (Burnham, 1997). The varying degrees of stress experienced by the child and situations in which the distress is experienced usually falls within one of these descriptions (Samuels & Sikorsky, 1990; Wicks-Nelson & Israel, 2003):

Social phobia

Separation anxiety disorder or school refusal

Generalized anxiety disorder

Panic disorder or panic attacks

Obsessive-compulsive disorder

Post-traumatic stress disorder

Achenback and Rescorla (2001), using the empirical approach, have described what they term the anxious/depressed syndrome, characterized by excessive crying, fears, school fears, fear of doing badly, perfectionism, feelings of being unloved, feelings of being worthless, nervousness, tenseness, guilt feelings, self-consciousness, easily hurt when criticized, possible talk of suicide, eagerness to please, fear of making mistakes, and generally worrying. Related are those syndromes of somatic complaints and withdrawal/depression. In the former, the child complains of illnesses or symptoms of illness; in the latter, the child may refuse to talk or withdraws (Wicks-Nelson & Israel, 2003).

Social Phobia

Another name for what parents describe as painfully "shy" is **social phobia**. The child has a fear of speaking, reading, writing, or performing in public. The child does not initiate conversations in social situations and when spoken to may avoid responding or answer in barely audible or short answers. The child has difficulty playing with other children in school and in the neighborhood. The child may express being seen in a negative way or being embarrassed. The child in the playroom may not interact with the therapist and may choose not to play. The child may be compliant but tentative in his or her exploration of the playroom. The rapport-building phase of therapy may be extended with a very silent child or one who does only what is asked in a slow and tentative manner. The child may also exhibit a need for reassurance that attempts at tasks are acceptable. The child may have drawings, stories, or other expressions that indicate low acceptance by peers and low self-worth. The child may be described by the parent as timid or shy. Selective mutism is a form of social phobia. These children do not speak in specific situations, like school or play activities. However, the child may speak easily with family members if no one else is present (Samuels & Sikorsky, 1990; Wicks-Nelson & Israel, 2003).

Separation Anxiety

Characterized in play therapy by crying after the age of about 3 or by refusing to accompany you to the playroom without the parent is a disorder called **separation anxiety.** The child may cling to the door and try to escape back to the parent, if you are not alert. In mild cases of separation anxiety, the child may ask to go to the bathroom or claim to be ill. In more extreme cases the child may relate that the parents are not returning because of an accident. The drawings and play themes are filled with various fears such as muggers, kidnappers, car accidents, and concerns about dying. The parent will usually report that the child has difficulty sleeping. Nightmares are very common or drawings and play themes that could be a nightmare (Wicks-Nelson & Israel, 2003).

Associated with separation anxiety is **school refusal,** which plays out with anxiety and somatic complaints. The child may become dizzy, nauseated, or have stomachaches, demanding to be kept at home. The child's pediatrician cannot usually find a source for these so-called illnesses. The parent may be very reluctant to send the apparently sick child to school because of the uncertainty of illness and the child's sincere anxiety. Most often the child is afraid of some part of the school. Children who are bullied at school, embarrassed by academic ability, or fearful of particular adults may develop these symptoms. When children cannot live up to expectations or demands for excellence in sports or physical activities, the child may develop school refusal. The child may also want to remain at home with the mother.

An example is Michael, who was fearful to come to school the day that both parents were in the home. During these times, spousal abuse was a common experience in his home. The parents would not become physically violent when Michael, their only child, was present. Therefore Michael saw his absence from the home as leaving one parent unprotected from the other. He became ill so he could control the violence (Wicks-Nelson & Israel, 2003).

School refusal is considered a separation anxiety because the fears are frequently associated with fear of separation from the primary caretaker. The school refusal may exacerbate when the child is given special treatment when he or she stays home. The special treatment could be as simple as getting to be with the caretaker alone to more complex treatment like new toys, special foods, or undivided attention from the caretaker (Samuels & Sikorsky, 1990; Wicks-Nelson & Israel, 2003).

According to Wicks-Nelson and Israel (2003), separation anxiety and school re-fusal are reported most often following some life-changing event (e.g., a death, an illness, a change of school, or a move). In the case of school refusal, the child needs to return to school as quickly as possible. In both cases, you and the parents need to work together to identify the underlying source of the child's separation anxiety.

Generalized Anxiety Disorder

A more unfocused kind of worrying is described as **generalized anxiety disorder**. The child may display excessive anxiety or worry, seem restless or feeling on edge, may express fatigue, have difficulty concentrating, be irritable, seem tense, or have dis-turbed sleep. In the playroom the child may talk about being afraid of ghosts, mon-sters, abandonment, war, guns, knives, strangers, or any number of things. The play themes are likely to center on these fears and trying to gain control over them. The child is likely reported by the parents as having sleep problems and needing a night light beyond a reasonable age (Wicks-Nelson & Israel, 2003).

The child may display excessive worrying and fearful behavior without a known stressor. The child will play out a theme and then react in a manner such as nail bit-ing, thumb sucking, or even pouting. Sometimes a particular object may cause a nerv-ous movement. The child may need to be reassured excessively. The body of the child is tense and rigid. The child may express worry about who will be seeing the play ses-sion or what will happen after it is over. The child may not play but rather ask ques-tions about the other children and what happened to them.

Panic Disorder

Panic disorder is not common in children under the age of 12 (Kearney & Silverman, 1992; Klein, Mannuzza, Chapman, & Fyer, 1992; Ollendick, 1998); however, be-tween the ages of 12 and 17, as many as 10% to 16% have been found to experience panic attacks in clinical samples (Alessi, Robbins, & Dilsaver, 1987; King, Ollendick, Mattis, Yang, & Tonge, 1997; Last & Strauss, 1989). Panic disorder must include recurrent and unexpected panic attacks, which results in a concern about the reoc-currence to the point that it changes the child or adolescent's behavior. Panic attacks are not considered a diagnostic category. However, in panic attacks the child may experience rapid pulse, sweating, trembling, loss of breath, choking, chest pain, nau-sea, abdominal distress, dizziness, derealization (feeling this is not real), or deper-sonalization (feeling you are leaving your body). Other symptoms can include feeling like you are going crazy, fear of dying, experiencing numbness or tingling, and feel-ing flushed or chilled (Wicks-Nelson & Israel, 2003).

Post-traumatic Stress Disorder

The reexperiencing, avoidance, and arousal following a traumatic event is called **post-traumatic stress disorder (PTSD)**. Trauma occurs when the child experiences something outside everyday experiences that would be distressing to almost anyone

(Wicks-Nelson & Israel, 2003). Traumatic experiences may include experiences of disasters, violence, or medical illnesses (Perrin, Smith, & Yuke, 2000). Salmon and Bryant (2002) have recommended that DSM-IV criteria be expanded to include that young children need only be exposed to traumatic events to be considered for PTSD. The extended criteria would include that children may not have any symptoms immediately following the event and may not have shown intense fear during the event. The number and types of symptoms currently in the DSM-IV criteria have not proven to be indicative of PTSD in young children. Aggression and new fears not related to the event have been suggested to be added to the criteria (Salmon & Bryant, 2002). The symptoms of PTSD can be any of those associated with the other anxiety disorders (Wicks-Nelson & Israel, 2003).

Obsessive-Compulsive Disorder

Obsessive-compulsive disorder (OCD) is defined in two separate terms. *Obsessions* are those thoughts that are "unwanted, repetitive, intrusive"; *compulsions* are repetitive stereotyped behaviors that the child feels forced to carry out to reduce stress or anxiety (Wicks-Nelson & Israel, 2003). The child need not be aware that the thoughts or acts are irrational. Because OCD may have an onset as early as 7, the child may have his or her own explanation for the unusual behavior or ideas. Significant adults usually become aware of the OCD behavior when the child's thoughts or behaviors begin to interfere significantly with routines, school, or relationships (Wicks-Nelson & Israel, 2003).

All children exhibit some of these symptoms from time to time and at different developmental stages. The child usually comes into play therapy as the result of a referral from the pediatrician, the school, or the parents when the child's OCD is disruptive and severe. See the following box for instruments used to assess Anxiety Disorders in children.

Anxiety Disorder Assessment Instruments

Anxiety Disorders Interview Schedule for Children (Albano & Silverman, 1996)

State-Trait Anxiety Inventory for Children (Spielberger, 1973)

Revised Children's Manifest Anxiety Scale (Reynolds & Richmond, 1985)

Multidimensional Anxiety Scale for Children (March, 1997)

The Negative Affectivity Self-Statement Questionnaire (Ronan, Kendall, & Rowe, 1994)

The Coping Questionnaire—Child Version (Kendall, Panichelli-Mindel, Sugarman, & Callahan, 1997)

The Revised Fear Survey for Children (Ollendick, 1983)

Social Phobia and Anxiety Inventory for Children (LaGreca & Stone, 1993)

Treatment

Behavioral and cognitive-behavioral approaches have been found to be most effective with anxiety disorders. **Relaxation and desensitization** has been used to help the child approach the threatening situation. The child is taught a relaxation technique and then asked to visualize the threatening situation. As the child's anxiety begins to rise, the child is reminded to use the relaxation technique. With repeated usage, the child is eventually able to control the anxiety around the situation or event. **Modeling** involves the child making a gradual approach to the feared object with the therapist or parent showing the child there is nothing to fear. **Contingency management** involves providing the child with a reward for approaching the fearful situation. Most important in the treatment is that the child learn to recognize the symptoms of anxious arousal, what thoughts go through the child's mind, and the strategies and skills for managing the anxious feelings (Wicks-Nelson & Israel, 2003). Based on the literature, cognitive-behavioral, behavioral and other structured theories of play therapy are recommended for treatment.

Pharmacological treatments are often used in addition to the behavioral approaches. Fluvoxamine, a selective serotonin reuptake inhibitor (SSRI), is often used to treat social phobia, separation anxiety disorder, or generalized anxiety disorder. Obsessive-compulsive disorder is more commonly treated with fluoxetin, sertraline,

Separation anxiety may take many forms. The child may cling to the door and may want to return to the mother. This child is looking to assure herself that mother is still waiting in the hall.

proxetine, and fluvoxamine. Although these drugs are used in the treatment, they have not been shown to be effective in treating OCD in children and adolescents (Wicks-Nelson & Israel, 2003).

MOOD DISORDERS

Mood disorders in children is a relatively new concept. Early in the 20th century, children were considered nervous or neurotic. The idea that a child could have a mood disorder was overshadowed by the concept that childhood is carefree and without stress. A child only came to the attention of a therapist when the child was a significant problem to the adults in the child's life.

As pioneers in the field of child development focused more and more on the emotional development of children, awareness of children's experience of moods surfaced. Children's normal moods can vary greatly from being elated to unusually sad. However, when these moods become extreme or persistent enough to interfere with the daily functioning of the child, as in mania or depression, direct intervention is needed.

Improvements in identifying and treating children's psychopathology have greatly advanced the investigation and diagnosis of mood disorders in children. Of major interest has been the investigation of depression in children, although some children may display both depression and mania, or bipolar disorder (Wicks-Nelson & Israel, 2003).

According to the DSM-IV, a major depressive episode is characterized by one or both features: depressed mood and loss of interest or pleasure in activities. A child experiencing a manic episode exhibits persistently elevated, expansive, or irritable mood. Mixed episode has to include the characteristics of both manic and major depressive episode. An episode in which the child experiences elevated, expansive, or irritable mood but does not experience impairment to functioning is termed a hypomanic manic episode. If the child experiences a less severe bout of depression, the term used is *dysthymic disorder*. Another diagnosis that may be given is that of adjustment disorder with depressed mood, especially when the child is reacting to a stressor that is not among those in the depressive disorder symptomatology.

Children with depression are likely to report or be reported by parents to experience depression for 1 year with two or more of the following: poor appetite, overeating, sleep disturbances, low energy, fatigue, low self-esteem, lack of concentration, lack of decision making, or feelings of hopelessness.

Bipolar Disorder

An affective condition in which the child exhibits manic and depressive states or moods is called **bipolar disorder**. *Cyclothymia* is an inclination to have relatively mild and uneven mood changes, varying from excitement and high energy to periods of depression and low energy levels (Corsini, 2002). The elevated mood of the manic phase can be described as "joyous," "real good," "high," or "cheerful," but the mood is considered excessive by caretakers or others close to the child (American Psychiatric Association, 2000). Adolescents experiencing manic episodes are likely to engage in antisocial behaviors, school truancy, academic failure, or substance use

---

Major Indicators of Bipolar Disorder in Children

1. Presence of mood shift or a mixed-state mood disorder
2. A predisposition to rage
3. Anxious hyperactivity and wild behavior (younger children)
4. Impulsivity and impaired judgment
5. Inattention and distractibility
6. Extreme irritable self-centeredness and combative behavior
7. Sleep issues: nighttime overarousal and morning underarousal
8. Seemingly malevolent enjoyment of knives, fire, and dangerous behavior
9. Morbid cognition and suicidal thinking
10. Tyrannical behavior
11. Hallucinations and other psychotic phenomena
12. Sexual hyperacuity
13. Severe energy reduction in the depressed phase
14. Affective illness in the family
15. Difficult or premature birth

Based on material from Lynn (2000).

(Wicks-Nelson & Israel, 2003). A large body of research helps provide indications of early-onset bipolar disorder in children (Biederman, 1998; Biederman et al., 1995; Post, 1999) (see the above box).

Other descriptors included in the possible diagnosis of bipolar disorder in children include persistent elevated mood, inflated self-esteem, thought racing, excessive pleasurable activities with negative consequences, poor appetite or overeating, low self-esteem, and feelings of hopelessness (Wicks-Nelson & Israel, 2003). Significant weight loss, diminished interest in pleasurable activities, not sleeping or sleeping excessively, restlessness or feeling slowed down, fatigue, feelings of worthlessness, and inappropriate guilt indicate the depressive state; inflated self-esteem, decreased need for sleep, talkativeness, flighty thoughts, distractibility, increase in goal-directed behavior, or excessive involvement in pleasure indicate the manic state (Papolos & Papolos, 2002).

A wide range of hormonal and metabolic disorders, infectious disease, neurological disorders, blood diseases, metal intoxications, nutritional disorders, cancers, genetic disorders, and other diseases can mimic the symptoms of bipolar disorder in children (Papolos & Papolos, 2002). Popper (1989) insists that attention-deficit/hyperactivity disorder closely resembles bipolar disorder and that ADHD should not be diagnosed until all mood disorders have been ruled out.

Bipolar disorder is thought to be rare in prepubescent children; however, as the ability of clinicians becomes more advanced in diagnosing bipolar disorder in children, the disorder may prove to be more common (Papolos & Papolos, 2002). Mood disorders, bipolar disorder, and depression have a greater chance of occurrence where there is a genetic predisposition or a biochemical imbalance. Separation and loss are common social-psychological influences (Wicks-Nelson & Israel, 2003). Learned helplessness has also been considered an explanation for mood disorders, specifically in depression (Seligman & Peterson, 1986).

In summary, mood disorders are still an area of research interest in terms of how they are manifested and how prevalent they are during the different developmental stages of children. Major depressive disorder appears to be the most prevalent of the mood disorders among children. Current theory about treatment and causes relies too heavily on theories and research based on adult subjects. The research suggests that although there appears to be a genetic component, the environment of the child seems to exert considerable influence on the development and degree of the disorder. Another trend in the research is based on findings in the biochemistry of children with depression as different from the biochemistry of adults with depression (Wicks-Nelson & Israel, 2003).

Separation and Loss

A key theme in theories about childhood depression is **separation and loss**. The child may also be exhibiting a type of learned helplessness, with symptoms similar to depression. A possible consideration with children is the presence of maternal depression, which does appear to be related to childhood mood disorders; however, present research has not clearly defined the exact relationship.

Suicide

Although **suicide** is still relatively rare among children, increased instances are creating a concern among professionals. Suicide ideation and behavior seems most related to depression (see nearby box for list of assessment instruments). A high-risk group is children with same-sex orientation. Other causes of suicidal behaviors may have multiple origins, including physical health, family dynamics, interpersonal relationships, and psychopathology (Wicks-Nelson & Israel, 2003).

Treatment

Antidepressant medications are used to treat mood disorders, but the long-range effects are unknown. Pharmacological treatment usually includes tricyclic antidepressants (TCAs) such as imipramine, amitriptyline, nortriptyline, and desipramine for depression. SSRIs such as fluoxetine and paroxetine are also used. Second-generation antidepressants such as bupropion and venlafaxine may be used with depressed youth (Sweeney & Tatum, 1995; Wicks-Nelson & Israel, 2003).

Treatments that have been found most promising with this population are behavioral, cognitive-behavioral, group, and family therapies. Among the relevant play therapy theories, all of them have merit in the treatment of depression and bipolar disorder, especially when they build up the child's self-esteem and feelings of competence.

> ### Assessment Instruments for Depression
>
> Child Behavior Checklist (Achenbach, 2002)
> The Children's Depression Inventory (CDI) (Kovacs, 1992)
> The Peer Nomination Inventory of Depression (Lefkowitz & Tesiny, 1980)

CONDUCT DISORDER

One of the most common complaints about child clients is one of noncompliant, aggressive, or antisocial behavior. Parents, teachers, siblings, peers, and significant adults in the child's life object loudly to fighting, lying, property destruction, and not following directions. The terms *acting out, disruptive, undercontrolled, impulsive, oppositional, defiant, antisocial, conduct disordered,* and *delinquent* describe the varying degrees of severity and tolerance for the child's behavior. These children usually fall under a diagnosis of conduct disorder, oppositional defiant, and/or juvenile delinquent, depending on how disruptive their behaviors are to family, school, and community.

One of your priorities is to establish if the behavior is developmentally appropriate. A child who is trying to establish independence may be described by the parent as noncompliant or oppositional. The parent may also have a low tolerance for a child's normal noncompliant or oppositional behavior. However, if the report comes from more than one source, the behavior is problematic and eventually will be problematic for the child. Many times children do not view these behaviors as problematic, however.

A **conduct disorder (CD)** is considered a persistent disruptive behavior that results in disturbance and destruction beyond what is commonly experienced with children. The behaviors may be inattention, hyperactivity, or oppositional behavior as a milder form of disruptive behavior. Aggression and oppositional behaviors represent the midrange of this disorder. The term *conduct disorder* is reserved for the more serious aggressive-antisocial behaviors (Wicks-Nelson & Israel, 2003).

CD has been divided into two syndromes: *aggressive behavior* and *rule-breaking behavior* (Achenbach & Rescorla, 2001). In *aggressive behaviors* children may argue, be intentionally mean to others, demand attention, destroy their own and others' property, be disobedient, physically attack others, threaten others, verbally attack others, become frustrated easily, be weary about others' intentions, display mood changes, appear sullen and stubborn, have temper tantrums, and be loud. The more of these behaviors the child displays, the more serious the conduct disorder. The child with *rule-breaking behaviors* is more likely to develop chemical dependency problems, choose bad company, prefer older kids, set fires, steal at home, use tobacco, engage in vandalism, have poor school attendance, exhibit high sexual interests or promiscuity, and lack a sense of guilty or remorse for actions. Conduct disorder can begin either in childhood or in adolescence.

The child's mother completes a children's behavior checklist describing the child's current behavior at home.

Conduct Disorder (CD) is a clinical term, whereas *delinquency* is a legal term for many of the same behaviors. Delinquency occurs when the child's behavior comes to the attention of law enforcement. Such behavior includes acts of violence toward people or animals, destruction of property, drug usage or selling, prostitution, sexual exploitation of others, stealing, repeated truancy, or similar legal difficulties (Jongsma, Peterson, & McInnis, 2000). Possession of a weapon (e.g., knife, gun, brick, bat, broken bottle, razor, box cutter), breaking and entering a house, and running away from home are also CD behaviors that might be considered delinquent (Rapoport & Ismond, 1996).

Oppositional Defiant Disorder (ODD)

Oppositional defiant disorder (ODD) is defined as a persistent pattern of negativistic, hostile, and defiant behavior toward most adults, lasting for a minimum of 6 months (American Psychiatric Association, 2000; Jongsma et al., 2000; Rapoport & Ismond, 1996; Wicks-Nelson & Israel, 2003). Wicks-Nelson and Israel (2003) state that ODD is the most common problem among both clinical and nonclinic children. ODD may be a precursor for CD; however, the exact nature of the relationship is not known and does not develop consistently in all children diagnosed as ODD (Hinshaw, Lahey, & Hart, 1993; Loeber, 1988; Loeber, Burke, Lahey, Winters, & Zerz, 2000; Loeber & Farrington, 2000; Loeber & Keenan, 1994; Loeber & Schmaling, 1985; Loeber & Stouthamer-Loeber, 1998; Loeber et al., 1993). See the following box.

Assessment for Conduct Disorder

Child Behavior Checklist (Achenbach, 2002)

The Behavioral Assessment System for Children (BASC) (Reynolds & Kamphaus, 1992)

Connors Rating Scales-Revised (Connors, Sitarenios, Parker, & Epstein, 1998)

Eyberg Child Behavior Inventory (EBCI) (Eyberg, 1992)

Sutter-Eyberg Student Behavior Inventory (SESBI) (Eyberg, 1992)

The Self-Report Delinquency Scale (SRD) (Elliott, Huizinga, & Ageton, 1985)

Treatment

Children with extreme aggressive and conduct-disordered behaviors are most often treated with mood stabilizers. Drugs such as lithium and carbamazepine have been used to treat children with severe aggression and explosiveness. The use of these drugs remains controversial but may be recommended when a multimodal treatment plan is used (Sweeney & Tatum, 1995; Wicks-Nelson & Israel, 2003).

In the multimodal treatment plan, parent training is recommended in conjunction with the treatment of the child (Wicks-Nelson & Israel, 2003). The recommended play therapy theories for these children would be ecosystemic, cognitive-behavioral, Adlerian, and Jungian. Family play therapies and their emphasis on parent training are especially viable with these children.

ATTENTION-DEFICIT/HYPERACTIVITY DISORDER (ADHD)

Attention-deficit/hyperactivity disorder (ADHD) has the primary features of inattention, hyperactivity, and impulsivity (see the following box for assessment tools). Current practice has divided this disorder into three subtypes: inattentive, hyperactive-impulsive, and combined. The inattentive child makes careless mistakes, fails to attend to details, lacks ability to sustain attention, appears not to listen when spoken to, does not follow directions, struggles to organize tasks or activities, dislikes and avoids tasks that require sustained attention, loses items, and is distracted and forgetful in daily activities. The child who is primarily hyperactive fidgets, squirms in seat, does not stay seated, runs or climbs inappropriately, seems restless, struggles to play quietly, is always on the move, and talks incessantly. Children who are impulsive tend to blurt out answers to questions inappropriately, struggle with turn taking, and interrupt or intrude on others. A combination of the inattention symptoms and the hyperactivity/impulsivity symptoms constitutes the combined type.

ADHD children often have a dual diagnosis of ODD, OCD, or learning disabilities. Some ADHD children are very aggressive and act out. Others may be well behaved but seem not to listen to simple instructions. Children observed in the playroom who are ADHD move rapidly from one activity to another. Drawings are

Assessment for ADHD

Connors Rating Scales—Revised (Connors et al., 1998)

Student Behavior Survey (Lachar, Wingenfeld, Kline, & Guber, 1998)

Personality Inventory for Children, 2nd ed. (Wirt, Lachar, Klinedinst, Seat, & Broen, 2001)

often not completed or play themes played out. Noises that would normally be ignored from outside the playroom are heard and distract the child from play. The child may not complete sentences because he or she has noticed something that attracts attention in the playroom. Limit setting becomes an ongoing challenge when attempting to help the child self-regulate. Inattentive types may complete a task, but their behavior is marked by their interrupting their work to talk or to notice something most children would ignore.

Treatment

ADHD children respond to medication in a paradoxical manner: Stimulants calm the child. The most common stimulants prescribed for ADHD are methylphenidate (Ritalin, Concerta), dextroamphetamine (Dexedrine), and the combination of dextroamphetamine and amphetamine (Adderall) (Wicks-Nelson & Israel, 2003). Antidepressants and antihypertensives may also be prescribed as an alternative choice to the more common stimulants. Rarely used are the anticonvulsants and antipsychotics for ADHD (Sweeney & Tatum, 1995; Wicks-Nelson & Israel, 2003). Any medication for children remains controversial when prescribed for behavioral disorders.

ADHD has been treated with success with all the different play therapy theories. Limit setting is often a significant part of therapy for the child with ADHD who cannot yet set limits on self. A tactic I employ when working with a ADHD child who becomes overstimulated by the toys and playroom is to allow the child to choose five toys. I take the child to another counseling room that has subdued colored walls, plain furniture, and a table. Then the next week the child is allowed to choose six toys, then seven the next week, and so on. When the child gets too stimulated by the toys, the number stays the same or I cut it back by one toy. The child does not have to choose the same toys each week. Some children never get to the point that they can enter the playroom without becoming overstimulated, but many are able to return to the playroom after a few weeks.

LANGUAGE AND LEARNING DISORDERS (LLD)

Language and learning disorders (LLD) are usually identified by the school when the child fails to learn at the rate of peers. Children are identified and provided special services that may involve tutors, special assignments, or attending special classes. Because of the current emphasis on inclusion, fewer children are assigned a separate classroom, except in the most extreme cases. The child usually comes to the play therapist because of social and/or behavioral problems in the home and at school.

Many children with LLD do very well socially and behaviorally; these children are at risk for behavioral or social problems, however (Wicks-Nelson & Israel, 2003). Children with LLD may have difficulty interpreting social situations or interacting with their peers. Teachers may view their special needs as problematic and often describe these children as anxious, immature, uncooperative, lacking self-control, hyperactive, or exhibiting other behavioral disorders (Wicks-Nelson & Israel, 2003). Low academic achievement and low self-esteem are the usual cause for referral to a clinic or play therapists.

Assessment is an extensive process usually carried out by the school psychologist or other individual trained to administer the battery of tests required to determine the presence and extent of the learning language disability. Specific individual education plans (IEPs) are drawn up to describe the type of learning activities and any accommodations the child will need. The child is then placed in the educational system in the least restrictive environment to accommodate his or her special needs.

Misdiagnosis of LLD can occur if the child's primary language is not English or if the child's speech is greatly influenced by cultural speech patterns. The language and dialects spoken in the home need to be considered in the assessment before a diagnosis of LLD is made. Children can appear to be fluent in English but may not have developed sufficient English-language skills to score at age level on an assessment designed primarily to establish dominant language. Although error usually occurs because the assessor does not realize English is not the child's primary language, the reverse can happen. An evaluator can assume the child is not English dominant when, in fact, the child's parents speak another language but the child does not. Error may occur in either direction, so it is best to test and ascertain the dominant language if there is any doubt.

Treatment

LLD treatment may include the drug treatment for inattention or hyperactivity. However, the actual treatment is a specially planned academic program, based on the IEP. Your main concern will be helping the child with self-esteem and behavioral problems. All theories of play therapy are effective with LLD. Theraplay and developmental play therapy may be most useful for the preschool child. Parent education therapies are often helpful for the significant others of the child with LLD.

MENTAL RETARDATION

Mentally retarded children are expected to develop more slowly than their peers. Depending on the severity of the delay in intellectual development, the child's social skills and functioning may be several months to years behind the norm for his or her age group. In spite of these children lacking academic achievement, most are sensitive to acceptance or rejection by others. Self-esteem and behavior issues do arise with the mentally retarded (Wicks-Nelson & Israel, 2003).

This child is being tested for learning disabilities. The process is a lengthy one in which a large battery of tests might be used to assess the child's intellectual functioning, auditory and visual processing, and achievement. The number of assessments used and the length of the evaluation varies with the individual child.

Assessment Instruments for Mental Retardation

Intelligence Tests
Bayley Scales of Infant Development–II (Bayley, 1993)
Stanford-Binet Intelligence Scale (S-B) (Thorndike, Hagen, & Sattler, 1986)
Wechsler Intelligence Scale for Children–III (Wechsler, 1991)
The Kaufman Assessment Battery for Children (K-ABC) (Kaufman & Kaufman, 1983)

Adaptive Behavior Assessments
Vineland Adaptive Behavior Scales (Sparrow, Balla, & Cicchetti, 1984)
AAMR Adaptive Behavior Scales (American Association on Mental Retardation, 1992)

You may be sought out because the child's developmental age may be appropriate for play therapy while the chronological age may be in the upper limits or beyond what you usually see in therapy. Expect the child to play at a much younger developmental age. A general guideline would be to treat the child at what level is appropriate to the child's developmental age. See the above box for a list of assessment tools.

Treatment

Treatment is a broad spectrum including educational, behavioral, and medical aspects as indicated by the individual case and its severity. Children with mild or moderate intellectual deficits may benefit from play therapy. Recommendations for play therapy require you to be directive and have specific goals for the session. Your language needs to be concrete and clear. The sessions should be short, frequent, and somewhat structured (Wicks-Nelson & Israel, 2003). All theories of play therapy work are recommended with this population, but each may have to accommodate for the child's limited abilities in creative play.

PERVASIVE DEVELOPMENTAL DISORDERS

Pervasive developmental disorder (PPD) describes a group of disorders including autism, Rett's disorder, childhood disintegrative disorder, and Asperger's disorder (see nearby box for assessment tools). These disorders are recognized as nonpsychotic and have been associated historically with schizophrenia and schizophrenia-like disorders but lack the psychotic characteristics of schizophrenia.

Autism

Autism is characterized by the child's impaired social interaction, communication, and limited preoccupations and stereotyped behaviors. The diagnosis is usually made before the age of 3. The child is not mentally retarded, although intellectual functioning may be low normal or below normal. Play therapy with this population has been limited in the literature. The Theraplay Institute has a videotape that depicts using its technique with an autistic child. Kenny and Winick (2000) provide a description of their adaptation of child-centered play therapy with an autistic child. Axline's (1964) classic description of play therapy with Dibs is a chronicle of play therapy with a child who would be diagnosed with autism today.

Rett's Disorder

As a result of **Rett's disorder,** head growth is decelerated at 5 to 48 months. The child usually displays poor coordinated gait, impaired language development, and severe psychomotor retardation. The condition is more common in females than in males. Autistic behaviors are present, but Rett's disorder has a more negative outcome than autism. The degree of disability is relatively stable after childhood (Wicks-Nelson & Israel, 2003). Whether the child is a candidate for play therapy depends on your training and the severity of the disorder in the child.

Childhood Disintegrative Disorder

In **childhood disintegrative disorder,** the child has at least 2 years of normal development with symptoms appearing before age 10. These children lack social and emotional engagement; have impaired communications, and engage in restrictive, repetitive interests and behaviors. The disorder is usually accompanied by severe mental retardation. Children with this disorder represent the lowest functioning of the PDD diagnosis (Wicks-Nelson & Israel, 2003). Play therapy, as described in this text, would not be recommended.

Asperger's Disorder

Children affected with **Asperger's disorder** present the repetitive, restrictive, and stereotyped interests of the child with autism. They do not possess a delay in language development, cognition, or adaptive behavior with the exception of social behavior. Many appear precocious and display excessive verbalization. Their deficit areas surface in the areas of nonverbal social gestures, emotional expression, and early sharing behaviors. Others experience them as socially awkward, inappropriate, lacking empathy, and insensitive. Their lives are marked by loneliness, even if there is some interest in relationships with others (Wicks-Nelson & Israel, 2003).

Assessment of PDD

The Childhood Autism Rating Scale (CARS) (Newsom & Hovanitz, 1997)

The Autism Diagnostic Observation Schedule (ADOS) (Lord, Risi, Lambrecht, Cook, Leventhal, & DiLavore, 2000)

Checklist for Autism in Toddlers (CHAT) (Baird et al., 2000; Scambler, Rogers, & Wehner, 2001)

Other assessment tools used to distinguish PDD from other disorders are intelligence tests and adaptive behavior scales. These instruments are listed under other disorders in this text.

Treatment

Pharmacological treatment is used as an adjunct to other treatments to reduce symptoms of autism and related behavior problems. Haloperidol (Haldol) is sometimes prescribed to reduce the agitation, aggression, perseveration, social withdrawal, emotional instability, and self-injurious behavior. Adverse side effects of this drug may occur in many children (e.g., involuntary movements of tongue, mouth, and jaw). Risperidone has been found to improve behavior. Naltrexone is one drug that has been found to reduce hyperactivity and restlessness/irritability. Drugs may provide some reduction in behaviors but have not been considered successful in treatment (Sweeney & Tatum, 1995; Wicks-Nelson & Israel, 2003).

Historically, child-centered play therapy has been successful with this population. The goal of therapy will determine whether a more directive play therapy approach is needed. The more specific the goal, the more directive the intervention in play therapy and the more directive the theory of play therapy used.

Summary

This chapter presented the more common types of disorders you may encounter in clinical practice. All theories of play therapy have been used with all types of disorders, but some may be more appropriate than others. At this time, little research has been conducted in looking at the efficacy of specific theories and their application to specific disorders. As you will see in Chapter 15, the efficacy of play therapy as a treatment for children is just now gaining recognition in the mental health field.

CHAPTER 15

THE LAW, ETHICS, AND RESEARCH

Play therapists must be mindful of the legal and ethical concerns in working with minor children. While this area is one of the least interesting, legal and ethical concerns are an area of the most responsibility to the child and his or her family.

This chapter surveys the current legal, professional, and ethical issues in the practice of play therapy. The information here does not in any way substitute for consultation with an attorney. Laws vary from state to state. What may appear to be an ethical or generally accepted practice is not always the legal practice in a specific state. In addition, the efficacy of the play therapy approach in helping children is discussed.

INTRODUCTION

In my 20 years of teaching play therapy, the telephone calls I get most often are from therapists wanting to consult about a legal or ethical course of action with a client. Although students have told me repeatedly that this section of study is the most boring in the field of play therapy, legal and ethical issues are potentially the most dangerous mistakes to make in your practice. One of my most often remembered adapted folkisms is "If you like the luxury of sleeping indoors, you had better understand the ethical and legal guidelines of our profession." The focus of ethics and law is on the welfare of the client and the protection of the therapeutic relationship. We can never know too much about the law or ethics.

Play therapy is a multidisciplinary therapeutic intervention for children. Although this means a wonderful montage of theories and strategies, the diversity brings more than one code of ethics, licensing board, and form of verifying competency into the professional identity. Most play therapists hold professional membership or follow one of the major codes of ethics for the mental health community: American Counseling Association (ACA), American Association of Marriage and Family Therapists (AAMFT), American Psychological Association (APA), or National Association of Social Work (NASW). Depending on the state, registered play therapists are usually licensed or certified by one of the state boards aligned with these professions. Many other licenses, certifications, and registrations exist within the play therapy field and the mental health community (e.g., child life, art therapist, music therapist, dance therapist). To address this diversity and establish a level playing field, the Association for Play Therapy developed a set of guidelines for practice (Appendix A). Registered play therapists are expected to adhere to these guidelines where they are not in conflict with state laws or ethical practice for the play therapist's field of mental health work.

LEGAL AND ETHICAL GUIDELINES

Social workers, professional counselors, and psychologists are part of the professional mental health workers governed by state boards in most states. The professional codes of conduct and standards of practice are usually reviewed and acted into law. Therefore when the code of ethics is violated by the mental health worker, a law is most often broken. The mental health worker's license is not only in danger of being revoked, but the licensee may be facing criminal charges under the state's legal code. A licensing board may hold a great deal of power granted by the state legislature. Many states require that a person hold a license, certification, or registration to practice independently in his or her professional field. When this document is revoked or sanctioned, the professional can no longer practice legally in that state.

The most common reason for losing a license or being sued is malpractice, legally defined as "professional misconduct or unreasonable lack of skill" (Black, 1990). Black's law (1990) explains further that the individual has failed to provide professional services to the degree of skill and learning commonly used within the professional community by the average, prudent, reputable member of the profession, which does not result in injury, loss, or damage. In addition, malpractice includes professional misconduct, lack of skill, misrepresenting the truth, evil practices, or illegal or immoral conduct. The professional code of ethics, standards of practice, and laws for practice for the play therapist's mental health field are the documents used to determine if malpractice has occurred. Therefore you must be familiar with what is generally considered ethical practice and children's rights for all mental health workers. Although the wording of the various codes of ethics and specific state statutes may differ, the common intent of these guidelines and laws are summarized here.

HISTORY OF CHILDREN'S RIGHTS

Historically, children were under the doctrine of *patriae potes,* or parental authority. The term comes from Roman civil law and meant those powers and rights that belonged to the head of the family with respect to wife and children (Black, 1990). This tradition of civil law allowed the father and, by extension, the mother to have absolute control over their children. Children were often abused, neglected, abandoned, sold into slavery, killed, and mutilated as the adults of the society wished (Hart & Paviovic, 1991). Children were considered chattel from the 15th to 18th centuries. The extreme of this legal position is illustrated by the Stubborn Child Act of 1638, which was part of Massachusetts state law. This law permitted parents to kill their child for the offense of disobedience (Halasz, 1996; Lawrence & Kurpius, 2000).

In the latter part of the 1800s and the early 1900s, laws were passed in an attempt to end dangerous health standards, exploitative labor, illiteracy, and abuse and neglect. One of the organizations founded during this time was the New York Children's Aid Society to relocate poor city children into the healthier countryside. Although the intentions behind the project were noble, the results forced many children into servitude.

In keeping with the growing consciousness about children, the first juvenile court system was established in Chicago, July 1, 1899, which resulted in children no longer being housed with adult offenders or judged by adult justice (Lawrence & Kurpius, 2000).

National child labor laws were enacted in 1904, which, without much success, proposed a shorter workday, minimum age for working, compulsory education, and banned dangerous jobs for children. Not until the Fair Labor Standards Act of 1938 enforced child labor guidelines for businesses engaging in interstate commerce was the minimum employment age set at 16. The first White House conference on Children in 1909 and the Compulsory Education Act of 1922 was another step in defining children's rights to be educated and to be safe. The Fifth Assembly of the League of Nations in 1924 established the doctrine of *parens patriae* (Halasz, 1996; Lawrence & Kurpius, 2000). The literal meaning is "parent of the country" and refers to the role of the state as guardian of people under legal disability, as in the case of minor children or the mentally ill. The term is used in child custody when the state acts to protect the best interests of the minor child (Black, 1990). This doctrine established the state's right and responsibility to protect the child when the parents failed to provide adequate protection for the child (Lawrence & Kupius, 2000).

Not until the latter half of the 20th century did the children's rights movement achieve notoriety as a social movement. In 1959 the United Nations Declaration of the Rights of the Child came to the forefront, declaring that the child is owed the best possible situation that humankind can provide. A year later, the White House Conference on Children and Youth provided an enumeration of children's rights. The civil rights movement addressed not only issues of diversity rights but also made inroads to secure rights, power, and protection for children (Halasz, 1996; Hart & Paviovic, 1991; Lawrence & Kurpius, 2000).

The All Handicapped Children's Act of 1975 (PL 94–142) established "free appropriate" education for children with disabilities. The 1989 United Nations Convention on the Rights of the Child made two major contributions to the welfare of children. First, the convention put forth a legal treaty that established that children were to be protected from physical and mental injury and abuse in all form. Second, the convention resulted in an urgent plea that prejudicial health practices toward children be abolished (Lawrence & Kurpius, 2000). The Young American Act of 1990 created an office within the Department of Health and Human Resources for Children, Youth, and Families that apportions grants to projects dealing with children's issues. These three acts have led to the increased recognition of children's legal and social rights.

LANDMARK COURT CASES IN CHILDREN'S RIGHTS

The right to an equal education was established by *Brown v. Board of Education* (1954), when segregated schools that were "separate but equal" in *Plessy v. Ferguson* (1896) was overturned (Fischer & Sorenson, 1996). The Supreme Court's basic contention was that separate is not equal based on the Fourteenth Amendment (Fischer & Sorenson, 1985). What was put into motion by this decision led to many years of controversy and reform in education and children's rights.

In re Gault (1967) became a landmark case solidifying the protection of minors under the Fourteenth Amendment. The minor child, Gerald Gault, was taken into custody by the local sheriff for making indecent telephone calls to a Mrs. Cook. No attempt was made to contact Gerald's parents, who were both at work, prior to his placement in a detention center. A hearing followed the next day, but no formal notification was provided to the parents. Neither Mrs. Cook nor any other witnesses appeared. No transcript or recording was made of the hearing. Gerald was returned to detention while the judge supposedly thought about the case. After a few days, Gerald was released without explanation. After Gerald's arrival home, his parents were informed of another hearing to be held the next week. Mrs. Cook was not at this hearing, and no consensus was established on what had occurred in the previous hearing. The case ended with the judge sentencing Gerald to the state industrial school until he was 21. Gerald, a minor, received a 6-year sentence for what would have cost an adult a $50 fine. Because Gerald was a minor, he had no right of appeal (Lawrence & Kurpius, 2000).

The U.S. Supreme Court ruled against Arizona and set Gerald free after serving 3 of the 6 years of his sentence. The Court ruled on the basis of denial of these civil rights: "(a) the right to counsel, (b) the right to be notified of charges, (c) the right to confront and to cross-examine witnesses, (d) the privilege against self-incrimination, (e) the right to appeal, and (f) the right to a transcript of proceedings" (Lawrence & Kurpius, 2000).

The Supreme Court granted the right to assemble and to freedom of speech to minors, which extended First Amendment rights to children, declaring them to be "persons" (*Tinker v. Des Moines Independent Community School District*, 1969). Through *Gault* and *Tinker*, minor children were first granted constitutional rights.

Other landmark cases providing rights to minor children include the right to terminate a pregnancy without parental consent if the minor is competent to make the decision (*Planned Parenthood of Central Mo. v. Danforth*, 1976). The mature minor is legally defined in 22 states and the District of Columbia (Griswold & Griswold, 2000). An example of that type of statute is from Alabama Code §22-8-4, which states "any minor who is age 14 or older, or has graduated from high school, or is married, or having been married is divorced or is pregnant may give effective consent to any legally authorized medical, dental, health or mental health services, and the consent of no other person shall be necessary."

Alabama Code §22-8-6 gives "any minor," regardless of age, the ability to "give effective consent for any . . . health services to determine the presence of, or to treat, pregnancy, venereal disease, drug dependency, alcohol toxicity, or any reportable disease." This statute provides minors with the right to privacy, independent of age, when specific health concerns are issues of immediacy, confidentiality, and important policy implications are present.

Alabama also protects health care providers from liability for treating a minor who is under the age of 14. Under Alabama Code §22-8-7 (2000), "any physician or other person who has relied in good faith upon the representations" of a minor who misrepresents herself will not be held liable for not gaining proper consent. Legal statutes vary from state to state concerning mature minors. A comparison chart describing minors' access to health care in the United States is available from the Legislative Initiative for Healthier Lives (Law Office # 2, 2002).

Minors' rights have both been expanded and limited in related Supreme Court decisions. The ability of parents to commit a minor to inpatient care against the child's will and without a hearing was established in *Parham v. J. R.* (1979). *H. L. v. Matherson* (1981) and *Planned Parenthood Association of Kansas City, Mo. v. Ashcroft* (1983) upheld the decision that minors have to notify and get consent for an abortion. *Ingraham v. Wright* (1977) upheld the ruling that no hearings are necessary to administer corporal punishment in public schools. The power for school authorities to search students without a warrant and to censor school newspapers was provided under *New Jersey v. T. L. O.* (1985) and *Hazelwood School District v. Kuhlmeier* (1988). The Supreme Court and the legal system as a whole has produced a quagmire in its efforts to balance the state's interest in social stability, the parent's interest in family autonomy and freedom of child rearing practices, and the child's interest in preservation of privacy, personal dignity and freedom from harm (Lawrence & Kurpius, 2000).

ETHICAL ISSUES IN PLAY THERAPY

Therapist competency to work with children is one of the first concerns of most codes of ethics. The Association for Play Therapy has established minimal training standards for registration at the level of Register Play Therapist (Appendix B) and Register Play Therapist Supervisor (Appendix C). Within these standards is an expressed belief that a competent therapist in play therapy will graduate from academic study within the areas of child development, theories of personality, principles of psychotherapy, child and adolescent psychopathology, and legal, ethical, and professional issues. In addition, the play therapist has specialized instruction in the history of play therapy, theories of play therapy, techniques or methods of play therapy, and applications of play therapy to special settings or populations. According to Lawrence and Kurpius (2000), therapists cannot take what they know of adult psychopathology and use the knowledge as a basis for treatment for children, nor can understanding adult concerns and problems lead to an understanding of childrens' issues and difficulties. This idea serves as a cornerstone of the minimal requirements for competency. Most state licensure boards require verification of a specialty, such as professional registration, prior to designating a specialty area of professional practice.

Do no harm has been the backbone of all professional codes of ethics in the field of mental health. Herlihy and Corey (1997) suggested guidelines to minimize the risk

Do no harm has been the backbone of any professional code of ethics in the field of mental health.

to the clients in the process of therapeutic services. These guidelines are paraphrased and extended specifically for child clients as follows:

1. Establish clear and definite boundaries about the therapist's participation in social and personal relationships with the child and the child's family at the onset of therapy.
2. Involve the child and the child's significant adults in establishing these boundaries with age-appropriate explanations to the child.
3. Discuss with the client, directly and openly, any potential problems that arise (e.g., need to disclose, referral to a physician, need for assessment, consultation with teachers and other significant adults).
4. Consult with professional colleagues to maintain objectivity and to forestall potential problems.
5. Work with a supervisor or consultant when the therapeutic relationship is complex or if the client is at risk.
6. Document interactions with the child and the legal guardian, recording in clinical case notes the therapeutic interventions with more complete notes when the child's behavior poses a higher risk.
7. Make referrals to other therapists or child specialists when necessary.

Clients' competency and **informed consent** to participate in their mental health treatment decisions have been neglected in work with children (Hall & Lin, 1995). Guidelines for deciding competency to participate have been established in most states with the decisions at what legal age and to what extent minor children become "mature minors" and can participate in the decision making about their treatment independent of parental consent (Law Office # 2, 2002). However, children need to be included in the treatment decisions at their ability to understand the procedures, even if they are not legally "mature minors." You are obligated ethically to explain the treatment to the child client in language appropriate to the child's developmental level of understanding and to secure the child's assent to care when reasonable to do so, even if the child cannot provide legal consent independent of parental consent (Griswold & Griswold, 2000; Halasz, 1996; Hall & Lin, 1995; Ledyard, 1998).

Informed consent is the formal contractual agreement that provides permission and describes the conditions under which treatment will begin (Lawrence & Kurpius, 2000). Elsewhere in this text, informed consent was discussed as necessary before beginning treatment. The APT Standards of Practice parallel other codes of ethics and standards of practice by stating that included in the informed consent are the purposes, goals, techniques, procedures, limitations, potential risks, and benefits of play therapy to the child. Access and use of diagnostic assessments are explained. Fees and billing arrangements are defined, including what charges will be expected for missed sessions. The limits of confidentiality are explained within the document. If someone other than the therapist has access to the records (e.g., supervisors, treatment teams, juvenile court), the access is clearly explained. If the child is a "mature minor" under the state law, the freedom of choice not to enter into the therapeutic relationship is explained. To whom and under what circumstances the records can be disclosed and/or confidentiality broken is explained. In the event the child is not a mature minor, the therapist works in the best interest of the child and with parental consent

(Appendix A, "APT Standards of Practice," A.3. a–c). The minor and the parents do not have to give consent in the case of a court order. A minor may usually enter into treatment in one of three ways: with parental consent, involuntarily at the parent's insistence, or by order of the juvenile court (Lawrence & Kurpius, 2000).

In the case of divorced parents, informed consent must be obtained from the custodial parent (Stein, 1990). The therapist is bound by the state statute as to what rights the noncustodial parent retains in regard to information concerning the treatment plan, releasing of information, and confidentiality in regard to the child. Many agencies request a copy of the divorce decree section that outlines these agreements for their records. Other therapists have handled this by asking the custodial parent to sign a release that grants the noncustodial parent full or limited access to information about the child. My preference is to do the latter when both parents are supportive of the child and not restricted by the divorce decree from such information. It is important for the therapist to clearly understand the noncustodial parent's rights.

Confidentiality or **confidential communication** is "privileged communication such as that between spouses, physician-patient, attorney-client, confessor-penitent, etc." (Black, 1990). A confidential communication is a statement or discussion that is meant to be heard only by the person to whom the information was disclosed. If a third party was present, whose presence is not reasonably necessary, the communication is not privileged (Black, 1990). In 1995 the Supreme Court ruled that the relationship between a psychotherapist and his or her client is privileged communication (*Jaffee v. Redmond*, 1995) in accordance with the rules for federal evidence ("Federal Evidence Code, Rule 501," 1975). Social workers, psychologists, and psychiatrists were specifically named as psychotherapists. The Supreme Court ruling "failed to define the parameters of the privilege and left the refinement of the common-law definition for the lower federal courts to make on a case-by-case basis" (Poulin, 1999).

As a general rule, do not disclose information gathered through the therapeutic relationship, unless you are court ordered to do so. When court ordered, seek the permission of the legal guardian to disclose or ask the court for privilege, when permission cannot be or is not given to disclose (American Association for Marriage and Family Therapy, 1991; American Counseling Association, 1995; American Psychological Association, 2002; Association for Play Therapy, 1998; National Association of Social Work, 1999). Ethical exceptions to this rule have been defined by Corey, Corey, and Callanan (1998):

1. The therapist has the legal guardian's permission to disclose.
2. The therapist has a *duty to warn* in order to protect the child or others.
3. The therapist must report under the law, as in child abuse.
4. The therapist perceives an emergency.
5. The therapist can disclose information in the event of being sued by the client or his or her legal representative.
6. The therapist may disclose the relationship in order to obtain payment or reimbursement for services.

Four points of view are identified in the literature in regard to minor children and confidentiality (Hendrix, 1991; Lawrence & Kurpius, 2000). The first of these stances is to divulge nothing to the parents about the child's treatment. The second position is to provide the child with limited confidentiality that the minor has assented to in advance and with the knowledge that what is said can be discussed openly with the parents or guardian. Another perspective is a forced informed consent: The therapist tells the minor children that a disclosure will be made to the parents, but the minor does not have any assent to what is to be disclosed. The final point of view is that no guarantee of confidentiality is made to the child.

The ethical codes and the law agree that confidentiality is broken when the therapist suspects child abuse, when the therapist knows of the child's attempts to harm himself or herself, and when the therapist knows of clear and imminent danger to a third party or property. Beyond these three instances, the ethical waters become murky as to the direction of the therapist in disclosures (Mitchell, Disque, & Robertson, 2002).

Minors do not have confidentiality rights under the law (Mitchell et al., 2002). The recent federal laws have been enacted to provide mature minors with confidentiality when they are receiving alcohol and drug treatment (Sealander, Schwiebert, Oren, & Weekley, 1999). A mature minor, a legal definition, has the right to confidentiality concerning birth control, pregnancy, abortion, and testing for sexually transmitted diseases in some states (Corey et al., 1998; Mitchell et al., 2002; Welfel, 2002). Children under the age of 12 years are not considered "mature minors" in any state at this time (Law Office # 2, 2002).

In lieu of a legal statute and within the intent of the codes of ethics, APT has stated,

> Play therapists respect the child's right to privacy and disclose to the parents/guardians/significant adults, except where otherwise provided by state law, only those concerns that are in the best interest of the child and avoid illegal and unwarranted disclosures of confidential information which might adversely affect the treatment of the client. (Association for Play Therapy, 1998)

Assent, in the legal sense, is authorizing something to be done or agreeing to a course of action (Black, 1990). Play therapists developing the APT Standards of Practice voiced a preference for the play therapist to seek assent from the child when the child is able developmentally to understand the need for the disclosure. Seeking assent conveys a respect to the child as the client. If the child were not to give assent, the therapist would act in the best interest of the child. The codes of ethics and APT have basically taken the stance that disclosure under any circumstance is minimal for the safety and best interest of the client and, by extension, to the child client (American Association for Marriage and Family Therapy, 1991; American Counseling Association, 1995; American Psychological Association, 2002; Association for Play Therapy, 1998; National Association of Social Work, 1999). This point of view appears to be the most logical, whether the therapist perceives the parent as an extension of the child as a client or not. As discussed elsewhere in this text, the confidentiality agreement needs to be clearly expressed in the written informed consent.

Duty to warn has extended to include minors. Therapists are liable for the protection of a third party, if the child makes a threat to a specific party and intends to carry out that threat as described in the famous Tarasoff case (*Tarasoff v. Regents of Univ. of CA.*, 1976) and extended by the Jablonski case to include duty to warn when there is a foreseeable danger (*Jablonski v. US,* 1978). Minors need to be told of this exception to confidentiality in developmental language that is appropriate to their understanding, and the legal guardian needs to be assured of this in the informed consent (Lawrence & Kurpius, 2000).

Peck v. Counseling Services of Addison County (1985) extended the duty to warn to the destruction of property. Peck disclosed to his counselor his intention of burning down his father's barn in retaliation for an argument with his father. The counselor was found to be negligent because she did not warn the prospective victim, she did not secure previous medical and social history in a timely manner, and she did not consult with other professionals concerning the potential danger (Harrar, VandCreek, & Knapp, 1990). In addition, the agency was found to be negligent in failing to have a written policy regarding consultation procedures when a client presents a serious danger (Harrar et al., 1990).

Child abuse reporting is mandatory in all 50 states for those people who are in professions that provide direct services in the care and treatment of children (e.g., teachers, doctors, therapists, nurses, social workers). A mandatory reporting law is required by a state to receive funding under the Child Abuse Prevention and Treatment Act (CAPTA). 1974; "Child Abuse Prevention and Treatment and Adoption Act Amendment," 1996).

CAPTA sets minimum definitions of child abuse and neglect as any recent act or a failure to act that results in risk of serious harm, death, serious physical or emotional harm, sexual abuse, or exploitation of a minor child by a parent or caretaker who is responsible for the child's welfare. CAPTA defines sexual abuse as the

> employment, use, persuasion, inducement, enticement, or coercion of any child to engage in, or assist any other person to engage in, any sexually explicit conduct or any simulation of such conduct for the purpose of producing any visual depiction of such conduct; or rape, and in cases of caretaker or inter-familial relationships, statutory rape, molestation, prostitution, or other form of sexual exploitations of children, or incest with children. (Child Abuse Prevention and Treatment Act (CAPTA), 1974)

Most states have followed the Model Child Protection Act that requires professionals and institutions, mental health care providers, teachers and school personnel, social workers, day care providers, and law enforcement personnel to report "suspected" child abuse. Some states extend this mandatory reporting to film developers. Eighteen states have extended their mandatory reporting laws to include "any person" to report. The basis of reporting can be "reasonable cause to believe" or "reasonable suspicion"; still others require the reporter to have a higher degree of knowledge by the words "know or suspect" (Smith, 2002).

CAPTA demands that the states include in their reporting laws immunity from prosecution arising out of the reporting of the abuse or neglect. Most of the states have included immunity for those persons reporting in "good faith" for both criminal and civil liability. Usually a health care attorney will advise the health care provider to report and face a civil action for reporting rather than face the consequences of not reporting, if the child is injured or killed as a result of not reporting (Smith, 2002). A reporter's confidentiality and privilege in reporting vary from state to state: generally, the privilege is abrogated or, more precisely, nonexistent. In some states the right of clergy to privilege is maintained, but in most states, even that privilege is abrogated. Because of the allegations of sexual abuse among the clergy, many states that allowed privilege to clergy have withdrawn privilege in sexual abuse cases. Attorney/client privilege stands in the defense of the accused, but the attorney serving in a role other than defending the accused may be required to report (Smith, 2002).

Because of the legal and ethical dilemmas posed by working with minors, Lawrence and Kupius (2000) have made suggestions to help the therapist navigate the difficult arena of working with minors. These suggestions are paraphrased here:

1. Practice within the limits of your training, education, and supervised expertise.
2. Be completely familiar with what constitutes privilege and its limitations within your state.
3. Develop a written informed consent that clarifies confidentiality for the child and the parents at the onset of therapy that asks for the child and parents' (legal guardian's) cooperation. The document needs to be signed by all parties and dated prior to the first treatment session.
4. Keep accurate and objective records of all interactions and play therapy sessions.
5. Secure malpractice insurance that will adequately cover costs in case of a suit.
6. Confer with colleagues or legal counsel when unsure of the proper ethical or legal procedure.
7. Even when all of the guidelines are followed and adhered to strictly, a person may still be sued. (Lawrence & Kurpius, 2000)

While the practice of play therapy is more than a century old and has enjoyed widespread acceptance, the treatment has failed to be examined extensively.

Being sued does not mean a violation has taken place, nor does it mean a conviction will be the outcome. However, because of the changing laws governing children and children's rights, you must remain cognizant of the law and ethics concerning the special practice. Always consult with an attorney who specializes in family law when faced with any legal questions. Many professional organizations offer free legal consultation at the national and state level. Use these professional resources and err on the side of being overly conservative in legal matters.

RESEARCH

The most recent emphasis within the field of play therapy has been to indicate the efficacy of play therapy as a therapeutic intervention in mental health treatment for children. Although the practice of play therapy is more than a century old and has enjoyed widespread acceptance, the treatment has failed to be examined extensively. Until the turn of the 21st century, research failed to provide adequate validation because of

> (a) inadequate definitions of what constitutes play therapy; (b) research methodology that often relied on case studies, small samples, and uncontrolled studies, and (c) inadequate or non-measurable determinants of treatment outcome. (LeBlanc & Ritchie, 2001)

Some of the best designed studies have been those by Elliot and Pumfrey (1972), Fall, Balvanz, Nelson, and Johnson (1994), and Constantino, Malgady, and Rogler (1986). Fall et al. (1994) indicated that children exposed to play therapy make a significant increase in self-efficacy scores but failed to find significant changes using behavioral measures. Elliot and Pumfrey (1972) found the child subjects assigned to nine play therapy sessions or to the control group did not improve significantly in reading. Constantino et al. (1986) compared three groups of children over 20 sessions. Two groups discussed Puerto Rican folktales or American-adapted folktales; the third group participated in an art/play therapy group. All three groups showed significant improvement on Constantino's Behavior Rating Scale and Trait Anxiety Scale. The outcome indicated that treatment was preferred to no treatment with the groups participating in the folklore discussion groups showing a significant increase in comprehension on the Weschler Intelligence Scale for Children—Revised.

The bulk of the research has been anecdotal and case study, reported by practitioners using play therapy as a treatment modality. Although these reports are at times compelling, the studies lack research rigor and are fraught with bias reporting. The studies have not followed the more rigorous qualitative methods and designs of case study inquiry as described by such authors as Yin (2003) or Stake (1995).

Bratton and Ray (2000) conducted a meta-analysis of the experimental research studies recorded in the literature, both published and unpublished, from the 1940s through the 1990s. The initial studies focused on intelligence and school achievement, shifting in the 1970s and 1980s to social adjustment and self-concept. Bratton and Ray (2000) found the latter studies to be more concerned with topics centered around the social concerns of spousal abuse, divorce, chemical dependency, sexual abuse, and the personal concerns of attention deficit, depression and conduct disorder. In this early study, they found that play therapy did appear to be effective in the areas of improving self-concept, fostering behavioral change, improving cognitive ability, improving social skills, and reducing anxiety.

In the initial study, criticism leveled at the 60 years of research examined was the sparseness and poverty of research into play therapy's effectiveness. Play therapy research had lacked the ability to be generalized to a broader population because of the small number included in many of the studies. Many of these study designs compared play therapy to no intervention, which does not allow play therapy to be compared to other interventions. Play therapists were basically left with the research stance from these studies that play therapy is better than no intervention, which prevented claims of preference over other child therapy interventions.

A further meta-analysis was conducted, using 94 play therapy studies taken from 1947 until 2001. In this expanded study of the effects of play therapy, Ray, Bratton, Rhine, and Jones (2001) found a substantial positive effect in treatment outcomes across modality, gender, clinical versus nonclinical populations, settings, and diverse play therapy theories. Parent involvement was found to be one of the greatest contributors to the child's treatment.

LeBlanc and Ritchie (2001) conducted a meta-analysis of 42 studies drawn from both outside and inside the United States. They found the two types of play therapy that proved most effective were filial therapy and parent-child interaction therapy. The commonality between these two forms of parental involvement was that parents who received live feedback, training, and supervision from professionals were more likely to have greater positive increases in their therapeutic interactions with their children (LeBlanc & Ritchie, 2001). Leblanc and Ritchie hypothesize that the inclusion of the parents may be the greater contribution than the modality. Filial therapy is considered a nondirective therapy, whereas parent-child interaction therapy is directive and behavioral.

Duration of therapy appeared to be a major contributor to the success of play therapy as an intervention. LeBlanc and Ritchie (2001) found that the benefits of play therapy increased over 30 sessions. However, they observed that treatment extending over 35 sessions appeared to decrease the benefits of therapy. The data was insufficient to draw any conclusive arguments about the long-term effects of play therapy. However, LeBlanc and Ritchie (2001) drew the logical conclusion that children who remained in therapy for a long period of time were doing so because of their failure to respond to treatment, which might be inappropriate to the child's situation.

SUMMARY

Children's rights remains an expanding field of legislature that demands play therapists stay apprised of the rapid changes taking place. More so than ever in history, children have come to the forefront as individuals to be respected. No longer are children seen as miniature adults, but rather a developmentally special population with unique problems and concerns to be addressed with equally unique interventions from the social, physical, cognitive, and legislative aspects of our world culture.

Professional and ethical behavior toward children is just beginning to be acknowledged. Organizations like the Association for Play Therapy are defining the child as the client, with rights and privileges apart from those of his or her parents.

Professional ethical behavior toward children is just beginning to be acknowledged. Organizations like the Association for Play Therapy are defining the child as the client with rights and privileges apart from those of his or her parents. Some of these practices are passing into law, but most are still being determined by the professional organizations that represent those therapists who work with children.

Research on the efficacy of play therapy continues to be a growing and fertile field for this century. What we have begun to learn only scratches the surface of what is to be learned. As research methods are improved, the study of what is the best treatment or treatments will be more focused. The effects of therapist experience, types of training, modalities of play therapy, and theories of play therapy remain as areas needing comparison.

Although play therapy has been used as an intervention with many types of childhood problems, little research has looked at what theories or techniques of play therapy are best with which population of children. The multicultural aspects of play therapy have not been examined to the degree that specific theories appear to be more salient for treatment. We have only just begun.

CHAPTER 16

CULTURAL SENSITIVITY AND PLAY THERAPY

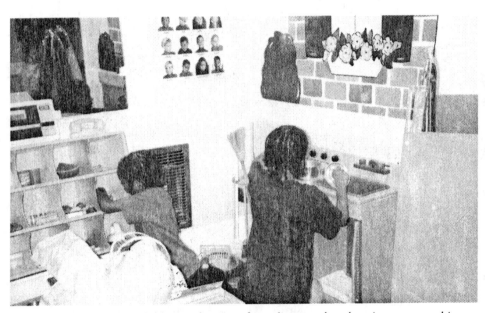

Play therapists encounter children and parents from diverse cultural environments seeking therapeutic services. The therapist needs to have knowledge of various cultures in order to provide appropriate treatment and interventions.

Play therapists serve children and parents from diverse cultural environments who are seeking therapeutic services. Through an awareness of culture differences, you can provide an enriched therapeutic milieu. This chapter offers a brief introduction of how to make play therapy more culturally sensitive.

INTRODUCTION

Cultures differ along specific boundaries of communication. Some of these boundaries become evident when we consider roles, status, inclusion, exclusion, trust, age, gender, religion, language, race, tribe, family, identity, self-concept, communication patterns, customs, time, and individualism (Pedersen & Carey, 2003; Sue & Sue,

2003; Triandis, 1987). To understand the role a child assumes in the play themes, you need to observe how each of these factors influences the cultural values of a given group. Understanding the traditional attitudes and customs of a particular culture, sect, or ethnic group is necessary to provide culturally sensitive play therapy and interventions.

One of the first questions you need to determine is the child's degree of acculturation. Asking the parents how "traditional" they consider themselves is one way to establish this cultural distinction. Another helpful question is to ask how many generations have passed since a parent or grandparent lived in the country of origin. How much contact do the parents and child have with people still immersed in the culture? Do the parents speak English or another language in the home? Another question for male-dominated cultures is whether or not the mother works and if the children have gone to day care, which appears to expedite the acculturation process for many cultures.

Families and children are acculturated at different levels because of the amount of contact with the world outside of the home and the type of community where the family lives. All people, even in the same family, may not share the same degree of acculturation or influence from the cultural milieu (Pedersen & Carey, 2003; Sue & Sue, 2003).

Triandis (1987) defined people according to two elements: *what people do* or *who people are*. He used spanking a child as an example. If the focus is on what people do, the observer from the culture may be horrified that one person is striking another. If the cultural emphasis is on who people are, the observer might say a mother has a right to spank her child. Although minorities in the United States tend to be more in tune to who people are, communities differ in their orientation of the emphasis, and the acculturation to the community will differ with individuals (Pedersen & Carey, 2003; Sue & Sue, 2003).

In every culture, whether the group is based on family, race, community, ethnicity, or other distinction, **in-groups** and **out-groups** exist. The out-groups may be based on historical events or on differing values. The in-groups are those that are seen as "most like us." The out-groups are those that are seen as "most different from us." This continuum of in-group to out-group defines the prejudices of each group. One of the most obvious ways to define the in-group is by racial characteristics. People who look alike are considered part of the in-group; those having different racial characteristics are considered the out-group. This dichotomy is the simplest and easiest way to discern possible prejudicial stances. However, biases are seldom so easily dichotomized or obvious to a person who may lack the experiences of the in-group (Pedersen & Carey, 2003; Sue & Sue, 2003).

Cultures differ in their perception of whom and how to *trust* others. Many cultures do not trust outside the family, below a certain maturity, or of a specific origin. Trust is won or earned. An easy way to find out what it takes is to ask the client, "How do you know you can trust someone?" In children, earning their trust is experiential. You behave in a consistent and accepting way to the child, and the child will trust. Trust is sacred to all cultures (Pedersen & Carey, 2003; Sue & Sue, 2003).

Age and *gender* form another tenet of cultural difference and are systematic beliefs in all cultures. The popular cry of the 1970s was "Don't trust anyone over the age of 30." Age can be considered as wisdom or as out of step. One gender can be considered superior to another. Being male is often considered a superior position, but in some cultures females are more valued and may dominate the household. In the United States the African American and Jewish cultures tend to be matriarchies. European cultures tend to be patriarchies. Eastern cultures tend to be age dominated. Middle Eastern cultures are usually male-dominated societies (Pedersen & Carey, 2003; Sue & Sue, 2003).

Religion, spirituality, and *philosophy* may define a culture or influence the development of a culture. The Muslims, Christians, Buddhists, and Jews throughout the world have religious-based cultures that may mediate the culture of the community or other differences. One of the problems plaguing the Catholic Church in North and South America is the blending of local spiritual beliefs with traditional beliefs of the church. Although Catholics and Protestant denominations share a common belief system and theological ideologies that set them apart from each other, each community may have additional practices that set them apart from the mainstream of their religious denomination or religious theology. Unique practices in one area may be commonplace in another, such as speaking in tongues, possession of demons, taking up the serpent, being slain in the spirit, dark-sided saints, foot washing, and encouragement of dissociation. These are all common in rural areas of the South and the Southwest (Pedersen & Carey, 2003; Sue & Sue, 2003).

Language contributes to diversity in a unique manner. Chomsky (1972) maintains that we cannot express what we do not have words to express. In other words, our cultural feeling is defined by the words of our language to express those feelings. Some languages do not have words to describe shadings of feelings or experiences. The child is perceived to have a limited realm of feelings because of a lack of vocabulary. Jargon is also a method to keep the in-group in and the out-group out. If a child uses jargon, tell the child, "I don't know what that means." Two reasons exist for not using the child's jargon: (1) using the jargon would be an intrusion by the therapist, and (2) jargon meanings are unique to the person using them (Pedersen & Carey, 2003; Sue & Sue, 2003; Triandis, 1987).

Racial differences are based on physical differences that cannot be changed. Remember that because a person has a particular racial appearance does not mean the person is culturally different. Race is a poor indicator of cultural differences and cultural experiences (Pedersen & Carey, 2003; Sue & Sue, 2003; Triandis, 1987).

When children come from a traditional *tribal* background, as do Native Americans and many Southeast Asians, the children are more responsive in groups. These tribal groups see the individual's problems as group problems. In cultures having extended families, it may be necessary to see grandparents, aunts, uncles, or other members outside the nuclear family. The primary caregivers are not always the biological parents. Although a child may be from a traditional extended family or tribe, the child may be acculturated to a different norm (Pedersen & Carey, 2003; Sue & Sue, 2003; Triandis, 1987).

Who is given *status* and how they are given it varies from culture to culture. Status may be based on age, gender, or earned. Many traditional Asians may take what a teacher, therapist, or doctor says without question because of the status afforded to such people in their culture. Another culture may ignore any suggestions from a female because women have no status in their culture (Pedersen & Carey, 2003; Sue & Sue, 2003; Triandis, 1987).

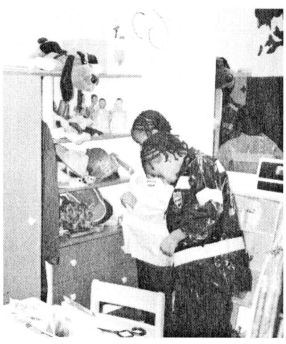

Who is given status and how they are given status varies from culture to culture.

Meta-communication is the tone or intention behind the content of a statement. Some children who may have limited language skills or who are bilingual focus on your tone, not on what you say. What is confusing about sarcasm is the incongruent message between the meta-communication and the content of the statement. The same incongruity leads many culturally different people to miss humor in satire. Make sure your communication is congruent because the child may focus on one aspect of language more than another (Pedersen & Carey, 2003; Sue & Sue, 2003; Triandis, 1987).

Self-concept is an oddity of Western European ideology and philosophy. The self-concept has to do with a related theme in cultures of individualism. Cultures focusing on self-concept and individualism look at what is good for the individual. Cultures that have a people's identity or collectivist orientation are not concerned about the individual but rather what is best for the whole. Western cultures tend to be self-concept/individualist oriented, whereas Eastern/South American cultures tend to be collectivist/people identity oriented (Pedersen & Carey, 2003; Sue & Sue, 2003; Triandis, 1987).

Customs present the final element of cultural differences. Customs and their adherence vary from family to family, individual to individual, and community to community. The best way to discover customs is to ask how people celebrate events in their lives. Most people gladly share their customs or traditions if the seeker appears sincere (Pedersen & Carey, 2003; Sue & Sue, 2003; Triandis, 1987).

Toy Selection

Toys reflect the culture and social environment of a culture. Toys are cultural artifacts that tell us a great deal about the culture's values and attitudes. The changing balance of social power is reflected in the toys. Toys generally reflect the attitudes of the dominant group and are used to legitimize the ideas, values, and experiences of that group while discrediting the ideas, values, and experiences of others (Nelson, 2004). Nelson describes that prior to the late 1960s, few toys were available that reflected the multicultural diversity of the United States. Based on her research for the Balch Institute of Ethnic Studies, the following guidelines are provided to determine whether toys selected for the playroom may be unintentionally biased or derogatory:

1. Do the images on the game board or other illustrations show ethnic diversity?
2. Do the dolls show ethnic characteristics and are not just "white" dolls painted or tinted different skin tones?
3. Are objects considered sacred to a group allowed to be used in a profane manner (e.g., drums, headdresses, shields, masks)?
4. Are stereotypes avoided in the selection of toys?

Nelson (2004) reported that a concerted effort has been made by toy makers to provide more culturally diverse versions of popular dolls. However, American Indian images in toys have remained unchanged, although fewer American Indian images are available. The Arab culture appears to have emerged as a new figure of derision since the fall of the World Trade Center and wars in the Middle East (Nelson, 2004).

Although you cannot change the world or even the views of many communities, we can be sure our playrooms do not reflect unhealthy biases and attitudes in the children with whom we work. Honoring all cultures is more than being politically correct. Honoring others' cultures teaches tolerance and acceptance of individual rights, respect for others and ourselves, and worthiness of others and ourselves. The world outside the playroom is one of diversity, and the playroom should reflect that diversity as closely as possible.

Gender bias is another consideration in selecting toys for a diverse playroom. Children often notice small images on objects that readily identify it as a "girl's toy." Examine any print on toys to see if there appears to a single representation of gender, boy or girl, man or woman. Although these indicators may be subtle to you, the child often quickly sees these minute differences in toys. Gender bias may show up in other areas as well. Male figurine or action figures are frequently more difficult to acquire, especially if you are looking for male figurines unassociated with aggression. Costumes are often another area that becomes unbalanced in the playroom. Strive to balance the playroom along gender lines as well as ethnic selections.

Role of the Therapist

Hinman (2003) suggests that the parents are a reliable source for knowledge of cultural traditions. However, she advises that you need to seek other sources of cultural traditions as well. Parents may not be forthcoming with information they feel may not be readily accepted by you. Most important is that you do not overgeneralize the child's cultural experience. Knowledge of the child's culture can assist you in building rapport with the child's parents and in providing a culturally inviting play therapy experience.

In a cross-cultural play therapy session, where you and the child are different races, you may have a more difficult time establishing rapport and trust than a same-race play therapist would. After a history of discrimination, minority clients are sensitive to signs of bias and discrimination in initial relationships. Reaction to this history of discrimination has resulted in anger that is often expressed in violence when active and in other ways when passive. You do not need to take the anger, whether passive or active, personally. Patience and understanding will help resolve the initially perceived adversarial relationship.

You may have to make minor changes to your standard operating procedures to accommodate cultural differences in clients. One example is extending confidentiality beyond the legal guardians and child. In discussing confidentiality, you may find it helpful to ask if the child and guardian want the confidentiality extended to other family members and caretakers. I might say something like this to the parents or legal guardian:

> I know that sometimes you might want me to talk to other members of the family about the child. I don't know all of your family. I will not share any information with any other family member without your permission. However, you are free to give me permission to share information with whomever you wish. Please tell me who I may share information with and sign a release for that person. I know that may sound silly to you, but I want to be sure I am doing what you want done for this child.

Because many cultures use traditional healers for both physical and mental health difficulties, you may find it advantageous to be familiar with various healers in the community. American Indians, Asian Americans, African Americans, and Latino Americans have a tradition that includes healers, herbalists, and folk medicines (Chandras, Eddy, & Spaulding, 1999). An understanding of this aspect of culture and its need for symbolism and ritual in therapy may provide you with intervention ideas that are compatible with these cultural values. Consultation with spiritual leaders, healers, and religious leaders becomes more important in those cultures that have a strong spiritual component (Hinman, 2003; Jackson-Brown, 1987; Lou & Takeuchi, 2001; Turner, 1979; Zhang, Snowden, & Sue, 1998).

Time is looked at as a present orientation. Long-term planning is not a traditional part of cultures that live at a survival level. Goal-setting behavior, behavioral reinforcement, baseline data, and many other concepts commonly used in therapy are not logical to cultures like the American Indian. Although the concepts of treatment planning with long-term and short-term treatment goals are readily understood by therapists, the American Indian client wants to tell you what is happening today. The focus is on the present without projection into the future. Many cultures that rely on fate or karma share this present orientation. Your role is to find that bridge between meeting the needs of health providers and governmental systems while conducting the session in a here-and-now format that meets the needs of the client.

Parental behavior does not always give you an indication of how a child expects to be treated by adults. The playfulness observed between Mexican American parents and their children does not carry over into the expectations of the therapeutic relationship. The Mexican American parent will expect a problem-solving, focused relationship with you. You will need to delineate clearly the behavioral expectations for the child between the playroom and the parent consultation sessions (Hinman, 2003; Martinez, 1988). This clarification of expectations is especially important at the beginning of a therapeutic relationship.

STRUCTURING THE SESSION

Nondirective play therapy is not usually successful with minority children. A more structured approach is advised. Carmichael (1991) found that children need to have items included in the playroom or toy selection that are culturally specific when possible. In addition, children may not be acculturated to the lack of structure in nondirective play therapy and may do much better with the structure of artwork to begin.

The cultural expectation may be for a much more formal atmosphere for therapy. One area where this formality may be important is in the showing of respect for oneself and for the clients. Hinman (2003) offers guidance about names. She suggests that you not introduce yourself to the child by your first name. Using one's first name is considered presumptuous in many cultures like the Asian American. The use of the surname indicates respect and affiliation to the family. For example, "Hello. I am Dr. Carmichael." Likewise to show respect to Asian American parents, you would refer to them by their title and surname. An example would be, "Mr. and Mrs. Tseo, I am pleased to meet you."

In addition to the more formal addressing of clients, the following treatment strategies are offered as general guidelines in working with clients from other cultures (Chandras et al., 1999):

1. Ask only relevant questions, avoiding personal questions when possible.
2. Explain what is to be done in the play therapy session, the stages of play therapy, need for verbal disclosure, problems that might be expected, the role of the therapist, child, and parents, misconceptions of therapy, and any other information that completely explains what is happening. If this explanation is written down in simple language or in the native language, the likelihood of continuation is increased. The more you can share with the child and parents about play therapy, the more interested and respectfully you are perceived. This perception of you adds to the parents' cooperation in making positive changes and adjustments.
3. Focus on specific problems and help the client develop short-term or immediate goals for therapy.
4. Be active and directive in the play therapy role. Many cultures, like Asian American, have an external locus of control.
5. Intervene with brief and focused concrete resolution to problems. (Chandras et al., 1999)

Behavioral reinforcement may be different for minority clients than for other clients. Thornton (2004) found African Americans expressed little concern for making money, economic security, and career focus. The order of their values from lowest to highest was religion, family, identity, career, social life, sex, economic security, sports, intellectual/artistic pursuits, helping others, vocational activities, and participation in community affairs (Thornton, 2004). Their values focused more on family and spiritual involvements. Your role is to recognize that the child may be reinforced by contingencies not shared by you.

Because of early responsibilities and expectations placed on the child in low-income families, the child may come to the session with a pseudo maturity and worldliness beyond what you expect for the child's age. However, if the child is from a middle-class family, the differences between this child and other middle-class children are minimal. Your role is to be aware of the impact of socioeconomic status on the child's acculturation and cultural experiences.

Nondirective play therapy is certainly one way to build rapport and help the child establish self-esteem. However, child-centered play therapy requires that the child engage in fantasy play. Cultural minority children are capable of fantasy, but their play may seem on a very realistic plane. Their play seems to reflect the no-nonsense atmosphere of their culture. The child may respond much better to therapy that has a clear expectation and allows the child to move gradually toward less directed and more creative fantasy play.

When you instruct the child that he or she may engage in free play, the child may experience emotional conflict. The conflict is that an authority figure is requesting the child to engage in a behavior that the child's parents (e.g., Japanese Americans) do not allow. The child does not know whether to not engage in

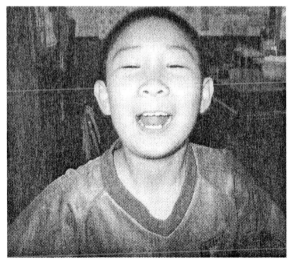

The Asian child may not know whether to refuse to engage in pretend play and disrespect an authority figure, or to embarrass his or her parents by engaging in inappropriate behavior.

pretend play and disrespect an authority figure or to embarrass his or her parents by engaging in inappropriate behavior. Hinman (2003) suggests that directed activities like art or other creative activities would better serve this and many other Asian populations.

The traditional Western approach to treatment of therapy is to remove obstacles that prevent the individual from being well or behaving well. The American Indian and Asian American tradition is to examine not only the illness, but underlying causes of the illness, understanding events from a spiritual perspective and then aligning the body, mind, and spirit into harmony. This alignment is believed to assist the individual to overcome the illness (Williams & Ellison, 1996). You need to understand this concept when the child or parents are providing what may seem like endless details of an event or experience. These cultural minorities are attempting to provide you with the complete experience, and they expect you to consider these important aspects in the treatment of the child.

Time is perceived in a very different manner than the traditional clock time that most therapists use in their practice. Working with cultures like the Mexican American and American Indian children and their families may require extending the therapeutic 50-minute hour as you listen quietly to what the family has to say. Remember there may be long pauses and a different speech cadence when the primary language spoken in the home is not English. The family's speech pattern may sound like the person is having difficulty finding the right word to say. The family may include more than just the parents in the interview. Everyone should be listened to and given time to speak. Do not interrupt anyone. The American Indian and Mexican American family is quickly put off by and interprets the strict adherence to the therapeutic hour as disinterest in helping the child and family. Remember that scheduling with some flexibility may be necessary in order to establish and maintain rapport with the family and child (Garwick, 2000; Tafoya, 1989).

Individualism and self-concept are not philosophical concepts prevalent within cultures that value stoicism, like Asian societies. Good mental health is typified by the ability to transcend the present emotional suffering to regain harmony and peace. Therefore emotional problems most often surface in somatic complaints that can be taken care of by doctors and healers (Chandras et al., 1999). Children are likely to show this kind of somatic distress through problems with sleep, elimination, and eating. This denial of emotional conflict and anxiety can aggravate chronic medical conditions like asthma and diabetes (Wicks-Nelson & Israel, 2003). Arab American and Asian American children are more likely than any other groups to display somatic symptoms (Hinman, 2003; Nassar-McMillan & Hakim-Larson, 2003).

However, not all cultural groups considered Asian are alike. The Indian American child in play therapy is most likely to attribute external causes like bias, favoritism, cheating, or another external cause to reasons for misbehaviors and social problems. This attribution to external causes results in the child not overvaluing the self, valuing the importance of other people in his or her life, and creating enhanced social ties to the cultural community. The use of praise or blame to attempt change may not be successful with Indian children. Because of their worldview, the Indian child may interpret the therapist's criticism to be bias while valuing praise much more than children from other cultures (Parameswaran & Hom, 2000). The more positive the interventions used in the structure of play therapy, the more likely the interventions will be successful.

The teachings of Islam for Arab Americans can be conceptualized as survival oriented as opposed to insight-oriented philosophy. Therapies that require insight may provoke a great deal of anxiety in the Islamic Arab American, leading to ineffective and counterproductive interventions and techniques. The emphasis on the individual may produce conflicts because the Arab American culture is a collective or tribal-based culture (Nassar-McMillan & Hakim-Larson, 2003).

Client-centered therapy has been argued to be universally effective by Patterson (1996), whereas Marsella (1998) found that standard psychodynamic therapy techniques and concepts were effective with Arab clients. Multimodal or eclectic methodology appears to be most effective in working with Arab Americans. Recommendations include family or systems approaches, cognitive-behavioral approaches, and problem-solving approaches that provide a focus on immediate and daily concerns (Nassar-McMillan & Hakim-Larson, 2003).

The primary determiner of successful therapy is the building of the relationships among the therapist, the child, and the adults in the Arab American family. The traditional therapeutic approaches that interpret and explore the client's issues are not as important as the relationship. The relationship valued in the Arab American culture tends to be paternalistic, benevolent, and authoritative. The Arab American comes to the therapist expecting to receive wisdom, not necessarily self-understanding. Consultation with religious leaders may be an important step in establishing rapport and trust because the Arab American culture is dominated by religious devotion. Acknowledging spiritual issues by consulting with priests and imams in the therapeutic process may ensure successful mental health interventions. Religious leaders as allies in the delivery of mental health services is important for most Arab Americans, but you cannot safely assume all Arab Americans are devoutly religious or follow a given theological philosophy (Nassar-McMillan & Hakim-Larson, 2003).

Because of issues of confidentiality and distrust, even of members within their own community, many Arab Americans do much better in individual counseling. However, the parents of a child may be reluctant to share personal information during the intake unless they understand how this information is necessary to working with the child. Those theories of play therapy that present the play therapist as a detached observer, who sees the child during the therapy hour once a week and excludes the parents from the sessions are not recommended. So much of the success of the therapy depends on the relationship to the family of the child within the Arab American culture that you may want to make home visits, seeing the child in his or her environment and interacting with all of the family. Creating a friendly and social relationship is recommended prior to discussing therapeutic concerns. The family may invite you to a family meal. You may have to depart from the clear delineations between therapeutic sessions and social interactions with clients and their families in order to accommodate the cultural differences demanded in rapport building with Arab American clients (Nassar-McMillan & Hakim-Larson, 2003).

LIMIT SETTING

Limit setting within the family is often characterized by strict rules and heavy responsibilities for the developmental ages of the children. The strictness and harshness of the discipline in the minority family may be seen by the middle-class American family as uncaring and authoritarian. However, the findings suggest that strictness is functional for the minority family when they reside in hostile environments (Nandi & Harris, 1999).

PARENT INVOLVEMENT

A first step in providing play therapy is to develop a working relationship or to join with the child's parents. The parents are important in the process because of their knowledge of the problem and the child, but also because their cooperation is needed for the success of the treatment. The parents or significant caregivers ultimately determine if the child continues in play therapy or not. One of the most common occurrence in working with culturally different clients is early withdrawal from therapy (Hinman, 2003).

A major concern of minority parents who are living in inner cities or impoverished areas is for the safety and support from the community for their children. Many minority children are reared in single-parent homes. Rearing a child as a single parent raises issues of lack of appropriate gender models. Children must look to outside sources within their community or to celebrity and sports figures. What is seen and heard about these gender role models provides a distorted view of traditional cultural values and may overemphasize sexuality, street culture, and violence (Parker, 2003).

In high-crime areas, resources are limited for the wholesome physical and emotional well-being of children. Medical facilities, cinemas, parks, and other facilities open to the middle-class neighborhood are absent. Taxis and buses often do not make stops convenient to the residents in these neighborhoods; therefore the children are denied access to libraries and other public educational services afforded their more fortunate peers. Lack of available and reliable transportation prevents adults in the family from sustaining employment unless the employment is within walking distance of their homes. Well-paying jobs are usually located far from crime-ridden neighborhoods, which make these better paying jobs inaccessible to the family that cannot afford to maintain a car. The neighborhood and its problems serve to isolate and maintain a status that is not conducive to improved education, employment, and escape (Nandi & Harris, 1999). This lack of public resources and community support may greatly affect the interventions that parents are willing to attempt within their financial and time allowances.

Many of the children seen by play therapists in private and agency practices are referred by child protection agencies. These children are usually from low-income families. Be prepared to work with the women of the family in order to assist the child. Parenting skills training programs that do not allow strict discipline may not be well accepted or applied by the caregiver. Helping parents to select activities for their children that prevent them from becoming involved in the criminal, drug, and violent street culture of many urban communities becomes paramount for intervention in the home environment (Jipguep & Sanders-Phillips, 2003).

Therapy with a clear focus that can be articulated to parents and caregivers may have an advantage in securing cooperation from the adults in the child's life. Questions from the adult caregivers may be more direct and appear more demanding than with other cultures. With the many other frustrations that impinge on this cultural group, frustration tolerance for yet another demand on their resources may be met with low frustration levels unless you can demonstrate how this therapeutic intervention can help lower other frustrations. Depending on the individual's resources, transportation and similar social support services may need to be secured, if the child is to be in therapy on a regular basis (Whaley, 2003).

Tribal or extended family traditions are more likely to respond to family therapy. Therefore the child may respond more appropriately to play therapy in a group or to one of the emerging family play therapies or filial therapy. The broad ethnic categories of persons who might be considered for this parent/family intervention are American Indians, Asian Americans, and African Americans (Brucker & Perry, 1998; Garwick, 2000).

No one can know all there is to know about a particular family or culture. Individual beliefs within the culture are often as diverse as the culture itself. So when parents seem to be reluctant or resistant to a suggestion, you may approach this resistance by saying, "I am not familiar with your traditions. Is there something about what I have asked you to do that will not work for you or that you find strange?"

As children, most Asians are taught to be compliant and respectful of authority figures. When any service is sought from a professional, he or she is expected to provide a directive and the directive is to be followed without question. Questioning the professional is considered disrespectful. Silence, however, does not mean the directive will be carried out. Asian Americans usually cope with these conflicts between being respectful and disagreeing with the professional by simply not returning to the sessions (Gong, Gage & Tacata, 2003; Yeung & Kung, 2004; Yick, Shibusawa, & Agbayani-Siewert, 2003).

Japanese Americans may enter the office of the play therapists with a sense of shame because they feel they have not met the needs of their child. The Japanese have historically viewed mental health problems as under personal control and an attempt to avoid responsibility. Failure to teach a child to take responsibility and to face life stoically results in failure as a parent. By creating a working relationship with the family and an atmosphere of confidentiality and support, you can help the family through the shame they are feeling. As trust is built, you can help the parents learn supportive interventions at home and help them overcome their sense of shame and loss of control (Hinman, 2003).

In the Vietnamese and Cambodian cultures, a request for help creates a debt. The debt to professionals is considered to cost a great deal. Therefore the parents of these children want to be assured the service is equal to the cost they are obligated to pay for the service. The initial intake is a opportunity for you to show your credibility and to negotiate with the parents about the treatment, its merits, and the expected

An American "grandfather" has been adopted by this Asian family as part of the acculturation process.

outcomes. While you are describing the service and the merits of the service toward helping the child, the parents will be determining if the cost, financially and emotionally, will be worth it to the child and family (Hinman, 2003).

Parenting practices vary greatly on the continuum from permissive to authoritarian, and they may differ markedly according to the gender of the child. Mexican Americans do not commonly participate in parenting classes, so their participation may be reluctant. To make parenting education more palatable to Mexican Americans, the parenting education appears to be more successful when informal from therapist to parents. Classroom formats have not been found effective with Mexican American parents (Martinez, 1988).

Arab Americans are likely to view seeing a play therapist as an attempt to cure a mental illness. Their culture is prone to the use of pharmacotherapy as opposed to talk therapies. Their concept of good mental health is complete submission to the will of Allah, whereas disintegration and disruption of inner harmony denotes the lack of moral and spiritual fiber, or "*gossonrfi al nazaa'aldeeneya*" (Sayed, 2003). Christian Arabs of North Africa believe traumatic events are brought upon people because they have sinned (Sayed, 2003).

TERMINATION

Termination is a special event for Asian Americans and American Indians. This special time requires some kind of honor to be bestowed on the child and family. Gifts and food need to be part of this time. The gifts need not be expensive, but they do need to carry with them the affirmations of self-worth and reminders of what the child has learned in the sessions. A worry stone, a smooth river stone of the child's choosing, may be a reminder that the irritations of the sand on the stone are what makes it beautiful and smooth. White smooth stones usually portray wisdom. A small painting, a bead project, a colorful votive candle, a poem written about the child, or anything symbolic of encouragement is a perfect gift for the child. The food served should be something the child likes. Work with the caregiver to know who will be expected and what kinds of activities and foods are appropriate for this type of passage. You may want to have the honor bestowed away from the office. A word of warning: With the extended family, this little honor can turn into a gathering with far more people than the novice therapist would ever expect (Herring, 1994).

ASSESSMENT

The American Psychiatric Association (1994) has included in the DSM-IV an Outline for Cultural Formulation. This instrument is intended to gather information that will assist you in understanding the client's cultural identity. In addition, the information helps in the assessment process to indicate the impact of cultural differences on testing and treatment. Three major areas are examined in the instrument: (1) determining the cultural identity of the individual, (2) identifying and clarifying symptoms within the cultural context, and (3) identifying social supports and stressors. The Outline for Cultural Formulation is provided in the appendixes of the DSM-IV. The outline was essentially intended for adult clients ("Towards Culturally Competent Care," 2004).

The Cultural Consultation Service ("Cultural Consultation Service," 2004) has expanded the original DSM-IV outline to address "common issues and experiences for immigrants, refugees, and members of ethnocultural minorities." Two versions of the document have been developed. Version A focuses on cultural formulation: version B is "designed as a semi-structured interview to be used by a researcher interviewing a clinician/consultant after the fact."

The cultural formulation outline includes gathering information about the cultural and religious groups with which each parent self-identifies, languages spoken at home, work, or childhood, cultural origin of peer group and siblings, degree of contact with culture of origin, and degree of contact with host culture. The instrument then explores the cultural explanations of the complaint and what kinds of help, both formal health care and traditional healers or other alternative services, the family has explored or intends to explore. Social support and social stressors are examined and compared to level of functioning and disability. A comparison is made between the therapist and the client in relation to ethnocultural background, language, cultural knowledge, and potential value conflicts.

The data collected is reviewed and a checklist is developed that summarizes the information. A treatment plan checklist concludes the instrument. The treatment plan checklist includes the type of medical referral, psychiatric intervention, religious involvement, legal requirements, community support, and previous treatment ("Cultural Consultation Service," 2004).

Version B is divided into sections with questions designed to stimulate you to reflect on the cultural needs of the client. This version of the instrument gets at the same information but is focused on looking at children in a reflective methodology. The sections are referral, triage process, evaluation, family narrative, course of treatment, and outcome questions. Version B is designed specifically for a children's hospital and may be more useful to the play therapist ("Cultural Consultation Service," 2004).

SUMMARY

Psychotherapy is a Western cultural concept with Western psychology its philosophical science (Dwairy, 1999; Marsella, 1998). The notion that entirely culture-free interventions, theories, or assessment instruments exist is a misguided perception because the basis of psychology and therapy is a Western schema of health and illness (Christopher, 1999). The client may use your ignorance of his or her culture as a defense when the client is not ready to engage in a therapeutic relationship (Sayed, 2003). Seeking therapy from a member of one's own cultural group may indeed be a symptom of mistrust and suspicion, which allows the individual to claim betrayal of the culturally similar therapist when the client remains resistant to therapy (Sayed, 2003).

Play therapy with its many adaptations can provide an intervention across cultures. The continuum of nondirective to directive is one of the most important aspects of play therapy to consider when working with other cultures. The continuum of nondirective to directive roughly coincides with the acculturation continuum with the less acculturated seeking more directive play therapy and the more acculturated seeking less directive play therapy.

Some cultural characteristics were presented in this chapter, but individuals vary greatly from these generalized cultural characteristics. Familiarity with the cultural features will allow you to make adaptations that are culturally sensitive and more likely to be helpful to the minority client.

The mother and children leave the therapy session.

APPENDIX A

ASSOCIATION FOR PLAY THERAPY STANDARDS OF PRACTICE

PREAMBLE

The Association for Play Therapy (APT) is a world-wide organization dedicated to the advancement of play therapy so that children in need may receive the best possible mental health services. Its members have a unique and distinctive preparation in play therapy.

Standards of Practice allow an association to clarify to current and future members, clients, and other professionals, their guidelines to the ethical provision of services and behavior of APT members.

SECTION A: THE THERAPEUTIC RELATIONSHIP

A.1. Commitments and Responsibilities to the Client

a. Primary Responsibilities

The primary responsibility of the play therapist is to conduct therapy that respects the dignity, recognizes the uniqueness, and promotes the best interests in the welfare of the child. The best interests may include education and/or other adjunct therapy for the significant adults in the child's life.

b. Optimal Growth and Development

Play therapists encourage the advancement of the psychosocial development and mental health of people through play and play therapy. Play therapists foster the clients' interest and welfare as well as the nurturing relationships in the child's life.

c. Therapeutic Plans

The play therapist explains the developmentally appropriate therapeutic plan in an understandable manner to the child and his/her legal representative. This plan is reviewed regularly to ensure viability, effectiveness, and the continued support of the child and the involvement of the adults in the therapeutic goals.

d. Documentation

Play therapists practicing independently shall document sessions with clients so that the most recent progress notes reflect the following:

- Current developmental level of functioning, i.e. cognitive, play, affective
- Long and short term goals of treatment
- Verbal content of sessions relevant to behavior and goals
- Observed play themes and materials used
- Graphic images relevant to client behavior and goals, i.e. sketches of sand trays, drawings, photographs, videotapes, etc.
- Changes in thought process, affect, play themes, and behavior
- Interventions with significant others, i.e. adjunct therapy, referrals, etc.
- Suicidal or homicidal intent or ideation
- Observations of child with significant others
- Level of family functioning and environment
- Conditions of termination

e. Educational Needs

Play therapists recognize that play is a child's inalienable right and school is the work of children. If qualified, the play therapist may work with the child and significant adults in considering educational placements that are consistent with the child client's overall abilities, physical restrictions, general temperament, interests, aptitudes, social skills, and other relevant individual differences and developmental needs. Play therapists are ever mindful of the best interests of the child's welfare in recommendation and placement of child clients.

A.2. Respecting Individual Differences

a. Nondiscrimination

Play therapists do not encourage or engage in discrimination based on age, color, culture, disability, ethnic group, gender, race, religion, sexual orientation, or socioeconomic status.

b. Respect of Individual Differences

Play therapists will actively participate in the providing of interventions that show understanding of the diverse cultural backgrounds of their clients, being cognizant of how their own cultural/ethnic/racial identity may influence interventions and therapeutic philosophy. Where appropriate, the play therapist should make every effort to support and maintain the culture and cultural identity of clients.

A.3. Rights of Clients

a. Disclosure Statement

The play therapist recognizes and respects that the child is the client; and thus, informs the child and his/her appropriate significant adults of the purposes, goals, techniques, procedures limitations, potential risks, and benefits of the services to be performed in age appropriate language for the understanding of the child client. The play therapist takes steps to ensure that the child-client and his/her appropriate significant adults understand the implications of diagnosis, the intention of tests and reports, fees and billing arrangements. The child client has the right to expect confidentiality and to be provided with an explanation of its limitations, including disclosure to appropriate significant adults, supervision and/or treatment teams, and to obtain clear information about their case records; to participate in the ongoing treatment plan as is appropriate to their developmental level.

b. Freedom of Choice

Play therapists recognize that minor children do not always have the freedom to choose whether they enter into the therapeutic relationship or with whom they enter into therapy. However, the play therapist will advise the legal guardians of the minor child with a rationale of play therapy to assist in choosing whether to enter into a therapeutic relationship and to determine which professional(s) may provide for the best interest of the child. Restrictions that limit choices of the clients are fully explained.

c. Inability to Give Consent

The play therapist acts in the best interest of the client in working with minor children or others unable to give voluntary informed consent.

A.4. Clients Served by Multiple Resources

The play therapist must carefully consider the client's welfare and treatment issues when the client is receiving services from another mental health, educational, or medical professional. The play therapist, with the permission from the legal representative, consults other professional providers to develop clear agreements to avoid confusion and reduce conflict for the client(s).

A.5. Therapist Needs and Values

a. Therapist Personal Needs

In a therapeutic relationship, the play therapist is responsible for maintaining respect for the client and to avoid actions that seek to meet personal needs at the expense of the child client.

b. Therapist Personal Values

Play therapists recognize the vulnerability of children and do not impose personal attitudes and beliefs on their child clients. However, this does not mean therapists attempt to conduct therapy free of values. Play therapists set limits when children's behavior presents a danger to the child or others. Further, the play therapist helps to redirect children whose behavior prevents them from getting their own needs met or significantly interferes with the ability of others to get their needs met. Play therapists should also be aware of how their own values, attitudes, and beliefs affect their clients. Lastly, play therapists should make every effort to convey to child clients and their parents the system or basis on which they, as therapists, make value judgments and decisions in therapy.

A.6. Dual Relationships

a. Avoidance

Play therapists are alert to and guard against dual relationships with clients and their significant adults that could impair professional judgment, increase the risk of harm to the client or exploit the client through personal, social, organizational, political, or religious relationships. Play therapists take appropriate professional precautions through informed consent, consultation, supervision, and/or documentation in an unavoidable dual relationship.

b. Superior/Subordinate Relationships

Play therapists do not accept as child clients the children of superiors or subordinates with whom they have administrative, supervisory, or evaluative relationships.

A.7. Sexual Intimacies

a. Current Clients

Play therapists do not have any type of sexual intimacies with child clients and do not counsel the children of persons with whom they have had or have a sexual relationship.

b. Encouragement of Intimacies

Play therapist do not encourage inappropriate intimacies from the child client or the child client's significant adults.

c. Requests for Nurturance

Play therapists respond professionally and responsibly to a child's spontaneous request for nurturance.

d. Therapeutic Touch

Play therapists recognize the importance of therapeutic touch, a form of non-sexual touch, as a valid intervention in play therapy. However, play therapists do not engage in any form of therapeutic touch without the informed consent of the child's legal representative.

e. Inappropriate Touching of Therapist by Child

Play therapists recognize that children who have been inappropriately sexualized may initiate inappropriate touching of the play therapist. A play therapist who has been inappropriately touched by a child should explain to the child that in the play therapy every person's body is respected and is not touched in a way that makes them uncomfortable or that is generally considered inappropriate by society. The incident and intervention should be documented.

f. Former Clients

Play therapists never engage in sexual intimacies with the parent, caregiver, legal guardian, or custodian of a child-client, when such a relationship would have an adverse impact on the child-client or children who were clients.

A.8. Multiple Clients

When the play therapist is providing services to two or more persons who have a relationship (siblings, parent and child, etc.), the play therapist clarifies at the beginning of therapy the nature of the relationship with each client. If the play therapist is called upon to perform potentially conflicting roles, the play therapist may clarify, adjust, or withdraw after informing the clients of the conflict.

A.9. Group Work

a. Screening

The play therapist selects clients for group play therapy whose needs are compatible and conducive to the therapeutic process and well-being of each child.

b. Protecting Clients

Play therapists using group play therapy take reasonable precautions in protecting clients from physical and psychological trauma.

c. Confidentiality in Groups

Play therapists explain to child-clients that confidentiality is to be maintained regarding group therapy sessions.

A.10. Payment

a. Fee Contract

Play therapists clarify the financial arrangements with the party responsible for the fee prior to entering into a therapeutic relationship with the child-client, including the use of collection agencies or legal measures for nonpayment.

b. Fee Structure

Play therapists consider the financial status of the legally responsible party and generally accepted fee for services within the community. When an established fee structure is inappropriate for the responsible party, assistance is provided in attempting to find comparable services of acceptable cost.

c. Bartering versus Pro Bono

Play therapists refrain from accepting goods or services from the party responsible for the fee. Pro Bono service is encouraged.

A.11. Termination and Referral

a. Abandonment

Play therapists do not abandon their clients. When a break in treatment occurs, the play therapist makes appropriate arrangements to avoid abandonment. When such a break is not initiated by the play therapist, the legal representative is advised to dangerous hazards and is provided an alternative referral/treatment source.

b. Inability to Assist Clients

Play therapists may sometimes find that they are unable to provide proper professional assistance to a client. In such situations, it is required that the play therapist provide appropriate referral sources. This is required even if the original referral source refuses the suggested alternative therapeutic sources.

c. Termination

Play therapists terminate a therapeutic relationship when it is reasonably clear that the client is no longer benefiting, when services are no longer required, when therapy no longer serves the client's needs or interests, when the responsible party fails to pay fees charged, or when agency or institution limits discontinue the therapeutic relationship. Play therapists do not allow an unreasonable unpaid fee to accumulate.

A.12. Computer Technology

a. Computer Usage

Play therapists using computer applications ensure that: (1) the client is developmentally capable of benefiting from the computer application; (2) the computer application meets the needs of the client; (3) the client understands the purpose and operation of the computer applications; (4) a follow-up of client use of a computer application is provided to clarify misconceptions, inappropriate use, and subsequent needs, and (5) use of the computer application is congruent with the treatment goals.

b. Computer Limitations
Play therapists inform clients of limitations of computer technology.

c. Computer Access
Play therapists provide appropriate access to computer applications congruent with treatment goals.

SECTION B: PARENTS AND FAMILY

B.1. Parents
a. Parents in Conflict
Play therapists comply with laws and local guidelines in assisting parents in conflict when the relationship interferes with the child-client's effectiveness and welfare.

b. Custodial and Non-custodial Parents
Play therapists are cognizant of, and recognize, that custodial and non-custodial parents may have specific and differing rights and responsibilities for the welfare of their children according to law or agreement.

B.2. Family
a. Family Involvement
Play therapists recognize that children have family members and other significant adults who have influence in the child's psychosocial growth and development and strive to gain understanding and involvement of these significant adults for positive support where appropriate and as according to the treatment plan.

b. Home-based Intervention
Play therapists make a reasonable effort to provide privacy for the child-client during home-based therapy sessions.

c. Family Interventions
Play therapists never disclose information about one family member to another member without informed consent.

SECTION C: CONFIDENTIALITY

C.1. Right to Privacy
a. Respect for Privacy
Play therapists respect the child's right to privacy and disclose to parents/guardians/significant adults, except where otherwise provided by state law. Only those concerns that are in the best interest of the child and avoid illegal and unwarranted disclosures of confidential information which might adversely affect the treatment of the client are disclosed.

b. Waiver of Client's Right
A minor child cannot waive their right to privacy, but disclosure of material that is in the best interest of the child may be waived by their legal representative. The minor child needs to be informed of the information being disclosed and the reason for the disclosure.

c. Exceptions to Confidentiality
Play therapists keep information confidential except when disclosure is required to prevent clear and imminent danger to the child-client or others. Play therapists responsibly consult with other health care professionals and child care providers when in doubt. Play therapists also become cognizant of state law related to confidentiality and comply with it.

d. Contagious Diseases
The play therapist is responsible for taking reasonable precautions to prevent the spread of contagious diseases and endangerment to others.

e. Court-ordered Disclosure
When court ordered to release confidential information without permission from the child's legal representative, play therapists request the court grant privilege.

f. Minimal Disclosure
When circumstances require the disclosure of confidential information, only essential information is revealed. Information which might adversely affect the treatment of the client requires a request for privileged communication. Play therapists also become cognizant of state law related to confidentiality and comply with it.

g. Limitations
The play therapist informs the child client and his/her legal representative of the limitations of confidentiality and identifies foreseeable situations in which confidentiality must be breached.

h. Subordinates
Play therapists implement reasonable precautions ensuring privacy and confidentiality of the client, including maintenance of all personnel privileged to client contact or information.

i. Treatment Teams
The existence of a treatment team and its composition are disclosed by the play therapist to the child client and legal representative.

C.2. Group
Play therapists who use group play therapy clarify limits of confidentiality and specify group parameters. Consequences for violation of the rules need to be explained and enforced.

C.3. Documents
a. Documentation
Play therapists maintain documentation as required by law, regulation, or agency or institutional proce-

dure to provide support for therapeutic intervention and rendering professional services.

b. Confidentiality of Documents
Play therapists are responsible for the safety and confidentiality of any documentation they create, maintain, transfer, or destroy, whether the records are written, taped, computerized, or stored in any other medium.

c. Permission to Electronically Document or Observe
Play therapists obtain permission from client's legal representatives before electronically documenting or observing the session.

d. Public Use and Reproduction of Client Expression and Therapy Sessions
Play therapists do not make or permit any public use or reproduction of the client's play, artwork, music, or other creative expression through videotaping, audio recording, photography, or otherwise duplicating or permitting a third-party observation in art galleries, mental health facilities, schools, or other public places without the written informed consent of the client and/or the legal representative of the client.

e. Client Access
Play therapists provide access to copies of the records when requested to do so by the legal representative of minor children, unless the records contain information that may not be in the best interest of the client. Access to documents are limited to those parts of the documents that do not include confidential information related to another client. When possible, play therapists should attempt to respond to a subpoena in a way that protects the best interest of the client.

f. Disclosure or Transfer
Play therapists obtain written permission from the legal representative of the client to disclose or transfer records to legitimate third parties unless exceptions to confidentiality exists.

C.4. Research and Training
a. Disguise Identity
Play therapists engaged in training, research, or publication are required to disguise the data to ensure the anonymity of the individuals involved.

b. Agreement for Identification
Public release of information regarding a specific client is permissible only when the client or legal representative is fully aware of the material and has reviewed the material and has agreed to its public release. Play therapists should receive specific written permission, depending upon the nature of the situation, for example, the play therapist should consider the type of audience, location of the audience, etc., when obtaining the written permission.

C.5. Consultation
a. Privacy
Play therapists discuss information from consultations with significant adults or other professionals only with those persons having a direct bearing on therapeutic intervention. Every effort is made to protect client identity and avoid undue invasion of privacy.

b. Cooperating Agencies
Prior to sharing information, play therapists take reasonable care to ensure that there are defined policies in other agencies serving the client that effectively protect the confidentiality of the client.

SECTION D: PROFESSIONAL RESPONSIBILITY
D.1. Knowledge of Standards
Play therapists are responsible for reading, understanding, and following the APT Standards of Practice.

D.2. Professional Competencies
a. Boundaries of Competence
Play therapists practice only within the boundaries of their competence. Competence is based on training; supervised experience; state, national, and international professional credentials; and professional experience. Play therapists commit to knowledge acquisition and skill development pertinent to working with a diverse client population.

b. New Areas of Specialty
Play therapists practice a new specialty after appropriate education, training, and supervised experience. Play therapists take steps to ensure the competence of their work while developing skills in the new specialty.

c. Employment Qualifications
Play therapists accept employment for positions for which they are qualified. Qualifications are determined by education, training, supervised experience, state, national, and international credentials, and professional experience. Play therapists hire only individuals who are qualified and competent.

d. Monitor Effectiveness
Play therapists monitor their effectiveness as professionals and pursue ongoing training, education, and supervision.

e. Ethical Consultation
Play therapists consult with knowledgeable professionals concerning questions regarding ethical obligations or professional practices.

f. Continuing Education/Training

Play therapists acquire continuing education to maintain awareness of current research in play therapy, being open to new procedures, and by keeping current with diverse and/or special populations with whom they work. The play therapist maintains competency through knowledge of new procedures and models of client diversity.

g. Therapist Impairment

Play therapists refrain from providing play therapy when their physical, mental, or emotional problems might harm a client or others. The play therapist is aware of signs of impairment, seeks assistance, limits, suspends, or terminates their professional responsibilities if necessary.

D.3. Advertising and Soliciting Clients

a. Accurate Advertising

Play therapists and their employees accurately represent their competency, education, training, and experience relevant to the practice of play therapy. Play therapists can only advertise the highest degree earned in a mental health or closely related field from a college or university that was accredited and recognized by the Council on Post-secondary Accreditation or recognized internationally as meeting equivalent academic accreditation standards.

b. Testimonials

Play therapists do not solicit or use testimonials.

c. Statements by Others

Play therapists ensure that statements made by others about them, their service, or the profession of play therapy are accurate.

d. Products and Training Advertisements

Play therapists do not inappropriately use the power of their positions to promote their services or training events. Play therapists may adopt textbooks and materials they have authored for instructional purposes.

e. Professional Association Involvement

Play therapists are actively involved in local, state, national, and international associations that promote the development and improvement of play therapy.

D.4. Credentials

a. Credentials Claimed

Play therapists represent only professional education/training earned and take responsibility for correcting any misrepresentations. Professional APT credentials include:

- J. Doe, Registered Play Therapist
- J. Doe, Registered Play Therapist-Supervisor

b. Credential Guidelines

Play therapists adhere to the guidelines of credentials that have been determined by credential issuing body or bodies.

c. Misrepresentation of Credentials

Play therapists never misrepresent their credentials.

d. Doctoral Degrees from Other Fields

Play therapists holding a master's degree in a mental health or closely related field, but holding a doctoral degree that is not in mental health or closely related field, cannot use the title "Dr." in their practices (i.e. Play therapist holds a masters in counseling and a doctorate in educational leadership would not use the Dr. in their play therapy practice).

D.5. Public Responsibility

a. Nondiscrimination

Play therapists do not discriminate against clients, students, or supervisees in a manner that has a negative impact based on their age, color, culture, disability, ethnic group, gender, race, religion, sexual orientation, or socioeconomic status, or for any legal reason.

b. Sexual Harassment

Play therapists never encourage or participate in sexual harassment. Sexual harassment is defined as undesired sexual advances, solicitation of sexual favors, unwanted physical contact, sexual solicitation, physical advances, or verbal or nonverbal conduct that is explicitly or implicitly sexual, that occurs within the professional activities or role, and that either (1) is unwanted, offensive, repeated, or interferes with the individual's therapy or work performance and creates a hostile workplace or therapeutic environment, and the play therapist is told this; or (2) is perceived as harassment to a reasonable third-party in the given circumstances. Sexual harassment may exist after a single intense or severe act or multiple persistent or pervasive acts.

c. Third Party Reports

Play therapists are unbiased, accurate, and honest in disclosing their professional activities and assessments to appropriate third parties.

d. Media Presentations

Play therapists providing advice or comment through public lectures, presentations, and media programs take precautionary measures to ensure that (1) information is based on research and current models of practice; (2) the information is consistent with the Standards of Practice; and (3) receiving the information does not mean that a professional therapeutic relationship has been established.

e. Exploitation
Play therapists never use the power of their positions to exploit their clients and their significant adults for unearned or unfair gains, advantages, goods or services.

D.6. Responsibility to Other Professionals
a. Different Approaches
Play therapists respect theoretical approaches to play therapy that diverge from their own. Play therapists are aware and acknowledge traditions and practices of other professional disciplines.

b. Personal Public Statement
Play therapists clarify that they are speaking from their personal perspectives and that they are not speaking on behalf of APT, state branches, or play therapists, when offering a personal statement in public context.

c. Clients Served by Others
Play therapists request a release from clients to inform other professionals and seek to establish collaborative professional relationships in the best interest of the child client.

SECTION E: RELATIONSHIPS WITH OTHER PROFESSIONALS
E.1. Relationships with Employers and Employees
a. Definition of Role
Play therapists delineate for their employers and employees the boundaries, limitations, and levels of their professional roles.

b. Covenants
Play therapists establish covenants with supervisors, colleagues, and subordinates regarding play therapy Standards of Practice, workload, and accountability. Covenants are specified and made known to those affected.

c. Disruptive or Damaging Conditions
Play therapists inform their employers about disruptive or damaging conditions affecting the play therapist's professional responsibilities.

d. Evaluation
Play therapists participate in professional review and evaluation by supervisor, employer, or peer group.

e. Professional Development
Play therapists are available for providing professional development to staff regarding the benefits and limitations of play therapy.

f. Goals
Play therapists' goals are communicated to staff and other professional associates when requested and/or when appropriate.

g. Discrimination
Play therapists do not engage or condone inhumane, illegal, or unjustifiable practices in the workplace.

h. Professional Conduct
Play therapists maintain high standards of professional conduct in the work setting.

i. Exploitive Relationships
Play therapists do not engage in exploitive relationships with supervisees, students, staff, or other subordinates.

j. Employer Policies
Play therapists strive to reach agreement regarding APT Standards of Practice that allow for changes in institutional policy conducive to the therapeutic relationship.

E.2. Consultation
a. Providing Consultation
Play therapists choosing to consult with other professionally competent people about their clients avoid placing the consultant in a conflict of interest. Play therapists employed in a work setting that compromises this consultation standard consult with other professionals whenever possible.

b. Consultant Competency
Play therapists ascertain the organization represented has competencies and resources to provide adequate consulting services and referral resources.

c. Consultant Role
Play therapists, who choose to serve as consultants to other mental health professionals, should develop a comprehensible understanding of the problem, goals for change, recommend and discuss possible outcomes for their client, and encourage growth in independent functioning.

E.3. Fees for Referral
a. Accepting Fees from Agencies
Play therapists refuse a private fee or remuneration for providing services to persons who are entitled to such services through the play therapist's employment setting.

b. Referral Fees
Play therapists do not accept referral fees.

E.4. Subcontracting
Play therapists subcontracting play therapy services to a third party inform clients of the limitations of confidentiality prior to or during the intake session.

Section F: Evaluation, Assessment, and Interpretation

F.1. General

Play therapists recognize the limitations of their competence and perform only those assessment services for which they are trained and in accordance with the ethical expectations of their primary licensing/certification body.

F.2. Proper Diagnosis of Mental Disorders

a. Proper Diagnosis

Play therapists take special care to provide proper diagnosis of mental disorders.

b. Sensitivity to Individual vs. Group Differences

Play therapists recognize that culture, gender, developmental age, and chronological age affect how clients' symptoms are defined. Clients' life experiences are considered in diagnosing mental, developmental, and educational disorders. Play therapists are sensitive to the impact of both individual and group differences on the context of the client's life and the manifestation of their symptoms.

Section G: Teaching, Training, and Supervision

G.1. Educators and Trainers

a. Educators as Teachers and Practitioners

Play therapists knowledgeably facilitate education and clinical training as described in the Standards of Practice.

b. Relationship Boundaries with Students and Supervisees

Play therapists clearly define and maintain ethical relationships with their students and supervisees. Being aware that a differential in power exists, play therapists explain to students and supervisees the potential for an exploitive relationship.

c. Sexual Relationships

Play therapists never engage in sexual intimacies with students or supervisees and never subject them to sexual harassment.

d. Contributions to Research

Play therapists properly credit students or supervisees for their contributions.

e. Close Relatives

Play therapists never provide, in a professional capacity, training, supervision, or education to close relatives.

f. Supervision Preparation

Play therapists offering clinical supervision services are adequately trained in supervision methods and supervisory skills.

g. Responsibility for Services to Clients

Play therapist supervisors ensure that play therapy services provided to clients are professional and high quality.

h. Recommendation

Play therapist supervisors do not recommend unqualified students or supervisees for certification, licensure, employment, or completion of an academic or training program.

G.2. Training Programs

a. Orientation

Play therapists orient beginning students to program expectations, including but not limited to the following; (1) knowledge and competency required for completion of the training, (2) theoretical model(s) to be covered, (3) basis for student evaluation, (4) experiences in self-growth and self-disclosure, (5) clinical experiences, sites, and supervision expectations, (6) dismissal procedures, and (7) current employment prospects for trainees.

b. Integration of Study and Practice

Play therapists provide training programs that require integration of academic study and supervised practice.

c. Teaching Ethics

Play therapist supervisors or trainers make students and supervisees aware of the ethical requirements and standards of the practice.

d. Peer Relationships

Play therapist supervisors ensure that trainees who are involved in peer supervision adhere to the same ethical obligations as play therapy supervisors.

e. Diversity Issues

When appropriate, play therapist clinical trainers include diversity issues into courses and/or presentations promoting the on-going development of play therapists.

G.3. Trainees and Supervisees

a. Limitations

Play therapy supervisors are aware of academic and/or personal limitations of the trainees and supervisees; and therefore, provide assistance and/or dismissal if appropriate.

b. Self-Disclosure

Play therapists make students and supervisees aware of the ramifications of self-disclosure.

c. Therapy for Trainees and Supervisees

If a play therapist trainee requests therapy, supervisors or trainers provide them with a minimum of three (3) appropriate resources, whenever possible.

d. Standards for Trainees and Supervisees
Play therapy trainees and supervisees preparing to become Registered Play Therapists adhere to the Standards of Practice and have the same obligations to clients and their legal representatives as those required of Registered Play Therapists.

SECTION H: RESEARCH AND PUBLICATION
H.1. Research Responsibilities
a. Use of Human Subjects
Play therapists follow guidelines of ethical principles, federal and state laws, institutional/agency regulations, and scientific protocol, when planning, conducting, and reporting research using human subjects.

b. Deviation from Standard Practices
Play therapists pursue consultation and abide by rigorous criteria to safeguard research participants when a research problem necessitates deviation from standard research practices.

c. Precautions to Avoid Injury
Play therapists conducting research are responsible for the subjects' welfare and take reasonable precautions to avoid injurious psychological, physical, social, and developmental effects and affects to their subjects.

d. Principal Researcher Responsibility
The principal play therapy researcher is responsible for ethical research practice; however, co-researchers share ethical obligations and responsibility for their actions.

e. Minimal Interference
Play therapist researchers take precautions to avoid disruptions in subjects' lives.

f. Diversity
Play therapist researchers take into consideration diversity in research issues with special populations.

H.2. Informed Consent
a. Topics Disclosed
Play therapist researchers use understandable, developmentally appropriate language in obtaining informed consent from research participants and that (1) specifically explains the research purpose and procedures; (2) identifies experimental or relatively untried procedures; (3) describes the possible discomforts and risks; (4) describes expected outcomes; (5) discloses possible alternatives for subjects; (6) answers any questions about the research procedures; (7) describes any limitations; and (8) advises the subjects about their legal rights to withdraw and discontinue at any time.

b. Deception
Play therapists never do research involving deception.

c. Voluntary Participation
Participation in research is typically voluntary and without penalty for refusal to participate.

d. Confidentiality of Research Data
Information obtained about research participants is confidential. When there is the possibility that others may obtain access to such information, ethical research practice requires that the possibility, together with the plans for protecting confidentiality, be explained to participants.

e. Persons Incapable of Giving Informed Consent
When a client is incapable of giving informed consent, play therapist researchers provide an explanation, and obtain agreement for participation and appropriate consent from the client's legal representative.

f. Commitments to Subjects
Play therapist researchers take measures to honor all commitments to research participants.

g. Explanations of Research Study
Play therapist researchers remove any misconceptions regarding the intent of the study and provide safeguards to avoid harm to the client through explanation of the study.

h. Agreements to Cooperate
Play therapists who agree to be co-researchers or co-authors have an obligation to be complete and accurate with information.

i. Informed Consent for Grant Providers
Play therapist researchers extend informed consent to and in accordance with grant providers guidelines. Play therapist researchers ensure that feedback and acknowledgment of research is given to grant providers.

H.3. Reporting Results
a. Information Affecting Outcome
Play therapist researchers clearly describe all relevant variables that may have affected the outcome of the study.

b. Honesty in Research
Play therapists avoid in engaging in fraudulent research or distorting or misrepresenting data to deliberately bias their results.

c. Reporting Research Results
Play therapists promote the growth of their profession by reporting negative and positive research results deemed to be of professional value.

d. Identity of Subjects
Play therapist researchers protect the identity of respective subjects.

e. Replication Studies
Play therapists cooperate with researchers wishing to replicate studies/research.

H.4. Publication
a. Recognition of Others
Play therapists do not intentionally commit plagiarism. Play therapists cite previous work on the topic, adhere to copyright laws, and give appropriate credit.

b. Contributors
Play therapists credit joint authorship, acknowledgments, citations, or other significant contributions to research or concept development. The first author is the primary contributor; minor technical and other authors are listed in order of their degree of contribution.

c. Student Research
The student is listed as the principal author of a manuscript as appropriate.

d. Professional Review
Play therapist reviewers must respect the confidentiality and proprietary rights of authors submitting manuscripts.

ACKNOWLEDGMENT
Reference documents, statements and sources for the development of the first draft of the APT code were as follows:

The Ethical Standards of the American Counseling Association (ACA)

American Psychological Association

American School Counselor Association

Ethical Standards for Art Therapists

NBCC Code of Ethics

American Board of Examiners of Clinical Social Work Code of Ethics

Principles of Practice of Child and Adolescent Psychiatry

American Association for Marriage and Family Therapists

APPENDIX B

HOW TO BECOME A REGISTERED PLAY THERAPIST

I. Academic Training
   A. A Masters degree in an appropriate Medical or Mental Health profession from a regionally accredited educational institution. Formal candidacy status of an educational institution for regional accreditation will be accepted if full accreditation of the institution is achieved within six years from the date of the granting of an applicant's graduate degree. Content areas of graduate study, from an accredited university, must include child development, theories of personality, principles of psychotherapy, child and adolescent psychopathology, and legal, ethical, and professional issues.
   B. A minimum of 150 clock hours of instruction in Play Therapy (all 150 hours may not be taken from the same instructor). Effective 1/1/99, all hours accumulated after this date must be granted by an APT approved Provider. Hours accumulated prior to 1/1/99 are not required to have APT approval. Content areas must include history, theory, techniques/methods, and applications to special settings or populations.

II. Clinical Experience
   A. Two years of supervised experience including 2,000 direct contact hours related to the area in which the applicant received a Masters. One year of this experience (1,000 hours of direct clinical work) must be at the post-Masters level.
      1. The pre-Master's degree hours may consist of a formal internship/practicum or appropriate fieldwork. This portion of the training may include up to 1,000 hours and must have been completed within a consecutive two-year or 24-month period. During this internship/practicum, it is expected that the applicant's status was that of "intern" or "trainee." The ratio of supervision to direct service time must be at least 1 to 10.
      2. The post-Master's degree hours must consist of a minimum of 1,000 hours of supervised experience; typically, this period follows the internship/practicum year and must occur after all requirements of the graduate program are completed. It is expected that the required post-Master's hours will have been completed within a consecutive 4-year period. "Trainee" status is not required for the postgraduate year of supervised experience. The ratio of supervision time to direct service time must be at least 1:10.
      3. The "supervised experience" in A.1 and A.2 must meet the requirements specified on the attachment entitled "Meeting the Supervision Requirements for Becoming a Registered Play Therapist."
   B. The applicant must have provided a minimum of 500 direct contact hours of Play Therapy under supervision.
      1. These hours may or may not represent a portion of the hours used to fulfill the overall requirement of 2,000 direct contact hours specified in Criteria II.A above.
      2. A minimum of 50 hours of play therapy supervision must have been accumulated during the time that the 500 direct contact hours of Play Therapy were provided. That is, the ratio of supervision hours to contact hours must be at least 1:10. While all of these hours may have been obtained in individual supervision a

maximum of fifteen (15) may have been obtained in a group of no more than 10 supervisees. For details regarding exceptions, supervisors, qualifying types of supervision, and so forth, please see the attachment entitled "Meeting the Supervision Requirements for Becoming a Registered Play Therapist."

III. Continuing Education

Once registered, Play Therapists will need to complete 36 hours of continuing education every 3 years in order to maintain their registration. Eighteen of these hours must be specifically in play therapy, and granted by an APT approved provider.

IV. Denial or Revocation of Registration: An application for Registration may be denied, or an existing Registration revoked, if any of the following is found to apply:

A. Falsification (by inclusion or omission) of information on the Registration Application or any supporting documents.

B. Breach of the ethical code(s) of the Mental Health Service group of which the Registrant is a member (e.g. Social Work, Counseling, etc.). Where no other ethical code applies, the Ethical Standards of Psychologists as set forth by the American Psychological Association shall serve as the standard.

C. Conviction of a crime related to the provision of Mental Health Services or would adversely affect the public image of the APT.

D. Failure to complete the requisite Continuing Education in a timely manner.

Policy Changes Effective Oct. 1, 2000:

Up to 120 of the 150 didactic play therapy training hours may be earned from the same instructor.

All registration applicants must receive at least 10 hours of supervision with one supervisor and applicants must be observed and supervised via video or in person for at least one hour by any supervisor who provides 10 or more hours of supervision.

Up to 30 of the 150 didactic play therapy training hours can be earned via non-contact training.

Up to 18 of the 36 continuing education hours required for registration renewal can be earned via non-contact training. However, not more than 9 of those 18 hours may be in play therapy.

Supervised General Clinical Experience:

The 2,000 hours of supervised general clinical experience required to meet Criteria II.A.1 and II.A.2 must meet the following requirements:

1. The applicant must have been supervised by a person with the following qualifications:

   a. Supervisors must be licensed/certified or have met the qualifications for independent practice in their respective professions.

   b. The professional qualifications of each direct supervisor must be appropriate to the services rendered. Applicants must provide evidence of the qualifications of all direct supervisors identified in the application.

   c. A supervisor, at the time of supervision, must not be in a dual relationship with the supervisee, e.g. be a spouse, other close relative, or therapist.

2. The supervision must consist of direct, formal contact with a senior person who is responsible for the educational development and guidance of the trainee or supervisee. Excluded are classwork or other course-related experience.

3. The supervision must be for the direct provision of mental health services by the applicant to individuals or groups of clients/patients. An applicant's own personal growth experience, i.e. personal therapy or encounter groups, is not acceptable. Supervision of others is also not acceptable.

Supervised Play Therapy Experience:

The following exceptions and restrictions apply to the 500 hours of supervised play therapy experience required to meet Criteria II.B. These exceptions and restrictions are subject to change without prior notice and the regulations in effect at the time the application is submitted apply.

1. The total number of hours of supervised play therapy experience required (500) may be reduced by obtaining supervision from a RPT-S.

   a. If all of the applicant's supervision is provided by an RPT-S then only 350 hours of supervised play therapy experience and 35 hours of supervision are required.

   b. If some supervision is provided by a RPT-S then the total number of hours of experience and supervision required are reduced accordingly. To estimate the reductions you count each hour of experience or supervision under an RPT-S as equal to 1.43 hours toward the 500 (experience) hours and 50 (supervision) hours. If you have received supervision from both an RPT-S and a non-RPT-S you may contact the APT Office directly for an exact reckoning of the hours you need to meet this requirement. Example: Dr. Bob has received 14 hours of supervision from an RPT-S who recently moved out of state. Dr. Bob wants to know how many hours of supervision he needs to receive from Dr. Bill (who is not an RPT) before he has met the Registration requirement.

Step 1: Dr. Bob calculates the number of supervision hours he has so far: 14 (Supervision received) × 1.43 (RPT-S factor) = 20 (Total of Step 1).

Step 2: Dr. Bob calculates the number he still needs: 50 (Supervision hours required) − 20 (Total from Step 1) = 30 (Hours still required).

Assuming Dr. Bob has been conducting at least 10 hours of play therapy for every hour of supervision he has received he could count 200 (Total of Step 1 × 10) of the contact hours he provided during the time he was supervised by the RPT-S and would need to acquire an additional 300 (Hours still required × 10) contact hours under Dr. Bill's supervision.

2. The following types of supervisory contact may be counted as individual supervision hours:

a. Face to Face: The supervisee and supervisor meet and discuss cases based on the therapist's report or notes of the sessions. Note: Every supervisor must observe at least one (1) session conducted by the supervisee sometime during the course of the entire supervision period. The supervisor may observe a live session or review a videotape to meet this requirement. There is no limit to the number of hours that may be obtained in this format.

b. Face to Face with Videotape Review: The supervisor and supervisee meet and review videotapes of the supervisee's play therapy sessions. There is no limit to the number of hours that may be obtained in this format.

c. Telephone:* The supervisee and supervisor discuss cases over the telephone based on the therapist's report or notes of the session. Note: Every supervisor must observe at least one (1) session conducted by the supervisee sometime during the course of the entire supervision period. The supervisor may observe a live session or review a videotape to meet this requirement. If the supervisor is not an RPT-S then no more than 8 of the 50 hours of supervision required may be in this category. If the supervisor is an RPT-S then no more than 5 of the 35 hours of supervision required may be in this category.

d. Telephone with Videotape Review:* The supervisee mails videotape(s) of play therapy session(s) to the supervisor who reviews these and then discusses the videotape(s) with the supervisee in a telephone session. Only the telephone time is counted toward the supervision hours. There is no limit to the number of hours that may be obtained in this format.

e. Telephone with Simultaneous Videotape Review:* The supervisee mails copies of videotapes of play therapy sessions to the supervisor who reviews these and then discusses the videotapes with the supervisee in a telephone session. During the telephone session the supervisor and supervisee make arrangements to actually review their copy of the tape on their own VCRs as the session proceeds. Again, only the telephone time is counted toward the supervision hours. There is no limit to the number of hours that may be obtained in this format.

3. The burden of documenting that the supervision he or she obtained meets the above criteria rests solely on the applicant.

*Note: With options c, d, and e the supervisor must verify the identity of the supervisee. This can be done in one of two ways.

Either (1) the supervisor and supervisee may meet face to face on at least one occasion during the course of the entire supervision period, or (2) the supervisee may provide the supervisor with a notarized copy of a picture form of identification.

APPENDIX C

HOW TO BECOME A REGISTERED PLAY THERAPIST SUPERVISOR

CRITERIA FOR REGISTRATION

I. Academic Training

    A. A Masters degree in an appropriate Medical or Mental Health profession from a regionally accredited educational institution. Formal candidacy status of an educational institution for regional accreditation will be accepted if full accreditation of the institution is achieved within six years from the date of the granting of an applicant's graduate degree. Content areas of graduate study, from an accredited university, must include child development, theories of personality, principles of psychotherapy, child and adolescent psychopathology, and legal, professional, and ethical issues.

    B. A minimum of 150 clock hours of instruction in Play Therapy (all 150 hours may not be taken from the same instructor). Effective 1/1/99, all hours accumulated after this date must be granted by an APT approved Provider. Hours accumulated prior to 1/1/99 are not required to have APT approval. Content areas must include history, theory, techniques/methods, and applications to special settings or populations.

II. Clinical Experience

    A. Licensure or Certification by a national or regional board in a Medical or Mental Health profession.

    B. A minimum of 5 years (5,000 hours) of direct contact hours after the receipt of the Masters degree in the field of the applicant's current license (e.g. an applicant who is applying for Registration under a Social Work license must have 5 years of related clinical practice since receiving the M.S.W. even if a Masters degree in another field was earned earlier).

    C. The applicant must have provided a minimum of 500 direct contact hours of Play Therapy under supervision.

        1. These hours may or may not represent a portion of the hours used to fulfill the overall requirement of 5,000 direct contact hours specified in Criteria II.B above. Use FORM 3 to document these hours.

        2. A minimum of 50 hours of play therapy supervision must have been accumulated during the time that the 500 direct contact hours of Play Therapy were provided. That is, the ratio of supervision hours to contact hours must be at least 1:10. While all of these hours may have been obtained in individual supervision, a maximum of fifteen (15) may have been obtained in a group of no more than 10 supervisees. For details regarding exceptions, supervisors, qualifying types of supervision, and so forth, please see the attachment entitled "Meeting the Supervision Requirements for Becoming a Registered Play Therapist and Supervisor."

    D. The applicant must have provided a minimum of 500 direct hours of Play Therapy experience in addition to that specified above.

III. Continuing Education

Once registered, Play Therapist Supervisors will need to complete 36 hours of continuing education every 3 years in order to maintain their registration. Eighteen of these hours must be specifically in play therapy, and granted by an APT approved provider.

IV. Denial or Revocation of Registration: An application for Registration may be denied, or an existing Registration revoked, if any of the following is found to apply:

A. Falsification (by inclusion or omission) of information on the Registration Application or any supporting documents.

B. Breach of the ethical code(s) of the Mental Health Service group of which the Registrant is a member (e.g. Social Work, Counseling, etc.). Where no other ethical code applies, the Ethical Standards of Psychologists as set forth by the American Psychological Association shall serve as the standard.

C. Conviction of a crime related to the provision of Mental Health Services or would adversely affect the public image of the APT.

D. Failure to complete the requisite Continuing Education in a timely manner.

Supervised General Clinical Experience: The requirements for meeting Criteria II.B on the RPT-S Application are delineated in the instructions on that form.

Supervised Play Therapy Experience: The following exceptions and restrictions apply to the 500 hours of supervised play therapy experience required to meet Criteria II.B. These exceptions and restrictions are subject to change without prior notice and the regulations in effect at the time the application is submitted apply.

1. The total number of hours of supervised play therapy experience required (500) may be reduced by obtaining supervision from a RPT-S.

   a. If all of the applicant's supervision is provided by an RPT-S, then only 350 hours of supervised play therapy experience and 35 hours of supervision are required.

   b. If some supervision is provided by a RPT-S, then the total number of hours of experience and supervision required are reduced accordingly. To estimate the reductions you count each hour of experience or supervision under an RPT-S as equal to 1.43 hours toward the 500 (experience) hours and 50 (supervision) hours. If you have received supervision from both an RPT-S and a non-RPT-S, you may contact the APT Office directly for an exact reckoning of the hours you need to meet this requirement. Example: Dr. Bob has received 14 hours of supervision from an RPT-S who recently moved out of state. Dr. Bob wants to know how many hours of supervision he needs to receive from Dr. Bill (who is not an RPT) before he has met the Registration requirement.

   Step 1: Dr. Bob calculates the number of supervision hours he has so far: 14 (Supervision received) $\times$ 1.43 (RPT-S factor) = 20 (Total of Step 1). Step 2: Dr. Bob calculates the number he still needs: 50 (Supervision hours required) $-$ 20 (Total from Step 1) = 30 (Hours still required).

Assuming Dr. Bob has been conducting at least 10 hours of play therapy for every hour of supervision he has received he could count 200 (Total of Step 1 $\times$ 10) of the contact hours he provided during the time he was supervised by the RPT-S and would need to acquire an additional 300 (Hours still required $\times$ 10) contact hours under Dr. Bill's supervision.

2. The following types of supervisory contact may be counted as individual supervision hours:

   a. Face to Face: The supervisee and supervisor meet and discuss cases based on the therapist's report or notes of the sessions. Note: Every supervisor must observe at least one (1) session conducted by the supervisee sometime during the course of the entire supervision period. The supervisor may observe a live session or review a videotape to meet this requirement. There is no limit to the number of hours that may be obtained in this format.

   b. Face to Face with Videotape Review: The supervisor and supervisee meet and review videotapes of the supervisee's play therapy sessions. There is no limit to the number of hours that may be obtained in this format.

   c. Telephone:* The supervisee and supervisor discuss cases over the telephone based on the therapist's report or notes of the session. Note: Every supervisor must observe at least one (1) session conducted by the supervisee sometime during the course of the entire supervision period. The supervisor may observe a live session or review a videotape to meet this requirement. If the supervisor is not an RPT-S then no more than 8 of the 50 hours of supervision required may be in this category. If the supervisor is an RPT-S then no more than 5 of the 35 hours of supervision required may be in this category.

d. Telephone with Videotape Review:* The supervisee mails videotape(s) of play therapy session(s) to the supervisor who reviews these and then discusses the videotape(s) with the supervisee in a telephone session. Only the telephone time is counted toward the supervision hours. There is no limit to the number of hours that may be obtained in this format.

e. Telephone with Simultaneous Videotape Review:* The supervisee mails copies of videotapes of play therapy sessions to the supervisor who reviews these and then discusses the videotapes with the supervisee in a telephone session. During the telephone session the supervisor and su-

pervisee make arrangements to actually review their copy of the tape on their own VCRs as the session proceeds. Again, only the telephone time is counted toward the supervision hours. There is no limit to the number of hours that may be obtained in this format.

3. The burden of documenting that the supervision he or she obtained meets the above criteria rests solely on the applicant.

*Note: With options c, d, and e the supervisor must verify the identity of the supervisee. This can be done in one of two ways. Either (1) the supervisor and supervisee may meet face to face on at least one occasion during the course of the entire supervision period, or (2) the supervisee may provide the supervisor with a notarized copy of a picture form of identification.

Appendixes A, B, and C reprinted with permission from:

Association for Play Therapy, Inc.
2050 N. Winery Ave., Suite 101, Fresno, CA 93703
Phone: (559) 252-2278 Fax: (559) 252-2297
Email: info@a4pt.org

Items are subject to revision without notice.

References

Achenbach, T. (1974). *Developmental psychopathology*. New York: Ronald Press.

Achenbach, T. (2002). *Child Behavior Checklist*. Burlington, VT: ASEBA.

Achenbach, T., & Edelbrock, C. (1982). *Manual for the child behavior checklist and child behavior profile*. Burlington, VT: Child Psychiatry, University of Vermont.

Achenbach, T., & Rescorla, L. (2001). *Manual for the ASEBA school-aged forms & profiles*. Burlington, VT: University of Vermont, Research Center for Children, Youth, & Families.

Ainsworth, M. (1963). The development of infant-mother interaction among the Ganda. In B. M. Foss (Ed.), *Determinants of infant behavior* (pp. 67–104). New York: Wiley.

Ainsworth, M. (1967). *Infancy in Uganda: Infant care and the growth of love*. Baltimore: Johns Hopkins Press.

Ainsworth, M. (1978). *Patterns of attachment: A psychological study of the strange situation*. Hillsdale, NJ, and New York: Lawrence Erlbaum Associates. Distributed by Halsted Press Division of Wiley.

Ainsworth, M., Bell, S., & Strayton, D. (1971). Individual differences in strange situation behavior of one-year-olds. In H. R. Schaffer (Ed.), *The origins of human social relations*. London: Cambridge University Press.

Ainsworth, M., Bell, S., & Strayton, D. (1974). Infant mother attachment and social development. In M. P. Richards (Ed.), *The introduction of the child into a social world* (pp. 99–135). London: Cambridge University Press.

Ainsworth, M., Blehar, M., Waters, E., & Wall, S. (1978). *Patterns of attachment: A psychological study of the strange situation*. Hillsdale, NJ: Lawrence Erlbaum Associates.

Ainsworth, M., & Bowlby, J. (1991). An ethological approach to personality development. *American Psychologist, 46*, 331–341.

Ainsworth, M., & Wittig, B. (1969). Attachment and the exploratoratory behavior of one-year-olds in a strange situation. In B. M. Foss (Ed.), *Determinants of infant behavior* (Vol. 4, pp. 113–136). London: Methuen.

Albano, A., & Silverman, W. (1996). *ADIS-Anxiety Disorders Interview Schedule for DSM-IV-Child Version*. Boulder, CO: Graywind.

Alessi, N., Robbins, D., & Dilsaver, S. (1987). Panic and depressive disorders among psychiatrically hospitalized adolescents. *Psychiatry Research, 20*, 275–283.

Alexander, F. (1964). School centered play therapy program. *Personnel and Guidance Journal, 43*, 56–261.

Alfred Adler Institute. (2004). *Alfred Adler Institutes of San Francisco and Northwestern Washington*. Retrieved February 8, 2005, from http://ourworld.compuserve.com/homepages/hstein/homepage.htm

Allan, J. (1988). *Inscapes of the child's world: Jungian counseling in schools and clinics*. Dallas: Spring Publications.

Allan, J. (1997). Jungian play psychotherapy. In K. O'Connor & L. Braverman (Eds.), *Play therapy theory and practice: A comparative presentation* (pp. 100–130). New York: Wiley.

Allan, J., & Bertoia, J. (1992). *Written pathways to healing: Education and Jungian child counseling.* Dallas: Spring Publications.

Allan, J., & Levin, S. (1993). Born on my bum: Jungian play therapy. In T. Kottman & C. Schaefer (Eds.), *Play therapy: A casebook for practitioners* (pp. 209–243). Northvale, NJ: J. Aronson.

Allen, F. (1939). Therapeutic work with children. *American Journal of Orthopsychiatry, 4,* 193–201.

Allen, F. (1942). *Psychotherapy with children.* New York: Norton.

Ambrosini, P. (2000). Practice parameters for the assessment and treatment of children and adolescents with depressive disorders. *Journal of the American Academy of Child and Adolescent Psychiatry, 37,* 635–835.

American Association for Marriage and Family Therapy. (1991). *AAMFT code of ethics.* Washington, DC: Author.

American Association on Mental Retardation. (1992). *Mental retardation: Definition, clasification, and systems of support* (9th ed.). Washington, DC: Author.

American Counseling Association. (1995). *ACA code of ethics and standards of practice.* Alexandria, VA: Author.

American Psychiatric Association. (1994). Appendix I. Outline for cultural formation and glossary of culture-bound syndromes. In *Diagnostic and Statistical Manual of Mental Disorders: DSM-IV,* pp. 483–489. Washington, DC: Author.

American Psychiatric Association. (2000). *Diagnostic and statistical manual of mental disorders* (4th ed.). Washington, DC: American Psychiatric Association.

American Psychological Association. (2002). *Ethical principles of psychologists and code of conduct.* Washington, DC: Author.

Ammen, S., Semrad, J., Soria, S., Limberg, E., Peterson, C., Moore, M., O'Neill, K., Picard, S., & Boley, S. (1996). The development of tools to research the color-your-life technique. *International Journal of Play Therapy, 5*(2), 21–39.

Anastasi, A., & Urbina, S. (1997). *Psychological testing* (7th ed.). Upper Saddle River, NJ: Prentice Hall.

Angold, A., Costello, E., & Erkanli, A. (1999). Comorbidity. *Journal of Child Psychology and Psychiatry, 40,* 57–87.

Ansbacher, H. (1974). *Adlerian psychology: A basic theory.* New York: J. Norton.

Ansbacher, H., & Ansbacher, R. (Eds.). (1956). *The individual psychology of Alfred Adler: A systematic presentation in selections from his writings.* San Francisco: Harper & Row.

Ariel, S. (1992). *Strategic family play therapy.* Chichester and New York: Wiley.

Ariel, S. (1997). Strategic family play therapy. In K. O'Connor & L. Braverman (Eds.), *Play therapy theory and practice: A comparative presentation* (pp. 368–395). New York: Wiley.

Association for Play Therapy. (1998). *APT Standards of practice.* Fresno, CA: Author.

Association for Play Therapy. (2000). *Practice guidelines.* Fresno, CA: AAPT.

Association for Play Therapy—About Play Therapy. Retrieved February 8, 2005, from www.a4apt.org

Axline, V. M. (1964). *Dibs: In search of self: Personality development in play therapy.* Boston: Houghton Mifflin.

Axline, V. M. (1969). *Play therapy.* New York: Ballantine.

Axline, V. M. (1989). *Play therapy.* Edinburgh and New York: Churchill Livingstone.

Axline, V. M., & Carmichael, L. (1947). *Play therapy: The inner dynamics of childhood.* Boston: Houghton Mifflin.

Baird, G., Charman, T., Baron-Cohen, S., Cox, A., Swettenham, J., Wheelwright, S., & Drew, S. (2000). A screening instrument of autism at 18 months of age: A 16-year follow-up study. *Journal of the American Academy of Child and Adolescent Psychiatry, 39,* 694–702.

Barnes, M. A. (1996). *The healing path with children: An exploration for parents and professionals.* Ontario, Canada and Clayton, NY: Viktoria, Fermoyle & Berrigan.

Bateson, G. (1972). A theory of play and fantasy. In *Steps to an ecology of mind: Collected essays in anthropology, psychiatry, evolution, and epistemology.* New York: Ballantine Books.

Bayley, N. (1993). *Bayley Scales of Infant Development: Birth to two years.* San Antonio, TX: Psychological Corporation.

Beck, A. T. (1976). *Cognitive therapy and the emotional disorders.* New York: International Universities Press.

Beck, A. T., Freeman, A. M., & Davis, D. D. (2003). *Cognitive therapy of personality disorders* (2nd ed.). New York: Guilford Press.

Beers, C. (1908). *The mind that found itself.* New York: Longmans, Green.

Bellak, L., & Bellak, S. (1949). *Children's Apperception Test (CAT)*. New York: CPS.

Bender, L. (1938). *A visual motor gestalt test and its clinical use*. New York: American Orthopsychiatric Association.

Benedict, H. (2003). Object relations/thematic play therapy. In C. Schaefer (Ed.), *Foundations of Play Therapy*. Hoboken, NJ: John Wiley & Sons.

Bergmann, T., & Freud, A. (1966). *Children in the hospital*. New York: International Universities Press.

Bettner, L., & Lew, A. (1989). *Raising kids who can: Using family meetings to nurture responsible, capable, caring, and happy children*. New York: Harper/Collins.

Biederman, J. (1998). Debate between Joseph Biederman, MD and Rachel G. Klein, Ph.D. Resolved [for debate]: "Mania is mistaken for ADHD in prepubertal children." *Journal of American Academy of Child and Adolescent Psychiatry, 37*, 10.

Biederman, J., Wozniak, J., Kiely, K., Abolon, S., Forone, S., Mick, E., Mundy, E., & Kraus, I. (1995). CBCL clinical scales discriminate prepubertal children with structured interview derived diagnosis of mania from those with ADHD. *Journal of the American Academy of Child and Adolescent Psychiatry, 34*(4), 94–96.

Bixler, R. (1949). Limits are therapy. In M. Haworth (Ed.), *Child Psychotherapy* (pp. 134–147). New York: Basic Books.

Black, H. (1990). *Black's Law Dictionary* (6th ed.). St. Paul, MN: West Group.

Boley, S., Ammen, S., O'Connor, K., & Miller, L. (1996). The use of the Color-Your-Life technique with pediatric cancer patients and their siblings. *International Journal of Play Therapy, 5*(2), 57–80.

Boley, S., Peterson, C., Miller, L., & Ammen, S. (1996). An investigation of the Color-Your-Life technique with childhood cancer patients. *International Journal of Play Therapy, 5*(2), 41–56.

Booth, P., & Koller, T. (1998). Training parents of failure-to-attach children. In J. M. Breismeister & C. E. Schaefer (Eds.), *Handbook of parent training: Parents as co-therapists* (pp. 308–342). New York: John Wiley & Sons.

Bowlby, J. (1951). *Maternal care and mental health*. Geneva: World Health Organization.

Bowlby, J. (1958). The nature of the child's tie to his mother. *International Journal of Psycho-analysis, 39*, 1–23.

Bowlby, J. (1959). Separation anxiety. *International Journal of Psycho-Analysis, 41*, 1–25.

Bowlby, J. (1960). Grief and mourning in infancy and early childhood. *The Psychoanalytic Study of the Child, 15*, 3–39.

Bowlby, J. (1962a). *Defences that follow loss: Causation and function*. Unpublished manuscript.

Bowlby, J. (1962b). *Loss, detachment and defence*. Unpublished manuscript.

Bowlby, J. (1982). *Attachment and loss* (Vol. 1, 2nd ed.). New York: Basic.

Bowlby, J., & Parkes, C. (1970). Separation and loss within the family. In E. J. Anthony & C. Koupernik (Eds.), *The child in his family: International Yearbook of Child Psychiatry and Allied Professions* (pp. 197–216). New York: Wiley.

Bratton, S., & Ray, D. (2000). What the research shows about play therapy. *International Journal of Play Therapy, 9*(1), 47–88.

Bretherton, I. (1992). The origins of attachment theory: John Bowlby and Mary Ainsworth. *Developmental Psychology, 28*, 759–775.

Brody, V. (1978). Developmental play: A relationship-focused program for children. *Journal of Child Welfare, 57*, 591–599.

Brody, V. (1993). *The dialogue of touch: Developmental play therapy*. Treasure Island, FL: Developmental Play Training Associates.

Brody, V. (1997). *The dialogue of touch: Developmental play therapy* (1997 softcover ed.). Northvale, NJ: J. Aronson.

Bromfield, R. (2003). Psychoanalytic play therapy. In C. Schaefer (Ed.), *Foundations of play therapy*. New York, NY: Wiley.

Brucker, P. S., & Perry, B. J. (1998). American Indians: Presenting concerns and considerations for family therapists. *American Journal of Family Therapy, 26*, 307.

Buck, J. (1948). The H-T-P technique: A qualitative and quantitative scoring manual. *Journal of Clinical Psychology, 4*, 397–405.

Buck, J. (1981). *The House-Tree-Person technique: A revised manual*. Los Angeles: Western Psychological Services.

Buck, J., & Hammer, E. (Eds.). (1969). *Advances in House-Tree-Person techniques: Variations and applications*. Los Angeles: Western Psychological Services.

Burks, H. (1978). *Imagine*. Huntington Beach, CA: Arden Press.

Burnham, J. J. G. (1997). The Fear Survey Schedule for Children II: A psychometric investigation with American data. *Behaviour Research & Therapy, 35*, 165.

Burns, R. (1987). *Kinetic-House-Tree-Person Drawings (K-H-T-P): An interpretation manual.* New York: Brunner/Mazel.

Burns, R., & Kaufman, S. (1970). *Kinetic Family Drawings (K-F-D): Research and application.* New York: Brunner/Mazel.

Burns, R., & Kaufman, S. (1972). *Actions, styles and symbols in Kinetic Family Drawings (K-F-D): An interpretive manual.* New York: Brunner/Mazel.

Cameron, S., & Turtle-Song, I. (2002). Learning to write case notes using the SOAP format. *Journal of Counseling and Development, 80*, 286–293.

Cantlay, L. (1996). *Detecting child abuse: Recognizing children at risk through drawings.* Santa Barbara, CA: Holly Press.

Carkhuff, R. (2003). *The skills of helping* (2nd ed.). Boston: Houghton Mifflin.

Carmichael, K. (1991). Play therapy with the culturally different. *Association for Play Therapy Newsletter, 10*(1), 1–3.

Carmichael, K. (1993). Preliminary development of an interaction matrix for observation of client-therapist relationships in play therapy. *International Journal of Play Therapy, 2*(2), 19–33.

Carmichael, K. (2002). Music play therapy. In C. Schaefer & D. M. Cangelosi (Eds.), *Play therapy techniques* (2nd ed.). Northvale, NJ: J. Aronson.

Carmichael, K. (2004). *Music play therapy.* Tuscaloosa, AL: Sky Dancer.

Carroll, F., & Oaklander, V. (1997). Gestalt play therapy. In K. O'Connor & L. Braverman (Eds.), *Play therapy theory and practice: A comparative presentation* (pp. 184–203). New York: Wiley.

Carson-Sabellil, L. (1998). Children's therapeutic puppet theatre—action, interaction, and cocreation. *International Journal of Action Methods, 51*, 91.

Chandras, K., Eddy, J. P., & Spaulding, D. J. (1999). Counseling Asian Americans: Implications for training. *Education, 120*, 239.

Chethik, M. (2000). *Techniques of child therapy.* New York: Guildford Press.

Child Abuse Prevention and Treatment Act (CAPTA), 42 U.S.C. 5101 et. seq. (1974).

Child Abuse Prevention and Treatment and Adoption Act Amendment, P.L. 104–235 (1996).

Chomsky, N. (1972). *Language and mind* (2nd ed.). New York: Harcourt Brace Jovanovich.

Christopher, J. (1999). Situating psychological well-being: Exploring the cultural roots of its theory and research. *Journal of Counseling and Development, 77*, 141–152.

Cipani, E. (1993). *The Cipani Behavioral Assessment and Diagnostic (C-BAD) System.* Visalia, CA: Cipani & Associates.

Connors, C. (1996). *Connors' Rating Scales—Revised (CRS—R), user's manual.* New York: The Psychological Corporation.

Connors, C., & Barkley, R. (1955). Rating scales and checklists for child psychopharmacology. *Psychopharmacology Bulletin, 21*, 809–815.

Connors, C., Sitarenios, G., Parker, J., & Epstein, J. (1998). *Revision and restandardization of the Connors Teacher Rating Scale (CTRS-R): Factor structure, reliability, and criterion validity.* Wilmington, DE: Wide Range.

Constantino, G., Malgady, R., & Rogler, L. (1986). Cuento therapy: A culturally sensitive modality for Puerto Rican children. *Journal of Consulting Psychology, 29*, 1–8.

Corey, G. (1991). *Theory and practice of counseling and psychotherapy.* Pacific Grove, CA: Brooks/Cole.

Corey, G., Corey, M., & Callanan, P. (1998). *Issues and ethics in the helping professions* (5th ed.). Pacific Grove, CA: Brooks/Cole.

Corsini, R. (2002). *The dictionary of psychology.* New York: Brunner/Routledge.

Cultural consultation service. (2004). Department of Psychiatry, McGill University. Retrieved June 29, 2004, from http://www.mcgill.ca/ccs/

Davis, N. (1990). *Once upon a time: Therapeutic stories.* Oxon Hill, MD: Psychological Associates of Oxon Hill.

Davis, N. (1996). *Once upon a time: Therapeutic stories that teach and heal.* Oxon Hill, MD: Nancy Davis.

de Domenico, G. (1994). Jungian play therapy techniques. In K. O'Connor & C. Schaefer (Eds.), *Handbook of play therapy* (Vol. 2, pp. 253–282). New York: Wiley.

Deren, S. (1975). An empirical evaluation of the validity of the Draw-a-Family. *Journal of Clinical Psychology, 31*, 47–52.

De Saussure, F. (1993). *Saussure's third course of lectures on general linguistics (1910–1911)* (W. Baskin, Trans.). New York: Pergamon Press.

DesLauriers, A. (1962). *The experience of reality in childhood schizophrenia.* New York: International Universities Press.

DesLauriers, A., & Carlson, C. (1969). *Your child is asleep—early infantile autism: Etiology, treatment, and parental influence.* Homewood, IL: Dorsey.

Developmental Therapy Institute. (1992). *Developmental teaching objectives for the Developmental Teaching Objectives Rating Form—Revised: Assessment and teaching of social emotional competence* (4th ed.). Athens, GA: Author.

Di Leo, J. (1973). *Children's drawings as diagnostic aids.* New York: Brunner/Mazel.

Dinkmeyer, D.C., & Dinkmeyer, J. D. (1977). Concise counseling assessment: The children's lifestyle guide. *Elementary School Guidance & Counseling, 12,* 117–124.

Dinkmeyer, D. C., Dinkmeyer, J. D., & Sperry, L. (1987). *Adlerian counseling and psychotherapy* (2nd ed.). Columbus: Merrill.

Dinkmeyer, D. C., & McKay, G. D. (1989). *The parent's handbook: STEP, systematic training for effective parenting* (3rd ed.). Circle Pines, MN: American Guidance Service.

Dinkmeyer, D. C., McKay, G., Dinkmeyer, J. D., Dinkmeyer, J., & McKay, J. (1987). *The effective parent.* Circle Pines, MN: American Guidance Service.

Dinkmeyer, D. C., McKay, G. D., & Dinkmeyer, J. S. (1989). *Parenting young children: Helpful strategies based on Systematic Training for Effective Parenting (STEP) for parents of children under six.* Circle Pines, MN: American Guidance Service.

DiPasquale, L. (2000). The Marschak interaction method. In E. Munns (Ed.), *Theraplay: Innovations in attachment enhancing play therapy* (pp. 27–51). Northvale, NJ: J. Aronson.

Dorfman, E. (1951). Play therapy. In C. S. Rogers (Ed.), *Client-centered therapy* (pp. 235–277). Boston: Houghton Mifflin.

Dreikurs, R. (1948). *The challenge of parenthood.* New York: Duell, Sloan & Pearce.

Dreikurs, R. (1953). *Fundamentals of Adlerian psychology.* Chicago: Alfred Adler Institute.

Dreikurs, R. (1967). *Psychodynamics, psychotherapy, and counseling.* Chicago: Alfred Adler Insitutute.

Dreikurs, R. (1989). *Fundamentals of Adlerian psychology.* Chicago: Alfred Adler Institute.

Dreikurs, R., & Cassel, P. (1972). *Discipline without tears.* Toronto: Alfred Adler Institute of Canada.

Dreikurs, R., & Soltz, V. (1984). *Children: The challenge.* New York: Hawthorn/Dutton.

Dwairy, M. (1999). Toward a psycho-cultural approach in Middle Eastern societies. *Clinical Psychology Review, 8,* 909–915.

Eckstein, D., Baruth, L., & Mehrer, D. (1992). *Lifestyle: What it is and how to do it* (3rd ed.). Dubuque, IA: Kendall/Hunt.

Elliot, G., & Pumfrey, P. (1972). The effects of nondirective play therapy on some maladjusted boys. *Educational Research, 14,* 157–163.

Elliott, D., Huizinga, D., & Ageton, S. (1985). *Explaining delinquency and drug use.* Beverly Hills, CA: Sage.

Erikson, E. (1950). *Childhood and society.* New York: Norton.

Erikson, E. (1958). *Young man Luther.* New York: Norton.

Erikson, E. (1964). *Insight and responsibility.* New York: Norton.

Erikson, E. (1968). *Identity: Youth and crisis.* New York: Norton.

Erikson, E. (1974). *Dimensions of a new identity.* New York: Norton.

Erikson, E. (1975). *Life history and the historical moment.* New York: Norton.

Exner, J. (1993). *The Rorschach: Basic foundations and principles of interpretation.* New York: John Wiley & Sons.

Exner, J., & Weiner, I. (1995). *The Rorschach: A comprehensive system, Assessment of children and adolescents* (2nd ed.). New York: John Wiley & Sons.

Eyberg, S. (1992). Parent and teacher behavior inventories of the assessment of conduct problem behaviors in children. In L. VandeCreek, S. Knapp, & T. Jackson (Eds.), *Innovations in clinical practice: A source book* (Vol. 2). Sarasota, FL: Professional Resource Exchange.

Fairbairn, W. (1952). *An object-relations theory of the personality.* New York: Basic.

Fall, M., Balvanz, J., Nelson, L., & Johnson, L. (1994). *The relationship of play therapy interventions to self-efficacy and classroom learning behaviors.* Paper presented at the North Central Association for Counsellor Education and Supervision, Milwaukee, WI.

Federal Evidence Code, Rule 501 (1975).

Fischer, L., & Sorenson, G. (1985). *School law for counselors, psychologist, and social workers.* New York: Longman.

Fischer, L., & Sorenson, G. (1996). *School law for counselors, psychologists, and social workers* (2nd ed.). New York: Longman.

Freed, K. (1985). *Red flag, green flag people: A personal safety program for children.* Fargo, ND: Rape & Abuse Crisis of Fargo Moorhead.

Freud, A. (1909/1955). *The case of "Little Hans" and the "Rat Man."* London: Hogarth Press.

Freud, A. (1928). *Introduction to the technic of child analysis* (L. P. Clark, Trans.). New York and Washington, DC: Nervous and Mental Disease Publishing. (Original work published 1895)

Freud, A. (1959). *The psycho-analytical treatment of children:* Technical lectures and essays. New York: International Universities Press.

Freud, A. (1964). *The psychoanalytical treatment of children:* Lectures and essays. New York: Schocken Books.

Freud, A. (1965). *Normality and pathology in childhood: Assessments of development.* New York: International Universities Press.

Freud, A. (1967). *The ego and the mechanisms of defense* (Rev. ed.). New York: International Universities Press.

Freud, A. (1975). *Introduction to the technic of child analysis.* (L. P. Clark, Trans.) New York: Arno Press. (Original work published 1895)

Freud, A., & Baines, C. (1946). *The ego and the mechanisms of defence.* New York: International Universities Press.

Freud, A., & Institute of Psycho-Analysis London. [from old catalog]. (1966). *Normality and pathology in childhood: Assessments of development.* London: Hogarth Press and the Institute of Psycho-Analysis.

Freud, A., & Low, B. (1931). *Introduction to psychoanalysis for teachers: Four lectures.* London: Allen & Unwin.

Freud, A., & Low, B. (1935). *Psycho-analysis for teachers and parents: Introductory lectures.* New York: Emerson Books, Inc.

Freud, S. (1909). Analysis of a phobia in a five-year-old boy. *Standard Edition* (Vol. 9). London: Hogarth Press.

Fujita, F., Diener, E., & Sanvik, E. (1991). Gender differences in negative affect and well-being: The case for emotional intensity. *Journal of Personality and Social Psychology, 61,* 427–434.

Gardner, R. (1968). The mutual storytelling technique: Use in alleviating childhood Oedipal problems. *Contemporary Psychoanalysis, 4,* 161–177.

Gardner, R. (1970). The mutual storytelling technique: Use in the pretreatment of a child with post-traumatic neurosis. *American Journal of Psychotherapy, 24,* 419–439.

Gardner, R. (1971). Mutual story telling: A technique in child psychotherapy. *Acta Paedopsychiatrica, 38,* 253–262.

Gardner, R. (1972a). The mutual storytelling technique in the treatment of anger inhibition problems. *International Journal of Child Psychotherapy, 1*(1), 34–64.

Gardner, R. (1972b). *Techniques of child psychotherapy* [Sound recording]. Fort Lee, NJ: Sigma Information.

Gardner, R. (1972c). "Once upon a time there was a doorknob and everybody used to make him all dirty with their fingerprints . . . " *Psychology Today, 5*(10), 67–71, 92.

Gardner, R. (1973). *The talking, feeling, and doing game.* Cresskill, NJ: Creative Therapeutics.

Gardner, R. (1974). The mutual story telling technique in the treatment of a psychogenic problems secondary to minimal brain dysfunction. *Journal of Learning Disabilities, 7,* 135–143.

Gardner, R. (1975). Dramatized storytelling in child psychotherapy. *Acta Paedopsychiatrica, 41*(3), 110–116.

Gardner, R. (2003). *The Gardner Children's Projective Battery: A diagnostic instrument for the assessment of the child's psychodynamics.* Creative Therapeutics. Retrieved July 21, 2003, from www.rgardner.com.

Garwick, A. (2000). What do providers need to know about American Indian culture? Recommendations from urban Indian family caregivers. *Families, Systems & Health: The Journal of Collaborative Family HealthCare, 18,* 177.

Getzel, J., & Csikszentmihalyi, M. (1976). *The creative version: A longitudinal study of problem finding in art.* New York: Wiley.

Gil, E. (1998). *Essentials of play therapy with abused children: Video manual.* New York: Guilford Press.

Ginott, H. G. (1959). The theory and practice of therapeutic intervention in child treatment. *Journal of Counseling Psychology, 23,* 160–166.

Ginott, H. G. (1961). *Group psychotherapy with children: The theory and practice of play-therapy.* New York: McGraw-Hill.

Ginott, H. G. (1965). *Between parent and child: New solutions to old problems.* New York: Macmillan.

Ginott, H. G. (1969a). *Between parent and child: New solutions to old problems* (Rev. ed.). London: Staples.

Ginott, H. G. (1969b). *Between parent and teenager.* New York: Macmillan.

Ginott, H. G. (1972). *Teacher and child: A book for parents and teachers.* New York: Macmillan.

Ginott, H. G. (1993). *Teacher and child: A book for parents and teachers* (1st Collier Books ed.). New York: Collier.

Ginott, H. G. (1994). *Group psychotherapy with children: The theory and practice of play-therapy* (1st softcover ed.). Northvale, NJ: J. Aronson.

Ginott, H. G., Ginott, A., & Goddard, H. W. (2003). *Between parent and child: The bestselling classic that revolutionized parent-child communication* (Rev. and updated ed.). New York: Three Rivers Press.

Ginott, H. G., & Lebo, D. (1963). Most and least used play therapy limits. *Journal of Genetic Psychology, 103,* 153–159.

Glasser, W. (1975). *Reality therapy.* New York: Harper & Row.

Gong, F., Gage, S. J. L., & Tacata, L. A., (2003). Helpseeking behavior among Filipino Americans: A cultural analysis of face and language. *Journal of Community Psychology, 31,* 469–488.

Goodenough, F. (1926). *Measurement of intelligence by drawings.* New York: Harcourt, Brace and World.

Gordon, I. (1985). Child abuse, gender, and the myth of family independence: A historical critique. *Child Welfare, 64,* 213–223.

Gregory, R. (2000). *Psychological testing* (3rd ed.). Boston: Allyn & Bacon.

Griff, M. (1983). Family play therapy. In C. Schaefer & K. O'Connor (Eds.), *Handbook of play therapy* (pp. 65–75). New York: Wiley.

Griffith, J., & Powers, R. (1984). *An Adlerian lexicon.* Chicago: America's Institute of Adlerian Studies.

Griswold, D. P., & Griswold, D. B. (2000). Minors: Rights to refuse medical treatment requested by their parents: Remaining issues. *Journal of the American Academy of Nurse Practitioners, 12*(8), 325–328.

Guerney, B. G. J. (1964). Filial therapy: Description and rationale. *Journal of Consulting Psychology, 28,* 303–310.

Guerney, L. F. (1976a). Filial therapy program. In D. H. Olson (Ed.), *Treating relationships* (pp. 67–91). Lake Mills, IA: Graphic Publishing.

Guerney, L. F. (1976b). Training manual for parents: Instruction in filial therapy. In C. E. Schaefer (Ed.), *Therapeutic use of child's play* (pp. 216–227). New York: J. Aronson.

Guerney, L. F. (1983a). Introduction to filial therapy: Training parents as therapists. In P. A. Keller & L. G. Ritt (Eds.), *Innovations in clinical practice: A source book* (Vol. 2, pp. 26–39). Sarasota, FL: Professional Resource Exchange.

Guerney, L. F. (1983b). Play therapy with learning disabled children. In C. E. Schaefer & K. J. O'Connor (Eds.), *Handbook of play therapy* (pp. 419–435). New York: Wiley.

Guerney, L. F. (1983c). Client-centered (nondirective) play therapy. In C. Schaefer & K. O'Connor (Eds.), *Handbook of play therapy* (pp. 21–64). New York: Wiley.

Guerney, L. F. (1987). *The parenting skills program: Leader's manual.* State College, PA: IDEAS.

Guerney, L. F. (1988). *Parenting: A skills training manual* (3rd ed.). State College, PA: IDEAS.

Guerney, L. F. (1991). Parents as partners in treating behavior problems in early childhood settings. *Topics in Early Childhood Special Education, 11,* 74.

Guerney, L. F. (2000). Filial therapy into the 21st century. *International Journal of Play Therapy, 9*(2), 1–17.

Guerney, L. F. (2001). Child-centered play therapy. *International Journal of Play Therapy, 10,* 13–31.

Guerney, L. F., & Guerney, B. G. (1987). Integrating child and family therapy. *Psychotherapy, 24,* 609–614.

Guerney, L. F., & Guerney, B. G. J. (1994). Child relationship enhancement: Family therapy and parent education. In C. E. Schaefer & L. J. Carey (Eds.), *Family play therapy* (pp. 127–137). Northvale, NJ: J. Aronson.

Guldner, C. A. (1991). Creating training contexts for interns in group psychotherapy and psychodrama with children. *Journal of Group Psychotherapy, Psychodrama & Sociometry, 43,* 156.

Halasz, G. (1996). The rights of the child in psychotherapy. *American Journal of Psychotherapy, 50*(3), 285–297.

Hall, A., & Lin, M. (1995). Theory and practice of children's rights: Implicatons for mental health counselors. *Journal of Mental Health Counseling, 17*(1), 63–81.

Hambridge, G. (1955). Structured play therapy. *American Journal of Orthospychiatry, 25,* 601–617.

Hammer, E. (1971). *The clinical application of projective drawings.* Springfield, IL: Charles C. Thomas.

Hardaway, T. G. I. (2000). Family play therapy and child psychiatry in an era of managed care. In H. G. Kaduson & C. E. Schaefer (Eds.), *Short-term play therapy for children.* New York: Guilford Press.

Harrar, W., VandCreek, L., & Knapp, S. (1990). Ethical and legal aspects of clinical supervision. *Psychology Research and Practice, 21*(1), 37–41.

Harris, D. (1963). *Children's drawings as measures of intellectual maturity.* New York: Harcourt, Brace and World.

Hart, S., & Paviovic, Z. (1991). Children's rights in education: Historical perspective. *School Psychology Review, 20,* 345–359.

Harvey, S. (1990). Dynamic play therapy: An integrated expressive arts approach to the family therapy of young children. *The Arts in Psychotherapy, 17,* 239–246.

Harvey, S. (1991). Creating a family: An integrated expressive approach to adoption. *The Arts in Psychotherapy, 18,* 213–222.

Harvey, S. (1993). Ann: Dynamic play therapy with ritual abuse. In T. Kottman & C. Schaefer (Eds.), *Play therapy in action: A casebook for practitioners.* New York: J. Aronson.

Harvey, S. (1994a). Dynamic play therapy: An integrated expressive arts approach to the treatment of infants and toddlers. *Zero to Three, 15,* 11–17.

Harvey, S. (1994b). Dynamic play therapy: Creating attachments. In B. James (Ed.), *Handbook for treatment of attachment-trauma problems in children.* New York: Lexington.

Harvey, S. (1994c). Dynamic play therapy: Expressive play interventions with families. In K. O'Connor & C. Schaefer (Eds.), *Handbook of play therapy* (Vol. 2, pp. 85–110). New York: Wiley.

Harvey, S. (1997). Dynamic family play therapy: A creative arts approach. In K. O'Connor & L. Braverman (Eds.), *Play therapy theory and practice: A comparative presentation* (pp. 341–367). New York: Wiley.

Harvey, S., & Kelly, E. (1993). The influence of the quality of early interaction in a three-year-old's play narratives: A longitudinal case study. *The Arts in Psychotherapy, 20,* 387–395.

Haworth, M. (Ed.). (1964). *Child psychotherapy.* New York: Basic.

Hazelwood School District v. Kuhlmeier, 484 U.S. 260 (1988).

Hendrix, D. (1991). Ethics and intrafamily confidentiality in counseling with children. *Journal of Mental Health Counseling, 13,* 323–358.

Herlihy, B., & Corey, G. (1997). *Boundary issues in counseling: Multiple roles and responsibilities.* Alexandria, VA: American Counseling Association.

Herring, R. D. (1994). The clown or contrary figure as a counseling intervention strategy with Native American Indians. *Journal of Multicultural Counseling & Development, 22,* 153.

Hinman, C. (2003). Multicultural considerations in the delivery of play therapy services. *International Journal of Play Therapy, 12,* 107–122.

Hinshaw, S., Lahey, B., & Hart, E. (1993). Issues of taxonomy and comorbidity in the development of conduct disorder. *Development and Psychopathology, 5,* 31–49.

H. L. v. Matherson, 450 U.S. 398 (1981).

Hodges, K., Cool, J., & McKnew, D. (1989). Test-retest reliability of a clinical research interview for children: The Child Assessment Schedule (CAS). *Psychological Assessment, 1,* 317–322.

Hulse, W. (1951). The emotionally disturbed child draws his family. *Quarterly Journal of Child Behavior, 3,* 152–174.

Hynes, A., & Hynes-Berry, M. (1986). *Bibliotherapy: The interactive process.* Boulder, CO: Westview.

In re Gault, 387 U.S.I (1967).

Ingraham v. Wright, 430 U.Sl 652 (97 S. St. 1401.51 1.ed.2d 711 (1977).

Ireton, H., & Thwing, E. (1972). *Minnesota Child Development Inventory.* New York: Guilford Press.

Irwin, E. (1991). The use of a puppet interview to understand children. In C. Schaefer, K. Gitlin, & A. Sandgrund (Eds.), *Play diagnosis and assessment* (pp. 617–635). New York: John Wiley & Sons.

Jablonski v. US, 712 FEd 2d 391 (1978).

Jackson-Brown, I. V. (1987). Liturgy and the arts: Toward a black cultural imperative. *Journal of Religious Thought, 44*, 55.

Jaffee v. Redmond, 518 U.S. 1, 13 (1995).

James, B. (1989). *Treating traumatized children: New insights and creative interventions*. Lexington, MA: Lexington.

James, O. (1997). *Play therapy: A comprehensive guide*. Northrale, NJ: Jason Aronson.

Jennings, S. (1999). *Introduction to developmental playtherapy: Playing and health*. London and Philadelphia: Jessica Kingsley.

Jernberg, A. (1979). *Theraplay: A new treatment using structured play for problem children and their families* (1st ed.). San Francisco: Jossey-Bass.

Jernberg, A., & Booth, P. (1999). *Theraplay: Helping parents and children build better relationships through attachment-based play* (2nd ed.). San Francisco: Jossey-Bass.

Jernberg, A., Booth, P., Koller, T., & Allert, A. (1991). *Manual for the administration and the clinical interpretation of the Marshak Interaction Method (MIM): Pre-school and school-aged* (rev.). Chicago: Theraplay Institute.

Jernberg, A., Hurst, T., & Lyman, C. (1969). *Here I am*. Chicago: Theraplay Institute.

Jernberg, A., Hurst, T., & Lyman, C. (1975). *There he goes*. Chicago: Theraplay Institute.

Jipguep, M. C., & Sanders-Phillips, K. (2003). The context of violence for children of color: Violence in the community and in the media. *Journal of Negro Education, 72*, 379–395.

Johnson, J., & Ironsmith, M. (1994). Assessing children's sociometric status: Issues and the application of social network analysis. *Journal of Group Psychotherapy, Psychodrama & Sociometry, 47*, 36.

Jolles, I. (1964). *A catalogue for the qualitative interpretation of the House-Tree-Person (H-T-P)*. Los Angeles: Western Psychological Services.

Jones, E. (1955). *The life and work of Sigmund Freud* (Vol. 2). New York: Basic.

Jongsma, A., Peterson, L. M., & McInnis, W. (2000). *The child psychotherapy treatment planner*. New York: Wiley.

Kanner, L. (1948). *Child psychiatry*. Springfield, IL: Charles C. Thomas.

Kaufman, A., & Kaufman, N. (1983). *Administration and scoring manual for the Kaufman Assessment Battery for Children*. Circle Pines, MN: AGS.

Kearney, C., & Silverman, W. (1992). Let's not push the "panic button": A critical analysis of panic and panic disorder in adolescents. *Clinical Psychology Review, 12*, 293–305.

Keith, D., & Whitaker, C. (1994). Play therapy: A paradigm for work with families. In C. E. Schaefer & L. J. Carey (Eds.), *Family play therapy* (pp. 185–202). Northvale, NJ: J. Aronson.

Kempe, R., & Kempe, C. (1984). *The common secret: Sexual abuse of children and adolescents*. New York: W. H. Freeman & Co.

Kendall, P., Panichelli-Mindel, S., Sugarman, A., & Callahan, S. (1997). Exposure to anxiety: Theory, research, and practice. *Clinical Psychology: Science and Practice, 4*, 29–39.

Kenny, M., & Winick, C. (2000). An integrative approach to play therapy with an autistic girl. *International Journal of Play Therapy, 9*, (111–133).

Kettenbach, G. (1995). *Writing SOAP notes*. Philadelphia: Davis.

King, N., Ollendick, T., Mattis, S., Yang, B., & Tonge, B. (1997). Nonclinical panic attacks in adolescents: Prevalence, symptomatology, and associated features. *Behavior Change, 13*, 495–507.

Kircher, C. J., & Catholic University of America. (1944). *Character formation through books, a bibliography: An application of bibliotherapy to the behavior problems of childhood*. Washington, DC: Catholic University of America.

Klein, D., Mannuzza, S., Chapman, T., & Fyer, A. (1992). Child panic revised. *Journal of the American Academy of Child and Adolescent Psychiatry, 31*, 112–113.

Klein, M. (1955). The psychoanalytic play technique. *American Journal of Orthospychiatry, 25*, 483–493.

Klein, M. (1975a). *Love, guilt, and reparation and other works, 1921–1945*. New York: Delacorte Press/Seymour Lawrence.

Klein, M. (1975b). *Envy and gratitude and other works 1946–1963*. New York: Delecorte Press/Seymour Lawrence.

Klein, M. (1984a). *Love, guilt, and reparation and other works, 1921–1945* (Free Press ed.). New York: Free Press.

Klein, M. (1984b). *Envy and gratitude and other works, 1946–1963* (Free Press ed.). New York: Free Press.

Klein, M., & Riviere, J. (1983). *Developments in psychoanalysis*. New York: Da Capo Press.

Klepsch, M., & Logie, L. (1982). *Children draw and tell*. New York: Brunner/Mazel.

Knell, S. M. (1993). *Cognitive-behavioral play therapy*. Northvale, NJ: J. Aronson.

Knell, S. M. (1997). Cognitive-behavioral play therapy. In K. O'Connor & L. Braverman (Eds.), *Play therapy theory and practice: A comparative presentation* (pp. 79–99). New York: Wiley.

Knell, S. M. (1998). Cognitive-behavioral play therapy. *Journal of Clinical Child Psychology, 27*, 28.

Knell, S. M., & Moore, D. J. (1990). Cognitive-behavioral play therapy in the treatment of encopresis. *Journal of Clinical Child Psychology, 19*, 55.

Koller, T., & Booth, P. (1997). Foster attachment through family theraplay. In K. O'Connor & L. Braverman (Eds.), *Play therapy theory and practice: A comparative presentation*. New York: Wiley.

Koppitz, E. (1964). *The Bender Gestalt Test for young children*. New York: Grune & Stratton.

Koppitz, E. (1968). *Psychological evaluation of children's human figure drawings*. New York: Grune & Stratton.

Koppitz, E. (1984). *Psychological evaluation of human figure drawings by middle school pupils*. New York: Grune & Stratton.

Kottman, T. (1995). *Partners in play: An Adlerian approach to play therapy*. Alexandria, VA: American Counseling Association.

Kottman, T. (2001a). *Play therapy: Basics and beyond*. Alexandria, VA: American Counseling Association.

Kottman, T. (2001b). *Art with children*. Paper presented at the Alabama Association for Play Therapy Spring Conference, Birmingham.

Kottman, T. (2003). *Partners in play: An Adlerian approach to play therapy* (2nd ed.). Alexandria, VA: American Counseling Association.

Kottman, T., & Schaefer, C. E. (1993). *Play therapy in action: A casebook for practitioners*. Northvale, NJ: J. Aronson.

Kovacs, M. (1992). *Children's Depression Inventory*. North Tonawanda, NY: Multi-Health Systems.

Kubler-Ross, E. (1970). *On death and dying*. London: Tavistock.

Kutnick, P. (1978). Children's drawings of their classrooms: Development and social maturity. *Child Study Journal, 8*, 175–185.

Lachar, D., Wingenfeld, S., Kline, R., & Guber, C. (1998). *Student Behavior Survey*. Los Angeles: Western Psychological Services.

LaGreca, A., & Stone, W. (1993). Social anxiety scale for children—revised: Factor structure and concurrent validity. *Journal of Clinical Child Psychology, 22*, 17–27.

Landreth, G. (1980). Class notes: Interpreting the HTP. Denton: University of North Texas.

Landreth, G. (1982). *Play therapy: Dynamics of the process of counseling with children*. Springfield, IL: Charles C. Thomas.

Landreth, G. (1987). Play therapy: Facilitative use of child's play in elementary school counseling. *Elementary School Guidance & Counseling, 21*, 253–261.

Landreth, G. (1991). *Play therapy: The art of the relationship*. Muncie, IN: Accelerated Development.

Landreth, G. (1996). *Play therapy interventions with children's problems*. Northvale, NJ: J. Aronson.

Landreth, G. (2001). *Innovations in play therapy: Issues, process, and special populations*. Philadelphia: Brunner-Routledge.

Landreth, G. (2002). *Play therapy: The art of the relationship* (2nd ed.). New York: Brunner-Routledge.

Landreth, G., Homeyer, L., & Bratton, S. (1993). *The world of play therapy literature: A definitive guide to the subjects and authors in the field*. Denton, TX: Center for Play Therapy.

Landreth, G., Jacquot, W., & Allen, L. (1969). A team approach to learning disabilities. *Journal of Learning Disabilities, 2*, 82–87.

Last, C., & Strauss, C. (1989). Panic disorder in children and adolescents. *Journal of Anxiety Disorders, 3*, 87–95.

Law Office # 2. (2002). *Justice Institute LCD Project: Legal rights for homeless youth*. Retrieved September 25, 2003, from http://www.bostoncoop.net/lcd/

Lawrence, G., & Kurpius, S. (2000). Legal and ethical issues involved when counseling minors in nonschool settings. *Journal of Counseling & Development, 78*, 130–136.

LeBlanc, M., & Ritchie, M. (2001). A meta-analysis of play therapy outcomes. *Counseling Psychology Quarterly, 14*(2), 149–163.

Lebo, D. (1955). The development of play as a form of therapy: From Rousseau to Rogers. *American Journal of Psychiatry, 110*, 104–109.

Ledyard, P. (1998). Counseling minors: Ethical and legal issues. *Counseling and Values, 42*, 171–178.

Lee, A. (1997). Psychoanalytic play therapy. In K. O'Connor & L. M. Braverman (Eds.), *Play therapy: Theory and practice (pp. 46–78). New York: Wiley.

Lefkowitz, M., & Tesiny, E. (1980). Assessment of childhood depression. *Journal of Consulting and Clinical Psychology, 48,* 43–50.

Lenkowsky, R. S. (1987). Bibliotherapy: A review and analysis of the literature. *Journal of Special Education, 21,* 123–132.

Levy, D. (1938). "Release Therapy" in young children. *Psychiatry, 1,* 387–389.

Loeber, R. (1988). Natural histories of conduct problems, delinquency, and associated substance use: Evidence for developmental progressions. In B. B. Lahey & A. E. Kazdin (Eds.), *Advances in clinical child psychology* (Vol. 11). New York: Plenum.

Loeber, R., Burke, J., Lahey, B., Winters, A., & Zerz, M. (2000). Oppositional defiant and conduct disorder: A review of the past 10 years, Part I. *American Academy of Child and Adolescent Psychiatry, 39,* 499–509.

Loeber, R., & Farrington, D. (2000). Young children who commit crime: Epidemiology, developmental origins, risk factors, early interventions, and policy implications. *Development and Psychopathology, 12,* 497–523.

Loeber, R., & Keenan, K. (1994). Interaction between conduct disorder and its comorbid conditions: Effects of age and gender. *Clinical Psychology Review, 14,* 497–523.

Loeber, R., & Schmaling, K. (1985). Empirical evidence for overt and covert patterns of antisocial conduct problems: A meta-analysis. *Journal of Abnormal Child Psychology, 13,* 337–354.

Loeber, R., & Stouthamer-Loeber, M. (1998). Development of juvenile aggression and violence: Some common misconceptions and controversies. *American Psychologist, 53,* 242–259.

Loeber, R., Wung, P., Keenan, K., Giroux, B., Stouthamer-Loeber, M., Van Kammen, W., & Maughan, B. (1993). Developmental pathways in disruptive child behavior. *Development and Psychopathology, 5,* 103–133.

Lord, C., Risi, S., Lambrecht, L., Cook, E., Levanthal, B., & DiLavore, P. (2000). The Autism Diagnostic Observation Schedule—Generic: A standard measure of social and communicative deficits associated with the spectrum of autism. *Journal of Autism and Pervasive Developmental Disorders, 30,* 205–223.

Lou, A., & Takeuchi, D. (2001). Cultural factors in help-seeking for child behavior problems: Value orientation, affective responding, and severity appraisals among Chinese-American parents. *Journal of Community Psychology, 29,* 675–692.

Lowenfeld, H., & Lowenfeld, M. (1923). *Back to prosperity: A new aspect of practical life.* London: E. Wilson.

Lowenfeld, M. (1935). *Play in childhood.* London: V. Gollancz.

Lowenfeld, M. (1949). *On the psychotherapy of children: A report of a conference held at the Institute of Child Psychology, London, August, 1948.*

Lowenfeld, M. (1954). *The Lowenfeld mosaic test.* London: Newman Neama.

Lowenfeld, M. (1979). *The world technique.* London and Boston: Allen & Unwin.

Lowenfeld, M. (1991). *Play in childhood.* London and New York: MacKeith Press. Distributed by Cambridge University Press.

Lowenfeld, M., Urwin, C., & Hood-Williams, J. (1988). *Child psychotherapy, war, and the normal child: Selected papers of Margaret Lowenfeld.* London: Free Association Books.

Lynn, G. (2000). *Survival strategies for parenting children with bipolar disorder.* Philadelphia: Jessica Kingsley.

Machover, K. (1949). *Personality projection in the drawing of the human figure (a method of personality investigation).* Springfield, IL: Charles C. Thomas.

Machover, K. (1951). Drawing of the human figure: A method of personality investigation. In H. Anderson & G. Anderson (Eds.), *An introduction to projective techniques.* New York: Prentice-Hall.

MacLean, G., & Rappen, U. (1991). *Hermine Hug-Hellmuth: Her life and work.* London: Routledge.

Magid, K., & McKelvey, C. (1988). *High risk: Children without a conscience.* New York: Bantam.

Mahler, M. S. (1968). *On human symbiosis and the vicissitudes of individuation.* New York: International Universities Press.

Mahler, M. S. (1979a). *Infantile psychosis and early contributions.* New York: J. Aronson.

Mahler, M. S. (1979b). *The selected papers of Margaret S. Mahler, M. D.* New York: J. Aronson.

Mahler, M. S. (1979c). *Separation-individuation.* New York: J. Aronson.

Mahler, M. S. (1994a). *Infantile psychosis and early contributions* (1st softcover ed.). Northvale, NJ: J. Aronson.

Mahler, M. S. (1994b). *The selected papers of Margaret S. Mahler, M. D.* (1st softcover ed.). Northvale, NJ: J. Aronson.

Mahler, M. S. (1994c). *Separation-individuation* (1st softcover ed.). Northvale, NJ: J. Aronson.

Mahler, M. S., & Stepansky, P. E. (1988). *The memoirs of Margaret S. Mahler.* New York: Collier Macmillan.

Mahler, M. S., Furer, M., & Institute of Psychoanalysis (Great Britain). (1969). *On human symbiosis and the vicissitudes of individuation.* London: Hogarth Press and the Institute of Psycho-Analysis.

Mahler, M. S., McDevitt, J. B., & Settlage, C. F. (1971). *Separation—individuation: Essays in honor of Margaret S. Mahler.* New York: International Universities Press.

Mahler, M. S., Pine, F., & Bergman, A. (1975). *The psychological birth of the human infant: Symbiosis and individuation.* London: Hutchinson.

March, J. (1997). *Multidimensional Anxiety Scale for Children (MASC).* San Antonio, TX: The Psychological Corporation.

Marsella, A. (1998). Toward a "global community psychology" meeting the needs of a changing world. *American Psychologist, 12,* 1282–1291.

Martinez, E. (1988). Child behavior in Mexican American/Chicano families: Maternal teaching and child-rearing practices. *Family Relations, 37,* 275–280.

Maslow, A. (1987). *Motivation and personality* (3rd ed.). New York: Addison-Wesley.

McArthur, D., & Roberts, G. (1982). *Robert's Apperception Test for Children manual.* Los Angeles: Western Psychological Services.

McCalla, C. (1994). A comparison of three play therapy theories: psychoanalytical, Jungian, and client-centered. *International Journal of Play Therapy, 3,* 1–10.

McGuire, D. K., & McGuire, D. E. (2000). *Linking parents to play therapy : A practical guide with applications, interventions, and case studies.* Philadelphia: Brunner/Routledge.

Miller, W. (1994). Family play therapy: History, theory and convergence. In C. Schaefer & L. Carey (Eds.), *Family play therapy* (pp. 3–19). Northvale, NJ: J. Aronson.

Mitchell, C., Disque, J., & Robertson, P. (2002). When parents want to know: Responding to parental demands for confidential information. *Professional School Counseling, 6*(2), 156–162.

Monte, C. (1987). *Beneath the mask: An introduction to theories of personality* (3rd ed., pp. 121–157). New York: Holt, Rinehart, & Winston.

Moreno, Z. T. (1990a). Healing the hidden wounds of war. *Journal of Group Psychotherapy, Psychodrama & Sociometry, 42,* 229.

Moreno, Z. T. (1990b). Applications of J. L. Moreno's legacy to contemporary life. *Journal of Group Psychotherapy, Psychodrama & Sociometry, 43,* 94.

Moreno, Z. T. (1991). More of Moreno's legacy. *Journal of Group Psychotherapy, Psychodrama & Sociometry, 44,* 95.

Morris, R., & Kratochwill, T. (1983). *The practice of child therapy.* New York: Pergamon Press.

Moustakas, C. E. (1953). *Children in play therapy.* New York and Ann Arbor: McGraw-Hill and University Microfilms.

Moustakas, C. E. (1955). Emotional adjustment and the process of play therapy. *Journal of Genetic Psychology, 86,* 309–325.

Moustakas, C. E. (1959). *Psychotherapy with children.* New York: Bantam.

Moustakas, C. E. (1973). *Children in play therapy.* New York: J. Aronson.

Moustakas, C. E. (1997). *Relationship play therapy.* Northvale, NJ: J. Aronson.

Moustakas, C. E., & Schalock, H. (1955). An analysis of therapist-child interaction. *Child Development, 26,* 143–157.

Munns, E. (2000). *Theraplay: Innovations in attachment-enhancing play therapy.* Northvale, N.J.: J. Aronson.

Muro, J. (1968). Play media in counseling: A brief report of experience and some opinions. *Elementary School Guidance & Counseling, 5,* 104–110.

Murray, H. (1943). *The thematic apperception test.* Cambridge, MA: Harvard University Press.

Myrick, R., & Holdin, W. (1971). A study of play process in counseling. *Elementary School Guidance & Counseling, 5,* 256–265.

Naglieri, J., McNeish, T., & Barbos, A. (1991). *Draw-A-Person: Screening procedure for emotional disturbance.* Austin, TX: ProEd.

Nandi, P. K., & Harris, H. (1999). The social world of female-headed black families: A study of quality of life in a marginalized neighborhood. *International Journal of Comparative Sociology, 40,* 195.

Nassar-McMillan, S. C., & Hakim-Larson, J. (2003). Counseling considerations among Arab Americans. *Journal of Counseling & Development, 81,* 150.

National Association of Social Work. (1999). *Code of ethics.* Washington, DC: Author.

Nelson, P. (2004). *Toys as history: Ethnic images and cultural change.* Retrieved May 31, 2004, from http://www.ferris.edu/news/jimcrow/links/toys

Nelson, R. (1966). Elementary school counseling with unstructured play media. *Personnel & Guidance Journal, 45,* 24–27.

Nemiroff, M. A., Annunziata, J. (1990). *A child's first book about play therapy* (1st ed.). Washington, DC, and Hyattsville, MD: American Psychological Association.

New Jersey v. T.L.O., 105 S. Ct. 733 (1985).

Newsom, C., & Hovanitz, C. (1997). Autistic disorder. In E. Mash & L. Terdal (Eds.), *Assessment of childhood disorders.* New York: Guilford Press.

Nordling, W., & Guerney, L. (1999). Typical stages in the child-centered play therapy process. *Journal for the Professional Counselor, 14,* 17–23.

Norton, C. C., & Norton, B. E. (1997). *Reaching children through play therapy: An experiential approach.* Denver: Publishing Cooperative.

Nystul, M. (1980). Nystulian play therapy: Applications of Adlerian psychology. *Elementary School Guidance & Counseling, 15,* 22–29.

Nystul, M. (1987). Strategies for parent-centered counseling of the young. *The Creative Child and Adult Quarterly, 12,* 103–110.

O'Brien, S. (1980). *Child abuse: A crying shame.* Provo, UT: Brigham Young University Press.

O'Connor, K. (1983). The color your life technique. In C. Schaefer & K. O'Connor (Eds.), *Handbook of play therapy* (pp. 251–257). New York: Wiley.

O'Connor, K. (1991). *The play therapy primer: An integration of theories and techniques.* New York: Wiley.

O'Connor, K. (1993). Child, protector, confidant: Structured group ecosystemic play therapy. In T. Kottman & C. Schaefer (Eds.), *Play therapy in action: A casebook for practitioners* (pp. 245–280). Northvale, NJ: J. Aronson.

O'Connor, K. (1994a). Ecosystemic play therapy. In K. O'Connor & C. Schaefer (Eds.), *Handbook of play therapy: Advances and innovations* (Vol. 2, pp. 61–84). New York: Wiley.

O'Connor, K. (1994b). Interpreting children's verbalizations in play therapy. In *Interviews with experts in child psychotherapy.* Plainview, NY: Center for Applied Psychology.

O'Connor, K. (1997). Ecosystemic play therapy. In K. O'Connor & L. Braverman (Eds.), *Play therapy theory and practice: A comparative presentation.* New York: Wiley.

O'Connor, K. (2001). Ecosystemic play therapy. *International Journal of Play Therapy, 10,* 33–44.

O'Connor, K. J., & Ammen, S. (1997). *Play therapy treatment planning and interventions: The ecosystemic model and workbook.* San Diego: Academic Press.

O'Connor, K. J., & Braverman, L. M. (1997). *Play therapy theory and practice: A comparative presentation.* New York: Wiley.

Oaklander, V. (1987). *A boy and his anger.* Long Beach, CA: Maxsound.

Oaklander, V. (1988). *Windows to our children.* Highland, NY: The Center for Gestalt Development.

Oaklander, V. (2000). Short-term Gestalt play therapy for grieving children. In H. G. Kaduson & C. Schaefer (Eds.), *Short-term play therapy for children* (pp. 28–52). New York: Guilford Press.

Oaklander, V. (2001). Gestalt play therapy. *International Journal of Play Therapy, 10,* 45–55.

Ogdon, D. (1982). *Psychodiagnostics and personality assessment: A handbook* (2nd ed.). Los Angeles: Western Psychological Services.

Ollendick, T. (1983). Reliability and validity of the Revised Fear Survey Schedule for Children. *Behavior Research and Therapy, 29,* 685–692.

Ollendick, T. (1998). Panic disorder in children and adolescents: New developments, new directions. *Journal of Clinical Child Psychology, 21,* 685–692.

Papolos, D., & Papolos, J. (2002). *The bipolar child: The definitive and reassuring guide to childhood's most misunderstood disorder.* New York: Broadway Books.

Parameswaran, G., & Hom, H. L. (2000). The lack of ability-related explanations in children from India. *Clearing House, 73,* 279.

Parham v. J.R., 442 U.S. 584 (1979).

Parker, S. (2003, August 7). Kobe already guilty of hurting black youth. *USA Today*, 11a.

Patterson, C. (1996). Multicultural counseling: From diversity to universality. *Journal of Counseling and Development, 74*, 227–231.

Peck v. Counseling Service of Addison County, 449 A. 2d (Vt. 1985).

Pedersen, P., & Carey, J. (2003). *Multicultural counseling in schools: A practical handbook*. Boston: Allyn & Bacon.

Peery, J. C. (2003). Jungian analytical play therapy. In C. Schaefer (Ed.), *Foundations of play therapy* (pp. 14–54). New York: Wiley.

Perls, F. S. (1951). *Gestalt therapy: Excitement and growth in the human personality*. New York: Julian Press.

Perls, F. S. (1968a). *Dream theory and demonstration* [Sound recording]. Tiburon, CA: Big Sur Recordings.

Perls, F. S. (1968b). *Neurosis, psychosis & dreams* [Sound recording]. Tiburon, CA: Big Sur Recordings.

Perls, F. S. (1968c). *Working with dreams* [Sound recording]. Tiburon, CA: Big Sur Recordings.

Perls, F. S. (1969a). *Ego, hunger, and aggression; The beginning of Gestalt therapy*. New York: Random House.

Perls, F. S. (1969b). *Gestalt therapy verbatim*. Lafayette, CA: Real People Press.

Perls, F. S. (1973). *The Gestalt approach & eyewitness to therapy*. Ben Lomond, CA: Science & Behavior Books.

Perls, L. (1973). *Gestalt workshop—contact & support* [Sound recording]. [n.p.]: Big Sur Recordings.

Perrin, S., Smith, P., & Yuke, W. (2000). The assessment and treatment of post-traumatic stress disorder in children and adolescents. *Journal of Child Psychology and Psychiatry, 41*, 277–289.

Perry, L., & Gerretsen, M. (2002). Theraplay: An attachment-foster intervention. *Envision: The Manitoba Journal of Child Welfare, 1*, 55–69.

Planned Parenthood Association of Kansas City, Mo. v. Ashcraft, 462 U.S. 476 (1983).

Planned Parenthood of Central Mo. v. Danforth, 428 U.S. 52, 74 (1976).

Popkin, M. (1982). *Active parenting*. Atlanta, GA: Active Parenting.

Popper, C. (1989). Diagnosing bipolar vs. ADHD. *Journal of the American Academy of Child and Adolescent Psychiatry, 28*, 5–6.

Post, R. (1999). Meeting highlights, early recognition and treatment of schizophrenia and bipolar disorder in children and adolescents. *Bipolar Network News*, NIMH Research Workshop, Bethesda, MD.

Poulin, A. (1999). *The psychotherapist-patient privilege after Jaffee v. Redmond: Where do we go from here? University Law Quarterly*. Retrieved September 26, 2003, from http://psa-uny.org/jr/articles/poulin

Powers, R., & Griffith, J. (1987). *Understanding lifestyle: The psychoclarity process*. Chicago: Americas Institute of Adlerian Studies.

Prieto, L., & Scheel, K. (2002). Using case documentation to strengthen counselor trainees' case conceptualization skills. *Journal of Counseling & Development, 80*, 11–22.

Prout, H., & Phillips, P. (1974). A clinical note: The Kinetic School Drawing. *Psychology in the Schools, 11*, 303–306.

Rank, O. (1936) *Will therapy*. New York: Knopf.

Rapoport, J., & Ismond, D. (1996). *DSM-IV training guide for diagnosis of childhood disorders*. New York: Brunner/Mazel.

Ray, D., Bratton, S., Rhine, T., & Jones, L. (2001). The effectiveness of play therapy: Responding to the critics. *International Journal of Play Therapy, 10*(1), 85–108.

Reich, W. (2000). Diagnostic Interview for Children and Adolescents (DICA). *Journal of the American Academy of Child and Adolescent Psychiatry, 39*, 59–66.

Reynolds, C., & Kamphaus, R. (1992). *The Behavior Assessment System for Children*. Circle Pines, MN: AGS.

Reynolds, C., & Richmond, B. (1985). *Revised Children's Manifest Anxiety Scale*. Los Angeles: Western Psychological Services.

Rezinkoff, M., & Rezinkoff, H. (1956). The family drawing test: A comparative study of children's drawings. *Journal of Consulting Psychology, 20*, 467–470.

Robertson, J., & Bowlby, J. (1952). Responses of young children to separation from their mothers. *Courier of the International Children's Centre, Paris, 2*, 131–140.

Rogers, C. (1942). *Counseling and psychotherapy.* Boston: Houghton Mifflin.

Rogers, C. (1951). *Client-centered therapy: Its current practice.* Boston: Houghton Mifflin.

Rogers, C. (1961). *On becoming a person.* Boston: Houghton Mifflin.

Ronan, K., Kendall, P., & Rowe, M. (1994). Negative affectivity in children: Development and validation of a self-statement questionnaire. *Cognitive Therapy and Research, 18,* 509–528.

Ross, P. (1991). The family puppet technique: For assessing parent-child and family interaction patterns. In C. Schaefer, K. Gitlin, & A. Sandgrund (Eds.), *Play diagnosis and assessment* (pp. 609–616). New York: Wiley.

Rubin, P. B., Tregay, J., & DaCosse, M. A. (1989). *Play with them—Theraplay groups in the classroom: A technique for professionals who work with children.* Springfield, IL: Charles C. Thomas.

Safer, D. (1965). Conjoint play therapy for the young child and his parent. *Archives of General Psychiatry, 13,* 320–326.

Salmon, K., & Bryant, R. (2002). Posttraumatic stress disorder in children: The influence of developmental factors. *Clinical Psychology Review, 22,* 163–188.

Salter, M. (1940). *An evaluation of adjustment based upon the concept of security.* Toronto, Ontario, Canada: University of Toronto Press.

Samuels, S., & Sikorsky, S. (1990). *Clinical evaluations of school-aged children: A structured approach to the diagnosis of child and adolescent mental disorders.* Sarasota, FL: Professional Resource Exchange.

Satir, V. (1967). *Conjoint family therapy.* Palo Alto, CA: Science and Behavior Books.

Satir, V. (1972). *Peoplemaking.* Palo Alto, CA: Science and Behavior Books.

Sayed, M. A. (2003). Psychotherapy of Arab patients in the West: Uniqueness, empathy, and "otherness." *American Journal of Psychotherapy, 57,* 445–459.

Scambler, D., Rogers, S., & Wehner, E. (2001). Can the Checklist for Autism in Toddlers differentiate young children with autism from those with developmental delay? *Journal of the American Academy of Child and Adolescent Psychiatry, 40,* 1457–1463.

Schaefer, C. (1993). *The therapeutic powers of play.* Northvale, NJ: J. Aronson.

Schaefer, C. E., & Carey, L. J. (1994). *Family play therapy.* Northvale, NJ: J. Aronson.

Scogin, F. R. (2003). Introduction: Integrating self-help into psychotherapy. *Journal of Clinical Psychology, 59,* 175–176.

Sealander, K., Schwiebert, V., Oren, T., & Weekley, J. (1999). Confidentiality and the law. *Professional School Counseling, 3,* 122–127.

Seligman, M., & Peterson, C. (1986). A learned helplessness perspective on childhood depression: Theory and research. In M. Rutter, C. E. Izard, & P. B. Read (Eds.), *Depression in young people: Developmental and clinical perspectives.* New York: Guilford Press.

Shaffer, D., Fisher, P., Lucas, C., Dulcan, M., & Schwab-Stone, M. (2000). NIMH Diagnostic Interview for Children Version IV (NIMH DISC-IV): Description, differences from previous versions, and reliability of some common diagnoses. *Journal of the American Academy of Child and Adolescent Psychiatry, 39,* 28–38.

Shank, F. (1982). Bibliotherapy as an elementary school counseling tool. *Elementary School Guidance & Counseling, 15,* 218–227.

Shelman, E., & Lazoritz, S. (2000). *Out of the darkenss: The story of Mary Ellen Wilson.* Lake Forest, CA: Dolphin Moon Publishing.

Sherril, J., & Kovacs, M. (2000). Interview Schedule for Children and Adolescents (ISCA). *Journal of the American Academy of Child and Adolescent Psychiatry, 39,* 67–75.

Shulman, B., & Mosak, H. (1988). *Manual for lifestyle assessment.* Muncie, IN: Accelerated Development.

Silverman, W., & Albano, A. (1997). *The anxiety disorders interview schedule for children (DSM-IV).* San Antonio, TX: Psychological Corporation.

Smith, S. (2002). *Mandatory reporting of child abuse and neglect.* Author. Retrieved September 27, 2003, from http://www.smith-lawfirm.com/mandatory_reporting.htm

Solomon, J. (1938). Active play therapy. *American Journal of Orthospsychiatry, 8,* 479–498.

Solomon, J. (1948). Play technique. *American Journal of Orthospsychiatry, 18,* 402–413.

Solomon, J. (1955). Play technique and the integrative process. *American Journal of Orthospsychiatry, 25,* 591–600.

Sparrow, S., Balla, D., & Cicchetti, D. (1984). *Vineland Adaptive Behavior Scales: Interview Edition Survey Form Manual*. Circle Pine, MN: AGS.

Spielberger, C. (1973). *Manual for the State-Trait Anxiety Inventory for Children*. Palo Alto, CA: Consulting Psychologists Press.

Stake, R. (1995). *The art of case study research*. Thousand Oaks, CA: Sage.

Stein, R. (1990). *Ethical issues in counseling*. Buffalo, NY: Prometheus.

Storr. A. (Ed.). (1983). *The essential Jung*. New York: MFJ Books.

Sue, D., & Sue, D. (2003). *Counseling the culturally diverse: Theory and practice* (4th ed.). New York: Wiley.

Sullivan, K. (1996). *Children's projective drawing battery*. Unpublished manuscript.

Sweeney, D., & Tatum, R. (1995). Play therapy and psychopharmacology: What the play therapist needs to know. *International Journal of Play Therapy, 4*(2), 41–57.

Swenson, L. (1993). *Psychology and law for the helping professions*. Pacific Grove, CA: Brooks/Cole.

Tafoya, T. (1989). Circles and cedar: Native Americans and family therapy. *Journal of Psychotherapy and the Family, 61*, 71–98.

Taft, J. (1933). *The dynamics of therapy in a controlled relationship*. New York: Macmillian.

Tarasoff v. Regents of Univ. of CA. (551 CA SC p 2d 334 (1976).

Taylor, B. B. (2004). Bibliotherapy. *Christian Century, 121*, 40–41).

Teglasi, H. (1993). *Clinical use of story telling: Emphasizing the TAT with children and adolescents*. Boston: Allyn & Bacon.

Teglasi, H. (2001). *Essentials of TAT and other storytelling techniques assessment*. New York: Wiley.

Thorndike, R., Hagen, E., & Sattler, J. (1986). *Stanford-Binet Intelligence Scale* (4th ed.). Chicago: Riverside.

Thornton, C. H. (2004). Value orientations: A study of black college students. *College Student Journal, 38*, 103–111.

Tinker v. Des Moines Independent Community School District, 393 U.S. 503, 89 S. Ct. 733, 21 L., ed.2d 731 (1969).

Towards culturally competent care. (2004). Retrieved June 28, 2004, from www.ncptsd.org/wsah booklet/33_towards_culturally_c.html - 12k - Jun 28, 2004

Triandis, H. (1987). Some major dimensions of cultural variation in client populations. In P. Pedersen (Ed.), *Handbook of cross-cultural counseling and therapy* (pp. 21–28). New York: Praeger.

Turner, P. R. (1979). Religious conversion and community development. *Journal for the Scientific Study of Religion, 18*, 252.

Urwin, C., & Hood-Williams, J. (1988). *Selected papers of Margaret Lowenfeld*. London: Free Association Books.

Van Fleet, R. (1994). *Filial therapy: Strengthening parent-child relationships through play*. Sarasota, FL: Professional Resource Press.

Van Fleet, R. (2004). *Filial therapy: Strengthening parent-child relationships through play* (2nd ed.). Sarasota, FL: Professional Resource Press.

Vare, J. W., & Norton, T. L. (2004). Bibliotherapy for gay and lesbian youth overcoming the structure of silence. *Clearing House, 77*, 190–194.

von Staabs, G. (1991). *The Sceno-test* (J. Smith, Trans.). Seattle: Hogrefe & Huber.

Warren, M. (2002). *Behavioral management guide: Essential treatment strategies for the psychotherapy of children, their parents, and families: A special treatment plan for critical incident stress management*. Northvale, NJ: J. Aronson.

Waterland, J. (1970). Actions instead of words: Play therapy for the young child. *Elementary School Guidance & Counseling, 4*, 180–197.

Webb, N. (1996). *Social work practice with children*. New York: Guilford Press.

Wechsler, D. (1991). *Manual for the Wechsler Intelligence Scale for Children—Third Edition (WISC—III)*. San Antonio, TX: The Psychological Corporation.

Weininger, O. (1982). *Out of the minds of babes: The strength of children's feelings*. Springfield, IL: Charles C. Thomas.

Weininger, O. (1984). *The clinical psychology of Melanie Klein*. Springfield, IL: Charles C. Thomas.

Weininger, O. (1989). *Children's phantasies: The shaping of relationships*. London: Karnac.

Welch, M. (1988). *Holding time*. New York: Simon & Schuster.

Welfel, E. (2002). *Ethics in counseling and psychotherapy*. Pacific Grove, CA: Brooks/Cole.

Weller, E., Weller, R., Fristad, M., Rooney, M., & Schecter, J. (2000). Children's interview for psychiatric syndromes (ChIPS). *Journal of the American Academy of Child and Adolescent Psychiatry, 39*, 76–84.

Wells, H. G. (1911). *Floor games.* London: Palmer.

West, J. (1992). *Child-centered play therapy.* London: Edward Arnold.

Westby, C. E. (1991). A scale for assessing children's pretend play. In C. Schaefer, K. Gitlin, & A. Sandgrund (Eds.), *Play diagnosis and assessment* (pp. 131–161). New York: Wiley.

Whaley, A. (2003). Cognitive-cultural model of identity and violence prevention for African American youth. *Genetic Social & General Psychology Monographs, 129*(2), 101–152.

Wicks-Nelson, R., & Israel, A. (2003). *Behavior disorders of childhood* (5th ed.). Upper Saddle River, NJ: Prentice Hall.

Williams, E. E., & Ellison, F. (1996). Culturally informed social work practice with American Indian clients: Guidelines for non-Indian social workers. *Social Work, 41,* 147.

Winnicott, D. (1958). Transitional objects and transitional phenomenon. In D. Winnicott (Ed.), *Collected papers* (pp. 229–242). New York: Basic.

Winnicott, D. (1965). *The maturational processes and the facilitating environment.* New York: International Universities Press.

Wirt, R., Lachar, D., Klinedinst, J., Seat, P., & Broen, W. (2001). *Personality Inventory for Children* (2nd ed.). Los Angeles: Western Psychological Services.

Wood, M. (1992a). *Developmental Teaching Objectives Rating Form—Revised technical report.* Athens, GA: Developmental Therapy Institute.

Yeung, A., & Kung, W. W. (2004). How culture impacts on the treatment of mental illnesses among Asian-Americans. *Psychiatric Times, 21,* 34–36.

Yick, A. G., Shibusawa, T., & Agbayani-Siewert, P. (2003). Partner violence, depression, and practice implications with families of Chinese descent. *Journal of Cultural Diversity, 10,* 96–104.

Yin, R. (2003). *Case study research: Design and methods* (3rd ed.). Thousand Oaks, CA: Sage.

Yura, M., & Galassi, M. (1974). Adlerian usage of children's play. *Journal of Individual Psychotherapy, 30,* 194–201.

Zakich, R. (1975). *The ungame.* Anaheim, CA: The Ungame Company.

Zakich, R., & Monroe, S. (1979). *Reunion.* Anaheim, CA: The Ungame Company.

Zhang, A. Y., Snowden, L. R., & Sue, S. (1998). Differences between Asian and White Americans' help seeking and utilization patterns in the Los Angeles area. *Journal of Community Psychology, 26,* 317–326.

Name Index

Achenbach, T., 3, 156, 157, 237, 245, 247
Agbayani-Siewert, P., 279
Ageton, S., 247
Ainsworth, M., 164, 165, 166–167
Albano, A., 234, 240
Alessi, N., 239
Alexander, F., 13
Alfred Adler Institute, 72, 88
Allan, J., 89, 90, 91, 92, 94, 95, 98, 99, 100, 101, 102, 103, 226
Allen, F., 10, 11, 155
Allen, L., 13
Allert, A., 184, 199
Ambrosini, P., 235
American Association for Marriage and Family Therapy, 261, 262
American Association on Mental Retardation, 250
American Counseling Association, 261, 262
American Psychiatric Association, 242, 246, 281
American Psychological Association, 261, 262
Ammen, S., 186, 189, 192, 195–196, 197, 198, 199, 226
Anastasi, A., 220–221, 223, 227, 228, 231
Angold, A., 235
Annunziata, J., 33, 154
Ansbacher, H., 71, 72
Ansbacher, R., 71, 72
Ariel, S., 201, 208–211

Association for Play Therapy (APT), 37–38, 261, 262, 283–292
Axline, V. M., 11, 42, 104, 105–107, 109, 113, 115–116, 155, 200, 251

Baines, C., 8
Baird, G., 252
Balla, D., 250
Balvanz, J., 265
Barbos, A., 221
Barkley, R., 197
Barnes, M. A., 22, 26
Baruth, L., 81
Bateson, G., 202
Bayley, N., 250
Beck, A. T., 150
Beers, C., 4
Bell, S., 166
Bellak, L., 157
Bellak, S., 157
Bender, L., 227
Benedict, H., 63
Bergman, A., 62
Bergmann, T., 48
Bertoia, J., 89, 90, 91, 94, 95, 98, 100
Bettner, L., 82
Biederman, J., 243
Bixler, R., 11, 12, 44–45, 80, 155–156, 179
Black, H., 255, 256, 261, 262
Blehar, M., 166
Boley, S., 226
Booth, P. B., 164, 172, 173, 174, 175, 176, 177, 178, 179, 180, 181, 183, 184, 199, 200
Bowlby, J., 164, 165–166, 205
Bratton, S., 265, 266
Braverman, L. M., 189
Bretherton, I., 165, 166
Brody, V. A., 164, 167, 168, 169, 170, 171, 172
Broen, W., 197, 248
Bromfield, R., 52, 64, 65, 67
Brucker, P. S., 279
Bryant, R., 240
Buck, J., 220, 221, 222, 223
Burke, J., 246
Burks, H., 189
Burnham, J. J. G., 237
Burns, R., 219, 220, 221, 223, 220, 225

Callahan, S., 240
Callanan, P., 261
Cameron, S., 36, 37
Cantlay, L., 199
Carey, J., 268, 269, 270, 271
Carey, L. J., 201
Carkhuff, R., 42
Carlson, C., 172
Carmichael, K., 24, 25, 49, 88, 274
Carmichael, L., 11, 42, 104, 105, 106–107, 200
Carroll, F., 122, 123
Carson-Sabellil, L., 88
Cassel, P., 71
Catholic University of America, 151, 163
Chandras, K., 273, 274, 276

Chapman, T., 8, 239

Chethik, M., 64, 65, 66, 67, 68, 69, 70

Child Abuse Prevention and Treatment Act (CAPTA), 263

Child Abuse Prevention and Treatment and Adoption Act Amendments, 263

Chomsky, N., 270

Christopher, J., 282

Cicchetti, D., 250

Cipani, E., 198

Clark, L. P., 8, 52, 200

Connors, C., 197, 247, 248

Constantino, G., 265

Cook, E., 252

Cool, J., 235

Corey, G., 127, 259–260, 261, 262

Corey, M., 261

Corsini, R., 208, 242

Costello, E., 235

Cox, C., 227

Csikszentmihalyi, M., 205

"Cultural Consultation Service," 281–282

DaCosse, M. A., 175

Davis, D. D., 150

Davis, N., 152

De Domenico, G., 89, 90, 91, 92, 93, 94, 95, 96, 97, 98, 99, 100

Deren, S., 224

De Saussure, F., 210

DesLauriers, A., 172

Developmental Therapy Institute, 196, 197

Diener, E., 95

DiLavore, P., 252

Di Leo, J., 224

Dilsaver, S., 239

Dinkmeyer, D. C., 13, 72, 73, 81, 82, 84, 86

Dinkmeyer, J., 82

Dinkmeyer, J. D., 72, 82, 84, 86

DiPasquale, L., 184, 185

Disque, J., 262

Dorfman, E., 11, 105

Dreikurs, R., 47, 71, 73, 82

Dulcan, M., 235

Dwairy, M., 282

Eckstein, D., 81

Eddy, J. P., 273

Edelbrock, C., 156, 157

Elliot, G., 265

Elliott, D., 247

Ellison, F., 276

Epstein, J., 197, 247

Erikson, E., 12, 54

Erkanli, A., 235

Exner, J., 199

Eysberg, S., 247

Fairbairn, W., 165

Fall, M., 265

Farrington, D., 246

"Federal Evidence Code, Rule 501," 261

Fischer, L., 257

Fisher, P., 235

Freed, K., 152

Freeman, A. M., 150

Freud, A., 8–9, 52, 57–60, 200

Freud, S., 52–54

Fristad, M., 235

Fujita, F., 95

Furer, M., 62

Fyer, A., 8, 239

Gage, S. J. L., 279

Galassi, M., 79

Gardner, R., 88, 103, 189, 232–233, 234

Garwick, A., 276, 279

Gerretsen, M., 172, 173, 174, 175, 177

Getzel, J., 205

Gil, E., 227

Ginott, A., 12, 155

Ginott, H. G., 12, 45, 52, 80, 155

Glasser, W., 200

Goddard, H. W., 12, 155

Gong, F., 279

Goodenough, F., 219, 220, 222

Gordon, I., 5

Gregory, R., 221, 222, 223

Griff, M., 202, 204–205

Griffith, J., 72, 81

Griswold, D. B., 258, 260

Griswold, D. P., 258, 260

Gruber, C., 248

Guerney, B. G. J., 201, 211

Guerney, L. F., 9, 105, 107, 108, 110, 112, 113, 114, 115–116, 201, 211, 213, 215

Guldner, C. A., 88

Hagen, E., 250

Hakim-Larson, J., 276, 277

Halasz, G., 256, 257, 260

Hall, A., 260

Hambridge, G., 10

Hammer, E., 220, 221

Hardaway, T. G. I., 201, 217

Harrar, W., 263

Harris, D., 219, 220, 221, 222

Harris, H., 278

Hart, E., 246

Hart, S., 256, 257

Harvey, S., 201, 205, 206, 207

Haworth, M., 117

Hazelwood School District v. Kuhlmeier, 258

Hendrix, D., 261

Herlihy, B., 259–260

Herring, R. D., 281

Hinman, C., 272, 273, 274, 276, 278, 279, 280

Hinshaw, S., 246

H. L. v. Matherson, 258

Hodges, K., 235

Holdin, W., 13, 42

Hom, H. L., 277

Hood-Williams, J., 8, 9, 60, 61

Hovanitz, C., 252

Hug-Hellmuth, H., 5–8

Huizinga, D., 247

Hulse, W., 220, 224

Hurst, T., 172

Hynes, A., 88

Hynes-Berry, M., 88

Ingraham v. Wright, 258

In re Gault, 257–258

Institute of Psycho-analysis (Great Britain), 62

Institute of Psycho-Analysis London, 57, 58
Ireton, H., 157
Ironsmith, M., 88
Irwin, E., 199, 228
Ismond, D., 246
Israel, A., 234, 235, 237, 238, 239–240, 241–244, 245, 246, 247, 248, 249, 251, 252, 276

Jablonski v. US, 263
Jackson-Brown, I. V., 273
Jacquot, W., 13
James, B., 38, 198
Jennings, S., 172
Jernberg, A., 164, 168, 169, 172, 173, 174, 175, 176, 177, 178, 179, 180, 181, 183, 184, 191, 199, 200
Jipguep, M. C., 279
Johnson, J., 88
Johnson, L., 265
Jolles, I., 220
Jones, E., 52, 54
Jones, L., 266
Jongsma, A., 246

Kamphaus, R., 247
Kanner, L., 3
Kaufman, A., 250
Kaufman, N., 250
Kaufman, S., 220, 225
Kearney, C., 239
Keenan, K., 246
Keith, D., 202, 203, 204
Kelly, E., 205
Kempe, C., 4
Kempe, R., 4
Kendall, P., 240
Kenny, M., 251
Kettenbach, G., 36
King, N., 239
Kircher, C. J., 151, 163
Klein, D., 8, 239
Klein, M., 8–9, 52, 55–56, 63, 64, 68, 200
Klepsch, M., 225, 226
Kline, R., 248
Klinedinst, J., 197, 248

Knapp, S., 263
Knell, S., 149, 150, 151, 152, 154, 155, 156, 157, 158, 160, 161, 162, 200
Koller, T., 172, 173, 174, 175, 176, 177, 178, 179, 184, 199
Koppitz, E., 220, 221, 227
Kottman, T., 71, 72, 74, 75, 76, 77, 78, 80, 81, 82, 84, 88, 222
Kovacs, M., 235, 245
Kratochwill, T., 3, 4, 5
Kubler-Ross, E., 166
Kung, W. W., 279
Kurpius, S., 256–257, 258, 259, 260, 261, 263, 264
Kutnick, P., 226

Lachar, D., 197, 248
LaGreca, A., 240
Lahey, B., 246
Lambrecht, L., 252
Landreth, G., 8, 13, 21, 22, 23–24, 25, 28, 44–45, 78, 80, 104, 105, 108, 109–110, 111, 112, 114, 116, 117, 118, 200, 222
Last, C., 239
Law Office # 2, 258, 260, 262
Lawrence, G., 256–257, 258, 259, 260, 261, 263, 264
Lazoritz, S., 4
LeBlanc, M., 265, 266
Lebo, D., 7, 8, 9, 45
Ledyard, P., 260
Lee, A., 64
Lefkowitz, M., 245
Lenkowsky, R. S., 151, 163
Levanthal, B., 252
Levin, S., 92, 100
Levy, D., 8, 9
Lew, A., 82
Lin, M., 260
Loeber, R., 246
Logie, L., 225, 226
Lord, C., 252
Lou, A., 273
Low, B., 8

Lowenfeld, H., 60
Lowenfeld, M., 60–63
Lucas, C., 235
Lyman, C., 172
Lynn, G., 243

Machover, K., 220, 221
MacLean, G., 5–8
Magid, K., 168, 169
Mahler, M. S., 62
Malgady, R., 265
Mannuzza, S., 8, 239
March, J., 240
Marsella, A., 277, 282
Martinez, E., 274, 280
Mattis, S., 239
McArthur, D., 157, 199
McCalla, C., 109, 112
McDevitt, J. B., 62
McGuire, D. E., 201, 216, 217
McGuire, D. K., 201, 216, 217
McInnis, W., 246
McKay, G., 73, 82
McKay, J., 82
McKelvey, C., 168, 169
McKnew, D., 235
McNeish, T., 221
Mehrer, D., 81
Miller, L., 226
Miller, W., 202
Mitchell, C., 262
Monroe, S., 189
Monte, C., 12, 56
Moore, D. J., 149, 150, 200
Moreno, Z. T., 88
Morris, R., 3, 4, 5
Mosak, H., 81
Moustakas, C. E., 10, 11, 80, 134–147, 148
Munns, E., 173
Muro, J., 13
Murray, H., 157
Myrick, R., 13, 42

Naglieri, J., 221
Nandi, P. K., 278
Nassar-McMillan, S. C., 276, 277
National Association of Social Work, 261, 262

Nelson, L., 265
Nelson, P., 272
Nelson, R., 13
Nemiroff, M. A., 33, 154
New Jersey v. T. L. O., 258
Newsom, C., 252
Nordling, W., 113
Norton, B. E., 21, 22, 23
Norton, C. C., 21, 22, 23
Norton, T. L., 151, 163
Nystul, M., 77–78

Oaklander, V., 120–123, 124, 125, 127, 129–130, 131–133
O'Brien, S., 5
O'Connor, K., 11–12, 186, 187–189, 190, 191, 192–193, 194–196, 197, 198, 199, 200, 226
Ogdon, D., 221, 222
Ollendick, T., 239, 240
Oren, T., 262

Panichelli-Mindel, S., 240
Papolos, D., 243
Papolos, J., 243
Parameswaran, G., 277
Parham v. J. R., 258
Parker, J., 197, 247
Parker, S., 278
Parkes, C., 166
Patterson, C., 277
Paviovic, Z., 256, 257
Peck v. Counseling Services of Addison County, 263
Pederson, P., 268, 269, 270, 271
Peery, J. C., 98, 101
Perls, F., 120
Perls, L., 120
Perrin, S., 240
Perry, B. J., 279
Perry, L., 172, 173, 174, 175, 177
Peterson, C., 226, 244
Peterson, L. M., 246
Phillips, P., 226
Pine, F., 62
Planned Parenthood Association of Kansas City, Mo. v. Ashcroft, 258

Planned Parenthood of Central Mo. v. Danforth, 258
Popkin, M., 82
Popper, C., 243
Post, R., 243
Poulin, A., 261
Powers, R., 72, 81
Prieto, L., 36, 37, 38
Prout, H., 226
Pumfrey, P., 265

Rank, O., 10
Rapoport, J., 246
Rappen, U., 5–8
Ray, D., 265, 266
Reich, W., 235
Rescorla, L., 237, 245
Reynolds, C., 240, 247
Reznikoff, H., 224
Reznikoff, M., 224
Rhine, T., 266
Richmond, B., 240
Risi, S., 252
Ritchie, M., 265, 266
Riviere, J., 52
Robbins, D., 239
Roberts, G., 157, 199
Robertson, J., 166
Robertson, P., 262
Rogers, C., 11, 104, 105, 111
Rogers, S., 252
Rogler, L., 265
Ronan, K., 240
Rooney, M., 235
Ross, P., 228
Rowe, M., 240
Rubin, P. B., 175

Safer, D., 204
Salmon, K., 240
Salter, M., 165
Samuels, S., 237, 238
Sanders-Phillips, K., 279
Sanvik, E., 95
Satir, V., 205
Sattler, J., 250
Sayed, M. A., 280, 282
Scambler, D., 252
Schaefer, C., 11–12, 71, 201, 205

Schalock, H., 10, 134
Schecter, J., 235
Scheel, K., 36, 37, 38
Schmaling, K., 246
Schwab-Stone, M., 235
Schwiebert, V., 262
Scogin, F. R., 151, 163
Scott, M., 33, 154
Sealander, K., 262
Seat, P., 197, 248
Seligman, M., 244
Settlage, C. F., 62
Shaffer, D., 235
Shank, F., 88
Shelman, E., 4
Sherril, J., 235
Shibusawa, T., 279
Shulman, B., 81
Sikorsky, S., 237, 238
Silverman, W., 234, 239, 240
Sitarenios, G., 197, 247
Smith, P., 240
Smith, S., 263, 264
Snowden, L. R., 273
Solomon, J., 9
Soltz, V., 71, 73, 82
Sorenson, G., 257
Sparrow, S., 250
Spaulding, D. J., 273
Sperry, L., 72, 84, 86
Spielberger, C., 240
Stake, R., 265
Stein, R., 261
Stepansky, P. E., 62
Stone, W., 240
Storr, A., 94
Stouthamer-Loeber, M., 246
Strauss, C., 239
Strayton, D., 166
Sue, D., 268–269, 270, 271
Sue, S., 273
Sugarman, A., 240
Sullivan, K., 199
Sweeney, D., 244, 247, 248, 252
Swenson, L., 36

Tacata, L. A., 279
Tafoya, T., 276
Taft, J., 10
Takeuchi, D., 273

Tarasoff v. Regents of Univ. of CA., 262
Tatum, R., 244, 247, 248, 252
Taylor, B. B., 151, 163
Teglasi, H., 199, 230, 231
Tesiny, E., 245
Thorndike, R., 250
Thornton, C. H., 275
Thwing, E., 157
Tonge, B., 239
"Towards Culturally Competent Care," 281
Tregay, J., 175
Triandis, H., 268–269, 270, 271
Turner, P. R., 273
Turtle-Song, I., 36, 37

Urbina, S., 220–221, 223, 227, 228, 231
Urwin, C., 8, 9, 60, 61

Van Fleet, R., 201, 211, 212, 213, 214, 215
VandCreek, L., 263
Vare, J. W., 151, 163
Von Staabs, G., 232

Wall, S., 166
Warren, M., 151, 163
Waterland, J., 13
Waters, E., 166
Webb, N., 234
Wechsler, D., 197, 250
Weekley, J., 262
Wehner, E., 252
Weiner, I., 199
Weininger, O., 52, 63, 64, 67, 68
Welch, M., 168, 169
Welfel, E., 262
Weller, E., 235
Weller, R., 235
Wells, H. G., 61
West, J., 108, 114–115
Westby, C. E., 199
Whaley, A., 279
Whitaker, C., 202, 203, 204
Wicks-Nelson, R., 234, 235, 237, 238, 239–240, 241–244, 245, 246, 247, 248, 249, 251, 252, 276
Williams, E. E., 276
Wingenfeld, S., 248
Winick, C., 251

Winnicott, D., 62, 165
Winters, A., 246
Wirt, R., 197, 248
Wittig, B., 166
Wood, M., 196, 197
World Health Organization (WHO), 165

Yang, B., 239
Yeung, A., 279
Yick, A. G., 279
Yin, R., 265
Yuke, W., 240
Yura, M., 79

Zakich, R., 189
Zerz, M., 246
Zhang, A. Y., 273

Subject Index

Acting out–aggressive toys, 110
Active Parenting (Popkin), 82
Active play therapy, 9–10
Activity scheduling, 162
Adaptive behavior
     assessments, 250
Adler, Alfred, 71, 72
Adlerian play therapy, 71–74
   assessment and techniques,
       84–88
   limits, 80–81
   parent involvement, 81–83
   session structure, 77–80
   termination, 83–84
   therapist role, 74–77
   toy selection, 74
Advising responses, 42
After-hour availability, 39
Age, 269–270
Agency, 95
Aggressive stage of CCPT, 113
Ainsworth, Mary Salter, 164,
       165–167
Akinetic School Drawing
       Technique (ASDT),
       225, 226
Allan, John, 14
All Handicapped Children's
       Act, 257
Ambrose, Tony, 165
American Association for
       Counseling and
       Development, 13
American Association of
       Marriage and Family
       Therapists (AAMFT), 255
American Counseling Association
       (ACA), 13, 255

American Psychological Associa-
       tion (APA), 255
Analysis, 43
*Analysis of a Phobia in a Five-
       Year-Old Boy* (Freud), 52
Analytical play therapy. *See*
       Jungian analytical play
       therapy
Anima, 95
Animus, 95
Announcement phase of
       Theraplay termination,
       182, 183
Anxiety disorders, 237–242
Anxiety Disorders Interview for
       Children (ADIS-IV),
       234–235
Archetypes, 90–91
Asperger's disorder, 252
Assessment, 218–219
   Adlerian play therapy, 84–88
   child-centered play
       therapy, 119
   cognitive-behavioral play
       therapy, 152, 157–163
   cultural sensitivity, 281–282
   developmental play
       therapy, 172
   drawing, 219–227
   ecosystems play therapy,
       195–199
   filial play therapy, 212, 213
   Gestalt play therapy, 131–133
   interview, 227–230
   Jungian analytical play therapy,
       101–103
   psychoanalytic play therapy,
       69–70

relationship play therapy, 148
storytelling, 230–234
structured interviews, 234–235
Theraplay, 174, 183–185
Association for Play Therapy
       (APT), 2, 14
   case notes and treatment
       planning, 37–38
   ecosystems play therapy,
       189–190
   ethical issues, 255, 259,
       260–261, 262, 267
   Standards of Practice, 283–292
Attachment theory, 62–63,
       165–167
Attention-deficit/hyperactivity
       disorder (ADHD),
       247–248
Attention getting, 82–83
Autism, 251
Availability, 39
Axline, Virginia, 105

Baby stage of developmental play
       therapy, 167, 168
Baltimore Project, 166
Behavior. *See* Limits
Behavioral rehearsal, 161
Behavioral techniques, in
       cognitive-behavioral play
       therapy, 159–161
Bender-Gestalt Test (BGT), 227
Bergh, Henry, 4
Berlin school, 9, 55–57
Between Parent and Child
       (Ginott), 12
Between Parents and Teenager
       (Monte), 12

Between Teachers and Children (Ginott), 12
Bibliotherapy, 152, 163
Bipolar disorder, 242–244
Bird's Nest Drawing, 227
Black's law, 255–256
Booth, Phyllis B., 164
Boston, Mary, 165
Bowlby, John, 164, 165–167
Boy and His Anger, A (video), 130
British Psychoanalytic Society, 165
Brody, Viola A., 164
Brown v. Board of Education, 257

Caregiver interviews, 196
Caring, communication of, 137, 138
Case notes, 36–38
Center for Play Therapy, 13, 104
Challenging activities, 174, 175, 176
Chanting, 168, 169
Checkup activities, 174, 175
Child Abuse Prevention and Treatment Act (CAPTA), 5, 263
Child abuse reporting, 263
Child and Adolescent Psychiatric Assessment (CAPA), 235
Child Assessment Scale (CAS), 235
Child Behavioral Checklist (CBCL), 156, 157
Child Care and the Growth of Love (Ainsworth), 165
Child-centered play therapy (CCPT), 104–108
    assessment and techniques, 119
    limits, 115–116
    parent involvement, 116
    session structure, 113–115
    termination, 117–118
    therapist role, 110–112
    toy selection, 109–110
Child developmental play therapies, 164–167
    developmental play therapy, 167–172
    Theraplay, 172–185

Child guidance movement, 4
Childhood disintegrative disorder, 251–252
Child labor laws, 256
Child psychotherapy timeline, 15–16
Child relationship enhancement family therapy (CREFT), 211–212
Children, cruelty to, 4–5
Children's Apperception Test (CAT), 157
Children's Interview for Psychiatric Syndromes (ChIPS), 235
"Children's Play" (Hug-Hellmuth), 7
Children's Projective Drawing Battery, 199
Children's rights, 256–258, 266
Children: The Challenge (Dreikurs and Soltz), 82
Child's First Book of Play Therapy, A (Nemiroff, Annunziata, and Scott), 33, 154
Choice making, 206
Cipani Behavioral Assessment and Diagnostic System (C-Bad), 198
Clarification, 67
Clarifying responses, 42
Client-Centered Therapy (Rogers), 11, 105
Clients' competency, 260
Cognitive-behavioral play therapy (CBPT), 149–151
    assessment and techniques, 157–163
    limits, 155–156
    parent involvement, 156
    session structure, 154–155
    termination, 156
    therapist role, 152–153
    toy selection, 151–152
Cognitive change strategies, 162
Cognitive techniques, in cognitive-behavioral play therapy, 161–163

Collateral therapeutic work, 193
Collective unconscious, 90
Color-Your-Life (CYL), 226
Communion, 95
Compulsions, 240
Compulsory Education Act, 256
Conduct disorder (CD), 245–247
Confidential communication, 261
Confidentiality, 33–35, 261–262
Confrontation, 67
Conjoint play therapy, 204
Connors Rating Scales (CRS), 197–198
Consent to treat, 33
Contact, 121, 123, 127
Contact-boundary disturbances, 123
Content, restating, 75
Contingency management, 160, 241
Coping self-assessments, 162
Court cases, 257–258
Cradling, 168, 170, 179
Creative drama, 103
Creative expression–emotional release toys, 110
Cruelty to children, prevention of, 4–5
Crying, 180
Cultural Consultation Service, 281–282
Cultural sensitivity, 268–271
    assessment, 281–282
    limits, 278
    parental involvement, 278–280
    session structure, 274–277
    termination, 280–281
    therapist role, 272–274
    toy selection, 272
Custody issues, 32
Customs, 271
Cyclothymia, 242

Dean Behavioral Checklist for Child and Adolescent Multiple Personality Disorder, 198
Delinquency, 246
DesLauriers, Austin, 172

Developmental play (DP) therapy, 167–172

Developmental Teaching Objectives Rating Form (DTORF—R), 196, 197

Diagnosis, 236–237, 253
  anxiety disorders, 237–242
  attention-deficit/hyperactivity disorder, 247–248
  conduct disorder, 245–247
  language and learning disorders, 248–249
  mental retardation, 249–251
  mood disorders, 242–245
  pervasive developmental disorders, 251–252

Diagnostic Interview for Children and Adolescents (DICA), 235

Dialogue of Touch, The (Brody), 164, 172

Dibs: In Search of Self (Axline), 104, 105

Differential reinforcement of other behavior (DRO), 161

Discriminative stimulus, 160–161

Dollhouse Interview, 229–230

Do no harm, 259–260

Draw-A-Family (DAF), 220, 224–225

Draw-A-Group (DAG), 225, 226

Draw-A-House, 199

Draw-A-Person (DAP), 199, 220

Draw-A-Person: Screening Procedure for Emotional Disturbance (DAP:SPED), 221

Draw a Picture of a Person Picking an Apple from a Tree, 227

Draw-A-Volcano, 227

Drawing assessments, 219–227

Drive assessment, 70

Duty to warn, 261, 262–263

Dynamic family play therapy (DFPT), 205–207

Dynamic psychiatry, 5. *See also* Psychoanalysis

Dysthymic disorder, 242

Ecosystems play therapy (EPT), 186–187
  assessment and techniques, 195–199
  limits, 192–193
  parent involvement, 193–194
  session structure, 190–192
  summary, 200
  termination, 194–195
  therapist role, 189–190
  toy selection, 187–189

Effective Parent, The (Dinkmeyer, McKay, Dinkmeyer, Dinkmeyer, and McKay), 82

Ego, 90, 91–92

Ego assessment, 70

Ego defenses, 91

Elementary School Guidance and Counseling Journal, 13

Emotive, 208

Encouragement, 44, 77, 83

Engaging activities, 174, 175, 176

Erikson, Erik, 12, 52

Ethics, 255–256, 259–265, 267

Evaluating responses, 42

Experiments, 124, 126–127

Exploration phase of Theraplay, 178

Fair Labor Standards Act, 256

Family interviews, 196–197

Family play observation, 213

Family play therapy, 201–202, 204–205
  dynamic, 205–207
  paradigm for, 202–204
  parents and, 215–217
  strategic, 208–211
  summary, 217
  See also Filial play therapy

Family programs, 209

Fear Survey Schedule for Children II, 237

Feedback, 183, 185

Feelings, reflecting, 75

Felling Scales/Drawings, 159

Figure-ground, 121, 122

Filial play therapy, 201–202, 211–215. *See also* Family play therapy

Floor Games (Wells), 61

Freedom, atmosphere of, 137, 138

Freud, Anna, 5, 8–9, 52, 57–60, 70

Freud, Sigmund, 5, 52–54, 57, 70, 90

Gardner Children's Protective Battery (GCPB), 232

Gender, 269–270

Gender bias, 272

Generalized anxiety disorder, 239

Generalized interpretation, 191

Genetic interpretation, 191

Genetic-dynamic formation, 70

Gestalt play therapy, 120–124
  assessment and techniques, 131–133
  limits, 129
  parent involvement, 129–130
  session structure, 127–129
  termination, 130–131
  therapist role, 124–127
  toy selection, 124

Ginott, Hiam, 52

Good-bye personal note, 50

Good-bye session, 49–50. *See also* Termination

Goodenough-Harris Drawing Test, 220–221

Greeting, 174, 175

Grief, 166

"Grief and Mourning in Infancy and Early Childhood" (Bowlby), 165

Growing and trusting phase of Theraplay, 178, 179

Guerney, Louise, 14

Head Start, 172

Health Insurance Portability and Accountability Act (HIPAA), 30, 31, 38

Healy, William, 4

Heinicke, Christoph, 165

Here I Am (Jernberg, Hurst, and Lyman), 172

History
   children's rights, 256–257
   play therapy, 3–13
Holding, 168–169, 179–180
Homeostasis, 208
House-Tree-Person (HTP)
   drawings, 219, 220,
   221–223
Hugging, 168, 170
Hug-Hellmuth, Hermine, 5–8
Human Figure Drawing (HFD),
   219, 221
Humor, 44

Identification, 208
Inadequacy, display of, 83
Informed consent, 30–31,
   260–261
In-groups, 269
Initial intake interview, 183
Intake, 30
Intelligence measures, 157–159
Intelligence tests, 250
Interaction, 76
Interpretation, 43, 67
Interpreting Children's Verbaliza-
   tions in Play Therapy
   (video), 194
Interpreting therapist, 180–181
Intersubjective stage of develop-
   mental play therapy,
   167, 168
Interventions, 66, 67, 152–153
Interview assessments, 227–230
Interviews
   caregiver, 196
   family, 196–197
   structured, 234–235
Interview Schedule for Children
   and Adolescents
   (ISCA), 235
Introduction phase of
   Theraplay, 178
Introduction stage of develop-
   mental play therapy, 167
Irwin, Eleanor, 14
Itard, Jean, 3
I/Thou relationships, 121,
   123–124, 125

Jernberg, Ann, 14, 164, 172
Jung, Carl Gustav, 90
Jungian analytical play therapy,
   89–92
   assessment and techniques,
    101–103
   limits, 100
   parent involvement, 100–101
   session structure, 98–100
   termination, 101
   therapist role, 94–97
   toy selection, 92–93

Kinetic Family Drawing (KFD),
   199, 219, 220, 225
Kinetic-House-Tree-Person
   (KHTP) drawing, 220,
   223–224
Kinetic School Drawing (KSD),
   225, 226
Kissing, 168, 169–170
Klein, Melanie, 5, 8–9, 52,
   55–57, 70
Koppitz Developmental Scoring
   System, 227

Landmark court cases, 257–258
Landreth, Garry, 13, 14
Language, 270
Language and learning disorders
   (LLD), 248–249
Legal guidelines for play therapy,
   255–256
Legislative Initiative for Healthier
   Lives, 258
Lifestyle, 77, 78–79
Lifestyle interview, 84–88
Limits, 12
   Adlerian play therapy, 80–81
   child-centered play therapy,
    115–116
   cognitive-behavioral play
    therapy, 155–156
   cultural sensitivity, 278
   developmental play therapy,
    170–171
   ecosystems play therapy,
    192–193
   Gestalt play therapy, 129

Jungian analytical play
   therapy, 100
   play therapy sessions, 44–47
   psychoanalytic play therapy, 67
   relationship play therapy,
    141–144
   Theraplay, 179–180
"Limits Are Therapy" (Bixler), 12
Listening, 137
Little Hans, 52–54, 146
Logical consequences, 83
Loss. *See* Separation and loss
Lowenfeld, Margaret, 5, 8, 9,
   60–63

Main and auxiliary moves, 211
Make A Picture Story
   (MAPS), 231
Make-believe play, 209–211
Manipulation, 47–48
Marschack Interaction Method
   (MIM), 173, 174,
   183–184, 199
Mastery stage of CCPT, 113
Materials, accessibility of, 137, 138
Maternal Care and Mental Health
   (Bowlby), 165
Mental health, child guidance
   movement and, 4
Mental hygiene movement, 4
Mental retardation, 249–251
Meta-communication, 271
Meyer, Adolph, 5
Mind That Found Itself, A
   (Beers), 4
Minnesota Child Development
   Inventory (MCDI), 157
Misbehavior, goals of, 82–83
Mock play sessions, 214
Model Child Protection Act, 263
Modeling, 161, 241
Mood disorders, 242–245
Mosaic test, 61–62
Mother-Child and Father-Child
   Drawing, 199
Mourning, 166

National Association of Social
   Work (NASW), 255

National Center on Child Abuse and Neglect, 5
National Committee for Mental Hygiene, 4
Natural consequences, 83
"Nature of the Child's Tie to His Mother, The" (Bowlby), 165
Negative reaction phase of Theraplay, 178–179
"New Ways to the Understanding of Youth" (Hug-Hellmuth), 7
New York Children's Aid Society, 256
Nickerson, Eileen, 14
NIMH Diagnostic Interview Schedule for Children Version IV (NIMH DISC-IV), 235
Nondirective play therapy. See Child-centered play therapy
Nondirective therapy, 11–12
Nonsexual touching, 168, 169
Nurturing activities, 174, 175, 176

Object relations, 62–63
Observation, 211
Obsessions, 240
Obsessive-compulsive disorder (OCD), 240
O'Connor, Kevin, 14
Once Upon a Time story series (Davis), 152
On Death and Dying (Kubler-Ross), 166
On the Sexual Theories of Children (Freud), 52
Oppositional defiant disorder (ODD), 246
Organismic self-regulation, 121, 122
Out-groups, 269
Outline for Cultural Formation, 281
Out of the Darkness: The Story of Mary Ellen Wilson (Shelman and Lazoritz), 4

Panic disorder, 239
Parapraxes, 58
Parens patriae, 256–257
Parental authority, 256
Parenting Young Children (Dinkmeyer, McKay, and Dinkmeyer), 82
Parent involvement
    Adlerian play therapy, 81–83
    child-centered play therapy, 116
    cognitive-behavioral play therapy, 156
    cultural sensitivity, 278–280
    custody issues and, 32
    developmental play therapy, 171
    ecosystems play therapy, 193–194
    family and filial play therapy, 215–217
    Gestalt play therapy, 129–130
    Jungian analytical play therapy, 100–101
    psychoanalytic play therapy, 67–68
    relationship play therapy, 144–147
    Theraplay, 180–182
Parent-report measures, 157
Parkes, Colin, 166
Parting, 174, 176, 182
Patriae potes, 256
Pattern interpretations, 191
Personality, 105–106
Personality Inventory for Children (PIC), 197
Personality measures, 157–159
Personal unconscious, 90
Person-centered therapy, 105
Pervasive developmental disorders (PDD), 251–252
Pharmacological treatments
    anxiety disorders, 241–242
    attention-deficit/hyperactivity disorder, 248
    conduct disorder, 247
    language and learning disorders, 249
    mood disorders, 244
    pervasive developmental disorders, 252

Phenomenology, 73
Philosophy, 270
Piaget, Jean, 17
Planning, 211
Play assessments, 159. See also Assessment
Playfulness, 208
Playroom setup, 25–29
Play therapist roles
    Adlerian play therapy, 74–77
    child-centered play therapy, 110–112
    cognitive-behavioral play therapy, 152–153
    cultural sensitivity, 272–274
    developmental play therapy, 167–168
    ecosystems play therapy, 189–190
    Gestalt play therapy, 124–127
    Jungian analytical play therapy, 94–97
    psychoanalytic play therapy, 64–65
    relationship play therapy, 136–137
    Theraplay, 173–174
Play therapists
    competency, 259
    conflict among, 8–9
    Registered Play Therapist, 259, 293–295
    Registered Play Therapist Supervisor, 259, 296–298
    responses, 42–44
Play therapy, 1
    children's rights history, 256–258, 266
    conjoint, 204
    defining, 2
    ethics, 255–256, 259–265, 267
    historical development, 3–13
    legal guidelines, 255–256
    parents and, 215–217
    professional identity, 13–18
    research, 265–266, 267
    timeline, 15–16
    See also Adlerian play therapy; Assessment; Child-centered play therapy;

Child developmental play therapies; Cognitive-behavioral play therapy; Cultural sensitivity; Diagnosis; Ecosystems play therapy; Family play therapy; Filial play therapy; Gestalt play therapy; Jungian analytical play therapy; Psychoanalytic play therapy; Relationship play therapy; Treatment

Play Therapy (Axline), 105

Play Therapy Foundation, 14

Play therapy sessions, 19
  Adlerian play therapy, 77–80
  child-centered play therapy, 113–115
  cognitive-behavioral play therapy, 154–155
  conducting, 39–50
  cultural sensitivity, 274–277
  developmental play therapy, 168–170
  ecosystems play therapy, 190–192
  filial play therapy, 212, 214–215
  Gestalt play therapy, 127–129
  Jungian analytical play therapy, 98–100
  playroom setup, 25–29
  professional disclosure, intake, and documentation, 30–39
  psychoanalytic play therapy, 66–67
  relationship play therapy, 137–141
  Theraplay, 174–179
  toy display organization, 29–30
  toy selection, 19–25

Play therapy theory, purpose of, 17–18

Plessy v. Ferguson, 257

POMR, 36

Portable toy kit list, 23

Posttraumatic stress disorder (PTSD), 239–240

Power struggles, 48–49, 83

Preparation phase of Theraplay termination, 182, 183

Preparatory moves, 211

Privacy. *See* Confidentiality; Informed consent

Professional identity, of play therapy, 13–18

Projective questions, 234

Psyche, 90

Psychoanalysis, beginnings of, 5–9

Psychoanalytic play therapy, 51
  assessment and techniques, 69–70
  Freud, Anna, 57–60
  Freud, Sigmund, 52–54
  Klein, Melanie, 55–57
  limits, 67
  Lowenfeld, Margaret, 60–63
  parent involvement, 67–68
  session structure, 66–67
  termination, 68
  toy selection, 63–65

Psychopathology, 91

Psychotherapy timeline. *See* Child psychotherapy timeline

Puppet Interview, 228–229

Puppet Sentence Completion Task, 158–159

Questions, 75–76

Racial differences, 270

Raising Kids Who Can (Bettner and Lew), 82

Rapprochement, 63

Realification, 208

Real-life toys, 110

Reassurance, 43

Red Flag, Green Flag (Freed), 152

Reflection, 191

Reflective listening, 82

Registered Play Therapist, 259, 293–295

Registered Play Therapist Supervisor, 259, 296–298

Regressive stage of CCPT, 113

Relationship building, 77

Relationship play therapy, 134–135
  assessment and techniques, 148

limits, 141–144
  parent involvement, 144–147
  session structure, 137–141
  termination, 147
  therapist role, 136–137
  toy selection, 135–136

Relationship therapy, 10–11

Relaxation and desensitization, 241

Release therapy, 9–10

Religion, 270

Research, 265–266, 267

Resistance, 66, 121, 123, 127

Rett's disorder, 251

Revenge, 83

Robert's Apperception Test for Children (RAT-C), 157, 199

Robertson, James, 165, 166

Rogers, Carl, 105

Role playing, 76

Rosebush visualization strategy, 226

Rosenbluth, Dian, 165

Rules. *See* Limits

Sarcasm, 44

Scenotest, 231–232

Schaefer, Charles, 14

Schaffer, Rudoplph, 165

Schedule for Affective Disorders and Schizophrenia for School-Age Children (K-SADS), 235

School refusal, 238

Schools, play therapy in, 13

Security theory, 165

Self, 90

Self-concept, 271

Self-monitoring, 161

Sentence Completion Test, 158

Separation and loss, 244

"Separation Anxiety" (Bowlby), 165

Separation anxiety, 166, 238–239

Serial drawing, 102

Sessions. *See* Play therapy sessions

Sexual Enlightenment of Children, The (Freud), 52

Shaping, 160
Signified, 210
Signifier, 210
Silence, 43
Simple dynamic
    interpretation, 191
Singing, 168, 170
SOAP, 36, 37, 38
Social interest, 79
Social phobia, 237–238
Society for the Prevention of
    Cruelty to Children, 5
Speaking, 168
Special education, 3
Spirituality, 270
Status, 270
Stimulus fading, 161
STIPS, 36–37, 38
Storytelling assessments, 230–234
Storytelling Card Game, 232–233
Strange Situation, 166–167
Strategic family play therapy
    (SFPT), 208–211
Structured interviews, 234–235
Structured items, 136
Structured play therapy, 10
Structuring activities, 174,
    175–176
Stubborn Child Act of 1638, 256
Successive approximations, 160
Suicide, 244
Summarizing, 43
Superego assessment, 70
System desensitization, 159–160
Systematic Training for Effective
    Parenting (STEP)
    (Dinkmeyer and
    McKay), 82
Syzergy, 95

Tactics, 211
Teaching responses, 42
Temenos, 94
Tentative acceptance phase of
    Theraplay, 178
Termination, 49–50
    Adlerian play therapy, 83–84
    child-centered play therapy,
        117–118

cognitive-behavioral play
    therapy, 156
cultural sensitivity, 280–281
developmental play therapy,
    167, 168, 171
ecosystems play therapy,
    194–195
Gestalt play therapy, 130–131
Jungian analytical play
    therapy, 101
psychoanalytic play therapy, 68
relationship play therapy, 147
Theraplay, 178, 179, 182–183
Thematic Apperception Test
    (TAT), 157
Therapeutic alliance, 66
Therapeutic playrooms, toy list
    for, 23–24
Therapist competency, 259
Therapist roles. *See* Play therapist
    roles
Therapists. *See* Play therapists
Theraplay, 172–173
    assessment and techniques,
        183–185
    limits, 179–180
    parent involvement, 180–182
    session structure, 174–179
    termination, 182–183
    therapist role, 173–174
    toy selection, 173
Theraplay Activities Flip Book
    and Group Activity
    Cards, 175
Theraplay Institute, 173, 175
There He Goes (Jernberg, Hurst,
    and Lyman), 172
Tickling, 170
Time-Out, 161
"Tote bag" toys, 23, 110
Touch, 167, 168–169
Toy display organization, 29–30
Toy selection, 19–25
    Adlerian play therapy, 74
    child-centered play therapy,
        109–110
    cognitive-behavioral play
        therapy, 151–152
    cultural sensitivity, 272

developmental play therapy, 167
ecosystems play therapy,
    187–189
Gestalt play therapy, 124
Jungian analytical play therapy,
    92–93
psychoanalytic play therapy,
    63–65
relationship play therapy,
    135–136
Theraplay, 173
Tracking, 75
Training, for parents, 212,
    213–214
Tranquility, atmosphere of,
    137, 138
Transference, 58–59
Transition, 174, 176–177
Treatment
    anxiety disorders, 241–242
    attention-deficit/hyperactivity
        disorder, 248
    conduct disorder, 247
    language and learning
        disorders, 249
    mental retardation, 251
    mood disorders, 244
    pervasive developmental
        disorders, 252
Treatment planning, 36–38
Tribal backgrounds, 270
Trust, 269

United Nations Convention
    on the Rights of the
    Child, 257
United Nations Declaration
    of the Rights of the
    Child, 257
U.S. Supreme Court cases,
    257–258
Unstructured items, 135

Vienna school, 9, 57–60

Warm-up stage of CCPT, 113
Wechsler Intelligence Scales for
    Children—Third Edition
    (WISC—III), 197

Weininger, Otto, 52
Westby Symbolic Play Scale, 199
Wheeler, Etta Angell, 4
White House Conference on
    Children (1909), 5, 256
White House Conference on
    Children and Youth
    (1960), 257

Wild Boy of Aveyron, 3
Wilson, Mary Ellen, 4
Windows to Our Children
    (Oaklander), 120, 132
Witmer, Lightner, 4
Working through, 67, 167–168

World Health Organization
    (WHO), 165
World technique, 61

Young American Act, 257